THE FATHERS OF THE CHURCH

MEDIAEVAL CONTINUATION

VOLUME 19

THE FATHERS OF THE CHURCH

MEDIAEVAL CONTINUATION

ST. ALBERT THE GREAT

ON JOB, VOLUME 1

Translated by

FRANKLIN T. HARKINS

THE CATHOLIC UNIVERSITY OF AMERICA PRESS
Washington, D.C.

The paper used in this publication meets the minimum requirements of the American National Standards for Information Science—Permanence of Paper for Printed Library Materials, ANSI Z39.48 - 1984.

∞

Library of Congress Cataloging-in-Publication Data
Names: Albertus, Magnus, Saint, 1193?–1280, author. |
Harkins, Franklin T., translator.
Title: St. Albert the Great On Job / translated by Franklin T. Harkins.
Other titles: B. Alberti Magni o. praed. ratisponensis episcopi
Commentarii in Iob. English Description: Washington, D.C. :
The Catholic University Of America Press, 2019. |
Series: The fathers of the church mediaeval continuation ;
Volume 19 | Includes bibliographical references and index.
Identifiers: LCCN 2019013230 | ISBN 9780813232188 (cloth : alk. paper)
Subjects: LCSH: Bible. Job—Commentaries—Early works to 1800.
Classification: LCC BS1415.53 .A4313 2019 | DDC 223/.107—dc23
LC record available at https://lccn.loc.gov/2019013230

To Angela and Joseph

CONTENTS

INDICES

ACKNOWLEDGMENTS

It is a pleasure to acknowledge a number of individuals and institutions whose assistance has enabled the following translation. First, I am indebted to the Boston College School of Theology and Ministry (BC STM) and my faculty colleagues for their support in various ways. Second, I am grateful to Dr. Thomas C. Chiles, Vice Provost for Research at Boston College, and to his office for a Research Incentive Grant (RIG), which supported work on this project during the summer of 2016 and academic year 2016–17. Third, thanks to Richard (Rick) Nichols, SJ, and Simon Brake, who served as my Research Assistants in 2016–17 and 2018–19, respectively, for their many able and conscientious labors. Fourth, several librarians and scholars at research institutes generously assisted me in procuring digital images of several manuscripts of Albert's *Super Iob,* against which I was able to check Melchior Weiss's printed edition at various points. I am indebted to Drs. Elisabeth Dlugosch and Tamara Lust of the Department of Manuscripts, Rare Books, and Graphic Collection at University Library Erlangen-Nürnberg for providing me with scans of MS Erlangen UB 58 (fols. 1ra–58vb), including a high-resolution image of fol. 1r to serve as the frontispiece for this volume. And I am grateful to BC STM for covering the cost of these digital scans. Thanks to Dr. Silvia Scipioni, Manuscripts Manager at the Laurentian Library (Biblioteca Medicea Laurenziana) in Florence, for her kind assistance with MS Florence Laur. Plut. 13,10. I am much obliged to Dr. Ruth Meyer and Prof. Hannes Möhle of the Albertus-Magnus-Institut in Cologne for granting me special access to the Institut's photographs of MS Koenigsberg UB 1308 (fols. 109ra–183va), a manuscript that unfortunately was destroyed in World War II. In addition, for Dr. Meyer's generous and expert assistance with several scholarly questions that arose in the course of my work on *Super Iob,* I remain very grateful. I am also much obliged to Prof. Irven Resnick, of the University of Tennessee at Chattanooga, for his learned aid, advice, and encouragement throughout the project. Fifth, my heartfelt thanks to Dr. Carole Burnett, Staff Editor at The Catholic University of America Press, for her keen editorial eye and extraordinary skill with the Latin language, which served to improve my translation at various points, and for her gracious guidance regarding other aspects of the book's production. Sixth, I would be terribly remiss if I did not thank my parents, Bill and Mary Harkins, who, by their own example, first inspired in me a love of Scripture and an appreciation for excellent commentary on it. Finally and above all, I am profoundly grateful to my wife, Angela, and to our son, Joseph, for their enduring love and unfailing support, which together constitute the *sine qua non* of all my scholarly work. As a small token of my deep gratitude to Angela and Joseph, who have shared me so generously with Albert over the past several years, I lovingly dedicate this work to them.

ABBREVIATIONS

General Abbreviations

CCSL	Corpus Christianorum Series Latina
ch(s).	chapter(s)
col(s).	column(s)
CSEL	Corpus Scriptorum Ecclesiasticorum Latinorum
Ep.	*Epistula*
FOTC	The Fathers of the Church
FOTC MC	The Fathers of the Church: Mediaeval Continuation
GO	*Glossa ordinaria (Biblia Latina cum Glossa ordinaria: Facsimile Reprint of the Editio Princeps Adolph Rusch of Strassburg 1480/81)*
Hom.	*homilia*
l(l).	line(s)
LCL	Loeb Classical Library
LXX	Septuagint
MS(S)	manuscript(s)
PG	Patrologia Cursus Completus. Series Graeca
PL	Patrologia Cursus Completus. Series Latina
v(v).	verse(s)
vol(s).	volume(s)
Vulg.	Vulgate

Abbreviations for Specific Works

Albert the Great

AL	*De animalibus*
Eth.	*Ethica*

In Am	*In Amos prophetam Enarratio*
NOA	*De natura et origine animae*
Ph.	*Physica*
QQ. AL	*Quaestiones super De animalibus*
ST	*Summa theologiae*
Super Ioh.	*Super Iohannem*
Super Matt.	*Super Matthaeum*
Top.	*Topica*
Veg.	*De vegetabilibus et plantis*

Anselm of Canterbury

Conc.	*De concordia praescientiae et praedestinationis et gratiae Dei cum libero arbitrio*
Mon.	*Monologion*

Aristotle

APr.	*Analytica Priora*
Cael.	*De caelo*
EN	*Ethica Nicomachea*
GA	*De generatione animalium*
GC	*De generatione et corruptione*
Metaph.	*Metaphysica*
Mete.	*Meteorologica*
Mund.	*De mundo*
Ph.	*Physica*
Pl.	*De plantis*
Pol.	*Politica*
SE	*De sophisticis elenchis*
Somn.	*De somno et vigilia*
Top.	*Topica*

Augustine of Hippo

Civ.	*De civitate Dei*
c. Iul.	*contra Iulianum*
En. Ps.	*Enarrationes in Psalmos*
mend.	*De mendacio*
vid. Deo	*De videndo Deo* (*Ep.* 147)

Basil the Great

HS *De hominis structura*

Bernard of Clairvaux

Cons. *De consideratione*

Boethius

CP *De consolatione philosophiae*

Cato

Dist. *Disticha de moribus ad filium*

Cicero

ND *De natura Deorum*

TD *Tusculanae Disputationes*

Dionysius the Areopagite

CH *De coelesti hierarchia*

DN *De divinis nominibus*

Fulgentius of Ruspe

AM *Ad Monimum*

Galen

DM *Definitiones medicae*

IHH *In Hippocratis de humoribus*

Gregory the Great

Hom. eu. *In euangelia homiliae*

Mor. *Moralia in Iob*

Horace

AP *De arte poetica*

Sat. *Satirae*

Hugh of St. Victor

De sacr. *De sacramentis Christianae fidei*

Isaac Israeli

Def.	*Liber de definitionibus*

Jerome

In Hos	*Commentarium in Osee prophetam*

John Damascene

F.o.	*De fide orthodoxa*

Macrobius

CSS	*Commentarius in Ciceronis Somnium Scipionis*
Satu.	*Saturnalia*

Moses Maimonides

Dux	*Dux seu director neutrorum sive perplexorum*

Origen

In Ex	*In Exodum*
In Lam	*In Threnos seu Lamentationes Ieremiae*

Ovid

Metam.	*Metamorphoseon libri*

Palladius

OA	*Opus agriculturae*

Peter Lombard

Sent.	*Sententiae in IV libris distinctae*

Plato

Parm.	*Parmenides*
Rep.	*Res publica* (*Republic*)
Ti.	*Timaeus*

Priscian

IG	*Institutiones grammaticae*

Ps.-Chrysostom

OIM	*Opus imperfectum in Matthaeum*

Suetonius

VC	*De vita Caesarum*

Thomas Aquinas

Exp. Iob	*Expositio super Iob ad litteram*

Virgil

Aen.	*Aeneis*
Georg.	*Georgica*

Abbreviations for Biblical Books

Old Testament

Genesis	Gn	Job	Jb
Exodus	Ex	Psalm(s)	Ps(s)
Leviticus	Lv	Proverbs	Prv
Numbers	Nm	Ecclesiastes	Eccl
Deuteronomy	Dt	Song of Songs	Song
Joshua	Jos	Wisdom	Wis
Judges	Jgs	Sirach	Sir
Ruth	Ru	Isaiah	Is
1 Samuel	1 Sm	Jeremiah	Jer
2 Samuel	2 Sm	Lamentations	Lam
1 Kings	1 Kgs	Baruch	Bar
2 Kings	2 Kgs	Ezekiel	Ezek
1 Chronicles	1 Chr	Daniel	Dn
2 Chronicles	2 Chr	Hosea	Hos
Ezra	Ezr	Joel	Jl
Nehemiah	Neh	Amos	Am
Tobit	Tb	Obadiah	Ob
Judith	Jdt	Jonah	Jon
Esther	Est	Micah	Mi
1 Maccabees	1 Mc	Nahum	Na
2 Maccabees	2 Mc	Habakkuk	Hab

Zephaniah	Zep	Zechariah	Zec
Haggai	Hg	Malachi	Mal

New Testament

Matthew	Mt	1 Timothy	1 Tm
Mark	Mk	2 Timothy	2 Tm
Luke	Lk	Titus	Ti
John	Jn	Philemon	Phlm
Acts of the Apostles	Acts	Hebrews	Heb
Romans	Rom	James	Jas
1 Corinthians	1 Cor	1 Peter	1 Pt
2 Corinthians	2 Cor	2 Peter	2 Pt
Galatians	Gal	1 John	1 Jn
Ephesians	Eph	2 John	2 Jn
Philippians	Phil	3 John	3 Jn
Colossians	Col	Jude	Jude
1 Thessalonians	1 Thes	Revelation	Rv
2 Thessalonians	2 Thes		

SELECT BIBLIOGRAPHY

Primary Sources

Albert the Great

B. Alberti Magni O. Praed. Commentarii in Iob: Additamentum ad Opera Omnia B. Alberti. Edited by Melchior Weiss. Freiburg: Herder, 1904.

Opera Omnia. Edited by A. Borgnet. 38 vols. Paris: L. Vivès, 1890–99.

Opera Omnia. Edited by Bernhard Geyer (after t. 37/2 [1978]: Edited by Wilhelm Kübel). Monasterii Westfalorum: Aschendorff, 1951– .

Questions concerning Aristotle's On Animals. Translated by Irven M. Resnick and Kenneth F. Kitchell, Jr. FOTC MC 9. Washington, DC: The Catholic University of America Press, 2011.

Aristotle

The Categories, On Interpretation, Prior Analytics. Translated by Harold P. Cooke and Hugh Tredennick. LCL 325. London: William Heinemann Ltd, 1973.

Generation of Animals. Translated by A. L. Peck. LCL 366. Cambridge, MA: Harvard University Press, 1942.

The Metaphysics. Translated by John H. McMahon. Buffalo, NY: Prometheus Books, 1991.

Minor Works: On Colours, On Things Heard, Physiognomics, On Plants, On Marvellous Things Heard, Mechanical Problems, On Indivisible Lines, Situations and Names of Winds, On Melissus, Xenophanes, and *Gorgias.* Translated by W. S. Hett. LCL 307. Cambridge, MA: Harvard University Press, 1963.

Nicomachean Ethics. Translated by Terence Irwin, second edition. Indianapolis: Hackett Publishing Company, Inc., 1999.

On Sleep and Dreams. Translated by David Gallop. Warminster, England: Aris & Phillips Ltd, 1996.

On Sophistical Refutations, On Coming-to-be and Passing-away, On the Cosmos. Translated by E. S. Forster and D. J. Furley. LCL 400. Cambridge, MA: Harvard University Press, 1955.

On the Heavens. Translated by W. K. C. Guthrie. LCL 338. Cambridge, MA: Harvard University Press, 1986.

Physics. Translated by C. D. C. Reeve. Indianapolis: Hackett Publishing Company, Inc., 2018.

Politics. Translated by Ernest Barker and revised by R. F. Stalley. Oxford: Oxford University Press, 1995.

Posterior Analytics, Topica. Edited and translated by Hugh Tredennick and E. S. Forster. LCL 391. Cambridge, MA: Harvard University Press, 1960.

The Works of Aristotle. Translated under the editorship of W. D. Ross. 12 vols. Oxford: Clarendon Press, 1908–1931.

Other Authors and Works

Abraham ibn Daud. *The Exalted Faith*. Translated by Norbert M. Samuelson and edited by Gershon Weiss. Rutherford: Associated University Presses, 1986.

Anselm of Canterbury. *Complete Philosophical and Theological Treatises of Anselm of Canterbury*. Translated by Jasper Hopkins and Herbert Richardson. Minneapolis: Arthur J. Banning, 2000.

Basil of Caesarea. *Exegetic Homilies*. Translated by Sister Agnes Clare Way, CDP. FOTC 46. Washington, DC: The Catholic University of America Press, 1963,

Bernard of Clairvaux. *Five Books on Consideration: Advice to a Pope*. Translated by John D. Anderson and Elizabeth T. Kennan. Kalamazoo, MI: Cistercian Publications, 1976.

Biblia Latina cum Glossa ordinaria: Facsimile Reprint of the Editio Princeps Adolph Rusch of Strassburg 1480/81. Intro. Karlfried Froehlich and Margaret T. Gibson, 4 vols. Turnhout: Brepols, 1992.

Boethius. *The Consolation of Philosophy*. Translated by David R. Slavitt. Cambridge, MA: Harvard University Press, 2008.

Cicero, Marcus Tullius. *The Nature of the Gods and On Divination*. Translated by C. D. Yonge. Amherst, NY: Prometheus Books, 1997.

———. *Tusculan Disputations*. Translated by J. E. King. LCL 141. London: William Heinemann, 1927.

Galen. *Definitiones medicae*. In *Clavdii Galeni Opera Omnia,* edited by C. G. Kühn, t. 19, 346–462. Hildesheim: Georg Olms Verlagsbuchhandlung, 1965.

———. *Exhortation à l'étude de la médecine: Art médical*. Edited and translated by Véronique Boudon, t. 2. Paris: Les Belles Lettres, 2000.

———. *Hippocratis de humoribus liber et Galeni in eum commentarii*. In *Clavdii Galeni Opera Omnia,* edited by C. G. Kühn, t. 16, 1–488. Hildesheim: Georg Olms Verlagsbuchhandlung, 1965.

Gregory the Great. *Moralia in Iob I–XXXV*. Edited by Marc Adriaen. CCSL 143, 143A, 143B. Turnhout: Brepols, 1979–1985.

Humbert of Romans. *Instructiones de officiis ordinis*. In *Opera de vita regulari,* vol. II, ed. Joachim Joseph Berthier, 179–371. Rome: A. Befani, 1889.

Isaac Israeli. "Isaac Israeli, *Liber de Definicionibus*." Edited by J. T. Muckle. *Archives d'histoire doctrinale et littéraire du moyen âge* 11 (1937–38): 299–340.

———. *Isaac Israeli: A Neoplatonic Philosopher of the Early Tenth Century, His*

Works. Translated by A. Altmann and S. M. Stern. Oxford: Oxford University Press, 1958. Reprint, Westport, CT: Greenwood Press, 1979.

John Damascene. *De fide orthodoxa: Versions of Burgundio and Cerbanus*. Edited by Eligius M. Buytaert, OFM. St. Bonaventure, NY: The Franciscan Institute, 1955. English translation: *Saint John of Damascus: Writings*. Translated by Frederic H. Chase, Jr. FOTC 37, 165–406. New York: Fathers of the Church, Inc., 1958.

Macrobius. *Commentary on the Dream of Scipio*. Translated by William Harris Stahl. New York: Columbia University Press, 1952. Reprint, 1990.

Moses Maimonides. *The Guide of the Perplexed*. Translated by Shlomo Pines with an introductory essay by Leo Strauss. Chicago: University of Chicago Press, 1963.

Plato. *Parmenides*. Translated by Samuel Scolnicov. Berkeley: University of California Press, 2003.

———. *Timaeus, Critias, Cleitophon, Menexenus, Epistles*. Translated by R. G. Bury. LCL 234. Cambridge, MA: Harvard University Press, 1929. Reprint, 2005.

Pseudo-Dionysius. *The Complete Works*. Translated by Colm Luibheid. The Classics of Western Spirituality. New York: Paulist Press, 1987.

Ratherius of Verona. *The Complete Works of Rather of Verona*. Translated by Peter L. D. Reid. Binghamton, NY: Medieval & Renaissance Texts and Studies, 1991.

Thomas Aquinas. *Expositio super Iob ad litteram*. Edited by Antoine Dondaine. Editio Leonina 26. Rome: Ad Sanctae Sabinae, 1965. Translation: *The Literal Exposition on Job: A Scriptural Commentary concerning Providence*. Translated by A. Damico. Interpretive essay and notes by Martin D. Yaffe. Atlanta: Scholars Press, 1989.

Secondary Sources

Anzulewicz, Henryk. "Metaphysics and its Relation to Theology in Albert's Thought." In *A Companion to Albert the Great: Theology, Philosophy, and the Sciences*, edited by Irven M. Resnick, 553–61. Leiden: Brill, 2013.

———."Pseudo-Dionysius Areopagita und das Strukturprinzip des Denkens von Albert dem Grossen." In *Die Dionysius-Rezeption im Mittelalter*, edited by Tzotcho Boiadjiev, Georgi Kapriev, and Andreas Speer, 251–95. Turnhout: Brepols, 2000.

Bazàn, Bernardo C. "Les questions disputées principalement dans les facultés de théologie." In *Les questions disputées et les questions quodlibétiques dans les facultés de théologie, de droit et de médecine*, edited by Bernardo C. Bazàn, John W. Wipple, Gérard Fransen, and Danielle Jacquart, 13–149. Turnhout: Brepols, 1985.

Blankenhorn, Bernhard, OP. *The Mystery of Union with God: Dionysian Mysticism in Albert the Great and Thomas Aquinas*. Washington, DC: The Catholic University of America Press, 2015.

Boureau, Alain. Introduction to *Petri Iohannis Olivi Postilla super Iob*. Edited by Alain Boureau, CCCM 275, pp. V–XXVII. Turnhout: Brepols, 2015.

Boyle, Leonard E., OP. "Notes on the Education of the *fratres communes* in the Dominican Order in the Thirteenth Century." In *Xenia medii aevi historiam illustrantia oblata Thomae Kaeppeli, O.P.*, 2 vols., edited by R. Creytons and P. Künzle, vol. 1, 249–67. Rome: Edizioni di storia e letteratura, 1978.

Brett, Edward Tracy. *Humbert of Romans: His Life and Views of Thirteenth-century Society*. Toronto: Pontifical Institute of Mediaeval Studies, 1984.

Burger, Maria. "Die Bedeutung der Aristotelesrezeption für das Verständnis der Theologie als Wissenschaft bei Albertus Magnus." In *Albertus Magnus and the Beginnings of the Medieval Reception of Aristotle in the Latin West,* edited by Ludger Honnefelder, 281–305. Münster: Aschendorff, 2005.

———. "*Fides et ratio* als Erkenntnisprizipien der Theologie bei Albertus Magnus." In *Via Alberti: Texte—Quellen—Interpretationen,* edited by Ludger Honnefelder, Hannes Möhle, and Susana Bullido del Barrio, 37–58. Münster: Aschendorff, 2009.

———. "Das Verhältnis von Philosophie und Theologie in den Dionysius-Kommentaren Alberts des Grossen." In *What is Philosophy in the Middle Ages?* edited by Jan A. Aertsen and Andreas Speer, 579–86. Berlin: de Gruyter, 1998.

Callus, Daniel M., OP. "The Writings of Albert the Great." *New Blackfriars* 13 (1932): 278–87.

Canty, Aaron. "Nicholas of Lyra's Literal Commentary on Job." In *A Companion on Job in the Middle Ages,* edited by Franklin T. Harkins and Aaron Canty, 225–53. Leiden: Brill, 2017.

Chenu, Marie-Dominique, OP. "The Revolutionary Intellectualism of St. Albert the Great." *Blackfriars* 19 (1938): 5–15.

Congar, Yves, OP. "St. Albert the Great: The Power and the Anguish of an Intellectual Vocation." In *Faith and Spiritual Life,* translated by A. Manson and L. C. Sheppard, 62–66. London: Darton, Longman & Todd, Ltd., 1969.

Courtenay, William J. "The Bible in Medieval Universities." In *The New Cambridge History of the Bible.* Vol. 2, *From 600 to 1450,* edited by Richard Marsden and E. Ann Matter, 555–78. Cambridge: Cambridge University Press, 2012.

———. *Schools & Scholars in Fourteenth-century England.* Princeton: Princeton University Press, 1987.

Dahan, Gilbert. *L'exégèse chrétienne de la Bible en Occident médiéval, XIIe–XIVe siècle.* Paris: Cerf, 1999.

Eisen, Robert. *The Book of Job in Medieval Jewish Philosophy.* Oxford: Oxford University Press, 2004.

Fauser, Winfried, SJ. *Die Werke des Albertus Magnus in ihrer Handschriftlichen Überlieferung. Tiel I: Die echten Werke / Codices Manuscripti Operum Alberti Magni. Pars I: Opera Genuina.* Münster: Aschendorff, 1982.

Fries, Albert. “Zur Entstehungszeit der Bibelkommentare Alberts des Grossen.” In *Albertus Magnus, Doctor universalis: 1280/1980,* edited by Gerbert Meyer, OP, and Albert Zimmermann, 119–39. Mainz: Matthias Grünewald, 1980.

Ginther, James R. “A Scholastic Idea of the Church: Robert Grosseteste’s Exposition of Psalm 86.” *Archives d’histoire doctrinale et littéraire du moyen âge* 66 (1999): 49–72.

———. “There is a Text in this Classroom: The Bible and Theology in the Medieval University.” In *Essays in Medieval Philosophy and Theology in Memory of Walter H. Principe, CSB: Fortresses and Launching Pads,* edited by James R. Ginther and Carl N. Still, 31–51. Aldershot: Ashgate, 2005.

Graham, William A. *Beyond the Written Word: Oral Aspects of Scripture in the History of Religion.* Cambridge: Cambridge University Press, 1987.

Hankinson, R. J., ed. *Cambridge Companion to Galen.* Cambridge: Cambridge University Press, 2008.

Harkins, Franklin T. “Christ and the Eternal Extent of Divine Providence in the *Expositio super Iob ad litteram* of Thomas Aquinas.” In *A Companion to Job in the Middle Ages,* edited by Franklin T. Harkins and Aaron Canty, 161–200. Leiden: Brill, 2017.

——— and Aaron Canty, eds. *A Companion to Job in the Middle Ages.* Leiden: Brill, 2017.

Hipp, Stephen A. *“Person” in Christian Tradition and the Conception of Saint Albert the Great: A Systematic Study of its Concept as Illuminated by the Mysteries of the Trinity and the Incarnation.* Münster: Aschendorff, 2001.

Honnefelder, Ludger. “Wisdom on the Way of Science: Christian Theology and the Universe of Sciences according to St. Albert the Great.” In *Via Alberti: Texte—Quellen—Interpretationen,* edited by Ludger Honnefelder, Hannes Möhle, and Susana Bullido del Barrio, 13–36. Münster: Aschendorff, 2009.

Hossfeld, Paul. *Albertus Magnus als Naturphilosoph und Naturwissenschaftler.* Bonn: Albertus-Magnus-Institut, 1983.

Kovach, Francis J., and Robert W. Shahan, eds. *Albert the Great: Commemorative Essays.* Norman: University of Oklahoma Press, 1980.

Kugel, James L. *Traditions of the Bible: A Guide to the Bible as it Was at the Start of the Common Era.* Cambridge, MA: Harvard University Press, 1998.

Lawn, Brian. *Rise and Decline of the Scholastic* Quaestio disputata*, with special emphasis on its use in the teaching of medicine and science.* Leiden: Brill, 1993.

Legaspi, Michael C. *The Death of Scripture and the Rise of Biblical Studies.* Oxford: Oxford University Press, 2010.

Leinsle, Ulrich G. *Introduction to Scholastic Theology.* Translated by Michael J. Miller. Washington, DC: The Catholic University of America Press, 2010.

Lienhard, Joseph T. “Reading the Bible and Learning to Read: The Influence of Education on St. Augustine's Exegesis." *Augustinian Studies* 27.1 (1996): 7–25.

Light, Laura. "French Bibles c. 1200–30: A New Look at the Origin of the Paris Bible." In *The Early Medieval Bible: Its Production, Decoration and Use,* edited by Richard Gameson, 155–76. Cambridge: Cambridge University Press, 1994.

———. "The Thirteenth Century and the Paris Bible." In *The New Cambridge History of the Bible.* Vol. 2, *From 600 to 1450,* edited by Richard Marsden and E. Ann Matter, 380–91. Cambridge: Cambridge University Press, 2012.

Martin, J. P. P. "Le texte parisien de la Vulgate latine." *Le Muséon* 8 (1889): 444–66; 9 (1890): 55–70, 301–16.

———. "La Vulgate latine au XIIIe siècle d'après Roger Bacon." *Le Muséon* 7 (1888): 88–107, 169–96, 277–91, 381–93.

Maurer, Armand, CSB. *Medieval Philosophy: An Introduction,* second edition. Toronto: Pontifical Institute of Mediaeval Studies, 1982.

Meyer, Gerbert, OP, and Albert Zimmermann, eds. *Albertus Magnus, Doctor universalis: 1280–1980.* Mainz: Matthias Grünewald Verlag, 1980.

Meyer, Ruth. "'Hanc autem disputationem solus Deus determinare potest': Das Buch Hiob als *disputatio* bei Albertus Magnus und Thomas von Aquin." In *Via Alberti. Texte—Quellen—Interpretationen,* edited by Ludger Honnefelder, Hannes Möhle, and Susana Bullido del Barrio, 325–83. Münster, 2009.

———. "A Passionate Dispute over Divine Providence: Albert the Great's Commentary on the Book of Job." In *A Companion to Job in the Middle Ages,* edited by Franklin T. Harkins and Aaron Canty, 201–24. Leiden: Brill, 2017.

Mikołaj Olszewski, "The Nature of Theology according to Albert the Great." In *A Companion to Albert the Great: Theology, Philosophy, and the Sciences,* edited by Irven M. Resnick, 69–104. Leiden: Brill, 2013.

Möhle, Hannes. *Albertus Magnus.* Münster: Aschendorff, 2015.

———. "Zum Verhältnis von Theologie und Philosophie bei Albert dem Grossen." In *Rheinisch—Kölnisch—Katholisch. Beiträge zur Kirchen- und Landesgeschichte sowie zur Geschichte des Buch- und Bibliothekswesens der Rheinlande. Festschrift für Heinz Finger zum 60. Geburtstag,* edited by Siegfried Schmidt, 147–62. Cologne: Erzbischöfliche Diözesan- und Dombibliothek, 2008.

———, Henryk Anzulewicz, Maria Burger, et al., eds. *Albertus Magnus und sein System der Wissenschaften. Schlüsseltexte in Übersetzung. Lateinisch—Deutsch.* Münster: Aschendorff, 2011.

Moonan, Lawrence. "What is a Negative Theology? Albert's Answer." In *Albertus Magnus: Zum Gedenken nach 800 Jahren: Neue Zugänge, Aspekte und Perspektiven,* edited by Walter Senner, OP, Henryk Anzulewicz, et al., 605–18. Berlin: Akademie Verlag, 2001.

Mulchahey, M. Michèle. *"First the bow is bent in study . . .": Dominican Education before 1350.* Toronto: Pontifical Institute of Mediaeval Studies, 1998.

Noone, Timothy B. "Scholasticism." In *A Companion to Philosophy in the Middle Ages,* edited by Jorge J. E. Gracia and Timothy B. Noone, 55–64. Malden, MA: Blackwell Publishing, 2003.

Prügl, Thomas. "Thomas Aquinas as Interpreter of Scripture." In *The Theology of Thomas Aquinas,* edited by Rik van Nieuwenhove and Joseph Wawrykow, 386–415. Notre Dame: University of Notre Dame Press, 2005.

Resnick, Irven M. "Albert the Great: Biographical Introduction." In *A Companion to Albert the Great: Theology, Philosophy, and the Sciences,* edited by Irven M. Resnick, 1–11. Leiden: Brill, 2013.

———, ed. *A Companion to Albert the Great: Theology, Philosophy, and the Sciences.* Leiden: Brill, 2013.

——— and Kenneth F. Kitchell, Jr. *Albert the Great: A Selectively Annotated Bibliography (1900–2000).* Tempe: Arizona Center for Medieval and Renaissance Studies, 2004.

Reynolds, Philip Lyndon. *Food and the Body: Some Peculiar Questions in High Medieval Theology.* Leiden: Brill, 1999.

Riché, Pierre, and Guy Lobrichon, eds. *Le Moyen Age et la Bible.* Paris: Éditions Beauchesne, 1984.

Senner, Walter, OP. *Alberts des Großen Verständnis von Theologie und Philosophie.* Münster: Aschendorff, 2009.

Smalley, Beryl. *The Study of the Bible in the Middle Ages.* Notre Dame: University of Notre Dame Press, 1964.

Smith, Lesley. *The* Glossa Ordinaria: *The Making of a Medieval Bible Commentary.* Leiden: Brill, 2009.

———. "Hugh of St. Cher and Medieval Collaboration." In *Transforming Relations: Essays on Jews and Christians throughout History in Honor of Michael A. Signer,* edited by Franklin T. Harkins, 241–64. Notre Dame: University of Notre Dame Press, 2010.

———. "Job in the *Glossa Ordinaria* on the Bible." In *A Companion to Job in the Middle Ages,* edited by Franklin T. Harkins and Aaron Canty, 101–28. Leiden: Brill, 2017.

Söder, Joachim R. "Albert the Great, 'The Astonishing Wonder.'" In *Albert the Great: Theologian and Scientist. Bibliographic Resources and Translated Essays,* edited and translated by Thomas F. O'Meara, OP, 26–28. Chicago: New Priory Press, 2013.

Straw, Carole. "Job's Sin in the *Moralia* of Gregory the Great." In *A Companion to Job in the Middle Ages,* edited by Franklin T. Harkins and Aaron Canty, 71–100. Leiden: Brill, 2017.

Theodossiou, Efstratios Th., Milan S. Dimitrijevic, Vassilios N. Manimanis, and Th. Grammenos, "*Hydor* from Ancient Greek Cosmogonies to Modern Astrophysics." *Transdisciplinarity in Science and Religion* 1 (2007): 137–52.

Tugwell, Simon, OP. "Introduction: I. The Life and Works of Albert." In *Albert & Thomas: Selected Writings,* edited and translated by Simon Tugwell, OP, 3–39. New York: Paulist Press, 1988.

Twetten, David, and Steven Baldner. "Introduction to Albert's Philosophical Work." In *A Companion to Albert the Great: Theology, Philosophy, and the Sciences,* edited by Irven M. Resnick, 165–72. Leiden: Brill, 2013.

Van Steenberghen, Fernand. "Saint Albert le Grand Docteur de Église." *Collecteana Mechliniensia* 21 (1932): 518–34.

Wéber, Édouard-Henri. "La relation de la philosophie et de la théologie selon Albert le Grand." *Archives de Philosophie* 43 (1980): 559–88.

Wei, Ian P. *Intellectual Culture in Medieval Paris: Theologians and the University, c. 1100–1330.* Cambridge: Cambridge University Press, 2012.

Weijers, Olga. *La 'disputatio' à la Faculté des arts de Paris (1200–1350 environ): Esquisse d'une typologie.* Turnhout: Brepols, 1995.

———. "The Various Kinds of Disputation in the Faculties of Arts, Theology, and Law." In *Disputatio 1200–1800. Form, Funktion und Wirkung eines Leitmediums universitärer Wissenskultur,* edited by Marion Grundhardt and Ursula Kundert, 21–32. Berlin, 2010.

Weisheipl, James A., OP. "Albertus Magnus." In *Dictionary of the Middle Ages,* vol. 1, edited by Joseph R. Strayer, 126–30. New York: Scribner, 1982.

———. "The Life and Works of St. Albert the Great." In *Albertus Magnus and the Sciences: Commemorative Essays 1980,* edited by James A. Weisheipl, OP, 13–51. Toronto: Pontifical Institute of Mediaeval Studies, 1980.

INTRODUCTION

INTRODUCTION

I. ALBERTUS MAGNUS: UNIVERSAL DOCTOR AND THEOLOGIAN

A. *Doctor universalis*

Even prior to his death on 15 November 1280, the Dominican master Albert of Lauingen (b. ca. 1200) was legendary on account of his erudition. He was widely recognized for the depth and breadth of his learning in the philosophical disciplines as well as in the study of God, earning him the titles *Doctor universalis* and *Doctor expertus*.[1] Indeed, one of his Dominican students, Ulrich of Strasbourg (d. 1277), described Albert as "so godlike (*divinus*) in every branch of knowledge that he can properly be called the wonder and marvel of our age."[2] Albert holds a distinctive place among scholastic masters in that he commented on all the works of Aristotle (including such falsely attributed works as *Liber de causis* and *De plantis*)—producing approximately forty commentaries and paraphrases between

1. See James A. Weisheipl, OP, "The Life and Works of St. Albert the Great," in *Albertus Magnus and the Sciences: Commemorative Essays 1980*, ed. James A. Weisheipl, OP (Toronto: Pontifical Institute of Mediaeval Studies, 1980), 13–51, esp. 46–47; and Simon Tugwell, OP, "Introduction: I. The Life and Works of Albert," in *Albert & Thomas: Selected Writings*, trans. and ed. Simon Tugwell, OP (New York: Paulist Press, 1988), 3–39, esp. 3.

2. Quoted in Tugwell, "Introduction," 3, and in Irven M. Resnick, "Albert the Great: Biographical Introduction," in *A Companion to Albert the Great: Theology, Philosophy, and the Sciences*, ed. Irven M. Resnick (Leiden: Brill, 2013), 1–11, at 1. See also Joachim R. Söder, "Albert the Great, 'The Astonishing Wonder,'" in *Albert the Great: Theologian and Scientist. Bibliographic Resources and Translated Essays*, trans. and ed. Thomas F. O'Meara, OP (Chicago: New Priory Press, 2013), 26–28.

1250 and 1270—as well as on the entire Dionysian corpus.[3] Before c. 1250, in addition to the commentaries on Dionysius, Albert penned a number of other theological works, including *De sacramentis, De incarnatione, De resurrectione, Quaestiones (theologicae),* and a massive commentary on Peter Lombard's *Sentences.* And from the late 1250s onward, Albert authored a series of scriptural commentaries—on Matthew, Isaiah, Mark, Luke, John, Jeremiah, Lamentations, Baruch, Ezekiel, Daniel, the minor prophets, and Job—in addition to *Summa theologiae, Super missam,* and *De corpore domini.*[4] Indeed, Fernand van Steenberghen identifies Albert as having produced "the most gigantic" (*la plus gigantesque*) literary corpus of the entire Middle Ages, a body of work that fills more than twenty thousand manuscript pages.[5] Beyond his sheer literary output, during his lifetime Albert's teaching achieved an authority in the schools on a par with that of the ancients, meriting him the moniker *Magnus,* an appellation bestowed on no other man of the High Middle Ages.[6]

Albert's "greatness"—in holiness of life and in theological

3. See Resnick, "Albert the Great," 9–10; Söder, "Albert the Great, 'The Astonishing Wonder,'" 27; and, for an overview, Hannes Möhle, *Albertus Magnus* (Münster: Aschendorff, 2015), 60–78. On the Aristotelian commentaries and paraphrases, see, e.g., David Twetten and Steven Baldner, "Introduction to Albert's Philosophical Work," in *A Companion to Albert the Great,* ed. Resnick, 165–72. On the Dionysian commentaries, see, e.g., Bernhard Blankenhorn, OP, *The Mystery of Union with God: Dionysian Mysticism in Albert the Great and Thomas Aquinas* (Washington, DC: The Catholic University of America Press, 2015), who identifies these commentaries as among "the most sophisticated theological works that Albert achieved" (xv).

4. For a chronology of Albert's works, see *Albertus Magnus und sein System der Wissenschaften. Schlüsseltexte in Übersetzung. Lateinisch–Deutsch,* ed. Hannes Möhle, Henryk Anzulewicz, Maria Burger, et al. (Münster: Aschendorff, 2011), 28–31.

5. Fernand van Steenberghen, "Saint Albert le Grand Docteur de l'Église," *Collecteana Mechliniensia* 21 (1932): 518–34, at 529; and, for this number of manuscript pages, see Resnick, "Albert the Great," 9, and Paul Hossfeld, *Albertus Magnus als Naturphilosoph und Naturwissenschaftler* (Bonn: Albertus-Magnus-Institut, 1983), 6.

6. James A. Weisheipl, "Albertus Magnus," in *Dictionary of the Middle Ages,* vol. 1, ed. Joseph R. Strayer (New York: Scribner, 1982), 126–30.

and philosophical learning—also has not gone unnoticed in modernity. On 16 December 1931, Albert was canonized and recognized as a Doctor of the Church in the decree *In thesauris sapientiae* of Pope Pius XI, who affirmed that the *Doctor universalis* knew everything that could be known.[7] Exactly one decade later, on 16 December 1941, by the decree *Ad Deum* Pope Pius XII proclaimed Albert the patron saint of scientists.[8] These papal declarations represent the contemporary Church's official recognition of the two general areas of Albert's most significant intellectual contributions, namely in theology and scriptural exegesis, on the one hand, and in natural science and philosophy, on the other. Of these two fields, scholarship on Albert in the twentieth and early twenty-first centuries evinces a relative neglect of Albert's theology and exegesis, focusing instead on various aspects of his philosophical and scientific thought.[9] Stephen A. Hipp's appraisal of the state of Albertine

7. Daniel M. Callus, OP, "The Writings of Albert the Great," *New Blackfriars* 13 (1932): 278–87, at 278. Near the beginning of *In thesauris sapientiae,* Pope Pius XI describes Albert thus: "Albertus ille, Ordinis Praedicatorum alumnus, in theologia magister, episcopus quondam Batisbonensis, qui, vitae contemplativae atque activae rationes miro modo consocians, aetatis suae hominibus posterisque vere magnus apparuit, sicut quoque ob doctrinae eminentiam ac multiplicem rerum omnium peritiam Magni cognomento insignitus est" (*Acta Apostolicae Sedis: Commentarium Officiale,* Vol. XXIV Num. 1 [30 Ianuarii 1932] [Rome: Typis Polyglottis Vaticanis, 1932], 5–17, at 6).

8. See Weisheipl, "Albertus Magnus," 129; Weisheipl, "Life and Works," 46–47; and Resnick, "Albert the Great," 2 and n. 9.

9. Though examples abound, two essay collections published on the seventh centenary of Albert's death epitomize this tendency: *Albertus Magnus and the Sciences,* ed. Weisheipl; and *Albert the Great: Commemorative Essays,* ed. Francis J. Kovach and Robert W. Shahan (Norman: University of Oklahoma Press, 1980). For an extensive list of twentieth-century publications on Albert on the sciences and philosophy, see Irven M. Resnick and Kenneth F. Kitchell, Jr., *Albert the Great: A Selectively Annotated Bibliography (1900–2000)* (Tempe: Arizona Center for Medieval and Renaissance Studies, 2004), 156–217 and 222–79. This scholarly inclination toward Albert the philosopher/scientist, and thus away from Albert the theologian, continues to the present day, witnessed to in Brill's *Companion to Albert the Great,* ed. Resnick (2013). In spite of the prominence of theology in the book's subtitle (*Theology, Philosophy, and the Sciences*), only four of the twenty-nine distinct thematic essays (fewer than 14%) in this otherwise excellent volume fall under this rubric.

scholarship remains as true today as when he penned it nearly two decades ago:

> Current literature abounds with a vast number of publications on the philosophical thought of Albert. Unfortunately, in theological matters, the thought of the Universal Doctor has suffered relative neglect, examined only occasionally, and usually with respect to particular points alone, despite the fact that the most refined expression of that thought resides in his theological works.[10]

This state of scholarly affairs reflects the modern tendency to divide the academic disciplines more or less strictly and to devote far less attention to their points of convergence and overarching unity than did Albert and other medieval scholastic thinkers. Albert's intellectual vision was universal and unified, bringing within its ambit all that is knowable by natural reason, on the one hand, and all that is apprehensible by revelation and faith, on the other. In a piece originally written in 1931 to note the scholastic master's canonization, Yves Congar described his vision thus:

> Albert believed in the mind. He considered that between the altitude of the divine life, that supreme world to which he aspired, and the world of science and of our finite reasoning, a profound harmony existed.... To this scholar who was to vindicate the autonomy of the pure sciences he [God] gave a special realisation of the unity of the world, a single supernatural realm in which the facts of nature as well as those of grace are incorporated.[11]

Scholars of Albert generally agree that his major intellectual contribution, which provided the foundation for subsequent

10. Stephen A. Hipp, *"Person" in Christian Tradition and the Conception of Saint Albert the Great: A Systematic Study of its Concept as Illuminated by the Mysteries of the Trinity and the Incarnation* (Münster: Aschendorff, 2001), 183.

11. Yves Congar, OP, "St. Albert the Great: The Power and the Anguish of an Intellectual Vocation," in *Faith and Spiritual Life,* translated by A. Manson and L. C. Sheppard (London: Darton, Longman & Todd, Ltd., 1969), 62–66, at 65. Similarly, Simon Tugwell, OP, described Albert as "almost the apotheosis of curiosity," noting that nothing seems to have escaped his interest (*Albert & Thomas,* xi and 29). Likewise, Armand Maurer identified Albert as "an intellectual giant, whose interests extended to almost all the areas of theology, philosophy, and science cultivated in his day" (Armand Maurer, CSB, *Medieval Philosophy: An Introduction,* 2nd ed. [Toronto: Pontifical Institute of Mediaeval Studies, 1982], 153).

scholasticism and indeed for Western culture more broadly, was his conception of the universe as a synthesis of theology and philosophy.[12] At the heart of medieval scholastic method stands the assumption that all truths, wherever they may be found—whether in non-Christian philosophical sources such as Aristotle and Averroes or in the divinely revealed books of the Old and New Testaments and Christian commentary on them—are ultimately one and reconcilable, having their source in God, who is Truth itself and Creator of all.[13] It is the Christian view of reality, then, that seems to demand the unity of all knowledge, as Ludger Honnefelder explains: "It is the same God who has both created reason, endowing the human being with intellect and will, and who also reveals his work of grace in the history of salvation. And if the source is at work in both ways, faith and reason cannot in principle contradict each

12. See, e.g., Ludger Honnefelder, "Wisdom on the Way of Science: Christian Theology and the Universe of Sciences according to St. Albert the Great," in *Via Alberti: Texte—Quellen—Interpretationen,* ed. Ludger Honnefelder, Hannes Möhle, and Susana Bullido del Barrio (Münster: Aschendorff, 2009), 13–36; Maria Burger, "*Fides et ratio* als Erkenntnisprinzipien der Theologie bei Albertus Magnus," in *Via Alberti: Texte—Quellen—Interpretationen,* 37–58; Édouard-Henri Wéber, "La relation de la philosophie et de la théologie selon Albert le Grand," *Archives de Philosophie* 43 (1980): 559–88; Maria Burger, "Das Verhältnis von Philosophie und Theologie in den Dionysius-Kommentaren Alberts des Grossen," in *What is Philosophy in the Middle Ages?* ed. Jan A. Aertsen and Andreas Speer (Berlin: de Gruyter, 1998), 579–86; and Hannes Möhle, "Zum Verhältnis von Theologie und Philosophie bei Albert dem Grossen," in *Rheinisch—Kölnisch—Katholisch. Beiträge zur Kirchen- und Landesgeschichte sowie zur Geschichte des Buch- und Bibliothekswesens der Rheinlande. Festschrift für Heinz Finger zum 60. Geburtstag,* ed. Siegfried Schmidt (Cologne: Erzbischöfliche Diözesan- und Dombibliothek, 2008), 147–62. See also the studies listed in Maria Burger, "Die Bedeutung der Aristotelesrezeption für das Verständnis der Theologie als Wissenschaft bei Albertus Magnus," in *Albertus Magnus and the Beginnings of the Medieval Reception of Aristotle in the Latin West,* ed. Ludger Honnefelder (Münster: Aschendorff, 2005), 281–305, at 304–5.

13. For an overview of the scholastic method and its educational contexts, see Timothy B. Noone, "Scholasticism," in *A Companion to Philosophy in the Middle Ages,* ed. Jorge J. E. Gracia and Timothy B. Noone (Malden, MA: Blackwell Publishing, 2003), 55–64, who identifies three defining features of scholasticism, namely reasoned argumentation (*ratio*), reliance on authority (*auctoritas*), and the harmony of faith and reason (*concordia*) (55).

other."[14] Understanding the necessary overlap between what can be known through reason and what can be apprehended by faith enabled Albert to develop a new and influential view of the compatibility of philosophy and theology, even as each maintains its own distinct method and sphere of authority.[15] On account of this universal vision of reality, Albert could affirm, "Indeed, for the human the whole world is theology, as long as *the heavens show forth the glory of God, and the firmament declares the works of His hands* [Ps 18.2]."[16]

Around the turn of the thirteenth century, theology developed from an academic discipline understood principally in terms of scriptural interpretation to a systematic body of knowledge conceived according to the concept of *scientia* set forth in Aristotle's *Posterior Analytics.* This development required university masters of theology like Albert and Thomas Aquinas to think carefully about theology as a science, in terms of its subject matter, its proof or method of proceeding, its principles, its concern with universals versus particulars, its theoretical or practical nature, and its certainty.[17]

B. The Science of Theology

At the outset of the *Commentary on the Sentences,* Book I, even before he asks whether theology is a science, Albert inquires

14. Honnefelder, "Wisdom on the Way of Science," 19.

15. See Burger, "*Fides et ratio*"; and Honnefelder, "Wisdom on the Way of Science." See also Marie-Dominique Chenu, OP, "The Revolutionary Intellectualism of St. Albert the Great," *Blackfriars* 19 (1938): 5–15, who describes Albert's "discovery of a new world, the discovery in Aristotle of the world of ancient wisdom" as "a revelation that would set the youthful University of Paris in a turmoil and soon draw the whole of Christianity in its train" (11). Chenu notes, for example, that Aquinas's "harmonious system" of faith and reason "lives only by the spirit of Albert, for it is born of that spirit" (15).

16. *Super Matt.,* on 13.35: "Totus enim mundus theologia est homini, dum 'caeli enarrant gloriam dei, et opera manuum eius annuntiat firmamentum'" (Ed. Colon. t. 21/1 p. 412 ll. 35–37).

17. Ulrich G. Leinsle, *Introduction to Scholastic Theology,* trans. Michael J. Miller (Washington, DC: The Catholic University of America Press, 2010), 120–81, here 132–33.

about its subject.[18] This is so, it seems, because of the long shadow cast by Augustine via Peter Lombard. Indeed, Albert's question begins exactly where the Lombard began, namely with things and signs. Because Augustine maintains that all Christian teaching treats things and signs, Albert's initial objection notes, the subject matter of theology must be "things" and "signs."[19] But all "things," or things universally, seem not to be the subject, for Hugh of St. Victor teaches that only the "works of restoration," and not the works of creation also, constitute the subject matter of Sacred Scripture.[20] In determining this crucial question, Albert notes that the subject of theology can be spoken of in two ways: in general (*generaliter*) and in particular (*specialiter*).

One speaks generally when everything that is called the subject is indeed part of the subject that theology treats. It is true that things and signs are the subject in this sense, Albert notes, though the theological science does not treat *res* and *signa* absolutely or as such. Rather, it does so "inasmuch as they in some way act toward participation in beatitude."[21] Theology examines things insofar as they are ordered to the perfection of beatitude or fruition, according to Albert. Some things are ordered to the beatific end as things that actually make humans happy; as such, these things are to be enjoyed. Other things are ordered as helping and disposing humans toward their ultimate end, and these are to be used on the journey. Similarly, theology considers signs not in an absolute way, but rather as they signify or reveal—either by containing and conveying or not containing and conveying—grace, which is "the proper disposition for beatitude."[22]

When speaking in particular or specifically (*specialiter*), the subject of theology embraces all the particulars that are accept-

18. *Comm. in I Sent.* d. 1 A a. 2: *Quid sit subjectum Theologiae?* (Borgn. vol. 25 p. 15).

19. *Comm. in I Sent.* d. 1 A a. 2 obj. 1 (Borgn. vol. 25 p. 15).

20. *Comm. in I Sent.* d. 1 A a. 2 obj. 2/s.c. (Borgn. vol. 25 p. 16).

21. *Comm. in I Sent.* d. 1 A a. 2 sol.: "... res et signa sunt subiectum: non tamen absolute in eo quod res, nec absolute in eo quod signa: sed in quantum faciunt aliquo modo ad beatitudinis participationem" (Borgn. vol. 25 p. 16).

22. *Comm. in I Sent.* d. 1 A a. 2 sol. (Borgn. vol. 25 p. 16).

ed as or shown to be true in the science itself. Included here are (1) the preambles of faith, which Albert calls "the believable generally accepted" (*credibile generaliter acceptum*), such as that God exists, that God is truthful, and that Sacred Scripture has been produced by the Holy Spirit; (2) the articles of faith, which are proposed in the Creed; and (3) moral precepts that follow from the preambles and articles of faith.[23] But among all these particulars that theology considers, the specific or "special" subject of the science is the one that is most worthy or dignified. This subject, Albert teaches, is God, from whom theology takes its name. God is this "special" subject not only absolutely or without qualification, but also insofar as He is the Alpha and the Omega, the beginning and the end (Rv 1.8). Albert explains:

> The things that are in God are considered in this science as principles originating from Him that manifest indications of the Maker Himself. In the same way, Augustine says that all things cry out, "He Himself has made us, and not we ourselves" [Ps 100.3, or 99.3 LXX]. Insofar as God is the end, on the other hand, they are considered as ordained by Him to that end, as ordering dispositions, such as the virtues, the gifts, the sacraments, and other such things.[24]

Theology, then, examines both things and signs in their relation to the discipline's central "thing" and "special" subject, God Himself, who is the beginning and end of all that is and who alone is to be enjoyed by humans. In the Neoplatonic pattern of exit and return (*exitus-reditus*), God is the source of all created things and signs, which He orders back to Himself. Human beings are first among these things that God leads back to Himself, to the perfection of beatitude and fruition, and He does so through the use of the things and signs that He has made.

Albert's understanding of the subject matter of theology

23. *Comm. in I Sent.* d. 1 A a. 2 sol. (Borgn. vol. 25 p. 16).

24. *Comm. in I Sent.* d. 1 A a. 2 sol.: "... ea quae sunt in ipso, considerantur in ista scientia, tamquam principia ab ipso, quae repraesentant indicia sui factoris: sicut dicit Augustinus, quod omnia clamant: 'Ipse fecit nos, et non ipsi nos.' Secundum autem quod ipse est finis, sic considerantur propter ipsum ordinata ad finem illum, ut dispositiones ordinantes, sicut virtutes, dona, sacramenta, et huiusmodi" (Borgn. vol. 25 p. 16).

seems to beg the prior question of whether the study of God is, or can be, a science at all. When Albert asks, in the first question of his *Summa theologiae,* whether theology is a science, several of the objections point to the role of faith, rather than knowledge, in the discipline as suggesting a negative response. For example, because theology treats the particular deeds of God and of Old and New Testament saints, "which deeds are described historically" in Sacred Scripture, and because, according to Augustine, history is always concerned with things believed rather than with things perceived or known, there seems not to be a science or body of knowledge concerning them. For every science, as Aristotle teaches in *Posterior Analytics* I, is of intelligible realities.[25] Aristotle and Augustine seem to agree, then, that because Scripture treats credible rather than intelligible realities and because *credibilia* come under the rubric of faith rather than of knowledge, there can be no theological science.[26] Indeed, faith is a mode of apprehending that is, as Richard of St. Victor teaches, higher than opinion, which concerns the merely probable, but lower than science, the realm of the intelligible.[27] This line of argument reaches its crescendo in the final objection, according to which Boethius, Ptolemy, and Dionysius converge in support of the view that there can be no perfect science concerning realities such as God and separated substances like the human soul, whose excessive perfection prevents them from being understood even by the keenest human intellect. In fact, as Dionysius notes in chapter 1 of *On the Divine Names,* "when we come to divine realities, we come to the perfect absence of reason" (*perfectam . . . irrationabilitatem*).[28]

On the contrary, Albert observes, what is known from or by reason of the first principle (*ex primo*) is known more truly or more certainly than what is known by reason of anything secondary or inferior. And because what is known by means of divine inspiration (*per inspirationem*) is known *ex primo,* theo-

25. Albert, *ST* Liber I Tract. 1 q. 1 obj. 1 (Ed. Colon. t. 34/1 p. 5 ll. 13–24).
26. *ST* I tr. 1 q. 1 obj. 3 (Ed. Colon. t. 34/1 p. 6 ll. 7–19).
27. *ST* I tr. 1 q. 1 obj. 4 (Ed. Colon. t. 34/1 p. 6 ll. 20–23).
28. *ST* I tr. 1 q. 1 obj. 6 (Ed. Colon. t. 34/1 p. 6 ll. 30–38).

logical knowledge is more certain knowledge than that of any other science. The contra argument further notes that what is known from unchanging things is known more truly than what is known from changing things; and because what is known by means of revelation (*per revelationem*) is known from "the most unchanging things" (*ex immobilissimis*), theology is a science most properly.[29] Albert's thoroughly metaphysical and hierarchical view of reality—profoundly shaped by the Christianized Neoplatonism of Pseudo-Dionysius—serves as the epistemological underlay to this argument. Here it is clear just how philosophical Albert's understanding of theology is, and, conversely, how theological is his philosophical vision.[30] Everything that exists, that possesses goodness, and that is intelligible has its being and existence, its goodness, and its intelligibility principally from God, who is the primary cause, the first goodness, and the first intelligence.[31] This truth enables Albert to hold the view that metaphysics, or First Philosophy, can also be described as a "divine" science and even as "theology," as he explains in the commentary on the *Metaphysics:*

> In First Philosophy all things are called "divine" because God falls within their definition.... All things come forth from the first divine principles and are in them just as things crafted (*artificiata*) are in the mind of the craftsman (*artificis*). And just as things crafted are traced back (*resolvuntur*) to the light of the first active intellect and are defined by it, so all things are traced back to the light of separated substances, and the separated substances themselves are traced back

29. *ST* I tr. 1 q. 1 contra (Ed. Colon. t. 34/1 p. 6 ll. 43–51).

30. See Henryk Anzulewicz, "Metaphysics and its Relation to Theology in Albert's Thought," in *A Companion to Albert the Great,* ed. Resnick, 553–61; and Henryk Anzulewicz, "Pseudo-Dionysius Areopagita und das Strukturprinzip des Denkens von Albert dem Grossen," in *Die Dionysius-Rezeption im Mittelalter,* ed. Tzotcho Boiadjiev, Georgi Kapriev, and Andreas Speer (Turnhout: Brepols, 2000), 251–95.

31. See, e.g., *De causis et processu universitatis a prima causa* II tr. 3 cap. 11 and 12, where Albert explains how every living thing lives by reason of the first life and how every intellectual nature knows through the first intelligence, respectively (Ed. Colon. t. 17/2 pp. 148–50); and *De bono* tr. 1 q. 1 a. 2 sol., where Albert teaches that everything good is good—so long as we are speaking in terms of exemplarity and creation or productivity—by a single, simple goodness, namely the First Goodness or the Highest Good (Ed. Colon. t. 28 p. 8 ll. 4–17).

to the light of the intellect of God, through which they subsist and by which they are defined as by a first principle. And this is the reason that this wisdom is called "divine" and "theology."[32]

Although metaphysics may be called "theology" because it traces things "crafted" by God back to the divine craftsman and so treats "unchanging and separated and simple divine realities,"[33] theology as such differs from metaphysics in its habit, mode of contemplation, and end.[34] First, the theologian considers God and things in relation to God by means of a light infused by God Himself, namely the virtue of faith, whereas the philosopher does so by an acquired habit. Second, and relatedly, the theologian contemplates God as existing beyond human reason, whereas the philosopher examines God according to reason, as a demonstrative conclusion. Third, theology's end is the supernatural vision of God attained in heavenly glory, that is, the beatific vision, whereas metaphysics aims at a natural, this-worldly understanding of the divine. Although the human intellect can in this life have an idea of God through simple intuition, Albert maintains that it can in no way comprehend God.[35] He warns, therefore, against imagining God as the definite and logically graspable subject of the metaphysical science.[36] Particularly on account of this natural epistemological limitation, apprehending the transcendent *artifex* and His *artificia* more fully and more certainly demands, for the practitioner of theology, divine revelation and faith. Even with these

32. Albert, *Metaph.* VI tr. 1 cap. 3 (Ed. Colon. t. 16/2 p. 305 ll. 38–49).

33. Albert, *Metaph.* VI tr. 1 cap. 3 (Ed. Colon. t. 16/2 p. 305 ll. 63–64).

34. Here see Anzulewicz, "Metaphysics and its Relation to Theology," 557–58, who explains that the two sciences "differ in habit, end, and object."

35. Albert, *ST* I tr. 3 q. 13 cap 1 resp.: "Dicimus ergo, quod notitia intellectus creati et humani deus et substantia divina attingitur per simplicem intuitum et diffunditur intellectus in ipso per intuitionis considerationem, sed non capitur per comprehensionem" (Ed. Colon. t. 34/1 p. 41 ll. 3–7).

36. See, e.g., *Metaph.* I tr. 1 cap. 2, where, over against "certain of the Latins of the logical persuasion" who maintain that God is the subject of metaphysics because He is the most noble, the first, the divine, and the highest of all things, Albert teaches that "being and the parts and principles of being" constitute its subject matter because—in view of the nature of all things—they are the most evident, the most divine, the most noble, and prior to all (Ed. Colon. t. 16/1 p. 5 ll. 34–58).

supernatural gifts in view, Albert's understanding and practice of theology allow considerable room for God's unknowability, that is, the *via negativa.*[37] For our present purposes, suffice it to reaffirm Albert's teaching that what is known by way of the perfectly immutable God, through revelation, is known more certainly than anything known from inferior causes.

In his solution to this question—whether theology is a science—Albert affirms: "It must be said that theology is most truly a science, and, what is more, it is wisdom on account of the fact that it is by means of the highest causes, which humans have difficulty understanding."[38] Because theology *is* on account of or through the highest causes, which are traced back to God Himself, Albert's emphasis on revelation and faith as the means whereby the theologian apprehends God is hardly surprising. In brief, Albert defines theology, in light of the words of Ti 1.1, as *scientia secundum pietatem,* a science according to or aiming at piety.[39] In reply to the first objection of the first question of his *Summa,* namely that a science of particular deeds recounted in Scripture seems impossible because historically mediated truths cannot be known (but rather must be believed), Albert makes clear that theology is a science of particulars, but not of particulars considered as such. Rather, the historical particulars that are revealed in Scripture serve this science according to piety by forming the theologian according to faith and the merit of works (*informans ad fidem et*

37. On Albert's negative theology vis-à-vis his understanding of theology as a science, see Lawrence Moonan, "What is a Negative Theology? Albert's Answer," in *Albertus Magnus: Zum Gedenken nach 800 Jahren: Neue Zugänge, Aspekte und Perspektiven,* ed. Walter Senner, OP, Henryk Anzulewicz, et al. (Berlin: Akademie Verlag, 2001), 605–18.

38. *ST* I tr. 1 q. 1 sol.: "Ad hoc dicendum, quod theologia verissime scientia est et quod plus est sapientia, eo quod per altissimas causas est, quas difficile est homini scire" (Ed. Colon. t. 34/1 p. 6 ll. 52–54).

39. Albert, *ST* I tr. 1 q. 2 sol. (Ed. Colon. t. 34/1 p. 8 ll. 47–48). See Mikołaj Olszewski, "The Nature of Theology according to Albert the Great," in *A Companion to Albert the Great,* 69–104, esp. 104, who notes the crucial status of Ti 1.1 for Albert's understanding of theology as a science. Furthermore, Olszewski observes: "There is no medieval theologian that based his reflection, to the same extent, on the nature of theology on any biblical quotation" (104).

meritum operum).[40] This is so, Albert explains, because "the ultimate perfection of such a science is in particular works and in those working in particular ways."[41] Piety, or the worship of God (*cultus dei*), finds its perfection, according to Augustine, in faith, hope, and love, and in prayer and sacrifice. As such, theology, which is *scientia secundum pietatem,* is the science of those things that pertain to salvation. And so it concerns neither what is knowable as such, nor everything that is knowable; rather, theology treats the knowable "inasmuch as it inclines toward piety."[42] Albert recognizes that such a science is believed to a greater extent by those who love and do works oriented toward cultic practice, and so toward salvation, than by those who are persuaded or convinced intellectually.[43] Faith working through love, then, apprehends the theologically knowable insofar as it inclines toward piety; and this science according to piety, in turn, forms the theologian in faith and works toward salvation. It is precisely to this kind of formation—of his Dominican brothers and of subsequent readers of his work—that Albert intends his commentary *On Job* to contribute.

II. *ON JOB*

A. Context

Albert completed his commentary on the book of Job, *Super Iob,* when he was over seventy years old in Cologne, at the Dominican Kloster of Heilige Kreuz, where he seems to have resided as *lector emeritus* of the Order from 1269 until his death in 1280.[44] The manuscript evidence provides two possible dates for the completion of *On Job,* 1272 or 1274. Rome Casanat-

40. *ST* I tr. 1 q. 1 ad 1 (Ed. Colon. t. 34/1 p. 6 ll. 60–62).

41. *ST* I tr. 1 q. 1 ad 1: "Talis autem scientiae perfectio ultima in operibus particularibus et particulariter operantibus est" (Ed. Colon. t. 34/1 p. 6 ll. 62–64).

42. *ST* I tr. 1 q. 2 sol. (Ed. Colon. t. 34/1 p. 8 ll. 46–54).

43. *ST* I tr. 1 q. 1 ad 1 (Ed. Colon. t. 34/1 p. 6 ll. 64–67).

44. See Ruth Meyer, "A Passionate Dispute Over Divine Providence: Albert the Great's Commentary on the Book of Job," in *A Companion to Job in the Middle Ages,* ed. Franklin T. Harkins and Aaron Canty (Leiden: Brill, 2017), 201–24, here 201.

ense MS 445 (XIII ex.) bears the following colophon: *scriptum super iob fratris alberti theutonici ... Capitulum lectum et scriptum anno domini M°CC°LXXII° in colonia ciuitate germanie.* Similarly, Munich Univ. MS 50 (1460–63) has: *scriptum super iob fratris alberti theotonici ... compilatum, lectum et scriptum anno millesimo cc°lxxIIII in colonia ciuitate germanie.*[45] As the language of both colophons suggests, Albert's commentary on Job, like his other scriptural commentaries, seems to have been the product of actual lectures, in this case to his Dominican confreres at Heilige Kreuz.[46] Furthermore, given that 1272 and 1274 seem to indicate dates for the completion of the commentary, Albert may also have lectured on Job in the years previous to his arrival in Cologne, 1264–68, while serving as lector at the Dominican convents in Würzburg and Strassburg.[47] The mid- to late 1260s were a period of great literary productivity for Albert, during which he composed a number of philosophical commentaries—on the *Metaphysica, De causis, Topica, De sophisticis elenchis,* and *Politica*—as well as scriptural ones—on Mark, Luke, John, Jeremiah, Lamentations, Baruch, Ezekiel, Daniel, and the minor prophets.[48] It is hardly surprising, then, that Albert regularly invokes these authoritative sources in *Super Iob.*[49]

Significantly, Albert may have been inspired to produce *On Job* by his most famous student, Thomas Aquinas, who had written his own Joban commentary, the *Expositio super Iob ad litteram,* while serving as conventual lector at San Domenico in Orvieto from 1261 to 1264.[50] Furthermore, Master Albert's ba-

45. Winfried Fauser, SJ, *Die Werke des Albertus Magnus in ihrer Handschriftlichen Überlieferung. Tiel I: Die echten Werke / Codices Manuscripti Operum Alberti Magni. Pars I: Opera Genuina* (Münster: Aschendorff, 1982), 213, MSS 6 and 5, respectively.

46. See Weisheipl, "Life and Works," 40.

47. The chronology of Albert's works in *Albertus Magnus und sein System der Wissenschaften,* 28–31, suggests this possibility.

48. *Albertus Magnus und sein System der Wissenschaften,* 28–31.

49. In the first half of the commentary alone, e.g., Albert invokes Jeremiah and Lamentations over 100 times each.

50. See Meyer, "A Passionate Dispute," 201; and Franklin T. Harkins, "Christ and the Eternal Extent of Divine Providence in the *Expositio super Iob ad litteram* of Thomas Aquinas," in *A Companion to Job in the Middle Ages,* 161–200, esp. 164–68.

sic assumption concerning the fundamental nature of the book of Job—namely that it is an academic disputation among Job and his friends about divine providence—appears to have been taken from Aquinas's *Exposition* and developed more fully in *On Job.* Indeed, as Ruth Meyer observes, Albert, having borrowed this idea from his disciple, "for the first and only time in the history of exegesis explicitly interprets the entire book of Job as a disputation."[51] We will consider Albert's understanding of the book of Job as a scholastic disputation in greater detail below. Suffice it here to indicate, however, that such an understanding points to the context of Dominican education and formation in which Albert's *On Job* originated, most likely as lectures to his confreres, and was initially used.

In imagining mendicant masters such as Albert and Thomas first and foremost as university professors (of philosophy quite often), modern scholarship has tended to retroject its own academic contexts and assumptions back into the thirteenth century, leading to anachronistic distortions of precisely what it seeks to understand. Lesley Smith highlights key aspects of this problem in her excellent 2010 essay on Hugh of St. Cher's *Postilla in totam bibliam,* the production of which, she insists, must be viewed not through the lens of modern authorship but rather in terms of practical purpose vis-à-vis Dominican formation and mission. "All of Hugh's life and work speaks of his practical bent," Smith explains. "As a Dominican, he was part of a religious order that thought of itself as truly fraternal, each working for the good of the whole rather than for himself. The entire schema of production at St. Jacques was aimed at the better fulfillment of the Dominican vocation."[52] Relatedly, it is signif-

51. Meyer, "A Passionate Dispute," 201 and n. 6.

52. Lesley Smith, "Hugh of St. Cher and Medieval Collaboration," in *Transforming Relations: Essays on Jews and Christians throughout History in Honor of Michael A. Signer,* ed. Franklin T. Harkins (Notre Dame: University of Notre Dame Press, 2010), 241–64, at 254. Relatedly, Smith maintains: "Particularly in the case of authorship, there is a tendency to wear Romantic spectacles, employing the notion of the author, be it of a text, a picture, a sculpture, or any piece of creative work, as an individual (and preferably tortured) genius. This is surely inimical to the medieval view of authorship, which was focused strongly on purpose, rather than on creation for its own sake" (255).

icant that the mendicant convents at Paris, such as St. Jacques, technically were not part of the university, nor were their friars university students strictly speaking.[53] Rather, most of the select few Dominicans whom the various provinces deemed sufficiently promising to send to St. Jacques were enrolled in the order's lectorate program, a three- to four-year educational plan intended to prepare them to be lectors at a local convent or *studium*, usually one in their home province.[54] Michèle Mulchahey puts it this way: "... in many instances the Dominicans were at the universities, but not of the universities; they operated in proximity to the secular *studia* but were not technically a part of them.... the Dominicans were much more concerned with creating a staged curriculum which met the needs of their pastoral work than with being at the universities *per se*."[55]

Preaching took center stage in this pastoral work, of course, which required Dominican *lectores* serving at all levels of the order's educational system (that is, in general, provincial, and local or conventual *studia*) not only to lecture regularly on Sacred Scripture but to do so with an eye toward what would be of practical use for their auditors. Humbert of Romans, who served as Master General of the Order of Preachers from 1254 to 1263, makes this clear in his description of the office and obligations of the lector in his *Instructiones de officiis*, penned in 1265.[56] Here Humbert explains:

53. William J. Courtenay, "The Bible in Medieval Universities," in *The New Cambridge History of the Bible*, vol. 2: *From 600 to 1450*, ed. Richard Marsden and E. Ann Matter (Cambridge: Cambridge University Press, 2012), 555–78, at 560–61.

54. See Courtenay, "The Bible in Medieval Universities," 560–61; M. Michèle Mulchahey, *"First the Bow is Bent in Study ...": Dominican Education before 1350* (Toronto: Pontifical Institute of Mediaeval Studies, 1998), 383–84; and Leonard E. Boyle, OP, "Notes on the Education of the *fratres communes* in the Dominican Order in the Thirteenth Century," in *Xenia medii aevi historiam illustrantia oblata Thomae Kaeppeli, OP*, ed. R. Creytons and P. Künzle, 2 vols. (Rome: Edizioni di storia e letteratura, 1978), vol. 1, 249–67, esp. 255.

55. Mulchahey, *"First the Bow is Bent in Study ...,"* 352. For a consideration of Dominican *studia generalia* and their course of study in relation to their secular equivalents, see Mulchahey, *"First the Bow is Bent in Study ...,"* 352–84.

56. Boyle, "Notes on the Education," 256–57. On Humbert and Dominican education in the thirteenth century, see also Edward Tracy Brett, *Humbert of*

The duty of the good lector is to conform himself to the ability of his hearers, and to read useful and expedient things to them with ease and understanding; to flee from new opinions and to hold to ancient and safer ones; never to speak things that he does not understand well; always to avoid nauseating prolixity, which customarily occurs as a result of the excessive repetition of the same point, becoming wrapped up in words, or other causes.[57]

The lector should read in such a way, Humbert continues, that his auditors might become proficient in understanding "the truth of books," "useful questions," and other things that are ordered to the edification of morals. Thus he is "to read the letter only (*litteram tantum legere*), leaving behind the multitude of those things that are able to be said about each word, so that the hearers under him might make progress in understanding the Bible and the *Histories* and the *Sentences*."[58] Humbert also held the view, which appears to have been directly informed by the position of Albert and Thomas on the relationship of philosophy to theology, that Scripture contains innumerable passages that cannot be understood except with the help of philosophy.[59]

Romans: His Life and Views of Thirteenth-century Society (Toronto: Pontifical Institute of Mediaeval Studies, 1984), 41–56.

57. Humbert of Romans, *Instructiones de officiis ordinis,* ch. 10, in *Opera de vita regulari,* vol. 2, ed. Joachim Joseph Berthier (Rome: A. Befani, 1889), 254: "Officium boni lectoris est conformare se capacitati auditorum; et utilia, et expedientia eis faciliter et intelligibiliter legere; opiniones novas refugere, et antiquas et securiores tenere; ea quae non bene intelligit nunquam dicere; a fastidiosa prolixitate, quae accidere solet ex nimia repetitione eiusdem, aut ex involutione verborum, vel ex aliis causis, cavere semper."

58. Humbert, *Instructiones de officiis,* ch. 10: "... litteram tantum legere, relicta multitudine eorum quae dici possunt ad singula; quod auditores sub eo proficiant ad sciendum *Bibliam,* et *Historias,* et *Sententias*" (254).

59. See Brett, *Humbert of Romans,* 48–51, who notes that a commission of five doctors of theology in the Order commissioned by Humbert—viz., Albert, Thomas, Florence of Hesdin, Bonhomme of Brittany, and Peter of Tarentaise—presented its recommendations concerning the incorporation of the new philosophical learning into the Dominican curriculum to the General Chapter at Valenciennes in 1259, where they were approved.

B. Exegetical Method: Five Key Features

Albert's general approach to the book of Job aligns well with Humbert's instructions for the Dominican lector in five fundamental ways, namely: (1) his emphasis on the practical utility of Job; (2) his preferential engagement with "older and safer" authorities over newer ones; (3) the continuous and cursory nature of his commenting; (4) his detailed division of the Joban text (*divisio textus*); and (5) his richly intertextual approach.

First, in line with his understanding of theology as *scientia secundum pietatem,* Albert is concerned to highlight the practical utility of Job, as is clear from the outset of his commentary. Indeed, at the beginning of his Prologue, Albert indicates that the opening words of Jas 5.10—*Take, brothers, as an example of the departure of evil*—teach Job's primary utility (*utilitas*): "The book of Job is useful for this purpose: to show how evil will pass away, that is, how it will come to an end, with a view to the good and to consolation."[60] On Albert's reading, the remainder of Jas 5.10—*and of longsuffering, of labor and of patience, the prophets, who spoke in the name of the Lord*—bespeaks the further usefulness of Job, for building up virtue in the hearer or reader, in his or her manner of life, moderation of mind, and fellowship with and imitation of good people.[61] Throughout *On Job,* Albert maintains a focus on *utilitas,* which appears in places and ways that may surprise modern readers. In commenting on Job's possessing seven thousand sheep prior to his temptation (1.3), for instance, Albert describes them principally in terms of their practical utility: "Their dung is useful for the earth, their milk and flesh are useful for food, their skin for shoes, their fleece for clothes, and their intestines are used to make strings for musical instruments."[62] Most often, though, Albert emphasizes what is useful for the edification of virtue and the moral life, just as Humbert had taught. For "what is useful for nothing and to no end is vain," Albert declares.[63]

60. Prol., p. 49 below.
61. Prol., pp. 49–50 below.
62. On 1.3, pp. 56–57 below.
63. *On Job* 11.11, p. 222 below.

A second major way that *On Job* comports with Humbert's instructions for lectors is in its preference for "older and safer" opinions as opposed to newer ones. Apart from Scripture itself, the authorities whom Albert calls upon most frequently to help him in reading Job are Aristotle, whom the scholastics identify simply as "the Philosopher," and Gregory the Great. *Super Iob* is suffused with the teaching of Aristotle on a wide range of philosophical, ethical, and natural-scientific topics, which is not at all surprising given Albert's view, treated above, of the complementarity of philosophy and theology. The Dominican master makes use of the Philosopher, for instance, on such wide-ranging matters as the simplicity of virtue (on 1.1), the nature of wisdom and the wise man (9.4; 12.12; 15.10, 18), the methods and features of skilled argumentation or disputation (4.1; 6.28; 11.2; 21.1), the relative quantities of frost and snow (6.16), the features of freshwater (8.16), the natural motion of a runner (9.25), plant regeneration (14.7, 8–9), the nature of tyranny (15.20), and the four virtues of a household (15.28; 1.3). In line with his thoroughly intertextual method of reading Scripture, about which we will say more below, Albert often highlights how Aristotelian teaching converges with and corroborates truths received by divine revelation. For example, in expounding Eliphaz's words in Jb 4.13, *In the horror of a nocturnal vision, when deep sleep customarily overtakes humans,* Albert invokes Aristotle's observation in *On Sleep and Wakefulness* that mental images are excited during wakefulness in order to make the point—confirmed by Gn 2.21, Song 5.2, Nm 24.3–4, and Jb 33.15–16—that during deep sleep the human intellect is operative to a greater extent and so more disposed to receive divine instruction by means of vision.[64] Foundational to such an exegetical approach is Albert's assumption, central to the scholastic method generally, that all truths, wherever they may be found, are ultimately one by virtue of their single divine source.

Unsurprisingly, Gregory the Great serves as the most privileged Christian authority in Albert's *Super Iob.* Indeed, the Dominican directly quotes, paraphrases, or alludes to Gregory's *Moralia* over seventy times in the first half of his commentary

64. *On Job* 4.13, pp. 125–26 below.

alone. Albert takes from Gregory various moral interpretations (for example, on 4.2; 5.21; 6.26), of course, but also insights into a wide range of textual and theological loci, including the process of Job's temptation (1.6), the angelic nature of the "sons of God" (1.6), the four modes of God's speaking to Satan (1.7), Original Sin (9.22), God's eternality and incorruptibility (11.9; 14.15; 15.8), the counsel of God (12.13), human persistence in evil against God (15.25), divine judgment and punishment (14.17; 20.27), the darkness and depth of hell (10.22; 17.16), and even the method of capturing lionesses (10.16)! That the *Moralia* is so encyclopedic in its reading of Job—so much so that Carole Straw has described it as "something of a loose, baggy monster"—seems to have had a particular appeal to the comprehensive mind of the Universal Doctor.[65]

Significantly, it is precisely in its thoroughgoing use of Gregory's influential work that Albert's *On Job* diverges from the earlier *Expositio super Iob ad litteram* of his student, Thomas Aquinas. For his part, Aquinas explicitly states in his Prologue that he will read Job *ad litteram,* noting that Gregory seems to have exhausted the book's tropological potential: "For we intend, insofar as we are able and having faith in divine help, briefly to expound this book that is entitled *Blessed Job* according to the literal sense, for blessed Pope Gregory has disclosed to us its mysteries (*mysteria*) so subtlely and clearly that it seems that nothing further needs to be added to them."[66] This does not mean, of course, that Aquinas offers no readings of Job other than the sort that modern historical critics might recognize as "literal." To the contrary, as I have shown elsewhere, Aqui-

65. Carole Straw, "Job's Sin in the *Moralia* of Gregory the Great," in *A Companion to Job in the Middle Ages,* 71–100, at 73.

66. Aquinas, *Expositio super Iob ad litteram,* Prol.: "Intendimus enim compendiose secundum nostrum possibilitatem, de divino auxilio fiduciam habentes, librum istum qui intitulatur *Beati Iob* secundum litteralem sensum exponere; eius enim mysteria tam subtiliter et diserte beatus papa Gregorius nobis aperuit ut his nihil ultra addendum videatur" (Leon. ed., 4). By virtue of his own exegetical intention, then, Aquinas seems to stand as a rare exception in the High Middle Ages to Lesley Smith's claim that "Gregory's exposition of Job was an inescapable landmark of interpretation that was impossible to ignore" (Lesley Smith, "Job in the *Glossa Ordinaria* on the Bible," in *A Companion to Job in the Middle Ages,* ed. Harkins and Canty, 101–28, at 105).

nas understands "according to the letter" (*ad litteram*) much more expansively (particularly where prophecy is concerned) than modern biblical criticism traditionally has, such that he recognizes Christ as within the ambit of the literal signification of Job.[67] Nevertheless, Aquinas follows through on his stated intention to read Job differently than had Gregory, as is evidenced by the fact that he mentions Gregory by name only one time in the whole of his commentary proper.[68] Albert, by contrast, nowhere disavows interest in the *Moralia,* and in fact makes regular use of Gregory's commentary in his own.

One centrally important question concerning the sources of *Super Iob* that remains virtually unstudied is whether Albert made direct use of Aquinas's *Expositio* and, if so, to what extent. In his preface to the Leonine edition of the *Expositio,* published in 1965, Antoine Dondaine noted that Aquinas's commentary antedates that of his teacher and posed the question of possible influence.[69] Although scholars remain uncertain concerning whether copies of Aquinas's *Expositio* circulated before his death, Dondaine interpreted a handful of brief textual parallels as evidence of literary dependency. In a 1980 essay on Albert's biblical commentaries, Albert Fries concurred with Dondaine, affirming more strongly the presence of signs indicating that the text of Aquinas's commentary sat before Albert as he wrote his.[70] It is noteworthy, however, that Fries himself brings forth no further evidence of this literary dependency; rather, he is satisfied simply to cite Dondaine's preface.[71] Fries proposes that Albert could have obtained a copy of his student's *Expositio* sometime between the spring of 1261 and the spring of 1263 when he was part of an illustrious circle of scholars and

67. See Harkins, "Christ and the Eternal Extent of Divine Providence," esp. 168–70 and 198–200.

68. Namely, in commenting on 17.6–7 (Leon. ed., 107).

69. For Dondaine's Preface, see Leon. ed., 1*–144*, here 33*. On the influence of Aquinas's *Expositio* on subsequent scholastic commentators, see pp. 33*–43*.

70. Albert Fries, "Zur Entstehungszeit der Bibelkommentare Alberts des Grossen," in *Albertus Magnus, Doctor universalis: 1280/1980,* ed. Gerbert Meyer, OP, and Albert Zimmermann (Mainz: Matthias Grünewald, 1980), 119–39, at 138–39.

71. Fries, "Zur Entstehungszeit," 138 n. 49.

biblical exegetes—including William of Moerbeke, Hugh of St. Cher, and Thomas Aquinas—around Pope Urban IV at Viterbo and Orvieto.[72]

For my part, I remain unconvinced by what Dondaine takes to be literary parallels—parallels that he himself describes as "fragile."[73] It must be noted in this regard that in the whole of *Super Iob,* which runs to 514 columns in the printed Latin edition of Melchior Weiss, Albert makes no explicit mention of Aquinas or of his *Expositio.* Furthermore, Aquinas's failure to appear in his master's commentary is particularly striking in light of the frequent and thoroughgoing use of Aquinas made by subsequent Franciscan commentators on Job, such as Matthew of Aquasparta, Peter John Olivi, and Nicholas of Lyra.[74] Indeed, Alain Boureau has gone so far as to affirm that the Joban commentary of Olivi seems "to offer, in the year 1290, a reprise of that of Thomas Aquinas," albeit one reinforced by the use of Gregory's *Moralia.*[75] In sum, although we cannot identify with any degree of certainty the reasons why Albert, in commenting on Job, might have remained silent about Aquinas and his *Expositio* (if, in fact, he had any knowledge of the existence of his student's commentary), we might wonder whether Humbert's injunction that the Dominican lector "flee from newer opinions" might have been somehow at play.

Humbert's instruction "to read the letter only" (*litteram tantum legere*), avoiding extraneous digressions from the text, so that auditors (and subsequent readers of the lectures or commentary, presumably) "might make progress in understanding the Bible," is reflected in the third, fourth, and fifth key features

72. Fries, "Zur Entstehungszeit," 138–39. Cf. Weisheipl, "Life and Works," 38–39.

73. Dondaine, Preface, vol. 26, pp. 33*–34*. Dondaine himself indicates that the influence, if there was any, of Aquinas's commentary on that of Albert was "restricted" and "did not result in indisputable literary borrowing" (33*).

74. See Dondaine, Preface, vol. 26, pp. 34*–43*; Alain Boureau, Introduction to *Petri Iohannis Olivi Postilla super Iob,* ed. Alain Boureau, CCCM 275 (Turnhout: Brepols, 2015), pp. V–XXVII, at VII–VIII; and Aaron Canty, "Nicholas of Lyra's Literal Commentary on Job," in *A Companion to Job in the Middle Ages,* ed. Harkins and Canty, 225–53.

75. Boureau, in Introduction to CCCM 275, p. V.

of Albert's exegetical method in *Super Iob,* namely the continuous and cursory nature of his comments, his detailed division of the Joban text, and his deeply intertextual approach. Third, then, Albert reads Job continuously and cursorily, often setting brief explanatory glosses between the textual lemmata. Although only one of the extant manuscripts identifies *Super Iob* as *postille,* this mode of reading is, of course, the essential feature of the *postilla,* the name and reality of which likely derive from the phrase *post illa verba.*[76] Very often Albert uses *i.e.* (*id est*), "that is," and *scilicet*—which I render variously as "namely," "in other words," and "of course"—to introduce short definitions, specify particular instances or examples, or otherwise offer succinct explanations of details in the Joban text. His mode of "running through" Job is so quick and concise that Albert frequently adds the singular imperative "supply" (*supple*) following the textual lemma as a note of instruction to the reader (and perhaps originally intended for a hearer of lectures) indicating what should be added for the sake of greater understanding. For example, on 3.19, a portion of Job's lamenting that he was ever born, in which he notes the advantages that death provides, our Dominican comments thus: "**[19]** ***The small and the great are there,*** supply: they are equals and they are resting equally.... ***and the slave,*** supply: formerly bound, ***is free from his master,*** supply: who does not have a master, but pleases only himself; the former slave and the former master find rest equally."[77]

It is noteworthy that, whereas Albert may indeed "read the letter only," as Humbert instructs, our Dominican master does

76. Basel MS Universitätsbibliothek B IV 14 (XIVin.) uniquely identifies Albert's work as *postille* (*Postille Alberti super Iob et Danielem*), though this identification appears in a later hand on a parchment tag affixed to the outside of the back cover (see Fauser, *Die Werke des Albertus Magnus,* 212 MS 1). On the genre of *postilla,* see Beryl Smalley, *The Study of the Bible in the Middle Ages* (Notre Dame: University of Notre Dame Press, 1964), 270–71. See also Bernard Schmidt, Prolegomena to *Super Matthaeum* (Ed. Colon. t. 21/1 pp. IX–X), who identifies Albert's Gospel commentary, like his commentary on Isaiah, as *postilla.*

77. On 3.19, p. 110 below. Here and throughout the translation itself, the text of Job appears in bold and italics.

not read Job only according to the letter or in some strictly literal way as determined or understood by modern interpreters. When, for instance, we read Daniel M. Callus, OP, who, writing in 1932, identified Albert as a "pioneer" in biblical studies, "the first among the Scholastics who insistently urged the interpretation of the literal sense," we must not anachronistically imagine that the Universal Doctor was somehow the first practitioner of higher criticism.[78] Rather, we should note Albert's careful attention to the textual letter and its potential significations, both literal and spiritual. As mentioned above, Albert makes thoroughgoing use of Gregory's *Moralia,* for instance, and he does so because he understands (1) theology as *scientia secundum pietatem* and (2) the book of Job as eminently useful for building up virtue. His comments on the opening words of the Joban text, *There was a man* (*Vir erat*), illustrate clearly how Albert's attentiveness to the letter provides the foundation for and bolsters moral interpretation rather than precluding or obstructing it. After introducing Gregory's teaching that Job "is a man in the perfection of mind" and setting forth several

78. Callus, "The Writings of Albert the Great," 285–86. See also Smalley, *The Study of the Bible,* 264–355, who, in introducing the exegetical work of thirteenth-century mendicant masters, straightforwardly claims: "In the spiritual [exposition] we shall find decay, in the literal originality and new developments" (281). Smalley reveals her anachronistic perspective when she affirms, for instance, that "the great schoolmen were not primarily biblical scholars.… St. Thomas and St. Bonaventure … came to the Bible as theologians, St. Albert as a philosopher" (329). She further explains: "St. Albert had a smattering of Greek and Hebrew but not enough to allow of his reading Scripture in the originals.… St. Thomas also knew a little Greek; there is no evidence that he knew any Hebrew" (329 n. 1). For a more recent corrective to this traditional vision of medieval theology and exegesis, see James R. Ginther, "There is a Text in this Classroom: The Bible and Theology in the Medieval University," in *Essays in Medieval Philosophy and Theology in Memory of Walter H. Principe, CSB: Fortresses and Launching Pads,* ed. James R. Ginther and Carl N. Still (Aldershot: Ashgate, 2005), 31–51, who affirms: "At the very least, modern scholars must accept that medieval theologians had a deep and abiding knowledge of Scripture. The memorization of Scripture was not simply an act of piety, nor were its contents of interest only to textual critics and those interested in biblical history; rather, the biblical text was the foundation for all theological reflection" (44).

interpretive intertexts from the Old Testament, Albert directs his mind's eye to the exact letter of the Vulgate text: "Here it does not say 'there used to be' (*fuit*) or 'there had been' (*fuerat*), but instead 'there was' (*erat*). For the imperfect past tense describes ongoing past action, so that it is here noted that Job was so excellent a person in the past and that he continued to be so, according to what is said in Gal 6[.9]: *Let us not cease in doing good*."[79] It is precisely in reading the *litteram tantum* here that Albert is able to draw out what is expedient for understanding the text, not only of Jb 1.1 but indeed of all of divine revelation, which is always relevant to its hearers and readers in any time and place.

A proper consideration and appreciation of *Super Iob* entails understanding certain basic assumptions regarding the nature and purpose of Sacred Scripture that Albert brings to his reading of Job. James Kugel has identified four fundamental assumptions of all ancient interpreters, whether Jewish or Christian, which assumptions Albert and other medieval scholastic exegetes took for granted. Namely, like his ancient counterparts, Albert assumes that Sacred Scripture is essentially (1) cryptic, and therefore a text containing meanings beyond those that are immediately apparent on the surface of the letter; (2) relevant, what Kugel calls "one great Book of Instruction," containing models of conduct and stories according to which later readers might live; (3) perfect and perfectly harmonious among its various books and parts; and (4) of divine provenance and divinely inspired.[80] All four of these assumptions are found *in nuce* in Albert's reading of *vir erat* in Jb 1.1: it is because of its divine authorship that even this seemingly simple, straightforward text is cryptic, relevant far beyond the context of human literary production and intention, and accords in its basic teaching with other scriptural texts such as Gal 6.9. Inherent in the very tense of the opening verb of the book of Job is, in Albert's view, the divine intention to encour-

79. On Jb 1.1, p. 53 below.

80. James L. Kugel, *Traditions of the Bible: A Guide to the Bible as It Was at the Start of the Common Era* (Cambridge, MA: Harvard University Press, 1998), 14–19.

age readers and hearers in every time and place to do good unceasingly. Sacred Scripture, then, is both univocal and "omnisignificant." That is, in all the texts of Scripture, of both Old and New Testaments, God speaks ultimately with a single voice; and every word and each detail of every text is effective in signifying the divine intention.[81] The assumption of textual "omnisignificance" stands at the heart of Albert's careful attention to the letter, as is clear throughout *Super Iob*. For present introductory purposes, though, one other example will suffice. In commenting on the opening phrase of Jb 1.6, *Now on a certain day* (*Quadam autem die*), which opens the celestial scene wherein the Lord grants Satan permission to tempt Job, Albert explains: "It says 'certain' in order to designate the particularly and singularly remarkable fact of so great a temptation. And indeed it says 'day' because in the midst of such great suffering Job did not fall from the light of reason or of grace, and he was going to be restored from darkness to light."[82] Read in such a theologically rich way, then, this phrase from Jb 1.6 harmonizes perfectly with the words of Jas 5.11 with which Albert opens his Prologue, *You have heard of the suffering of Job, and you have seen the end of the Lord.* These New Testament words, according to our Dominican exegete, disclose the mode and order of the book of Job, namely how through tribulations endured at the beginning he attains to the glory of body and soul in the end.[83]

A fourth key feature of Albert's interpretive approach to Job is the *divisio textus,* the detailed division of the sacred text. As was the ordinary practice of high-scholastic exegetes, Albert divides the Joban text from the top down, as it were: that is,

81. See Kugel, *Traditions of the Bible,* 17, who explains: "... this same view of Scripture's perfection ultimately led to the doctrine of 'omnisignificance,' whereby nothing in Scripture is said in vain or for rhetorical flourish: every detail is important, everything is intended to impart some teaching." See also Joseph T. Lienhard, "Reading the Bible and Learning to Read: The Influence of Education on St. Augustine's Exegesis," *Augustinian Studies* 27.1 (1996): 7–25, who describes Augustine's approach to Scripture in precisely these terms: "Every word in the Bible was important, because the Holy Spirit had inspired it. The Holy Spirit was never wrong and never trite, and the Holy Spirit always said something useful to us" (16).

82. On Jb 1.6, p. 62 below.

83. *Super Iob* Prol., p. 51 below.

beginning from the macro-level of the book as a whole and moving down to collections of chapters and individual chapters, and from there down further still to groups of verses, to individual verses, and even to phrases and particular words that are constitutive thereof. Such a holistic and intricate division, in which there is a place for everything and everything has its place, aims not only at the isolation of smaller and smaller units for the sake of more effective analysis, but also—and more importantly—at the (re)unification of these parts in order to reveal the logic and structure of the whole.[84] Scholastic interpreters understood this logic to be inherent in the text, having been established there by its divine author. And so the *divisio textus,* according to its medieval practitioners, was an authentically exegetical exercise necessary for elucidating the sacred text; it was not, as the modern mind may be tempted to imagine, the occasion for the scholastic reader to impose eisegetically a foreign, non-biblical structure onto an ancient text and the putative intention of its human author.

Albert divides the text of Job most broadly into three parts: the first part, consisting of chapters 1 and 2, describes Job's state prior to his temptation; the second part, running from chapter 3 through chapter 41, contains "a disputation on the cause of his temptation"; and the third part, confined to chapter 42, tells of "Job's state after his temptation."[85] The *divisio textus* that Albert unfurls from here is so comprehensive and conceptually sophisticated that it may be considered a sort of commentary-in-brief in its own right. The level of detail characterizing Albert's entire *divisio textus* is intimated by his partitioning of the opening chapter, which is outlined thus:

84. On the scholastic *divisio textus* generally, see, e.g., Gilbert Dahan, *L'exégèse chrétienne de la Bible en Occident médiéval XIIe–XIVe siècle* (Paris: Cerf, 1999), 271–75; and on Albert's employment of the technique, see Schmidt, Prolegomena to *Super Matthaeum* (Ed. Colon. t. 21/1 pp. X–XI).

85. On Jb 1.1, p. 52 below.

- I. The state of Job's prosperity in soul and body (1.1–5)
  - A. Job's excellence in relation to other humans (1.1–4)
    - 1. With regard to the monastic good (v. 1)
      - a. According to the perfection of nature
      - b. According to the fame of his native land
      - c. According to the prophetic significance of his name
      - d. According to every perfection of justice
    - 2. With regard to the economic good (vv. 2–3a)
    - 3. With regard to the political good (vv. 3b–4)
  - B. Job's excellence in relation to God (1.5)
- II. The process of Job's temptation (1.6–2.13)
  - A. Temptations pertaining to property (1.6–22)
    - 1. Satan receives permission to tempt Job (vv. 6–12a)
      - a. Satan appears before God (vv. 6–8)
      - b. Satan obscures the good deeds of the saints (vv. 9–10)
      - c. Satan asks God for permission to tempt Job (v. 11)
      - d. Satan obtains permission (v. 12a)
    - 2. Description of the perfection of the temptation (vv. 12b–19)
      - a. Satan's departure from God (v. 12b)
      - b. The process of the temptation (vv. 13–19)
        - i. Concerning Job's property
          - α. Property pertaining to use and work
            - (*i*) In its timing (vv. 13–14a)
            - (*ii*) In Job's loss of property (vv. 14b–15)
            - (*iii*) In Job's despairing of regaining it (v. 15)
          - β. Property pertaining to use alone (v. 16)
          - γ. Property pertaining to work alone (v. 17)
        - ii. Concerning Job's children (vv. 18–19)
      - c. How Job made the best use of the temptation (vv. 20–22)
        - i. The use of misfortunes (vv. 20–21)
          - α. In his experience of being stricken (v. 20)

β. In his contempt for earthly realities (v. 21a)
γ. In his recognition of God's righteousness (v. 21b)
ii. The commendation of the one using them (v. 22)
3. Job is shown to withstand all trials (vv. 20–22)
B. Temptations pertaining to the body (2.1–13)

Such a thorough division of ch. 1 makes manifest Albert's assumption of the perfect harmony of the Joban text in all of its constitutive elements, a perfection that is consequential upon its divine authorship and intention. Furthermore, such a *divisio* is necessary for the reader on account of the cryptic nature of the book, even here in the seemingly straightforward narration of Job's excellence and temptation. Perhaps particularly here, in the account of Job's temptation, Albert understands the need to emphasize the perfect order of God's dealings with Job, which order is revealed and reflected in the scriptural text. Additionally, the above *divisio* indicates Albert's recognition that Job is a profoundly *theological* book and should be read as such: that is, like theology itself, Job examines "things" insofar as they are ordered to the beatific end of the human, whether things that actually make humans happy and thus are to be enjoyed, on the one hand, or things that help and dispose humans toward their end and so are to be used along the way, on the other. On Albert's reading of 1.20–22 (and indeed of the book as a whole), Job's temptation and misfortunes fall into this latter category: they are things of which Job makes good use toward beatitude. In so doing, Job provides a model for all subsequent hearers and readers of his tale of loss, suffering, and ultimate redemption. Thus Albert's *divisio* also bespeaks Job's timeless theological relevance.

A fifth and final feature of Albert's method in *Super Iob* that aligns with Humbert's instructions for lectors, particularly his injunction to "read the letter only" so that auditors "might make progress in understanding the Bible," is his deeply intertextual approach. Intertextuality is a characteristic mark of Albert's scriptural exegesis generally, also appearing prominently in his commentaries on Matthew and Isaiah, for instance.[86] And perhaps more than any other exegetical feature, including his more frequent engagement with Gregory's *Moralia,* Albert's thoroughgoing intertextual reading distinguishes the *Super Iob* from the literal *Expositio* of Aquinas. In commenting on ch. 1 alone, for example, Albert invokes approximately 140 other scriptural passages, most of which he quotes directly. Twelve of these interpretive intertexts appear in his treatment of vv. 20–21, which describe, on Albert's reading, the good use Job made of his temptation. On v. 20 (*Then Job arose and tore his clothes; and having shaved his head, he fell on the ground and worshiped*), Albert comments thus:

> ***Then Job arose,*** that is, he raised himself up. Col 3[.2]: *Contemplate the things that are above.* ***and tore his clothes,*** for it was the custom of the ancients, in time of sorrow, to rip apart the things that they used in caring for their bodies and to throw them aside. Thus Gn 37[.34] says of Jacob after Joseph's death had been reported to him: *Tearing his clothes, he put on sackcloth.* ***and having shaved his head,*** so that he might alter the pleasing appearance of his head as a sign of sadness. Ezek 5[.1]: *Son of man, take for yourself a sharp knife that shaves the hair, pick it up, and guide it over your head and through your beard.* ***he fell on the ground,*** namely face down, so that he would remember that he was nothing and that nothing had come forth from him. 1 Cor 14[.25]: *So, falling down on the ground, he will worship.*
>
> And this is what follows: ***and worshiped,*** namely God, who raises up from nothing whom He wills. Ps [145.8]: *The Lord raises up the broken.* Ex 4[.31]: *They worshiped face down on the ground.*[87]

Here, as throughout *Super Iob,* Albert not only underlines the univocity and interconnectedness of all of Sacred Scripture, both Old and New Testaments, but also thereby highlights its continuing relevance for his Christian hearers and readers. His use of Col 3.2 to interpret *Then Job arose* (*Tunc surrexit Iob*) of Jb 1.20 provides a clear example. Though Albert does not quote Col 3.1 here, he surely assumes that his auditor or reader will bring it to mind once v. 2 is introduced. He takes for grant-

86. See Schmidt, Prolegomena to *Super Matthaeum* (Ed. Colon. t. 21/1 p. XI and n. 46); and Callus, "The Writings of Albert the Great," 285, who identifies "reference on a large scale to similar passages of the Bible" as a defining feature of Albert's method.

87. On Jb 1.20, pp. 76–77 below.

ed that v. 1 makes explicit, both verbally and theologically, the connection between Job's "use" of his temptation and suffering toward final restoration, on the one hand, and Christ's resurrection and the new life of the faithful enabled by it, on the other: *If you have risen with Christ* (si consurrexistis cum Christo), *seek the things that are above, where Christ is sitting at the right hand of God* (Col 3.1). Thus Albert presents Job not only as a prefiguration of Christ, but also as a model for Christian behavior in the midst of suffering, as his use of Eccl 5.1 and Jas 3.2 to elucidate Jb 1.22 makes manifest.

Super Iob is replete with such intertextual interpretation, by means of which Albert lays open to view the essential nature of Sacred Scripture as *text* (in the most basic sense of the Latin *textus*), that is, as an elaborately woven fabric of divine revelation. To the modern reader (particularly one unfamiliar with scholastic exegesis and its assumptions), Albert may seem to lift particular scriptural passages from their larger texts and original contexts and to force them together artificially, perhaps even violently. James R. Ginther describes the fundamental difficulty of our encounter with the work of scholastic exegetes thus:

> Their construction is of such a foreign fabric, so alien are they to our modern way of reading and interpreting texts, that we often proceed down their corridors of reasoning and explanation in a partially blind state. It is sometimes unclear why we encounter so many disparate ideas in one book, and thus we are unsure how to bring together these ideas to form a coherent and unified pattern of exposition.[88]

Our experience of reading Albert's *On Job* may indeed serve as a stark reminder that scholastic theology and exegesis is, in Ginther's words, "ultimately an alien world to the modern scholar."[89] *On Job* challenges us to consider, however, that this perceived strangeness may be due more to our own assumptions and approaches to the Bible—that is, our own "partially blind state"—than to those of Albert.[90] But if Albert's commentary draws our attention to this basic problem of foreignness, it

88. Ginther, "There is a Text in this Classroom," 37.

89. Ibid., 44.

90. On these assumptions and approaches and their historical development, see, for example, Michael C. Legaspi, *The Death of Scripture and the Rise of Biblical Studies* (Oxford: Oxford University Press, 2010).

also provides something of a solution, precisely in its intertextuality. For although *On Job* may be, to use Ginther's phrase, "a foreign fabric," it is nevertheless a fabric, a *textus*. The attentive reader who approaches *On Job* with a basic familiarity with divine revelation as a whole and with some of the basic principles of pre-modern (Christian) reading (as outlined above) will surely discover a beautiful and profound tapestry intricately woven from a staggering diversity of scriptural threads. Careful examination of the rich scriptural tapestry that Albert here spreads out before us promises to contribute much to our understanding of the Bible generally, as Humbert indicates the exegetical work of the Dominican lector should.

C. The Book of Job as Scholastic Disputation

As noted earlier, Albert occupies a unique position in the history of the interpretation of Job: namely, he is the first and only exegete in history who explicitly reads the whole book as a debate in the mode of an academic or scholastic disputation.[91] Whereas Aquinas had several times compared the debate among Job and his friends to that of academic interlocutors, Albert takes the scholastic disputation as the structural principle of and interpretive key to the book as a whole.[92] Indeed, at the outset of his comments on ch. 3, he announces: "It must be said in advance that in this book there is a complete disputation among five people—namely, Job, Eliphaz, Bildad, Zophar, and Elihu—concerning the all-encompassing providence or care by which the Creator rules and governs human affairs."[93] Similarly, Aquinas had noted in the Prologue to his *Expositio* that the problem to which the book of Job responds is a fundamentally epistemological and theological one, namely that humans may not naturally or easily apprehend the truth that divine prov-

91. Meyer, "A Passionate Dispute," 201 and n. 6.

92. Ibid., 201 and n. 5; and Harkins, "Christ and the Eternal Extent of Divine Providence," 167–68. The following summary consideration of the disputation among Job and his friends, as Albert understands it, is indebted to Meyer's excellent and more detailed study.

93. On Jb 3.1, p. 93 below.

idence extends to human affairs.[94] On Albert's reading, Job's suffering raises three overarching questions pertaining to divine providence vis-à-vis human affairs that Job and his interlocutors take up: (1) whether humans can gain any insight into the nature of divine providence; (2) whether the working of providence reaches each individual creature; and (3) whether suffering is always a just punishment for guilt.[95] In introducing the disputation, Albert makes clear that the five disputants, in treating these questions, agree on three essential points. First, they agree that God, the Creator and Governor, possesses perfect knowledge of all human affairs. Second, they concur that there is absolutely no unfairness or sin (*nulla prorsus est iniquitas vel peccatum*) in God's care for and governing of all things. Finally, they agree that, in Albert's words, "God considers human actions more intimately than does the human himself who performs the actions, and therefore He sometimes grasps a defect in those actions that actually escapes the notice of the human himself."[96]

Beyond these basic points of correspondence, the views of the interlocutors variously diverge. Eliphaz endorses a straightforward act-consequence model, maintaining that God governs human affairs according to merits, repaying good people with good things and bad people with bad things, though he acknowledges that human sinfulness and demerit sometimes remain hidden from humans themselves.[97] Bildad, in contrast, denies that divine providence rules human affairs according to merits; rather, God always governs with an eye toward what is best in relation to the end of human happiness. Albert explains Bildad's teleological perspective thus: "And so, if God sometimes brings forth bad things for good people, He compensates for this by giving them many good things in the end; and if He sometimes brings forth good things for bad people, it is so that

94. See Harkins, "Christ and the Eternal Extent of Divine Providence," 165–68.

95. See Meyer, "A Passionate Dispute," 215–22, who notes that Zophar and Elihu treat the first question, Job and Eliphaz the second, and Eliphaz and Bildad the third (216).

96. On Jb 3.1, p. 93 below.

97. On Jb 3.1, pp. 94–95 below; and Meyer, "A Passionate Dispute," 218–19.

their condemnation might be more just."[98] In distinction from both Eliphaz and Bildad, Zophar holds that "divine governance is according to God's will alone," the cause of which cannot be known and therefore should not be sought by humans.[99] Like Zophar, Elihu, who enters the debate only in ch. 32, maintains that no human is able completely to understand the operations of divine providence. To Zophar's position, though, Elihu adds that God sometimes grants to particular humans—through dreams, angelic mediation, or discipline—a degree of insight into His will and thus into "how human affairs are bound to be in harmony with divine realities."[100]

Such propositional variation notwithstanding, Albert understands Eliphaz, Bildad, Zophar, and Elihu as standing together in fundamental agreement over against the position at which Job finally arrives at the conclusion of the disputation. Although they differ among themselves concerning (1) when humans will be repaid for their merits (whether in this life or the next) and (2) the extent to which humans can discern God's will and the workings of divine providence, Job's three friends and Elihu assume that God governs human life on the basis of a consideration of "inferior and temporal merits."[101] Job, by contrast, completely denies such a claim, holding instead that God's rule is "dissimilar to every human rule and looks to nothing temporal for governing human life."[102] But Job returns to such a proper understanding (*ad intellectum verum*) of divine justice only at the end of the disputation and in light of God's

98. On Jb 3.1, p. 95 below; and Meyer, "A Passionate Dispute," 219–20, who indicates Albert's own agreement with this doctrine, which he received from Moses Maimonides.

99. On Jb 3.1, p. 95 below; and Meyer, "A Passionate Dispute," 216–17.

100. On Jb 3.1, p. 95 below; and Meyer, "A Passionate Dispute," 216–17.

101. On Jb 37.24: "Hoc igitur est determinatio disputationis, et omnes supponunt quod ex respectu ad inferiora et temporalia merita regimen sit humanae vitae, …" (Weiss ed., col. 440 ll. 1–4). See also on Jb 38.1 (Weiss ed., col. 441 ll. 5–12).

102. On Jb 37.24: "Iob autem solus negat hoc, quod respiciendo ad merita hominum provideat et gubernet Deus humanam vitam, sed regimen suum dissimile sit omni regimini humano et ad nihil temporale respiciat gubernando vitam humanam" (Weiss ed., col. 440 ll. 18–24). See also on Jb 38.1 (Weiss ed., col. 441 ll. 12–14).

own determination.[103] Prior to this, Job had imagined what his interlocutors also took for granted, that the order of divine justice, according to which God governs human affairs, always stands in perfect harmony with the order of human justice.[104]

Following Elihu's protracted speech in chs. 32–37, Albert understands the human interlocutors to have reached a stalemate, a disputational deadlock that can be overcome only by divine intervention. "God alone is able to determine this disputation," and He does so *out of the whirlwind* (38.1), which phrase Albert takes as a reference to "the clash" of the positions of the interlocutors.[105] And God, as the "judge" (*iudex*) and master of the question under consideration, decides in favor of Job and against his friends. That is, God reveals that He rules human life without consideration of human merits; in this way God's governing of human affairs differs essentially from any mode of human rule.[106] Significantly, Albert notes how God's magisterial determination here dovetails with what God has revealed elsewhere in Scripture concerning His providential governing of human affairs. Indeed, our Dominican exegete explains how the divine solution to the *quaestio* of Job "is established on a certain proposition presupposed by all the saints, which is this: that nothing temporal can be the cause of the eternal."[107] On Albert's reading, Paul, for example, clearly sets forth this proposition in Rom 9.11–13, where he says of Esau and Jacob: *For before they had been born or had done anything good or evil, so that the purpose of God according to election might remain, not by works but by Him who calls, it was said to her* [*Rebecca*]: *The elder will serve the younger.* And in v. 16, concerning the cause of election and

103. On Jb 3.1, pp. 93–94 below.

104. On Jb 3.1, pp. 93–94 below. For a fuller consideration of Job's change of position, on Albert's reading, see Meyer, "A Passionate Dispute," 209–12.

105. On Jb 37.24: "Hanc autem disputationem solus Deus determinare potest, et ideo inducitur ut determinans eam" (Weiss ed., col. 440 ll. 24–26); and on Jb 38.1: "… *de turbine,* hoc est de conflictu huius disputationis, …" (Weiss ed., col. 442 ll 15–16).

106. On Jb 38.1 (Weiss ed., col. 440 ll. 32–39).

107. On Jb 38.1: "… et fundatur hoc super quandam propositionem ab omnibus sanctis suppositam, quae est haec, quod nihil temporale potest esse causa aeterni …" (Weiss ed., col. 440 ll. 39–42).

salvation, the Apostle declares: *Therefore, it is not of him who wills nor of him who runs, but of God who shows mercy.*[108] From such Scriptures, Albert maintains, one learns that God does not govern human affairs according to temporal merits, a truth that Eliphaz, Bildad, Zophar, and Elihu failed properly to grasp, thus necessitating God's final determination of the disputed question.[109]

Ruth Meyer has noted well how Albert presents Job as an exemplary practitioner and teacher of theological science, particularly in light of his special role at the end of the disputation.[110] What distinguishes Job from his friends is that he understands that in order to arrive at theological truth he must, as Meyer puts it, "allow himself to be taught by the Word of God."[111] At the beginning of ch. 42 Job acknowledges that he has spoken unwisely about divine realities that exceed his natural human understanding (v. 3).[112] Now, in contrast, he will interrogate God, and God will respond to him (v. 4). Albert reads this latter verse as indicating that Job sought the truth about divine providence from God Himself, hoping that God might illuminate him by grace, and indicating that God responded precisely with this supernatural gift of illumination.[113] Job seems to have understood the nature of theology as Albert himself conceives it in the *Summa theologiae,* namely that this science is wisdom properly speaking on account of the fact that it is through the highest causes (*per altissimas causas*), which are difficult for the human to know.[114] When Job asks, *But where is wisdom to be found, and where is the place of understanding?* (28.12), Albert notes that the word "wisdom" (*sapientia*) is used in two ways: generally and properly. Understood generally (*communiter*), "wisdom" is the power or excellence of any particular science or art, that

108. On Jb 38.1 (Weiss ed., col. 440 l. 42–col. 441 l. 5).

109. On Jb 38.1 (Weiss ed., col. 441 ll. 5–15).

110. See Meyer, "A Passionate Dispute," 209–15; quotation at 224.

111. Ibid., 209.

112. On Jb 42.3 (Weiss ed., col. 505 ll. 20–33).

113. On Jb 42.4 (Weiss ed., col. 505 l. 40–col. 506 l. 3). See also Meyer, "A Passionate Dispute," 209 and n. 48.

114. See *ST* I tr. 1 q. 1 sol. (Ed. Colon. t. 34/1 p. 6 ll. 52–54) and our treatment of this question above.

is, the understanding of what is highest and best in that body of knowledge, the attainment of the *ratio* according to which all other things in it are ordered and disposed.[115] Understood properly (*proprie*), on the other hand, "wisdom" is the apprehension of what is highest and best absolutely, the reception in the intellect of "the first things, the highest things, the most difficult things for the human to know on account of the fact that they are most distant from sensible perception." The only such things, Albert affirms, are God and divine realities, *Deus et divina*.[116] It is wisdom in this proper sense that Job inquires about in 28.12a; indeed, he seeks to know God in Himself, in His distinctions and properties, and in His effects.[117]

Similarly, when Job asks about the place of "understanding" in 28.12b, he intends by *intelligentia* the acceptance of the principles of investigation of divine matters or of wisdom properly speaking. These principles of the search for wisdom—that is, the starting points of theological inquiry—are received, Albert affirms, only "through revelation or through Scripture."[118] Furthermore, God graciously imprints these divine truths on "the clearest and purest intellect[s],"[119] of the sort that Job, who was *simple and upright* (1.1), possessed.[120] In reading the closing chapter of Job, Albert makes explicit the connection between Job's having spoken what is right about God's providence, on the one hand, and his worthiness to offer sacrifice and prayer for his friends, on the other.[121] After Job's intercession had reconciled his three primary interlocutors to God, all of his

115. On Jb 28.12 (Weiss ed. col. 316 ll. 3–24).

116. On Jb 28.12: "Proprie dicitur sapientia, ut in primo Metaphysicae dicit Aristoteles, acceptio intellectus de primis, altissimis, difficillimis homini scire eo, quod remotissima sunt a sensuum acceptione.... Talia autem non sunt nisi Deus et divina, secundum quod divina sunt" (Weiss ed. col. 315 ll. 28–42).

117. On Jb 28.12 (Weiss ed. col. 316 ll. 25–29).

118. On Jb 28.12: "Intelligentia autem acceptio principiorum est, quae in divinis esse non potest nisi per auctoritatem revelationi innixam et fultam. Unde talis principiorum acceptio per revelationem vel per scripturam dicitur intelligentia" (Weiss ed. col. 316 ll. 29–34).

119. On Jb 28.12: "Sapientia enim est acceptio divinorum a Deo impressa intellectui limpidissimo et purissimo" (Weiss ed. col. 317 l. 43–col. 318 l. 1).

120. Jb 1.1 and the commentary on it, pp. 52–56 below.

121. On Jb 42.7–8 (Weiss ed. cols. 507–8).

friends and siblings gathered at his house to eat with and comfort him concerning his past tribulation (42.11): each guest gave Job a single ewe, which Albert reads as "a sign of the innocence and simplicity" of Job, and one gold earring, "which, given to a wise man, signifies obedience to God more than it is a gift."[122]

At the beginning and end of the book bearing his name, then, Job is offered as a model theologian according to Albert's understanding of the nature and purpose of theology. He seeks wisdom proper—that is, God in Himself and divine realities that are most remote from sensible perception—on the basis of divine revelation and the infused virtue of faith rather than on the basis of fallible human reason in the manner of a philosopher. That Job's interlocutors fail to speak rightly concerning divine providence precisely because they assume that it operates according to the temporal merits of human agents serves as a clarion call to recognize that the First Cause and His ways stand finally beyond the reach of metaphysical science and its rational mode. Finally, Job reveals, in both his actions and his words, the nature of theology as *scientia secundum pietatem,* a science that treats the knowable, in Albert's words, "inasmuch as it inclines toward piety."[123]

In her well-known monograph *The Study of the Bible in the Middle Ages,* Beryl Smalley described Albert's *Super Iob* thus: "One has the impression of an experiment in exegesis, less attractive than it might have been because the argument between Job and his friends has been ruthlessly, tediously forced into the framework of a scholastic disputation, which God eventually 'determines' in favour of Job."[124] Such a harsh critique betrays a certain myopia concerning the Dominican pedagogical context that, as we have suggested above, likely gave rise to *Super Iob* and the formational and pastoral purposes for which Albert

122. On Jb 42.11: "... *et dederunt ei unusquisque ovem unam,* quae potius fuit signum innocentiae et simplicitatis, quam munus.... *et inaurem auream unam,* quae sapienti data magis significat oboedientiam Dei, quam munus sit" (Weiss ed. col. 510 ll. 27–34).

123. *ST* I tr. 1 q. 2 sol. (Ed. Colon. t. 34/1 p. 8 ll. 46–54).

124. Smalley, *The Study of the Bible,* 302.

seems to have intended his work. For Albert and scholastic masters like him, the disputation was most certainly not, as some modern historians have imagined, an exercise in logic-chopping and drawing meaningless distinctions wherein the ideas under debate were rarely given serious consideration.[125] Rather, even for ordinary Dominicans whose education remained confined to local *studia,* disputing was an essential task related to their learning of and formation according to Sacred Scripture.[126] Disputation provided the context wherein theological truths, having been revealed in the sacred text, could be rationally examined in various ways and their pastoral and pragmatic implications drawn out. Indeed, in his *Super Psalterium,* Robert Grosseteste, the thirteenth-century English scholastic and bishop of Lincoln, describes the leaders of the Church as the mouth of the ecclesial body in that they consume the food of Scripture for the entire body and masticate it through disputation so that its saving truths can be digested by the whole Church. As the mouth, these leaders also speak the words of God to the rest of the ecclesial body.[127]

Grosseteste's analogy promises to shed light both on Albert's understanding of Job as theologian and teacher and on the pedagogical purpose and pastoral potential of the Dominican master's reading the entire book of Job as a scholastic disputation. Job is fully aware, as we have seen, that wisdom properly speaking—the intellectual apprehension of "the first, highest, and most difficult things for the human to know," such as the mode of God's providential governance of human affairs—comes from God alone "through revelation or through Scrip-

125. See William J. Courtenay, *Schools & Scholars in Fourteenth-century England* (Princeton: Princeton University Press, 1987), 30.

126. See ibid., 61–66; and Ginther, "There is a Text in this Classroom," 39–43.

127. See Ginther, "There is a Text in this Classroom," 43; and James R. Ginther, "A Scholastic Idea of the Church: Robert Grosseteste's Exposition of Psalm 86," *Archives d'histoire doctrinale et littéraire du moyen âge* 66 (1999): 49–72, at 65–66. In this latter article, Ginther observes (p. 66 n. 66) that the image of chewing over Scripture in disputation comes from Peter the Chanter, *Verbum abbreviatum* (PL 205:25).

ture."[128] On Albert's reading, then, God necessarily determines the question under dispute so that Job—and his friends, by extension—might know what God also revealed to the human writers of other scriptural texts, namely that no temporal reality can be the cause of an eternal one. The words of Paul in Rom 9.11–13, 16 clearly attest to this profound theological truth.[129] More broadly, Albert's thoroughly intertextual reading of Job aims to highlight the perfect consistency of God's self-revelation throughout history as well as the transhistorical relevance of this divine revelation. If, as we have suggested, Albert's *Super Iob* originated as conventual lectures to his Dominican brothers in Cologne (and perhaps in Würzburg and Strassburg earlier), the general purpose of his framing the entire book as a scholastic disputation concerning divine providence seems clear enough. As a theological master lecturing on Job, Albert is inquiring into God and His ways on the basis of the divinely revealed text under consideration, just as the Job about whom he reads sought "wisdom" and "understanding" concerning providence from God Himself (Jb 28.12). Furthermore, in their own thirteenth-century context of religious formation, Albert's students are, with respect to this difficult theological question, likely engaging in the very exercise of disputation with which Job, Eliphaz, Bildad, Zophar, and Elihu were occupied so many centuries earlier. Thus the interpretive framework of a scholastic disputation within which Albert reads Job doubtless would have resonated deeply with his Dominican auditors. In combination with other aspects of *Super Iob,* such as its emphasis on practical utility and its employment of (Gregorian) moral readings, this overarching framework also would have had a particular appeal to Albert's initial hearers and readers. Ruth Meyer has observed, for instance, that Albert's interpretation of the end of Job "could be read as an appeal by the elderly Dominican to his readers, schooled in disputation as they were, to reach, through rational insight, a unanimous recognition of the truth, particularly when engaged in passion-

128. On Jb 28.12 (Weiss ed. col. 315 ll. 29–42 and col. 316 ll. 29–34).
129. On Jb 38.1 (Weiss ed. col. 440 l. 32–col. 441 l. 15).

ate disputation."[130] In short, by finding their own disputational exercise mirrored in the Sacred Scripture being commented upon by their conventual lector, Albert's Dominican hearers and readers were surely encouraged to consume and masticate the food of divine revelation in order that they might, in turn, preach it in such a way as to be digested easily and lived out by the body of Christian believers.

Situating *Super Iob* thus in its original Dominican context and reading it in terms of its putative formational purpose enables us to see how impoverished and anachronistic was Beryl Smalley's assessment. *On Job* must not be read as an "experiment in exegesis" that represents a "less attractive" stage of interpretation en route to the literal reading that modern historical critics have too easily assumed as objectively reflecting the original intention of the human author. It is only with this modern assumption of a biblical text's single, objectively knowable meaning in hand that Smalley could imagine that Albert had "ruthlessly, tediously forced" the argument between Job and his friends into the obviously foreign framework of a scholastic disputation.[131] In sharp contrast to Smalley, however, Albert understands the framework of scholastic disputation as anything but foreign to the book of Job, wherein Job and his friends are explicitly engaged in debate in their search for wisdom concerning divine providence. Equipped with the premodern assumptions that Job, like all of Sacred Scripture, is divinely authored, perfect, cryptic, and universally relevant, Albert knows that this sacred text speaks directly to his own scholastic educational context and to his Dominican students.[132] Bearing in mind Albert's context, purpose, and assumptions will surely aid the modern reader of *On Job* in recognizing and appreciating this commentary as a brilliant work of consummate exegetical and pedagogical skill.

130. Meyer, "A Passionate Dispute," 223.

131. Smalley, *The Study of the Bible,* 302.

132. See Legaspi, *The Death of Scripture,* who observes: "To scholastic theologians, the Bible was the source of theology. It contained timeless truths that needed to be clarified and organized by reason. These truths transcended historical and cultural boundaries" (11).

D. A Note on the Latin Text and the Present Translation

The following English translation of the first half of Albert's *Super Iob,* on chs. 1–21, is, to my knowledge, the first rendering of this work into any modern language. A translation of the second half of *Super Iob* will appear in a subsequent volume of the Fathers of the Church Mediaeval Continuation series. The Latin text of *Super Iob* from which the present translation has been made is the only modern edition of the text published to date: *B. Alberti Magni O. Praed. Ratisbonensis Episcopi Commentarii in Iob: Additamentum ad opera omnia B. Alberti* (Freiburg im Breisgau: Herder, 1904). Weiss produced his edition on the basis of five manuscript witnesses, which he describes briefly in the Prolegomena to his text and designates with the sigla E, T, B, F, and M.[133] Most often my translation follows the base text as established by Weiss, though in some instances I prefer alternate manuscript readings, either provided in Weiss's critical apparatus or supplied by my own consulting of particular manuscript witnesses. Such cases are indicated in the footnotes to the translation, and I refer to the manuscripts according to Weiss's sigla, of course.

Finally, a note concerning Albert's manner of quoting and paraphrasing scriptural texts is in order. The scriptural text of which Albert made use in his teaching and writing is commonly known as the Paris Bible, a version or general textual type of the Latin Vulgate that was copied in Paris beginning in the second quarter of the thirteenth century.[134] The scholarly use

133. Weiss ed., Prolegomena, VIII–X. Cf. the list of extant manuscripts attesting to *Super Iob* in Fauser, *Die Werke des Albertus Magnus,* 212–13.

134. On Albert's scriptural text and his general mode of using it, see Schmidt, Prolegomena to *Super Matthaeum* (Ed. Colon. t. 21/1 p. XXIV). On the Paris Bible or Paris Vulgate, see J. P. P. Martin, "La Vulgate latine au XIIIe siècle d'après Roger Bacon," *Le Muséon* 7 (1888): 88–107, 169–96, 277–91, 381–93; idem, "Le texte parisien de la Vulgate latine," *Le Muséon* 8 (1889): 444–66; 9 (1890): 55–70, 301–16; and, more recently, Laura Light, "The Thirteenth Century and the Paris Bible," in *The New Cambridge History of the Bible: From 600 to 1450,* vol. 2, ed. Richard Marsden and E. Ann Matter (Cambridge: Cambridge University Press, 2012), 380–91; and eadem, "French Bibles

of the term "Paris Bible" or "Paris Vulgate" ought not tempt us to imagine a single, absolutely fixed text across its manuscript witnesses; indeed, all texts transmitted via manuscripts exhibit a certain degree of fluidity.[135] Furthermore, in his practice of commenting on Scripture Albert often brings forth textual lemmata from memory, which sometimes results, for instance, in what appears to modern readers as the inappropriate conflation of two or more texts and the incorrect citation of the book or chapter from which these texts are taken. For many modern readers—who imagine the Bible exclusively as a written "text" that is uniformly printed, perfectly fixed, and very easily accessible—these elements of Albert's commentary may appear as infelicitous challenges.[136] We must bear in mind, though, the assumption that Albert makes manifest in various ways throughout *On Job,* namely that divine revelation is not reducible to a written text, nor is it intelligible apart from the divine economy of salvation and signification.[137] Indeed, William Graham has noted that in the medieval West "[a]t the most basic level, the oral text was the 'base text,' if only because reading a manuscript text virtually demanded prior knowledge of the text."[138] Albert surely did not have numerous individual scriptural manuscripts on his lectern or desk, each witnessing exact-

---

c. 1200–30: A New Look at the Origin of the Paris Bible," in *The Early Medieval Bible: Its Production, Decoration and Use,* ed. Richard Gameson (Cambridge: Cambridge University Press, 1994), 155–76.

135. Laura Light observes, for example: "Although it has often been stated that the great achievement of the thirteenth century was introducing order and uniformity into the chaotic history of the post-Carolingian Vulgate, uniformity was not in fact a characteristic of the thirteenth-century Bible—at least, not uniformity in the modern sense of the word" ("The Thirteenth Century and the Paris Bible," 383).

136. See, e.g., William A. Graham, *Beyond the Written Word: Oral Aspects of Scripture in the History of Religion* (Cambridge: Cambridge University Press, 1987), who affirms: "... it is especially the ubiquity of printed copies of the Bible ... that has reinforced our notion of scripture as a concrete and often commonplace object belonging to the physical paraphernalia of religious life and practice" (ix–x).

137. See Legaspi, *The Death of Scripture,* 3.

138. Graham, *Beyond the Written Word,* 36. He explains further: "Books were meant for ears as much as or more than for eyes, and authors wrote them with that explicitly or implicitly in mind" (38).

ly to a particular verse or constellation of verses—whether of Job or of the many other biblical books invoked—that appears in his commentary. In fact, there is no extant medieval codex that contains even the text of Job exactly as Albert sets it forth in *Super Iob*.[139] In addition to his own recollection from memory, Albert sometimes seems to draw on the liturgical use of a particular scriptural element or to take it from Gregory's *Moralia* or the *Glossa ordinaria*. Each of these serves as an important source for Albert's understanding of the divine economy of salvation and signification. So too does the book of Job. Let us turn, then, to Albert's magisterial reading of this divinely revealed account of a disputation concerning God's providence occasioned by a particularly poignant case of human suffering.

139. See Schmidt, Prolegomena to *Super Matthaeum* (Ed. Colon. t. 21/1 p. XXIV), who makes the same observation about Albert's commentary on Matthew.

ON JOB, VOLUME 1

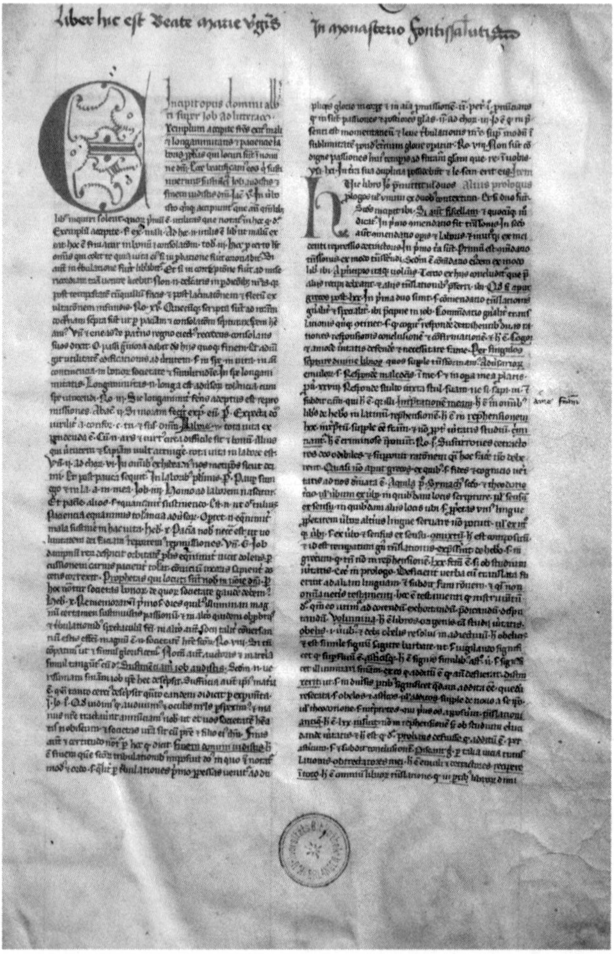

University Library Erlangen-Nürnberg, MS 58, fol. 1r.
Reproduced by permission.

THE PROLOGUE OF BLESSED ALBERT

TAKE, BROTHERS, *as an example of the departure of evil and of longsuffering, of labor and of patience, the prophets, who spoke in the name of the Lord. Behold, we count those blessed who have endured. You have heard of the suffering of Job, and you have seen the end of the Lord,* Jas 5.[1]

In this passage we learn five things that are customarily examined before reading any book whatsoever. The first of these is its utility, which is indicated when it says this: *Take, brothers, as an example of the departure of evil.* The book of Job is useful for this purpose: to show how evil will pass away, that is, how it will come to an end, with a view to the good and to consolation. Tb 3:[2] *Everyone who worships you holds this with certainty: that his life, if it is in the midst of trial, will be crowned; and if it is in the midst of tribulation, it will be liberated; and if it is in the midst of corruption, it will be allowed to come to your compassion. For you do not delight in our destruction, because after a storm you bring about tranquility, and after weeping and tears you infuse joy.* Rom 15:[3] *Whatever has been written has been written for our instruction, so that through patience and the consolation of the Scriptures we might have hope.* Hence even Aeneas, having been cast out of his father's kingdom and leaving it behind, comforted his crew, saying, "O you who have suffered more burdensome things, God will grant an end to these as well."[4]

And it adds Job's utility for the building up of virtue, namely in appearance, in manner of life, in moderation of the mind,

1. Jas 5.10–11.
2. Tb 3.21–22.
3. Rom 15.4.
4. Virgil, *Aen.* 1.199.

and in the fellowship with and imitation of good people. As to appearance, it says "of longsuffering." For longsuffering is the endurance of one's adversaries for a long time in the hope of conquering them. Heb 6:[5] *So with longsuffering he obtained the promise.* Hab 2:[6] *If it delays, wait for it.* Ps:[7] *Wait for the Lord, do so manfully; may your heart be strengthened, and wait for the Lord.*

With respect to manner of life the text says "of labor," in which one's entire life must be spent. Indeed, since art and virtue pertain to the difficult and the good, respectively, whoever wishes to attain to virtue and wisdom must occupy his entire life with labor. Hence 2 Cor 6:[8] *In all things let us show ourselves ministers of God.* And after a few words it follows:[9] *in a great number of labors.* Ps:[10] *I am poor, and in the midst of labors from my youth.* Jb 5:[11] *The human is born to labor.*

With respect to moderation of the mind the text has "and of patience," namely enduring others with equanimity. "For patience," as Cicero says, "is the calm toleration of adversaries."[12] Indeed, it is necessary to endure evil ones with equanimity in this life. Heb 10[13] says: *You need patience to do the will of God and to receive the promises.* Hence, blessed Job thought nothing of the loss of his property. Grieving with equanimity, he overcame the loss of his children. He patiently tolerated his flesh being stricken, and he corrected his wife's rebuke with wise teaching.

With regard to fellowship the text says, "the prophets, who spoke to us in the name of the Lord." This phrase indicates the community of the good, in whose fellowship we ought to rejoice. Heb 10:[14] *Call to mind the former days, after you had been enlightened, when you endured a great struggle with suffering. And indeed, on the one hand, you were made a spectacle by reproaches and*

5. Heb 6.15.
6. Hab 2.3.
7. Ps 26.14. All Psalm references use Vulg. numbering.
8. 2 Cor 6.4.
9. 2 Cor 6.5.
10. Ps 87.16.
11. Jb 5.7.
12. Quotation not found.
13. Heb 10.36.
14. Heb 10.32–33.

tribulations; but, on the other hand, you were made the companions of those who are treated this way. Indeed, it is great to have a community. Rom 8:[15] *If we suffer with Him, so too may we be glorified with Him.*

Moreover, the name of the author and the subject matter are simultaneously mentioned when it says, "You have heard of the suffering of Job." For, according to the most reliable opinion, Job himself has described these things. And the suffering of this very man is the subject matter, which he has described more certainly because he has learned it by experience. 1 Jn 1:[16] *What we have seen, what we have heard and have observed with our own eyes and what our hands have touched, we announce to you, so that you also may have fellowship with us, and [so that] our fellowship may be with the Father and with His Son Jesus Christ.*

The end and the truth of the book of Job are also indicated by the phrase that says, "You have seen the end of the Lord," that is, the end that the Lord has put to the tribulations of the saints. In this phrase too is indicated the mode and order of the book of Job, namely how through tribulations endured at the beginning he attains to the promise of a twofold glory, in body and in soul. 1 Pt 1:[17] *Announcing in advance the sufferings in store for Christ and the glories that follow.* 2 Cor 4[18] says: *For what is at present for us a momentary and slight tribulation is working in us an eternal weight of glory beyond measure in its sublimity.* Rom 8:[19] *The sufferings of this present time are not worthy to be compared to the future glory that will be revealed in us.* Is 61:[20] *They will possess double in their land, and everlasting joy will be theirs.*

15. Rom 8.17.
16. 1 Jn 1.1–3.
17. 1 Pt 1.11.
18. 2 Cor 4.17.
19. Rom 8.18.
20. Is 61.7.

CHAPTER 1

THERE WAS A MAN.

This book is divided into three parts: the first part describes Job's state before his temptation; the second part contains a disputation on the cause of his temptation, and begins further along in chapter 3, in this place:[1] *After these things Job opened his mouth;* and the third part describes Job's state after his temptation, beginning below in chapter 42, in this place:[2] *Then Job answered the Lord and said.*

The first of these parts is divided into two. The first describes the state of Job's prosperity, as much in the goods of the soul as in the goods of the body. The second recounts the process of his temptation, at this place in chapter 1:[3] *Now on a certain day.*

The first of these divisions is subdivided into two. The first describes how excellent a person Job was in relation to other humans; and the second how excellent he was in relation to God, at this place in chapter 1:[4] *And when the days of their feasting had run their course.*

The first of these subdivisions describes how excellent a person Job was with regard to the monastic good, which is the good of the individual human; the second describes how excellent he was with regard to the economic good, which is the stewardship of his household, at this place in chapter 1:[5] *And there were born to him.* The third describes how excellent he was with regard to the good of his people, which is called the po-

1. Jb 3.1.
2. Jb 42.1.
3. Jb 1.6.
4. Jb 1.5.
5. Jb 1.2.

litical good and consists in the governing of the city and the people, at this place in chapter 1:[6] *And that man was great.*

In the first of these subdivisions, Job is described according to the perfection of nature, the fame of his native land, the prophetic significance of his name, and every perfection of justice. And that is: ***a man,*** according to the perfection of mind, of nature, and of sex. ***There was:*** "He is a man in the perfection of mind," as Gregory says, "who fortifies himself with single-minded constancy while fighting back against the twofold attack of fortune. Since fortune favors him with prosperity at one moment, but at the next comes leaping upon him in a rage with adversities, mocking him, he fights back with uniform constancy, such that he is neither struck down in adversity nor raised up in prosperity."[7] Eccl 7:[8] *One man among a thousand I have found, a woman among them all I have not found.* Such a one was Hannah according to 1 Sm 1:[9] *And her countenance was no longer changed by different circumstances.* Jer 17:[10] *Blessed is the man who trusts in the Lord, and the Lord will be his confidence, for he will be like a vigorous tree,* and in this way it designates a man according to the perfection of nature and sex because he is vigorous and sprouts forth.

Here it does not say "there used to be" (*fuit*) or "there had been" (*fuerat*), but instead "there was" (*erat*). For the imperfect past tense describes ongoing past action, so that it is here noted that Job was so excellent a person in the past and that he continued to be so, according to what is said in Gal 6:[11] *Let us not cease in doing good.*

It commends Job for his native land, saying: ***in the land of Uz,*** which, in the literal sense, is in the region of Edom and Arabia. So, since he was of the stock of Edom, also known as Esau, he was an Edomite, as it is written in Gn 36.[12] Moreover, Uz is translated as "counsel," because that land was renowned for its

6. Jb 1.3.
7. Quotation not found.
8. Eccl 7.29.
9. 1 Sm 1.18.
10. Jer 17.7–8.
11. Gal 6.9.
12. Gn 36.43.

wisdom. Prv 8:[13] *I, wisdom, dwell in counsel, and I am present in learned thoughts.*

And the text adds a commendation on account of his name: ***whose name was Job.*** Gregory: "For previously his name was Jobab, and he was the son of a certain Zerah, who was the paternal grandson of Esau, and he was born of a certain woman named Borra. And so he was of the fifth generation from Esau, or of the fourth according to a different way of counting; but he was of the sixth or seventh generation from Abraham."[14] And it is said that he was the king of that land, and indeed its second king. For before him Bela reigned, and after him Husham is said to have reigned.[15] To be sure, the name Job means "he suffers," inasmuch as he suffered both in prosperity and in adversity. Hence below in the third chapter[16] he says: *I sigh before I eat, and my groanings are as overflowing water, because the fear which I feared has come upon me, and what I dreaded has befallen me.* Jb 31:[17] *I have always feared the Lord, as waves swelling over me,* so Job's name is prophetic.

And it adds a commendation concerning the perfection of his soul for having both parts of justice: ***and that man was.*** His soul's perfection will be shown in accordance with every distinction of the Psalm:[18] *Blessed is the man who has not walked in the counsel of the wicked.*

simple in intention, virtue, and prudence. In intention, because he directed his life toward the Lord alone, according to Mt 6:[19] *If your eye is simple, your whole body will be full of light.* Opposed to this simplicity is the duplicity of wishing both to reign with Christ and to prosper in this world. Sir 2:[20] *Woe to the sinner who walks the earth in two ways.* Dionysius and Aristotle say that the simplicity of virtue comes from the fact that virtue is from one cause, single and complete, whereas vice or sin is

13. Prv 8.12.
14. See Gregory the Great, *Mor.*, Preface, ch. 1. For Jobab, see Gn 36.33.
15. See Gn 36.33–34.
16. Jb 3.24–25.
17. Jb 31.23.
18. Ps 1.1.
19. Mt 6.22.
20. Sir 2.14.

of all sorts; and just as virtue touches upon the mean only, vice separates in every way.[21] Prv 11:[22] *The simplicity of the upright will guide them.*

Opposed to this simplicity is the multiplicity of sin. Jas 1:[23] *The double-minded man is inconstant in all his ways.* The simplicity of prudence is without the ambiguity (*sine plica*) of cunning and the subterfuge of evil. 1 Cor 14:[24] *I want you to be simple in evil and wise in good.*

and upright, supply:[25] in works. "He is upright," as Ambrose says, "who conforms his will to the divine will. He wills in every case what God wills for him to will, and with the same charity with which God wills. Whatever he wills, he has the same end that God does, which is the glory of God, and he wills it, as God does, according to the substance of the thing willed."[26] Song 1[27] says: *The upright love you.* "For a thing is upright," as Plato says, "which, having been joined to what is right, everywhere touches it and is touched by it."[28] Ps 111:[29] *The generation of the upright will be blessed.*

The text then adds a commendation concerning the other part of justice, which is to avoid evil both in habit and in act. In habit: ***and fearing God.*** Eccl 7:[30] *He who fears God neglects nothing.* Ps 13:[31] *There is no fear of God before their eyes.* Ps:[32] *Their ways are polluted at all times.*

and withdrawing from evil, in act, supply: universally, that is, from every evil, which is evil simply; for this is nothing other

21. See Dionysius, *DN* 4.31; and Aristotle, *EN* 2.6.

22. Prv 11.3.

23. Jas 1.8.

24. The quotation is actually from Rom 16.19. Surely working from memory, Albert seems to have confused this passage with 1 Cor 14.20.

25. Throughout his commentary, Albert often adds the word "supply" (*supple*) as a note of instruction to the reader indicating what he or she should add in order fully to understand the biblical text.

26. Quotation not found.

27. Song 1.3.

28. Plato, *Parm.* 137e.

29. Ps 111.2.

30. Eccl 7.19.

31. Ps 13.3.

32. Ps 9.26.

than mortal sin. Sir 1:[33] *The fear of the Lord drives out sin. For he who is without fear cannot be justified.* Jb 28:[34] *Behold the fear of the Lord is wisdom, and to withdraw from evil is understanding.*

[2] ***And there were born to him.***

Here it touches upon how excellent a person Job was with regard to the economic good, namely to his sons and daughters, his possessions, and his entire household.

And that is:[35] ***There were born to him,*** not to another. Here it touches on the fidelity of his marriage bed, which had no place for any adulterer, from whom sons might have been born. Heb 13:[36] *Let marriage be honorable, and the marriage bed be kept undefiled.* Wis 3:[37] *She who has not sinned in the marriage bed will be fruitful at the judgment of holy souls.* Is 28:[38] *The bed is so narrow that one or the other falls out, and the cover too short to cover both of them.*

seven sons. Seven pertains to holiness on account of the seven gifts of the Holy Spirit, as in Is 11,[39] and their sex pertains to perfection.

and three daughters. Three pertains to virtue on account of faith, hope, and charity, and their sex pertains to fruitfulness. Prv 31:[40] *Her children rose up and called her most blessed.* Wis 7:[41] *She is the mother of every good thing.*

And the text adds concerning his possessions: [3] ***And he possessed,*** as if he had placed them under his feet (*pedum positio*), because they were at his command and subject to his wishes, but he did not dominate them. ***seven thousand sheep,*** which are useful and gentle and simple animals. Their dung is useful for the earth, their milk and flesh are useful for food, their skin for

33. Sir 1.27–28.
34. Jb 28.28.
35. Throughout his commentary, Albert often, following the textual lemma, provides a brief summary of the theme(s) of the following section of text, immediately after which he adds the phrase “And that is” (*Et hoc est*) as an initial indicator of how precisely the text proceeds to present the identified theme(s).
36. Heb 13.4.
37. Wis 3.13.
38. Is 28.20.
39. Is 11.2–3.
40. Prv 31.28.
41. Wis 7.12.

shoes, their fleece for clothes, and their intestines are used to make strings for musical instruments. The number seven signifies the sum of all things, and one thousand signifies perfection because a thousand is a cube number.[42]

and three thousand camels, which carried heavier loads from place to place, loads of food and drink and treasures. Maybe that is why there were three thousand. But because the management of his household depended entirely on the fruit of the earth each year, the text adds: ***and five hundred yoke of oxen,*** which make one thousand oxen for plowing and cultivating the land. Prv 14:[43] *The strength of the ox is manifest where there is much wheat.* ***and five hundred donkeys,*** which carried the separated grain and the chaff crushed by the feet of animals from the fields to the barns. ***and an exceedingly large household,*** namely of workers and servants. The text calls the household exceedingly abundant, beyond the number necessary to manage the house, so that some workers might be on hand to step in for those who grow tired and falter and need to rest.

It must be noted that a household is managed with four virtues, none of which was neglected here. First, marital virtue, which is the knowledge and practice of making use of one's wife, is observed when the text says, *There were born to him,* considering that the wife is in her home as a queen is in her kingdom. Second, fraternal virtue, which is the virtue of treating one's children like senators in a kingdom, is observed where it says *seven sons and three daughters.* Third, chrematistic or economic virtue is observed where it says: *and he possessed.* And finally magisterial virtue, which is knowing how to use one's servants and handmaids, is observed where it says: *and an exceedingly large household.* In all these virtues Job was perfect with regard to the economic good.

But because, as the Philosopher says in Book I of the *Ethics,*[44] the good of an individual human is good, but the good of a household is better, and the good of a city and of a people is

42. A cube number, also called a perfect cube or simply a cube, is a number that is the cube of an integer. One thousand is the cube of ten (10^3=1000).

43. Prv 14.4.

44. Aristotle, *EN* 1.2.8.

best and most sacred, the text adds a description of how excellent a person Job was with regard to the good of his city and his people. And it does so in a threefold way, namely: by describing his excellence (1) toward his fellow-citizens, (2) toward God, in this place:[45] *And when the days of their feasting had run their course,* and (3) throughout the entire course of his life, in this place:[46] *Job did this every day.* The text describes his excellence toward his fellow-citizens in a twofold way, namely by explaining how he surpassed all in dignity and integrity, and how from his household he bound his city and his people together.

And that is: ***And this man,*** in particular, ***was great*** in virtue, integrity, and fame. The Gloss: "He was richer than the rich, because it is well known that those from the East are very rich."[47] Eustratius: "He is great who is universally renowned, whom no one surpasses in wealth, whom no one surpasses in moral integrity, whom no one surpasses in propriety of household, and whom no one surpasses in civic affairs."[48] 2 Chr 9:[49] *King Solomon was greatly esteemed above all the kings of the whole world for his wealth and glory.* **[*among all the people of the east* (orientales).]**[50] The people of the east are they from whom God's grace especially shines forth. Zec 6:[51] *Behold a Man, the Orient is his name; and under him he will arise.*

The text then adds how from his own household Job was building up the city in friendship and peace: **[4]** ***And his sons,*** who came forth from his house, ***were going,*** namely by making progress. Ps:[52] *They will go from virtue to virtue.* Is 27:[53] *When they go out from Jacob, Israel will blossom and bud.*[54] ***and preparing feasts,*** by means of which they restored themselves for the sake of the

45. Jb 1.5.
46. Ibid.
47. *GO* on Jb 1.3.
48. Quotation not found.
49. 2 Chr 9.22.
50. Albert omits this textual lemma, though his comments that follow depend upon it.
51. Zec 6.12.
52. Ps 83.8.
53. Is 27.6.
54. In the Vulg. Is 27.6 has *ad Iacob,* "to Jacob," rather than Albert's *ex Iacob* here. Albert, surely working from memory, seems to be recalling (whether

good and fortified one another ***at their homes***, that is, each one in turn. The preparation of sumptuous food is called a feast, according to which ***each one*** placed sumptuous food [before his brothers] so that they might be more refreshed and roused to virtue.

in his day, that is, when they wanted to display the bright light of their own fame. This is similar to Gn 43:[55] *Bring men into the house, slaughter animals, and prepare a feast, because they are going to eat with me at noon.* ***And***, lest members of the weaker sex imagine that they are looked down upon, ***they would send and invite their three sisters***. For Dionysius says that the divine Law brings those in the last rank of each hierarchy back to the divine majesty by those in the middle rank, and it brings those in the middle rank back by those in the first rank.[56] Rom 14:[57] *Welcome the one who is weak in faith, but not for the purpose of disputing over opinions.* ***to eat*** for strength, ***and drink*** for pleasure ***with them***. Song 5:[58] *Eat, friends, and drink, and become inebriated, dearly beloved.*

After this the text adds a description of Job's perfection toward God in the stewardship of his household: **[5]** ***And when the days of their feasting had run their course***, that is, when they had gone full circle. Ps 26:[59] *I will go around, and I will offer in His tabernacle a sacrifice of jubilation.*

Job would send to them, namely a priest and a sacrifice. Ps:[60] *The Lord has sent redemption to His people.* ***and sanctify them***, that is, he would atone for their sins, [according to the injunction in] Lv 19:[61] *Be holy, because I, the Lord your God, am holy.*

The text mentions the urgency and compulsion with which Job would do this: ***rising up at dawn***. Sir 5:[62] *Do not delay being*

---

intentionally or not) this text in a way that is more in accordance with the going forth of Job's sons from his house.

55. Gn 43.16.
56. See Dionysius, *CH* 4.3.
57. Rom 14.1.
58. Song 5.1.
59. Ps 26.6.
60. Ps 110.9.
61. Lv 19.2.
62. Sir 5.8.

converted to the Lord from day to day. Sir 39:[63] *The just man will surrender his heart at dawn to watch for the Lord who made him.*

he offered burnt offerings for each of them, seven burnt offerings for his seven sons. Ps:[64] *Seven times a day I have given praise to you.* The text also adds by what compulsion Job was offering these sacrifices: ***For Job said*** according to his own heart's judgment, [in line with] Rom 11:[65] *Do not be proud, but fear.* Gregory: "It is characteristic of a good mind to acknowledge a fault where there is no fault."[66] ***Lest perhaps,*** he says "perhaps" lest he judge his sons rashly. Lk 6:[67] *Do not judge! For you will be judged with the same judgment with which you judge.*[68]

my sons have sinned. 1 Jn 1:[69] *If we say that we have no sin, we deceive ourselves and the truth is not in us.* ***and have blessed God,*** this is said by antiphrasis, meaning they have cursed Him ***in their hearts,*** namely through gluttonous desire and through unbridled, loquacious speech, which are the two vices that customarily abound at feasts, as Gregory says and as Lk 16.24 proves.[70] The tongue of the rich man was tormented on account of his feasting.[71] And indeed it must be observed that he who has cleansed even the sins of his heart ought to loathe his sins of speech and action much more.

The text then adds praise for Job's continual perseverance: ***Job did this,*** unremitting in making progress in good deeds, ***every day.*** Mt 24:[72] *He who perseveres to the end will be saved.* Tb 4:[73] *Bless the Lord at all times.* Ps:[74] *I will bless you every day.*

[6] ***Now on a certain day.***

63. Sir 39.6.

64. Ps 118.164.

65. Rom 11.20.

66. *Regist. Epist. 64 Ad Augustinum Episcopum Anglorum* (PL 77:1195). See also Gregory, *Mor.* 32.1.1.

67. Lk 6.37.

68. Whereas the opening injunction here, *nolite iudicare,* is also in Lk 6.37, Albert appears to be quoting from Mt 7.1–2.

69. 1 Jn 1.8.

70. See Gregory, *Hom eu.* 40.5.

71. See Lk 16.

72. Mt 24.13.

73. Tb 4.20.

74. Ps 144.2.

Here the text recounts the process of Job's temptation, both from the perspective of the tempter and from the perspective of the one tempted, and it has two parts: first, temptations pertaining to property, and, second, temptations pertaining to the body. And this second part begins below in this place:[75] *And it happened, when on a certain day.*

The first part is divided into three. The first division mentions Satan's receiving permission to tempt Job. The second describes how perfect the temptation was in its aim to provoke and drive blessed Job to sin during his experience of temptation. In the third division Job, perfect in virtue, is shown to withstand, in the name of the Lord, any trials whatsoever, in this place:[76] *Then Job arose and tore his garments.*

And note the process of his temptation according to blessed Gregory.[77] First his property is snatched away, then his children, because Job was concerned to preserve his property as an inheritance for his children, and at its loss, his suffering was greater on their behalf. Concerning the loss of property, Job first loses his oxen, which are aids to his work, so that he might remain anxious about the cultivation of his land. Afterwards he loses his sheep, intended to nourish his household, so that he might remain anxious about his household. Finally, he loses his camels, so that he might remain anxious about how to transport those material things that providence already had prepared and provided for him.

The first division, on Satan's receiving permission to tempt Job, consists of four subdivisions. The first shows how the tempter appeared before God, and the second how he obscured the good deeds of the saints, in this place:[78] *Can it be that Job fears God for no reason?* In the third subdivision Satan asked God for permission to tempt Job, in this place:[79] *But stretch out your hand.* And the fourth subdivision relates how he obtained permission, in this place:[80] *Behold all.*

75. Jb 2.1.
76. Jb 1.20.
77. See Gregory, *Mor.* 2.12.26.
78. Jb 1.9.
79. Jb 1.11.
80. Jb 1.12.

The first subdivision begins in this way: ***Now on a certain day.*** It says "certain" in order to designate the particularly and singularly remarkable fact of so great a temptation. And indeed it says "day" because in the midst of such great suffering Job did not fall from the light of reason or of grace, and he was going to be restored from darkness to light. Mi 7:[81] *Do not rejoice, my enemy, over me because I have fallen; I will arise. When I sit in darkness, the Lord is my light.* And just after this:[82] *He will bring me forth into the light. I will see His face. And my enemy will see me, and she will be covered with confusion.* Later Job himself says:[83] *For I have not been destroyed by the darkness that hangs over me, nor has the gloom covered my face.* **when the sons of God came.** "Angels are called the sons of God," as Gregory says, "because the likeness of the image of God (*similitudinem imaginis Dei*) has been imprinted more deeply in them."[84] Hence the higher angel, who fell, is praised in Ezek 28[85] in this way: *You were the seal of the likeness, full of wisdom and perfect in beauty; you were in the midst of the pleasures of your God,* where Gregory says that a seal is a deep impression.[86] And for that reason this angel is called a seal, because he possessed a deeper likeness of the image of God in himself. Also in Dn 3[87] it is said of the angel who appeared with the three young men [in the fiery furnace] that his likeness (*species*) was similar to the Son of God.[88] These angels are said to have come when they have finished their ministry among humans, and they reveal, with divine light, the completion of their service, as [Raphael says] in Tb 12.20: *It is time that I return*

81. Mi 7.8.
82. Mi 7.9, 10.
83. Jb 23.17.
84. Gregory, *Mor.* 2.3.3.
85. Ezek 28.12–13.
86. See *Mor.* 32.23.47.
87. Dn 3.49, 92.
88. Standing behind Albert's, and Gregory's, exposition here is the ancient Christian doctrine that the divine Son, the second Person of the Trinity, is Himself the very image of God, according to which (Gn 1.27: … *ad imaginem Dei*. . . .) God made rational creatures (i.e., both angels and humans). In comparison with humans, angels are the "more profound" likeness of the image of God.

to Him who sent me, but as for you: bless the Lord and tell of all of His wonderful works.

And it is said in Bar 3[89] concerning the angels, described under the likeness of the stars: *And the stars have given light on their watches, and they rejoiced. They were called, and they said: We are here; and with delight they shined forth to Him who made them.* And this is what follows: ***to stand before the Lord.*** They "stand" because they are present to the face of God by the most intimate contemplation, and they reveal what they have accomplished in their own ministry and learn through illumination what they are going to do next. And that the text says "to stand" indicates that they bring themselves entirely into the divine light, without ever being distracted. And that it says "before the Lord" indicates that they conceal none of their desires or actions from God. Sir 23:[90] *The eyes of the Lord are far brighter than the sun, looking around and seeing all the ways of men.*

Satan, namely the adversary[91] of man, the devil, ***also appeared among them.*** And the text does not say that he came or that he was called, but rather that he, as if compelled, appeared, because he was not able to conceal himself from the divine light, just as he who is in the light sees by scattering the darkness. Jn 1:[92] *The light shines in the darkness.* Chrysostom explains that Satan himself is said to scatter the darkness because he is the adversary of all the elect, who make progress because they are guarded by the angels.[93] Zec 3:[94] *The Lord showed me the high priest Jesus, standing before the angel of the Lord, and Satan was standing at his right hand in order to be his adversary.*[95]

And the text says "among them" and not "with them," nor "before them," nor "after them." He was not "with them" because he was not united with them in will; he was not "before them" because he did not prevail in hindering their progress;

89. Bar 3.34, 35.
90. Sir 23.28.
91. In late Hebrew and Aramaic the word *Satan* means adversary.
92. Jn 1.5.
93. See Chrysostom, *Hom. 23* on Jn 1.11.
94. Zec 3.1.
95. In the immediate context of this text from Zechariah, Jesus or Joshua is the name of the high priest who was the son of Jehozadak (see Zec 6.11).

he was not "after them" because he was not able to make a treacherous attack on those angels who had been confirmed in obedience. Rather, he was "among them" because he sowed evil in the midst of their progress in ministry among humans. Mt 13:[96] *While they were asleep, his enemy came and sowed tares among the wheat.*

[7] ***The Lord said to him.*** Blessed Gregory says that these utterances were not produced by the exhalation of the voice, since God and the angels and Satan are incorporeal substances, but rather that for God to speak is to scrutinize thoroughly Satan's evils with His own light and to reveal them to Satan's conscience.[97] Ps:[98] *I will convict you, and I will set your evil deeds before your face.* That is, I will convict you by revealing you to yourself. Hence blessed Gregory says that God speaks to Satan according to four modes, namely by reproving his ways, by displaying the righteousness of His own elect against him, by permitting him to tempt an innocent person, and by preventing him from daring to go further.[99] And, in fact, these four modes of divine speech will be revealed in the scriptural text in that order. Satan, however, speaks to God according to three modes, namely by insinuating his own ways among others, by accusing the innocent of having committed sins, and by demanding permission to tempt an innocent person.[100] The Lord speaks to the good angels by inspiring them to do His will; the angels speak by admiring the God above them; holy souls speak to God through their desires, which are always in harmony with God.[101] But Gregory maintains that all these modes of speech occurred through demonstrations of illumination and not verbally. Indeed I call it a demonstration of illumination whenever by means of the will an intellectual substance, whether lower or higher, reveals its own concepts and desires that are in the light of its own understanding to another intellectual substance. Basil says as much in a certain little book on faith in the divine:

96. Mt 13.25.
97. See Gregory, *Mor.* 2.7.12.
98. Ps 49.21.
99. See Gregory, *Mor.* 2.7.12.
100. Ibid.
101. See Gregory, *Mor.* 2.7.10, 11.

"God has bestowed on us the use of speech so that we, existing as corporeal beings, might reveal our desires to one another. If, however, we were able to use the naked and bare soul to communicate with one another, we would not need speech, but rather we would see our own desires in each other."[102] Gregory also teaches this when he says: "We, who rest in the secret place of the heart behind the wall of the body, as it were, come out by means of the tongue."[103] Here Gregory wishes to say that, just as a person who stands behind a wall is not seen unless he goes out into the presence of another, so too the desire of the heart, hidden from another by the wall of the body, is not seen unless it goes out by the vehicle of the voice. If, however, there were not this wall between individuals, it would not be necessary for one to go out to the other in this way.

Now the first mode according to which God speaks to Satan is by reproving his ways in His own light, and He does this when He asks: ***Where do you come from?*** But this is not the question of one who is ignorant, but rather of one who is reproving, as if to say: "See, you come from so many indecencies and you have accomplished so many wicked deeds." Gn 3[104] is similar: *Adam, where are you?* that is, In what great misery are you? Jer 2:[105] *Your own wicked deeds will reprove you, and your apostasy will rebuke you.* Thus, when God utters this question, Satan's own wicked deeds are revealed to him in the divine light.

Concerning the first mode of Satan's speaking to God, which is by insinuating his own ways among others, the text then adds: ***He answered and said***. For Satan to answer here is to be unable to hide his ways from the divine light. ***I have gone around the earth* (Circuivi terram),** that is, I have frequented the hearts of those on the earth with crooked steps (*curvo gressu*). Ps 11:[106] *The wicked walk in circles* (in circuitu). Is 51:[107] *They have said to your soul: Bend down* (incurvare), *so that we may go over.*

and I have walked through it. He "walks through" who leaves

102. Basil, *Hom.* 15 (*de fide;* PG 31:464).
103. See Gregory, *Mor.* 2.7.8.
104. Gn 3.9.
105. Jer 2.19.
106. Ps 11.9.
107. Is 51.23.

footprints behind everywhere. But the footprints of the devil are sins, [as in] the Psalm:[108] *Have mercy on me, O God, for man has trampled me underfoot.* The devil is here called man because he has conquered man, just as Priscian says, "Scipio was called an African because he conquered Africa."[109] Ps:[110] *My enemies have trampled me underfoot all day.* The devil's walking is twisted, and the plodding of his feet is heavy. Is 27:[111] *The Lord will punish Leviathan the bar-like serpent and Leviathan who twists like a bar.* Like a bar, the devil is rigid when impressing his footing, and he twists when, by guile, he makes steps crooked and diverts man from the straight path of virtue.

Concerning the second mode of God's speaking to Satan, namely by revealing to him in His own light the righteousness of the elect, the text then adds: **[8]** ***And the Lord said to Satan: Can it be that you have considered my servant Job?*** "Can it be that" appears at the beginning of questions to which the answer is "no." And "to consider" means to focus the light of the star (*sideris*) of the understanding or of the eyes onto something with undivided attention and full effort, so that it is comprehended perfectly, and here the manner of considering is not without the disposition of love. For love, as Augustine says, fixes the eye.[112] Note that, although Satan sees good people by the light of his understanding, he nevertheless does not see them with the eye of love because, by turning himself away from them through envy and by being indignant toward them, he does not approve of their good deeds. Ps:[113] *The sinner will see and will be angry, and he will gnash his teeth and waste away.* That is why God enumerates Job's good deeds. When He says "my servant," He commends his obedience to the commandments. Wis 9:[114] *I am your servant, and the son of your handmaid.* When He says "Job," He commends him for his suffering on behalf of sinners and

108. Ps 55.2.
109. Priscian, *IG* 2.58.
110. Ps 55.3.
111. Is 27.1.
112. See Augustine, *En. Ps.* 149 sect. 3 (on v. 2).
113. Ps 111.10.
114. Wis 9.5.

for his compassion on the afflicted. Jb 30:[115] *In days past I wept for the afflicted, and my soul had compassion on the poor.*

Then God commends him for his eminent holiness and perfection: ***there is no one like him on the earth.*** Sir 44:[116] *There was not found one like him, who kept the law of the Most High.* Dt 33:[117] *Blessed are you, O Israel; who is like you, O people, you who are saved by the Lord?*

a simple man, this was explained earlier.[118] Mt 10:[119] *Be simple, as doves.* 2 Cor 1:[120] *In Him [Christ] it is not "Yes" and "No." Rather, in Him it is "Yes."* Prv 11:[121] *The righteousness of the simple man will order his way.* ***and upright,*** by every rectitude of virtue. Ps:[122] *The righteousness of the Lord is upright, delighting hearts.*

who fears God. Is 11:[123] *The spirit of fear will fill him.* ***and withdraws from evil:*** not only from sin itself, but even from the circumstances and occasions of sin. Gn 19:[124] *Do not remain anywhere in the whole region, but save yourself on the mountain.* Is 54:[125] *Withdraw far away from false accusations, for you will not be afraid, and from terror, for it will not come near you.*

But when the saints are praised, Satan rages against them more fiercely. And therefore his second mode of speaking, that is, obscuring the good deeds of the saints, is introduced: **[9]** ***Satan answered Him.*** Gregory: "He who does not find evil deeds that he can accuse turns good deeds into evil, as if they did not arise from a good soul. And so, for this sort, to speak is nothing other than to utter a complaint against good people, to envy their progress in the good, and to seek their destruction by harming them."[126]

115. Jb 30.25.
116. Sir 44.20.
117. Dt 33.29.
118. That is, on v. 1 above.
119. Mt 10.16.
120. 2 Cor 1.18, 19.
121. Prv 11.5.
122. Ps 18.9.
123. Is 11.3.
124. Gn 19.17.
125. Is 54.14.
126. Gregory, *Mor.* 2.8.14.

Can it be that Job fears God for no reason? that is, without hope of earthly reward. Gn 29:[127] *Can it be that you will serve me without payment simply because you are my brother? Tell me, what payment will you accept?*

The text then enumerates the rewards for which Job was said to hope, both in the preservation of goods that he had already acquired and in the increase of goods that he was going to acquire. That is: **[10]** ***Have you not built a rampart around him,*** that is, around his person. Is 26:[128] *Zion, the city of our strength; a savior will be set within it, a wall and a bulwark.* ***and his house,*** that is, his family. Ps:[129] *Unless the Lord builds the house, those who construct it labor in vain.* ***and all of his resources around him,*** namely his resources of wealth**?** Wis 10:[130] *Wisdom kept him safe from his enemies, and defended him from seducers.* ***Have you not blessed the work of his hands,*** that is, by multiplying it? Gn 22:[131] *By blessing I will bless you, and by multiplying I will multiply you.* ***and,*** supply: thus ***his possessions in the land have increased?*** that is, they have multiplied. 2 Sm 23:[132] *He is my entire salvation, from whom all things sprout forth.*

Here it adds the third mode of Satan's speaking to God, which is to demand permission to tempt Job. That is: **[11]** ***But stretch out your hand a little,*** namely so that you might not hold him in your protecting hand. But he says "a little" in order that God might expand his freedom to tempt Job to include his material resources, but not his person. And this is clear in what follows: ***and touch everything that he possesses,*** that is, permit my evil ways to touch them. For many who have a fear of this world are incited against the Lord when they lose their possessions. And this is why the text adds: ***and will he not refuse to bless you to your face?*** Here the presence in external goods of the illumination of grace is called "the face," and "to bless God to his face" is to venerate God for the presence of external prosperity. Ps:[133] *He will praise you when you bless him.*

127. Gn 29.15.
128. Is 26.1.
129. Ps 126.1.
130. Wis 10.12.
131. Gn 22.17.
132. 2 Sm 23.5.
133. Ps 48.19.

The text then adds the words of the Lord whereby He permits or extends to Satan the power to tempt an innocent holy person. That is: **[12]** ***Therefore, the Lord said to Satan,*** namely by revealing through illumination that the power to tempt Job had been granted. Hence Gregory says: "The face of the Lord is the consideration of His grace."[134] Satan says, then, to God that if you take away the things that you have given Job, which he loves, he will not seek your consideration, meaning the favor of your grace, but rather will scorn you by cursing you.

Continuing in the third mode of the Lord's speaking, which is allowing Satan the power to tempt an innocent person, the text adds: ***Behold, all that he has is in your hand,*** that is, in your power of tempting. Jb 9:[135] *The earth has been given into the hands of the wicked.* Jb 16:[136] *God has delivered me into the hands of the wicked.*

And it adds the fourth mode of God's speaking, which is to restrain Satan from tempting Job beyond his strength, when it says: ***only do not stretch out your hand,*** that is, your power to tempt, ***against him personally,*** that is, against his person, namely his body or soul. 1 Cor 10:[137] *God is faithful, and He will not allow you to be tempted beyond your strength, but together with the temptation He will provide some success, so that you may be able to endure it.*

The Jews and our Judaizing heretics interpret the words set forth here in a different way. For they say that "on a certain day,"[138] that is, in the light of divine providence, the angels or sons of God stand before God. These refer to good creatures, those who act in accord with an upright intellect. But Satan still attends to evil, and he represents evil creatures, those that are given to sensuality and to passions. And thus it is said that every human has a good angel on his right, and a bad angel on his left. The Lord's question to Satan, "Where do you come from?" is indefinite because evil itself is also indefinite. And when Satan is speaking, it is really matter with privation that is speak-

134. Gregory, *Mor.* 2.10.18.
135. Jb 9.24.
136. Jb 16.12.
137. 1 Cor 10.13.
138. Jb 1.6.

ing; so when he says, "I have gone around the earth,"[139] it was to spread the evil of privation everywhere. For Satan has no place in heaven, because there is neither generation there nor corruption. According to these interpreters, when the Lord says, "Can it be that you have considered," etc.,[140] and the demon says, "Stretch out," etc.,[141] it signifies the search by certain incorruptible realities for corruption and perversion. Thus Ovid, in the story of Phaeton,[142] says that Phaeton steered the chariot of the sun wrongly and burned up heaven and earth. This is interpreted as referring to the deviations of the planets in their orbits around the earth, or to the perversion of the upright by the wickedness of privation, or to the wickedness of a span of misfortune allowed to visit itself upon a household that had been enjoying prosperity. And this is summed up in the third part of the book of Rabbi Moses entitled the *Guide of the Perplexed,* ch. 24.[143] Abraham, Isaac, Moses the Egyptian, and the philosophers of the Jews agree with Rabbi Moses in affirming that angels are intelligences that are in every place and time, and thus cannot be sent. They maintain, however, that the sending of angels refers to the presence of their effects in lower creatures, or in humans who, by a spirit of prophecy, foretell future events, whether for good or for evil.

The former interpretation accords with Catholic truth, but as for the latter nonsense, that is none of our concern.

And Satan went out from the face of the Lord. Here the text discusses the process of Satan's temptation in taking Job's property away, and it mentions three things: [first,] the departure of the tempter; [second,] the process of his temptation, in this place: *Now;*[144] and [third,] how he who was tempted made the best use of the temptation, in this place: *Then Job arose.*[145] So, firstly: ***And Satan,*** namely the adversary of every good, ***went out,***

139. Jb 1.7.
140. Jb 1.8.
141. Jb 1.11.
142. Ovid, *Metam.* 2 ll. 47–328.
143. Moses Maimonides, *Dux* 3.22.
144. Jb 1.13.
145. Jb 1.20.

[in accordance with] Mt 4:[146] *Go, Satan.* Mt 16:[147] *Get behind me, Satan.* ***from the face of the Lord.*** Here the presence of the majesty and power of the one repressing and restraining the unjust will of the tempter is called "the face of the Lord." And the "going out" of Satan is his departure from the constraints of that power, so that he could exercise the wickedness of his will unencumbered. Is 10:[148] *His indignation is in my hand,* that is, in God's power to contain the wickedness of the will. Jer 15:[149] *Cast them out from my presence, and let them go forth,* that is, from the presence of God's power to restrain the freedom of the evil will. Secondly the text treats the process of Job's temptation, first concerning his property and then concerning his children. It treats the temptation concerning his property in three parts: the property that pertains both to use and to assistance in work, the property that pertains to use alone, and the property that pertains to work alone.

Concerning the first of these, the temptation befell Job in three ways, namely in its timing, in his loss of property, and in his despairing of regaining his property. That is: **[13]** ***Now on a certain,*** that is, remarkable on account of the magnitude of what happened, ***day,*** the experience of temptation is shown by the nature of the time, namely that it is a falling away from the light of reason. Wis 18:[150] *Your saints had a very great light.* Jn 8:[151] *He who follows me will not walk in darkness.* ***when his sons and daughters,*** which we interpreted according to the spiritual sense above.[152] ***were eating,*** that is, being restored by the sweetness of grace, ***and drinking wine*** of spiritual delight. Is 4:[153] *On that day seven women will seize one man, saying: We will eat our own bread and wear our own clothes.* ***in the oldest brother's house,*** namely whose turn to host the feast had come and who was second in his father's household because he was more distinguished than

146. Mt 4.10.
147. Mt 16.23.
148. Is 10.5.
149. Jer 15.1.
150. Wis 18.1.
151. Jn 8.12.
152. That is, on v. 2.
153. Is 4.1.

his siblings by birth. Moreover, the text says "brother's" in order to increase the sorrow, because a father's sorrow is increased by heaping a brother's sorrow onto it. Jer 6:[154] *Mourn as for an only son.*

[14] ***a messenger came to Job,*** so that the report and the knowledge of the disaster would afflict Job more than if he had remained unaware. 2 Sm 18:[155] *You will not be the messenger this day, but you will deliver the message another day. Today I do not want you to deliver the message because the king's son is dead.* ***and said,*** that is, by announcing a disaster he threw the household into confusion. ***The oxen were plowing,*** they are useful in a twofold way, as food and as help in work. ***and the donkeys were grazing beside them,*** beside the oxen. It says this because food for donkeys is produced from the work of oxen; thus the destruction of oxen would result in a desperate situation for donkeys because they are not able to forage for food. Is 30:[156] *The colts of donkeys will eat mixed grain, as it was winnowed on the threshing floor.*

[15] ***and the Sabeans,*** that is, bandits, those who take others captive, ***rushed in.*** And it says "rushed in" because they could not have been anticipated in such a way that the property damage that they inflicted could have been prevented, and because their javelins were all the more deadly, striking by surprise. ***and carried all of them off,*** so that there would be no hope at all after everything had been taken away. Ps:[157] *They said: Plunder it, plunder it all the way to its foundation.* And to show the futility of any hope for assistance, the text adds: ***and killed the servants with the sword,*** namely those who could have followed the bandits and recovered the lost property, ***and I alone have escaped,*** that is, I was permitted to escape, ***to tell you.*** This must be read with horror. And this is the sense: They allowed me to escape not only to tell you that they plundered your oxen and donkeys to alleviate their own poverty, but also, to add insult to injury, so that you might know that these things had been done. According to the spiritual sense, however, sad things are announced on a

154. Jer 6.26.
155. 2 Sm 18.20.
156. Is 30.24.
157. Ps 136.7.

day of exuberant joy because, as Gregory says, "the pleasure of being glutted is a forewarning of tribulation."[158] Ps:[159] *Even while their food was in their mouths, the wrath of God came upon them.* Prv 14:[160] *Laughter will be mingled with sorrow, and mourning waits at joy's end.* And the wheel of fortune, which first lifts a person up to the highest place, always drops him to the lowest. And this happened in the house of the firstborn son because when prelates are engaged in gluttony, firstly oxen, that is, those who are useful in the Church, and secondly donkeys, that is, the simple, are driven away by demons. The servants are the virtues that stand guard, such as reason and understanding and the intellectual faculties. Or they are the clerics and the laity who are only watchful outwardly, because they are killed with the sword of diabolical temptation. Jer 4:[161] *Behold, the sword reaches even to the soul.* The messenger who escapes is either the word of Scripture that convicts, or the worm of conscience that gnaws constantly. This is signified in Gn 4,[162] where the word of the Lord convicts Cain, saying: *What have you done?* At the end of Is:[163] *Their worm will not die,* that is, their gnawing conscience.

[16] ***And while.*** The second stage of the temptation concerns that property that pertains to use but not to assistance in work. And without interruption, even before the report of one disaster comes to an end, another one is announced, lest through any intervening time the mind dispose itself to patience. That is: ***he was still speaking,*** he had not yet completed his words when ***another came and said,*** doubling the disasters. Gregory: "Adversities, if they are many, strike more intensely if they are also announced in quick succession."[164]

The fire, which consumes everything and leaves nothing behind. Jb 31:[165] *It is a fire devouring all the way to consumption, and rooting out my entire harvest.* ***of God,*** namely whom you worship,

158. Gregory, *Mor.* 2.13.22.
159. Ps 77.30–31.
160. Prv 14.13.
161. Jer 4.10.
162. Gn 4.10.
163. Is 66.24.
164. Gregory, *Mor.* 2.13.22.
165. Jb 31.12.

fell unexpectedly, so that nothing could be saved, neither wool, nor skin, nor flesh. ***from heaven***, namely through bolts of lightning, so that you might know that even heaven strives against you. Jb 20:[166] *A fire that is not kindled will devour him; what is left in his tent will be consumed. The heavens will reveal his iniquity, and the earth will rise up against him.*

and burned up all the sheep, so that not one was left behind to serve as the seed for future generations, ***and the servants,*** so that there would be no hope of a rescuer of the sheep, ***and I alone have escaped,*** not to comfort, but ***to tell you*** that both heaven and the God of heaven strive against you. But according to the spiritual sense sheep are the gentle and simple members of the Church who are consumed by the fire of desire when prelates give rein to their appetites and to revelry. Am 6:[167] *Alas for those who drink wine from bowls and anoint themselves with the finest oils, but are not grieved over the affliction of Joseph.* The spiritual meanings of other things in the text are not changed.

[17] ***And while.*** Here the text touches on what was lost from those things that pertain to work alone. ***he was still speaking,*** he had not yet finished his words, ***another came and said:*** Jb 20:[168] *The terrible ones will rush and come upon him.* ***The Chaldeans formed three squadrons,*** so that they would accomplish with three what they were not able to do with either two or one, ***and attacked the camels,*** which are wild especially at the time of sexual intercourse, ***and,*** having thoroughly tamed the camels, ***carried them off,*** that is, they swept them away. Lam 1:[169] *They have gone away without strength before the face of the pursuer.* ***Moreover, they have killed the servants with the sword,*** so that there would be no hope of recovery. Jb 20:[170] *The sword is drawn forth and comes out of its scabbard, and it flashes in his bitterness.*

and, supply: not for your comfort, ***I alone have escaped to tell you*** that the Chaldeans did these things not to relieve their own poverty, but to spite you. Is 21:[171] *A harsh vision was revealed to*

166. Jb 20.26–27.
167. Am 6.6.
168. Jb 20.25.
169. Lam 1.6.
170. Jb 20.25.
171. Is 21.2.

me. According to the spiritual sense camels signify the wealthy members of the Church, who are driven away by demons through the injustice of prelates. Is 30:[172] *They carried their riches on the backs of pack-mules, and their treasures on the humps of camels.* The spiritual meanings of other things in the text are not changed.

Satan carried away Job's riches so that a greater concern might remain in Job for his children, by whose violent removal Satan tempts him, bereaving him of his children. And this is: **[18]** ***While he was still speaking,*** so that the disaster, having been interrupted, could not be mitigated by any consolation, ***behold another came in and said.*** Jb 16:[173] *He has struck me with wound upon wound; he has rushed in upon me like a giant.* ***Your sons,*** who are perfect, ***and your daughters,*** who are imperfect and weak, ***were eating*** with pleasure ***and drinking wine*** with joy. Ps:[174] *Wine gladdens the human heart.* ***in the oldest brother's house,*** who after Job was second in directing the household. Song 5:[175] *Eat, friends, and drink, and become inebriated, dearly beloved.* In this same way Joseph's brothers were feasting in his presence, according to Gn 43.[176]

[19] ***suddenly a violent wind,*** which no one had any chance of escaping, ***blew across the desert,*** in such a way that no obstacle impeded the violence of its blowing. Wis 4:[177] *Not standing firmly, they will be shaken by the wind, and they will be rooted out by the excessive strength of the wind.* ***shook the four corners of the house,*** so that the corners collapsed inwardly rather than outwardly, and therefore it must have been a whirlwind. Ezek 1:[178] *A whirlwind came out of the north, and a great cloud.* ***which collapsed*** in on itself. Mt 7:[179] *The winds blew and the floods came, and they beat upon that house and it fell, and great was its fall.* ***and crushed your children*** **(liberos)**, who were born of a free woman (*libera*) and not of

172. Is 30.6.
173. Jb 16.15.
174. Ps 103.15.
175. Song 5.1.
176. Gn 43.32–34.
177. Wis 4.4.
178. Ezek 1.4.
179. Mt 7.27.

a female slave. And lest there be any hope of freeing (*liberari*) them from the rubble, the messenger adds: ***and they are dead.*** Hence below Jb:[180] *I, who was once so wealthy, am now suddenly crushed to pieces.* ***I alone have escaped,*** supply: not for your consolation, but rather for your desolation, in order to increase your suffering, ***to tell you*** that not only humans, but also the entire earth strives against you. Wis 5:[181] *The entire earth will fight with him against those who are senseless.*

In this temptation, the wind is the persuasion of the devil, the children of Job are the virtues, the house is the building of the virtues, the four corners are the four cardinal virtues, the falling is the consent to mortal sin, the violent force pressing down on the children is the suffocation of the virtues. In terms of introducing authorities, these spiritual interpretations are sufficient, and the spiritual meanings of other things in the text are not changed.

[20] ***Then Job arose.***

Here the text touches on how blessed and very noble Job was in making the very best use of his misfortunes. For Aristotle says, in Book I of the *Ethics,* that the mark of a blessed person is to make proper use of both prosperity and adversity.[182] And two things are treated here, namely the use of misfortunes and the commendation of the one using them, in this place: *In all this.*[183] The use is treated in three ways, namely: in his experience of being stricken, for it is a defect not to feel a blow; in his contempt for destruction; and in his recognition of the righteousness of the One who gives liberally.

Then Job arose, that is, he raised himself up. Col 3:[184] *Contemplate the things that are above.* ***and tore his clothes,*** for it was the custom of the ancients, in time of sorrow, to rip apart the things that they used in caring for their bodies and to throw them aside. Thus, Gn 37[185] says of Jacob after Joseph's death had been reported to him: *Tearing his clothes, he put on sackcloth.*

180. Jb 16.13.
181. Wis 5.21.
182. Aristotle, *EN* 1.10.14.
183. Jb 1.22 below.
184. Col 3.2.
185. Gn 37.34.

and having shaved his head, so that he might alter the pleasing appearance of his head as a sign of sadness. Ezek 5:[186] *Son of man, take for yourself a sharp knife that shaves the hair, pick it up, and guide it over your head and through your beard.* ***he fell on the ground,*** namely face down, so that he would remember that he was nothing and that nothing had come forth from him. 1 Cor 14:[187] *So, falling down on the ground, he will worship.*

And this is what follows: ***and worshiped,*** namely God, who raises up from nothing whom He wills. Ps:[188] *The Lord raises up the broken.* Ex 4:[189] *They worshiped face down on the ground.* **[21]** ***And he said,*** adding a description of his contempt for earthly realities: ***Naked I came,*** namely carrying nothing with me; hence these external things are accidental because they were not born with me. ***from my mother's womb,*** namely from the earth, which is the first mother who conceives all, hence Gn 3:[190] *Adam called his wife Eve because she was the mother of all the living.* ***and naked will I return there,*** namely into the womb of the first mother, that is, into the earth. Sir 40:[191] *A great labor is allotted to all humans, and a heavy yoke is upon the children of Adam, from the day they come out of their mother's womb until the day of their burial in the mother of all.* 1 Tm 6:[192] *We brought nothing into this world, and without a doubt we cannot carry anything out.* Job then adds his recognition of the One who gives liberally and of his debt to Him: the former when he says: ***the Lord has given,*** supply: freely. Jas 1:[193] *He gives to all abundantly, and He does not reproach.* 1 Chr 29:[194] *We have given to you what we received from your hand.* Then Job adds his recognition of his debt to God when he says: ***and the Lord has taken away,*** for it was His own, and when He willed to take it away, He was able to do so. ***as it***

186. Ezek 5.1.
187. 1 Cor 14.25.
188. Ps 145.8.
189. Ex 4.31.
190. Gn 3.20.
191. Sir 40.1.
192. 1 Tm 6.7.
193. Jas 1.5.
194. 1 Chr 29.14.

has pleased the Lord, so it has been done, in giving and in taking away, of course. Lk 16:[195] *Give an account of your stewardship.*

Giving thanks, therefore, for gifts received, Job adds: ***blessed be the name of the Lord.*** Ps:[196] *Blessed be the name of the Lord, now and forever.* And Job made such graceful use of his misfortunes that he is commended when the text adds: **[22]** ***In all this, Job did not sin with his lips,*** that is, by impaticncc and murmuring in the midst of so many and such great disasters.

And to explain these words, the text adds: ***nor did he say anything foolish,*** that is, anything, ***against the Lord.*** Eccl 5:[197] *Do not say anything rashly, and do not allow your heart to be quick to utter a word before God, for God is in heaven and you are on the earth. Therefore, let your words be few.* Jas 3:[198] *If anyone does not offend in speech, he is a perfect man.*

195. Lk 16.2.
196. Ps 112.2.
197. Eccl 5.1.
198. Jas 3.2.

CHAPTER 2

AND IT HAPPENED.

The temptation of Job has been considered, both regarding his possessions and his children. Although the mind of the resolute man is not troubled by the loss of possessions, it is, however, disturbed by the loss of children, because, just as Aristotle says, a father has another self in his son.[1] Therefore, Job was also proven in being deprived of his children, and he was found steadfast because he neither thought, nor spoke, nor did anything unseemly. To be sure, a person is especially proven who is found to be steadfast in his very self, and who does not depart from an evenness of mind and who is most steadfast even if it happens that trials befall him physically.

Therefore, this chapter is introduced so that Job might be proven to be perfectly steadfast, according to what the Stoics have shown to be the case concerning the wise man, namely that no disturbance that befalls the wise man regarding his possessions, his children, or his person causes him to think, say, or do anything unseemly.[2] And so it was necessary that Job prove himself amidst physical trials, trials regarding his reputation, and trials regarding his honor. This chapter, then, is divided into three parts. First, Job is tested by physical trials. Second, he is tested by trials regarding his reputation, in this place:[3] *And his wife said to him.* And third, he is tested by trials regarding his honor:[4] *Now when his three friends heard.* This hap-

1. Aristotle, *EN* 13.12.2.
2. See Augustine, *Civ.* 14.8.1, 3.
3. Jb 2.9.
4. Jb 2.11.

pened so that in all three what is said in Sir 46[5] might be true: *In his faith he was proven.*

The first part has five divisions, namely concerning the manifestation of the tempter, his asking God for permission to tempt, the manner in which Job might be tempted, the granting of permission, and the completion of the temptation.

There are three points in the first of these divisions, namely the appearance of the tempter, his refutation, and the praising of the innocent man. That is: **[1]** ***And it happened,*** by the divine dispensation, of course. Wis 11:[6] *You have disposed all things according to number and weight and measure.* ***when on a certain day,*** a remarkable day because of an extraordinary deed. The daytime signifies that the one being tempted must not lose the light of reason. Jn 3:[7] *He who does evil hates the light.* Jn 1:[8] *The light shines in the darkness, and the darkness did not comprehend it,* that is, great darkness does not overtake the light of reason in the holy person in such a way that he is led away from a uniform constancy of mind. ***the sons of God,*** that is, the angels, who, for the reasons indicated above, are called the sons of God. Ps:[9] *I have said: You are gods, and all of you sons of the Most High.* ***came,*** namely to the divine light in order to report on the execution of their own ministries, just as the evenings report back to the mornings. Jb 25:[10] *Upon whom does His light not arise?* ***and stood,*** upright in understanding, love, and works, ***before the Lord,*** that is, before the divine veil and illuminated by God's light. Tb 12:[11] *For I am the angel Raphael, one of the seven who stand before the Lord.* Rv 1:[12] *From the seven spirits who are before His throne.* ***and Satan came,*** as an impediment to the good, ***among them,*** in order to hinder the progress of their ministry, as was said above

5. Sir 46.17.
6. Wis 11.21.
7. Jn 3.20.
8. Jn 1.5.
9. Ps 81.6.
10. Jb 25.3.
11. Tb 12.15.
12. Rv 1.4.

concerning the text's not having "before them."[13] The enemy of the good always insinuates himself among the good by *sowing his tares [among the wheat]*.[14]

and stood, obstinate in the wickedness of his will, and rigid. Zec 3:[15] *Satan stood at his right hand.* ***in His sight,*** going to be scattered by his own actions, just as darkness is scattered by the light. Wis 1:[16] *He who speaks unjust things is not able to hide, neither will the rebuking judgment of God pass him by. For an inquiry will be made into the thoughts of the wicked.* Hence Gregory: He stood in His sight so that he might be seen by God, not so that he himself might see God, because one who is impure in heart will not see God.[17] Is 26[18] according to the Septuagint: *Let the wicked one be destroyed, lest he see the glory of God.*

[2] ***That the Lord said to Satan,*** with that mode of speaking by which He disclosed Satan's ways: ***From where do you come?*** that is, carefully consider the perversity of your coming. Wis 1:[19] *A report of the words of that one,* that is, the unjust one, *will come to God, and He will rebuke his iniquity.* ***He,*** namely Satan, ***answered and said,*** with that mode of speaking that he used when insinuating his ways, which he cannot hide from God. Wis 1:[20] *He who speaks unjust things is not able to hide.*

I have gone around the earth, with curved and perverse steps I have gone around the hearts of the earthly, ***and I have walked through it,*** leaving behind the footprints of sin everywhere. Hence, as Is 37[21] says in passing: *With the steps of my feet I have dried up all the streams of the banks,* that is, every flow of grace and piety that ought to irrigate the field of the heart. This is sig-

13. On 1.6 above. Albert's point here, in conjunction with his interpretation of 1.6 above, seems to be that although Satan came "among them" for the purpose of hindering their ministerial progress, in fact he did not succeed in doing so, which explains why the text does not read "before them."

14. Mt 13.25.

15. Zec 3.1.

16. Wis 1.8–9.

17. Gregory, *Mor.* 2.4.4.

18. Is 26.10.

19. Wis 1.9.

20. Wis 1.8.

21. Is 37.25.

nified in Jgs 16,[22] where the Philistines captured Samson and made him grind by milling around a massive stone. Ps:[23] *My God, make them like a wheel.*

[3] ***And the Lord said to Satan,*** with that mode of speaking by which God speaks when he sets forth the righteousness of His own elect against the devil; that is, He makes them so excellent that Satan can be envious: ***Can it be that you have considered my servant Job?*** as if he had said: "You have looked upon him not with the eye of one who is pleased, but as one turning away and scorning him." Mt 20:[24] *Is your eye wicked?* Sir 31:[25] *What has been created more wicked than the eye?*

There is no one like him on earth, because he himself is in heaven. Phil 3:[26] *Our conversation is in heaven.* ***a man simple,*** a "man" by the perfection of natural endowment, in which there is nothing feminine, nothing able to be seduced like a woman. 1 Tm 2:[27] *The man was not seduced, but the woman, having been seduced, transgressed.* And he was "simple" in terms of virtue and intention. 1 Chr 29:[28] *In the simplicity of my heart I have joyfully offered all these things.* Gn 25:[29] *Jacob was a simple man, living in tents.* ***and upright*** in works. Is 26:[30] *The way of the just is upright; the path of the just is right to walk in.* ***who,*** in turning aside from evil, ***fears God*** in his heart. Eccl 12:[31] *Fear God and keep His commandments; this is the duty of every human.* Sir 2:[32] *Those who fear the Lord will seek the things that are pleasing to Him.* ***and withdraws from evil,*** in his works and in his actions, of course. Is 52:[33] *Withdraw, withdraw, refuse to touch anything unclean.* ***and who still,*** after so many and such great temptations regarding his resources and children, ***keeps his innocence,*** so that he does nothing against God.

22. Jgs 16.21.
23. Ps 82.14.
24. Mt 20.15.
25. Sir 31.15.
26. Phil 3.20.
27. 1 Tm 2.14.
28. 1 Chr 29.17.
29. Gn 25.27.
30. Is 26.7.
31. Eccl 12.13.
32. Sir 2.19.
33. Is 52.11.

Sir 31:[34] *He who has been tested in that way and found to be perfect will have eternal glory.*

And God turned decisively to Satan, and He refuted him: ***But you*** by the unjust wickedness of your will ***have provoked me*** as one with human feelings (*anthropopathos*);[35] that is, you have moved me to expose him to your temptation. Ps:[36] *He delivered them into the hands of the nations, and those who hated them had dominion over them.*

so that I would afflict him, that is, so that I would permit him to be afflicted. Prv 3:[37] *He scourges every son whom He accepts.* ***in vain,*** but not from the point of view of the Lord, who does nothing in vain, but with respect to the intention of Satan, who did not achieve his own purpose in afflicting Job. Indeed, as Aristotle says in the second book of the *Physics,*[38] that which in regard to some purpose that is outside itself is described as being "in vain," differs from something that is "spontaneous," in that what is spontaneous neither has a purpose nor pursues a purpose, like the motion of a finger when it is moved for no reason. Human acts may be done for some purpose in five ways, as Rabbi Moses says in Part III ch. 24 of the *Guide of the Perplexed.*[39] For they are done because they are honorable, or because they are delightful, or because they are useful, or for sport, and they may achieve the purpose for which they are done; or they are done for some purpose but do not achieve it, and so they are done in vain. If, for example, someone goes to the market in order to receive money but does not receive the money that he intended to receive, he has walked to the market in vain. But things in which nothing is intended are spontaneous. In the works of God, however, there are the honorable, the useful, and the delightful; but there is nothing for sport because the sporting man is soft, as Aristotle says in Book VII

34. Sir 31.10.

35. Albert will use this word again, to indicate the scriptural text's anthropomorphic way of speaking about God, in commenting on Job's description of God as "remembering all things" in 10.13 below.

36. Ps 105.41.

37. Prv 3.12 LXX. Cf. Heb 12.6.

38. See Aristotle, *Ph.* 2.6.6; cf. Albert, *Ph.* 2.2.17.

39. See Moses Maimonides, *Dux* 3.25 rather than ch. 24.

of the *Ethics*,[40] but God is not soft. God does nothing in vain, because He brings everything back to Himself. And nothing is spontaneous, because in all things He aims at His very self. Prv 12:[41] *He who is vain and foolish will lie open to contempt.*

Hence Satan was able to say, Is 49:[42] *I have labored in vain; I have spent my strength without cause and in vain.*

[4] ***Satan answered him and said,*** according to that mode of speaking whereby he accuses the innocent with false charges: ***Skin for skin.*** He intends to say that, just as rougher skin is exposed instead of more delicate skin, and as the hand is raised before the eye if a blow comes toward the eye, thus a human exposes what is less precious instead of what is more precious. It is as if he is saying: "Job has easily despised all the possessions that he had, lest murmuring against you he lose his life; but he has done this not for your sake, but only for himself."

And this is what follows: ***and all that a human has*** in external possessions ***he will give,*** that is, he would despise easily, ***for his soul* (anima)*,*** that is, his animate life (*animali vita*), supply: to be saved. For he loves life more than riches. And it is as if Satan is saying that Job has not murmured about lost riches for fear that, if he murmured, he might lose his life. Prv 13:[43] *The ransom of a man's soul is his own riches.*

And concerning Satan's request for permission to tempt, the text adds: [5] ***In any case,*** supply: if this is not so, or if it does not seem to you to be so, ***stretch out your hand,*** that is, loosen and relax the power by which you protect him, ***and touch his bone and his flesh.*** In Book II of the *Posterior Analytics,* Aristotle says: "In bones and muscles there are strength and vigor, whereas in flesh there is sensibility."[44] That is: strike even his sense perception and then his vigor may crumble, ***and then you will see,*** that is, you will cause humans to see, ***that to your face,*** this is not so except on account of the presence of grace in external things, ***he will bless you,*** that is, he will give you thanks in his heart, in

40. Aristotle, *EN* 7.4.4.
41. Prv 12.8.
42. Is 49.4.
43. Prv 13.8.
44. Rather, see Aristotle, *Top.* 3.1.13; cf. Aristotle, *GA* 2.5.

his speech, and in his works. Hence, below:[45] *My inner parts have boiled up without any rest.* And a little further:[46] *My skin has been made black on me, and my bones have dried up.* For the face of God means the presence of grace given freely in external things in which it arises. Ps:[47] *He will praise you when you help him.*

[6] ***Then the Lord said to Satan,*** according to that mode of speaking by which He expands the power of the tempter: ***Behold, he is in your hand,*** that is, within the power of your wickedness. Lam 1:[48] *The enemy has stretched out his hand to all her desirable things.* ***nevertheless, preserve his soul,*** that is, his life, lest Satan have the power to kill Job. Jb 16:[49] *He gave me into the hands of the wicked.* The situation is a good one, however, because Job's soul is preserved. As to the preservation of the soul after death, Rabbi Moses [Maimonides] has the view that, after death, the intellect, which understands, is joined to what he calls the First Mover.[50] But this is heretical, because the entire soul endures after death. And so the earlier interpretation is better. Jn 10:[51] *No one will snatch them from my hand.* Wis 3:[52] *The souls of the saints are in the hand of God, and the torment of death will not touch them.*

And concerning the progress of the temptation, the text adds: [7] ***So Satan went out,*** namely from the presence of the divine power that checks the wickedness of his will. And that is: ***from the face of the Lord.*** Gn 4:[53] *I will be hidden from your face.* ***and struck Job with the worst type of ulcer.*** An ulcer with a hot and moist center, putrefying at the sources of the bodily members is leprosy bubbling up, as Galen says.[54] This type of ulcer is said to be the worst because it originates from the corruption of all

45. Jb 30.27.
46. Jb 30.30.
47. Ps 48.19.
48. Lam 1.10.
49. Jb 16.12.
50. See Moses Maimonides, *Dux* 3.22.
51. Jn 10.28.
52. Wis 3.1.
53. Gn 4.14.
54. Cf. Galen, *DM* ch. 374. For more on Galen, see the *Cambridge Companion to Galen,* ed. R. J. Hankinson (Cambridge: Cambridge University Press, 2008).

the humors. Jer 30:[55] *Your wound is the worst; who will heal you?* But I think that it was lupus[56] with which Satan tempted him, for that kind of ulcer gnaws away at the flesh and bones, as Galen says.[57] ***from the sole of his foot all the way to the top of his head.*** Is 1:[58] *From the sole of his foot all the way to the top of his head, there is no health in him.*

[8] ***And he,*** namely Job, in order to help the hand that was wounding him, ***scraped,*** rather than wiping it clean, in order to draw attention to the rigor (*duritiam*) of his penance, ***the discharged pus*** that was bubbling out of his flesh ***with a potsherd,*** that is, something hard, lest by using a softer implement he might bear a lighter trial. Ps:[59] *My strength has dried up like a potsherd.*

while sitting on a dung heap. "Dung heap" signifies the pus that was coming out of his body. He did not have even a straw cloth to wipe away the discharge. Hence it says below:[60] *I have said to rottenness: You are my father; to worms: you are my mother and my sister.* Jb 30:[61] *At night my bones are pierced with pain, and those who eat away at me do not sleep.* Therefore, in 1 Mc 2[62] Mattathias says concerning the proud: *The glory of the sinful man is dung and worms: he is extolled today, but tomorrow will not be found.*

[9] ***And his wife said to him.***

Having concluded the account of the temptation that Satan accomplished by himself and through others, the text here sets forth how Job was tempted by his wife, just as in Gn 3[63] Satan attacked Adam by means of his wife, because he was not able to overcome him by himself. Here Satan tempts with regard to reputation and the fruit of life; for Job was renowned for his

55. Jer 30.12.

56. The name of the disease given by Albert here is *herpes esthiomenus*, which is known today as systemic lupus erythematosus (SLE) or simply lupus.

57. Galen, *DM* ch. 295; and *IHH* 3.20.

58. Is 1.6.

59. Ps 21.16.

60. Jb 17.14.

61. Jb 30.17.

62. 1 Mc 2.62–63.

63. Gn 3.6.

fruitful life, but his wife says the fruit of his life is tribulation and death.[64]

And there are two parts here: one on the temptation by Job's wife, and the other on the commendation of the one tempted. In the temptation there are two things: namely the completion of the temptation on the part of the temptress, and the usefulness of the temptation for the one tempted. And that is: ***And his wife said to him,*** with ridiculing words. Because she had been joined together with him in the inseparable intimacy of life, it was altogether inappropriate that she mocked Job, as when Tobit's wife said to him in Tb 2:[65] *Now your hope and your almsgiving,* which you have done, *are clearly in vain,* and as Adam's wife spoke to him concerning the transgression in Gn 3.[66]

Do you still continue in your simplicity? This should be read with indignation and mockery, as if she were saying: "See the fruit of your simplicity, that you have borne no fruit but tribulation and death." Hence Job himself continues in ch. 19[67] below: *My wife shuddered at my breath.*

Then she introduces the sting of the temptation: ***bless God,*** namely in your heart, in your words, and in your works, ***and die.*** In other words, you will bear no fruit but death. It is as if she were saying: "If you would take the opposite path and curse God, you would live." This was the case concerning those of whom it is said in Is 28:[68] *We have put our hope in lies, and we have*

64. Instead of *vita fructuosa,* "fruitful life," MSS EFM read *vita virtuosa,* "virtuous life." In an effort to retain the thematic connection to the fruit of Gn 3 and to convey the general blessedness of Job's life prior to his temptation (in terms of his large family, many possessions, and great wealth, e.g.), I read *vita fructuosa* with the Weiss edition. On the other hand, an equally strong case could be made for "virtuous life." It is, after all, Job's virtue (i.e., his continuing in his "simplicity" before God), which is one—indeed, perhaps the primary—manifestation of his "fruitful life," for which his wife here chastises him.

65. Tb 2.22.

66. Although Gn 3 recounts no specific words spoken by Eve to Adam, Albert may be assuming that some mocking words of Eve must have precipitated Adam's succumbing to Satan's temptation, perhaps on the basis of v. 17, where God says to Adam: *Quia audisti vocem uxoris tuae, et comedisti de lingo . . .*

67. Jb 19.17.

68. Is 28.15.

made a pact with hell; and in Mal 3:[69] *You have said: He who serves God labors in vain. And what advantage is it that we, who are sorrowful, have walked in the presence of the Lord?*

Then the text mentions the usefulness of the temptation. And because Job owed his wife correction and instruction, and because he would have sinned if he had withdrawn from her quietly, it follows: **[10]** ***And he said to her,*** that is, to correct her: ***You have spoken like one of the foolish women.*** He does not say, "of the women," lest he assign a defect to her gender, but "of the foolish women"; nor does he say "of the evil women," suggesting that he considers a certain beclouding of her mind by stupidity to be her sin. Sir 10:[70] *Pride was not created for human beings, nor a hot temper for the race of women.* Is 32:[71] *The fool will say foolish things, and his heart will work iniquity.*

Job then adds instruction to counter his wife's foolishness: ***If we receive good things,*** together and individually, you and I, ***from the hand of the Lord,*** who bestows all good things. Ps:[72] *You open your hand and fill every living thing with blessing.* ***why should we not bear,*** another text[73] reads: receive, ***evil things,*** namely these scourges now? Gregory: There is great comfort in calling to mind good things in the midst of misfortunes, lest there be total hopelessness. In the same way, foreseeing misfortune in joyful times tempers one's excitement.[74] Hence it is said in Sir 11:[75] *On the day of good things do not forget evil things, and on the day of evil things do not forget good things.* Is 63:[76] *I will remember the compassion of the Lord, the praise of the Lord for all the things that the Lord has given to us.*

69. Mal 3.14.

70. Sir 10.22.

71. Is 32.6.

72. Ps 144.16.

73. By *alia littera,* "another text," here Albert seems to mean another manuscript reading, rather than another official version, as *suscipiamus* ("receive") reflects the Vulg., LXX, and Hebrew readings. The manuscript from which Albert is working appears to have *sustineamus* instead. On Albert's general method of exposition, including the scriptural text he used, see the Introduction above.

74. See Gregory, *Mor.* 3.9.16.

75. Sir 11.27.

76. Is 63.7.

Then the text adds a commendation of the one tempted: ***In all these things***, that is to say, in so many and such great temptations, ***Job did not sin with his lips,*** neither by speaking against God foolishly, nor by keeping a damnable silence, withholding a word of salvation from his wife, whom he was responsible for correcting and instructing. 2 Tm 4:[77] *Reprove, entreat, rebuke with the utmost patience and learning.*

[11] ***Now when his three friends heard.***

The temptation of Job by his friends concerning his honor is introduced in order to complete his testing. It is shameful to be buffeted for vice or sin, but noble and even blessed to suffer as one of the just, whom the devil and the world persecute. But Job's friends were laying into him, asserting that he was suffering for his sins and vices, since according to civil law punishment is the recompense for sin, whereas honor is the reward for virtue. And therefore he was tempted by them with regard to his honor. Just as he was proven in the loss of his possessions, the bereavement of his children, and the disapproval of his wife, after which he neither thought, nor said, nor did anything unseemly—in the same way it is proven that in the face of a trial concerning his honor he does nothing unseemly. 1 Pt 4:[78] *May none of you suffer as though you were a murderer, a thief, or one who covets another's possessions. But if you suffer as a Christian, do not be ashamed; rather, glorify God on account of this name.*

Four things are mentioned concerning this temptation, namely who came, for what purpose they came, how they made themselves agreeable to the one who was suffering, and how they wisely awaited a more suitable time for consolation. And that is: ***Now,*** this is the beginning, ***when Job's three friends heard,*** for the report of such a serious event spread far and wide. The text says "three" because it is demonstrated in Book IX of the *Ethics* that true friendship is in two or three or even more.[79] For it is impossible to give your whole self to many people; but it is possible to give your whole self to one person. And if one more person is admitted, who functions like a bond that cements the

77. 2 Tm 4.2.
78. 1 Pt 4.15–16.
79. See Aristotle, *EN* 9.10.

friendship, then it will be like natural friendship, wherein the male is given entirely to the female and vice versa, and their child is the bond that unifies their love.

all the misfortune, considered according to the three classes treated above, that is, in his possessions, his offspring, and his honor. In Book I of *On Heaven and Earth,* Aristotle says: We classify all things according to three in the first place.[80]

that had befallen him, through the humans whom Satan incited. Jgs 6:[81] *The Lord is with us, so why have so many misfortunes come upon us?* ***each one came,*** because each one individually was reflecting upon Job's own misfortunes, ***from his own place,*** that is, from his proper residence. For they had to run to meet the one who had been afflicted. Mt 25:[82] *I was sick and you came to me.* Eccl 7:[83] *It is better to go to the house of mourning than to the house of feasting.* Sir 7:[84] *A friend is shown to be a true friend in times of need.* And in the same place:[85] *Do not fail to comfort those who are weeping, and walk with those who are grieving; do not be reluctant to visit the sick: for by these deeds you will be confirmed in love.*

Eliphaz the Temanite, Eliphaz means "contempt of the Lord"; Teman is "the south." So his name indicates that he was destined to slip and fall from consolation into contempt, and to refute his friend, just as the south wind smashes whatever is in its path by blowing from the south. ***and Bildad the Shuhite.*** By itself Bildad means "old age," and Shuhite means "speaking." So his name foretells that he was destined to speak according to old age, and to spread himself out in loquacity more than in wisdom. On the contrary, it is written in Eph 4:[86] *Take off the old man, who is corrupted by wandering desires.* ***and Zophar***

80. See Aristotle, *Cael.* 1.1. Aristotle means that three is the first number to which the term "all" is appropriated. 1 man = "the man"; 2 men = "both men"; 3 men = "all the men."

81. Jgs 6.13.

82. Mt 25.36.

83. Eccl 7.3.

84. This is not a direct quotation from Sir 7, but rather seems to be a general summary statement of sorts that Albert makes with a view to vv. 38–39, which he quotes immediately hereafter.

85. Sir 7.38–39.

86. Eph 4.22.

the Naamathite, Zophar means "the scattering of hope," and Naamathite means "beautiful." So his name prefigures that he is going to scatter hope for the truth by means of the beauty of his eloquence, against which it is said in 1 Cor 2:[87] *My speech and my preaching were not in the ignorant words of human wisdom, but in the teaching of the Spirit.*

Then the text describes their intention: ***For they agreed,*** united with one another in the love that they had for Job, of course, ***to go together,*** at one time so that they might do together what they were unable to do separately. ***to visit him,*** so that they might examine his suffering with their own eyes. Lk 1:[88] *Through the depths of the mercy of our God, in which He has visited us.* Lam 1:[89] *O all of you who pass by the road, look and see if there is any sorrow like my sorrow.* ***and comfort him.*** Is 40:[90] *Be comforted, my people, be comforted.*

The text then adds how they made themselves sympathetic to the one who had been stricken. Gregory: "You cannot comfort someone who is suffering unless you are sympathetic to his suffering."[91] To lead someone beyond his pain you must influence him, and to influence him you must reach out to him, but you cannot reach out to him without sympathy.

And that is: **[12]** ***And when they lifted up their eyes from far away,*** they lifted them up at a distance, before they came near, because for the one who is in great need nothing is quick enough. There is a parallel in Tb 10,[92] where Tobit's mother wandered through all the streets by which there was any hope of his coming, and she opened her eyes so that she might see him coming from a long way off before he drew near. ***they did not recognize him*** on account of the difference between his situation in misfortune and his preceding situation in the midst of good things. Is 53[93] is similar: *We have seen him, but there was nothing in his appearance that we should desire him. Despised and the*

87. 1 Cor 2.4.
88. Lk 1.78.
89. Lam 1.12.
90. Is 40.1.
91. Gregory, *Mor.* 3.12.20.
92. Tb 10.7.
93. Is 53.2–3.

least of men, a man of sorrows and acquainted with infirmity; his face was hidden and despised; hence we did not esteem him.

and shouted out, in order to reveal their internal sorrow, ***they wept aloud.*** Jer 9:[94] *Who will offer water for my head, and a fountain of tears for my eyes? And I will weep day and night for the slain of the daughter of my people.*

and tearing their clothes, in order to show their sympathy in their nakedness. Jon 3[95] is similar: *The news reached the king of Nineveh; and he rose from his throne, removed his clothes, and dressed himself in sackcloth.* ***they threw dust up on their heads,*** in order to show their sympathy with their hair cut off and their heads filthy, ***toward heaven,*** placing their only hope for consolation in the God of heaven, just as the king of Nineveh did when he *sat in ashes* according to Jon 3,[96] and as Jer 41[97] relates [concerning the eighty men from Shechem and Shiloh and Samaria]: *With their beards shaven, their clothes torn, and their bodies filthy, and with offerings and frankincense in their hands to offer in the house of the Lord. And they came upon Ishmael.*

Then the text adds how they awaited the best time. **[13]** ***And they sat with him on the ground*** on account of humility. Is 47:[98] *Come down, sit in the dust.* ***for seven days and seven nights,*** which indicates their support and patience. Sir 2:[99] *Bear up in sorrow and have patience in humiliation.* ***and no one spoke a word to him,*** that is, they refrained from speaking while waiting to take a cue from his words. Eccl 3:[100] *There is a time to speak and a time to remain silent.* And the text adds the reason: ***for they saw that his suffering was severe,*** and consequently it had made him impatient. Thus, also, the tempter does not try his prey when compunction for sins is ardent. Ps:[101] *I became silent and I did not speak after good things; and my sorrow was renewed.*

94. Jer 9.1.
95. Jon 3.6.
96. Ibid.
97. Jer 41.5.
98. Is 47.1.
99. Sir 2.4.
100. Eccl 3.7.
101. Ps 38.3.

CHAPTER 3

AFTER THESE THINGS JOB OPENED HIS MOUTH.

It must be said in advance that in this book there is a complete disputation among five people—namely, Job, Eliphaz, Bildad, Zophar, and Elihu—concerning the all-encompassing providence or care by which the Creator rules and governs human affairs. And all of the disputants agree that God, the Creator and Governor, possesses perfect knowledge of all human affairs, as it is said below:[1] *You indeed have numbered my steps.* Similarly, all of the disputants agree that in God's care and directing and governing of all things there is absolutely no unfairness or sin. Likewise, they all agree on this: that God considers human actions more intimately than does the human himself who performs the actions, and therefore He sometimes grasps a defect in those actions that actually escapes the notice of the human himself. They disagree, however, over the matter of Job's first complaint, that his own deeds were not judged according to human reason and foresight. Hence below he says:[2] *If I will be judged, I will be found just;* and also:[3] *If only my sins, for which I deserved wrath, and the calamity that I suffer were weighed out on scales!* And:[4] *Let the one who judges write a book, and I will carry it on my shoulder.* From his speech it is clear that Job maintains his own righteousness in every case. And it follows that the three men set aside their own arguments because Job seemed to himself to be just. It seemed to Job that God ought to have governed as if the justice of human governance was the exemplar of the order of divine justice; and so it

1. Jb 14.16.
2. Jb 13.18.
3. Jb 6.2.
4. Jb 31.35–36.

seemed that the latter should have been in harmony with the former, and that nothing would be in one that would not be in the other. Hence divine justice is named from what has been heard and handed down about the order of human justice. But when the Lord finally settles the disputation, Job realizes that the order of divine justice is utterly different from the order of human justice. For the human person, who is created from mud, is not so dignified that God should be obliged by the order of human justice. Therefore, returning to a proper understanding of divine justice at the end, he says:[5] *With the hearing of the ear I heard you,* as if described according to the order of human justice; *but now my eye sees you,* he adds,[6] as if he were saying, "Because of your determination, I have returned to understanding and have recognized that your governance is different from that of humans." So he says:[7] *Therefore, I blame myself and I do penance.* And Job reveals what penance he might do when he says,[8] *There is one thing that I have said,* which I wish I had not said: *He condemns both the innocent and the wicked,* which would certainly be unjust if God's governance proceeded according to the order of human justice. Gn 18:[9] *Far be it from you, you who judge the entire earth, that you should condemn the just with the wicked.* These two, then, are the different positions held by Job, the one at the beginning and the other subsequently.

Eliphaz, however, maintains that divine governance of human affairs is according to merits, that good things happen to good people and bad things happen to the wicked. But sometimes it remains hidden from humans that they are wicked by their own merits, and that on account of the baseness of their nature humans are not able to be without sin. Hence he says:[10] *Nothing on earth happens without a cause;* and:[11] *In His angels He finds perverseness. How much more will those who* [*live in clay houses, which*] *have their foundation on earth be consumed, as if by moths.*

5. Jb 42.5.
6. Ibid.
7. Jb 42.6.
8. Jb 9.22.
9. Gn 18.25.
10. Jb 5.6.
11. Jb 4.18–20.

And because no one understands, all will similarly perish. And Eliphaz never departs from this intention.

Bildad maintains that divine governance takes place not according to merits, but rather according to the best order in relation to the end of human happiness. And so, if God sometimes brings forth bad things for good people, He compensates for this by giving them many good things in the end; and if He sometimes brings forth good things for bad people, it is so that their condemnation might be more just. And Bildad expresses this in his own words, when he says at the end of his speech:[12] *God will not reject the simple, nor stretch out His hand to evildoers, until your mouth is filled with laughter and your lips with rejoicing;* and:[13] *Those who hate you will be covered with confusion, and the tent of the wicked will not stand.*

Zophar, however, maintains that divine governance is according to God's will alone and the cause of that will must not be sought, because it cannot be known by humans. Therefore, he says:[14] *Will you, by chance, comprehend the steps of God, and will you get to know the Almighty perfectly?* And:[15] *He is higher than heaven, so what will you do?* And:[16] *If He should overturn all things or press them together into one, who will speak against Him?* And Zophar never departs from this sort of intention.

After these positions have been set forth, the position of Elihu is introduced. His position is in agreement with the three previous speeches, and especially with the position of Zophar. Therefore, he says,[17] *He will crush many men, beyond counting,* but the cause of this must not be sought. And Elihu does not add anything more about this divine intention, except that God sometimes teaches, either through a mediator or by Himself, how human affairs are bound to be in harmony with divine realities, and therefore he says,[18] *If there will be an angel, one of*

12. Jb 8.20–21.
13. Jb 8.22.
14. Jb 11.7.
15. Jb 11.8.
16. Jb 11.10.
17. Jb 34.24.
18. Jb 33.23.

thousands, speaking for Him,[19] and that in the night God teaches the hearts of men and instructs them with discipline.[20] Nevertheless, Elihu boasts of God's wisdom, he comes upon this after all the others [namely Eliphaz, Bildad, and Zophar], and he extols that wisdom in the clouds and in the lightning and in other things of this sort.[21]

Although these are their principal intentions, the five disputants add certain other remarks, sometimes reproving a companion in the disputation, sometimes praising the wisdom that they have found in another's speech, and sometimes complaining that a companion has not rightly understood what was said. Job wished, for example, that his words, which resound with impatience, not be attributed to his unwillingness to endure suffering,[22] and that his friends not proudly boast of their own wisdom.[23] But the others thought this statement was offensive and said that he had slighted them.[24] And they add other words of this kind, which to this day have become customary in the struggle among disputants.

This part of the book[25] is divided into two subparts. The disputation is set forth in the first of these; and the determination is contained in the second, which begins below with the words:[26] *And responding to Job out of a whirlwind, the Lord said.* The first subpart, which contains the disputation, is further divided into two: the disputation among the four [namely Job and his three friends, Eliphaz, Bildad, and Zophar] is set forth in the first of these; in the second, the opinion of the last dispu-

19. Although the *pro eo* in the Vulg. text here appears to have the human person who is suffering (seemingly unjustly) as its antecedent (Elihu is imagining an angel interceding on his behalf), Albert reads this phrase as referring to God, for whom this angel and thousands of others speak as mediators.

20. See Jb 33.16.

21. See Jb 33.27–30.

22. See Jb 16.7.

23. See Jb 17.1–10, esp. v. 10.

24. See Jb 18.3.

25. That is, the second major part, containing the disputation on the cause of Job's temptation, which occupies chapters 3–41. See the general threefold division of the book with which Albert begins commenting on 1.1.

26. Jb 38.1.

tant [namely Elihu] is introduced, further along in this place:[27] *But these three men ceased to answer Job.* The first of these is again divided into two: in the first, the four dispute; in the second, with one of them, namely Zophar, conceding, Job gains the upper hand, below at:[28] *Job also added.* The first of these is divided yet again into two: in the first of these, the disputation among the four is set forth according to their proposed intentions; in the second, the disputation among two, namely Eliphaz and Bildad, is set forth, and the third [namely Zophar] concedes, below at:[29] *Then responding, Job said: Hear, I beg you, my words.* The first of these is divided into two parts according to two cycles of speeches of the four disputants. The first cycle concludes at chapter 12,[30] in this place below: *Then responding, Job said: Therefore, are you alone humans?* The second cycle concludes at 21,[31] in this place below: *Then responding, Job said: Hear, I beg you, my words.* In all of these disputations, however, Job debates with each person individually, and each one individually disputes with him. The first of these individual disputations is divided into two: in the first of these parts, Job's words of complaint about the works of Satan are revealed; the second part contains the disputation itself, which begins below in chapter 4,[32] in this place: *Then Eliphaz, responding.*

After these things.

In this chapter Job, in order to provide the subject matter for the disputation, utters his complaint concerning daylight, which is a principle of life, which Satan takes into his power to change into sadness, with regard to Job's resources, his children, his person, and his friends.

And the chapter is divided into two parts. In the first part, Job brings forth his curse against that day; and in the second, the reason [for his curse], in this place:[33] *Why did I not die in the womb?* The first part is further subdivided into two: in the

27. Jb 32.1.
28. Jb 27.1.
29. Jb 21.1–2.
30. Jb 12.1–2.
31. Jb 21.1.
32. Jb 4.1.
33. Jb 3.11.

first subdivision, Job jointly curses the day of his birth from the womb and the night of his conception in the womb; in the second, he curses the day and the night individually, in this place:[34] *Let that day turn into darkness.* The first subdivision has two further parts, having to do with how he spoke and what he said.

And that is: ***After these things,*** by which he was proven, in both fortune and misfortune, to be perfect, as much in himself as with regard to his household and to his city. ***Job opened his mouth,*** in order to provide the topic of the disputation for the disputants and to speak openly so as to begin the disputation. And on account of this the text says, "He opened his mouth." This phrase indicates that his style of speaking was accessible and that he was going to speak about great things. There is a parallel in 2 Cor 6:[35] *Our mouth is open to you, O you Corinthians.* Mt 5:[36] *And, opening His mouth, He taught them, saying.* Prv 31:[37] *She has opened her mouth to wisdom.* And it says "his," not that of another, so that it would be known that Job was speaking from his very own experience. Ps:[38] *Open your mouth and I will fill it.* ***and he cursed his own day.*** Gregory: There are two modes of cursing, namely "with the judgment of justice" or "with the spite of vengeance."[39] The former is praised, the latter is forbidden. God uses the former, as in Gn 3:[40] *Cursed is the earth in your work*; and Gn 12, addressing Abraham:[41] *I will curse those who curse you.* The saints also use this mode of cursing: Peter in Acts 8:[42] *May your money go with you into perdition.* And Elijah in 2 Kgs 1:[43] *If I am a man of God, let fire come down and consume you.* Hence the curse of Job is not wickedness, but justice; nor is it the arousal of anger, but rather instruction. And every inter-

34. Jb 3.4.
35. 2 Cor 6.11.
36. Mt 5.2.
37. Prv 31.26.
38. Ps 80.11.
39. See Gregory, *Mor.* 4.1.2.
40. Gn 3.17.
41. Gn 12.3.
42. Acts 8.20.
43. 2 Kgs 1.10.

pretation, whether literal or allegorical,[44] agrees on this. For it belongs to wisdom to curse neither oneself nor another. Jgs 5:[45] *Curse the land of Meroz, said the angel of the Lord; curse its inhabitants because they have not come to the help of the Lord.* Meroz means "multitude" or "of the multitude," and it signifies that the multitude, which pursues the pleasures of the senses, should be cursed because they have not come to the help of God through the work of virtue. Eccl 1:[46] *The perverse are difficult to correct, and the number of fools is infinite.*

[2] *And he said:* [3] *Let the day on which I was born perish;* the "day" is by nature the beginning of the life of the one who comes forth from the womb into the light. And the entire span of Job's life—in which Satan receives the power to exercise the wickedness of his own will with regard to Job's property, his children, his person, and his friends, whom Satan turns into adversaries—cannot be wished for, except so that it might perish. For if it perishes, it will not heap up sadness and misfortune. If, however, it proceeds from morning to midday and from midday to evening, it will consume that selfsame life with many afflictions.[47] And therefore it should not be wished for, except so that it might perish. Job does not curse the day inasmuch as it is one single day, but rather inasmuch as it is the beginning of his entire life, which is going to run its course among the torments of Satan.

and the night, supply: let it perish, ***in which it was said, "A human being has been conceived!"*** Just as it is wished that the external day, as the beginning of external life in the light of this

44. Like other medieval exegetes, Albert intends to signify allegorical exposition here by the word *mystica*, which is that second-level meaning, built on the foundation of the literal, that pertains to the sacred mysteries of the Christian faith. Because the word "mystical" carries connotations in modern usage that are somewhat different, I will translate *mystica* as "allegorical" throughout the commentary.

45. Jgs 5.23.

46. Eccl 1.15.

47. Albert here offers a striking image of Satan's nearly comprehensive power over Job's life and its destructive potential. The Adversary has been given such control over the holy man's life that, if this life should continue from day to day, it actually will devour its very self through many torments and great suffering.

world, might perish, so too the night, which, through the one conceived, is the beginning of the conception of such a child, cannot be wished for except so that it might perish, inasmuch as in this night Satan receives power over all things during the entire span of this life. For Satan does not do anything other than transform life into bitterness, just as in Ex 1[48] the Egyptians made the lives of the children of Israel bitter by mocking and afflicting them. There is a parallel in Jer 20:[49] *Cursed be the day on which I was born! Let the day on which my mother bore me not be blessed!* Likewise, in the same place[50] he says: *Cursed be the man who brought the news to my father, saying, "A boy has been born to you."* Wis 3:[51] *Cursed is their offspring.* And after a few lines:[52] *And even if they live a long life, they will be regarded as nothing, and their extraordinary old age will be without honor. And if they die quickly, they will have neither hope nor a consoling speech on the day of judgment. For curses are the consummation of an unjust people.* And Job speaks of the day of his birth and the night of his conception because the night, with its coolness coming on by degrees, closes the body's air passages so that the seeds, having been received (*concepta*) internally, by overflowing with life and heat to a more intimate place, might grow warmer. But when the light of day, which is infused with heat, returns, bodies relax and open up in their passages and permeability, and so they are disposed to expel what has been received (*conceptum est*). Therefore, for the sake of symmetry it ought to be called the day of birth and the night of conception. Jer 15:[53] *Woe is me, my mother! Why have you given birth to me, a man of strife, a man of contention to the whole earth?* And after a few words:[54] *All people curse me.*

The interpretation of Gregory does not differ from this one, except that Gregory describes the progress of sin, but we are describing the progress of Satan's torments.[55]

48. Ex 1.13–14.
49. Jer 20.14.
50. Jer 20.15.
51. Wis 3.13.
52. Wis 3.17–19.
53. Jer 15.10.
54. Ibid.
55. See Gregory, *Mor.* 4.1.6.

Then Job adds a specific curse first for the day; and afterwards one for the night, in this place:[56] *That night.* In the first of these, two things are mentioned, namely: an obstructing of the day, so that it might not exist; and an obstructing of its effect, in this place:[57] *Let darkness conceal it.* In the first of these, four things are designated, namely: the removal of the day, the search for it by the human who counts the days of his life, the recollection of the one who lives, whose day it is, and the obstruction of its illumination. And that is: [4] ***Let that day,*** namely that life which was given into the power of Satan, ***be turned into darkness,*** so that the effect of Satan would never be seen, never appear, and never come to light. Concerning this it is said,[58] *From the height of the day I will fear,* because the higher the light of the day climbs, the more calamities it heaps up; but the human person is concealed from these calamities if the disastrous day does not arise in his presence. Mi 7:[59] *As long as I sit in darkness, the Lord is my light.* Ps:[60] *Night will be my illumination in my delights.* For he calculates his delights if a disastrous life does not dawn.

let God not count it from above, for God governs what is lower by means of what is higher, and He has established the lengths and limits of human life and the number of their days. Ps:[61] *You have established a boundary, which they will not pass over.* And if one day is missing, it will be accounted for by God, the ordainer of life. Ps:[62] *I spoke with my tongue: Enable me to know my end, Lord, and what the number of my days is, so that I might know when I will die. Behold, you have made my days measurable.* Job asks that the day of Satan's power not be counted among the number of his days. There is a parallel in [another] Ps:[63] *May I never sleep in death, lest at any time my enemy say: I have prevailed against him.*

and let it not be in the recollection,[64] supply: of the living. For

56. Jb 3.6.
57. Jb 3.5.
58. Ps 55.4.
59. Mi 7.8.
60. Ps 138.11.
61. Ps 103.9.
62. Ps 38.5–6.
63. Ps 12.4–5.
64. This phrase is not found in the Vulg. text as it has come down to us.

if it is not in the recollection, then it was never in past life. The recollection of disaster negatively affects the soul and moves it toward sadness. Is 38:[65] *I will recount to you all my years in the bitterness of my soul.*

nor let the light shine upon it, in order that the disastrous things of life might be revealed by more abundant light, seeing that it is more advantageous for such things to fall away than to be illuminated. Jn 3:[66] *He who does evil hates the light.* So Adam, when he experienced the effect of Satan in himself, hid himself from the light, according to Gn 3:[67] *I heard your voice and I hid myself.*

Then Job mentions impediments to Satan's progress: **[5]** ***Let darkness conceal it.*** "Darkness" arises from the lower bodies and signifies the dispositions by which the ominous light is removed from both body and soul. Sometimes, in fact, an ominous star recurs and enkindles a disease that arises and advances in the body. For example, according to the study of medicine, blood is let from a patient suffering from quartan fever[68] every fourth day to prevent the recurrence of symptoms. So too in the soul, when it is concealed by devotion or compunction, the ominous light of Satan is prevented from arising either by the providence of wisdom or even by the merit of justice. The things that prevent ominous light are called "darkness" through their effect. There is a parallel in Is 26:[69] *Go, my people, go into your bedrooms and close the doors behind you, until my anger subsides.*

and the shadows of death, supply: let them conceal it. The calling to mind of death or the loathing of the ominous light, desiring to destroy it, is called "the shadow of death." Sir 7:[70] *In all your works remember your last day, and you will never sin.* Eccl 11:[71] *If a person lives for many years and rejoices in them all, he must nev-*

65. Is 38.15.
66. Jn 3.20.
67. Gn 3.10.
68. Quartan fever is also known as quartan malaria because this type of malaria, caused by the parasitic protozoa *plasmodium malariae*, produces fevers that recur approximately every fourth day.
69. Is 26.20.
70. Sir 7.40.
71. Eccl 11.8.

ertheless remember the dark time and the many days that, when they come, will accuse the past of vanity.

let thick fog seize it. This is a very powerful and dense disposition, by contrast. For thick fog is made by misty vapor, by dense darkness obstructing the light and hindering it; and it signifies the thick disposition of the wise man or the merit of the good man against the light of Satan. Ex 10:[72] *Let there be darkness so thick that they can touch it.* But this is the disposition of the wise man, as the Philosopher says,[73] or of the penitent, as Gregory says.[74] What deprives one of all light is not called "thick fog," but only what hinders that ominous light of Satan. Thus Ex 20:[75] *Moses entered into the thick fog,* so that all things seen in the light of this world would fall away and he alone would be glorious in the light of God.

and let it be enveloped in bitterness, so that the ominous light might be so wrapped up by the bitterness of the contrary disposition in the body or in the soul or in both that it is not able to diffuse itself through my life. Lam 3:[76] *God has filled me with bitterness, He has inebriated me with wormwood.* One who is inebriated does not feel anything.

Then Job comes to the night of conception, which was the beginning of the formation of the life that was given into Satan's power:

[6] ***That night,*** in which the seeds for forming the one conceived came together into a disastrous life—***let a dark whirlwind seize it.*** A "whirlwind" is a wind that blows in a circular pattern, and it signifies dispositions of the heart and of work that are composed of many things, dispositions that ruin and restrain Satan's effect. Hence when God spoke to Abraham about the blessings that He would give him, Gn 15[77] says in advance [of God's making the covenant with him]: *And when the sun had set, fear rushed upon Abraham, and a very great and gloomy horror seized*

72. Ex 10.21.
73. See Aristotle, *Metaph.* 1.2.
74. See *Mor.* 4.4.9.
75. Ex 20.21.
76. Lam 3.15.
77. Gn 15.12.

him, by which the work of Satan was driven back, lest, otherwise, it spread itself widely.

Let it not be counted among the days of the year, that is, of the cycle of life, so that it might be missing from the computation of days in the whole life because it introduces the evils of life. Eph 5:[78] *Redeeming the time, because the days are evil.* ***nor numbered among the months.*** On account of its proximity to the earth, the moon has greater power in human affairs, and through the passing of each month the moon produces the spring, summer, autumn, and winter, the cycle of seasons that the sun produces in a year. Job here is asking, then, that Satan's effect not be able to diffuse itself among the particular changes of his life. Sir 43:[79] *The moon is the sign of a festal day, a light that diminishes in its perfection. "Month" is derived from the word "moon," increasing wonderfully in its perfection.*

And so he adds: **[7]** ***Let that night be solitary and not worthy of praise.*** The order of the text should be changed to read, "and let that night, not worthy of praise, be solitary," to make clear that the second is the cause of the first, and the latter is the cause of the former. Because the night is not worthy of praise, Job should desire that it be solitary, lest by repetition it should spread throughout his life. Sir 23:[80] *Lest you, having made a fool of yourself through repetition, suffer reproach, and wish that you had not been born and curse the day of your birth.*

And because he spoke separately about the night and the day, here he speaks of them together: **[8]** ***Let those,*** supply: wise people, ***curse it,*** namely such a day and night, ***who curse the day,*** that is, those who are familiar with and have experience cursing such a day, which is poisoned by the wickedness of Satan. Dt 27:[81] *Cursed is he who has not continued in all the works of this law, and has not fulfilled them in his work. And all the people shall say, Amen.*

who are prepared to awaken Leviathan. According to the philosopher Abraham the Jew and according to Rabbi Moses

78. Eph 5.16.
79. Sir 43.7–8.
80. Sir 23.19.
81. Dt 27.26.

[Maimonides],[82] Satan is called Leviathan. He spreads his venom from the first day of life through all the subsequent days, months, and years; he adds evil to evil and in this way infects the whole cycle of our life. As a serpent he slithers, and as a crowbar he rigidly stands in our way, and his tongue spews forth venom, as it is said in Jas 3:[83] *The tongue defiles the whole body and inflames the cycle of our birth, being set on fire by hell.* But those, on the other hand, who would struggle and make a stand against the serpent must rouse themselves and put their own strength to the test. Just as the Lord also says in Gn 3:[84] *I will put enmity between you and the woman, and between your offspring and the offspring of the woman; she will crush your head, and you will lie in wait for her heel.*

[9] ***Let the stars be darkened by its thick fog.*** Job is referring to stars whose twinkling forebodes ill, which he desires to be concealed by the thick fog of a contrary disposition, as has been said previously. For a foul exterior light is kept away by an interior darkness. Lam 3:[85] *He has driven me and He has led me into darkness, and not into light.*

Concerning how it would happen, he adds: ***let it expect light,*** in other words, let Satan wait for the appearance of the ominous light, ***but not see*** that light, because when that star is rising I desire its setting, lest it shine on the day of human birth. Jer 15:[86] *Her sun goes down while it is still daytime,* that is, when the

82. See Moses Maimonides, *Dux* 3.22, 24. Like Weiss, I have been unable to locate this allusion to "the philosopher Abraham the Jew" or even to identify this Abraham with certainty. Albert may be referring to Abraham ibn Daud (d. 1180), whom Weiss identifies as the "Abraham of Spain" whom Albert mentions among several Jewish philosophers in commenting on the name *Leviathan* in Jb 40.20 (Weiss, col. 485). Here Weiss references Ibn Daud's work *Ha-Emunah ha-Ramah* (*The Exalted Faith*). For more on Ibn Daud, see Resianne Fontaine, "Abraham Ibn Daud," *The Stanford Encyclopedia of Philosophy* (Fall 2018 edition), ed. Edward N. Zalta (URL: *https://plato.stanford.edu/archives/fall2018/entries/abraham-daud*); and Gad Freudenthal, "Abraham Ibn Daud, Avendauth, Dominicus Gundissalinus and Practical Mathematics in Mid-Twelfth Century Toledo," *Aleph* 16/1 (2016): 61–106.

83. Jas 3.6.

84. Gn 3.15.

85. Lam 3.2.

86. Jer 15.9.

day was just beginning. ***nor,*** supply: may it see ***the beginning of the dawn rising.*** Dawn is when the rays of the sun have mixed themselves with the darkness of night; and so the dawn of ominous light is when that light first mixes itself with the days of human life. Job hopes that such a dawn does not rise, as it also says in Wis 5:[87] *All the things of the wicked pass over into hell like a shadow, and like a messenger running ahead.* And after a few lines:[88] *So too we, having been born, immediately ceased to be; and indeed we have been unable to show any sign of virtue. On the contrary, we have been consumed in our malice.* Hence it should be desired that such a day not arise.

Then Job adds the reason for such a great curse: **[10]** ***because it did not shut the doors of the womb,*** in order that, with the doors having been shut, I might have died in the womb, and my mother would not have brought me forth into this ominous light. Lk 23:[89] *Blessed are the barren, and the wombs that have not given birth.* By way of exposition, Job adds: ***nor removed evils from my eyes,*** that is, the trials I have experienced, which I designate "evils," which Satan infuses into the whole cycle of life. Jer 20:[90] *Cursed is he who did not kill me from the womb, so that my mother might have become my grave and her womb an everlasting conception! Why have I come out of the womb, in order to see suffering and hardship, and so that my days might be swallowed up in confusion?*

[11] ***Why did I not die in the womb?***

Here Job touches on the reason why he curses the day, and it is divided into two parts. In the first place he sets forth the usefulness of being deprived of that day, and secondly he adapts this to himself in this place:[91] *Before I eat.*

There are three things in the first part. First, he shows that the things of which he is deprived in this life are not useful *per se;* secondly, that the longed-for setting of that day frees people from many worries and evils, in this place:[92] *The wicked have*

87. Wis 5.9.
88. Wis 5.13.
89. Lk 23.29.
90. Jer 20.15–18.
91. Jb 3.24.
92. Jb 3.17.

ceased from tumult; thirdly, that the light of this life does not benefit anyone born in misery, in this place:[93] *Why has light been given to one who is in misery?* And that is: ***Why did I not die in the womb,*** so that I would not have experienced the evils of Satan, nor seen them, but would have been carried away from his venom at the very beginning. Mt 26:[94] *It would have been better for him if he had not been born.* ***why did I not perish immediately when I came forth from the womb?*** That is, why did I not perish at once, because then I would not have experienced the evils of Satan? But then I would not have discerned through the power of reasoning. Ps:[95] *Blessed is he who will take your infants and dash them against a stone.*

[12] ***Why was I received upon the knees?*** that is, from the knees of my mother I have been brought forth by the midwife while crying over the evils of Satan. Wis 7:[96] *The first sound that I uttered was crying, like all others.* ***Why was I nursed (*lactatus*) at the breasts?*** since that nourishment would lead, inexorably, to experiences of Satan's evil. Therefore, indeed, it is cruel to feed an infant. Jer 15:[97] *She who gave birth was perplexed and ashamed, because I will give those who survive from her to the sword in the sight of their enemies.* Lam 4:[98] *Even witches lay bare their breasts and nurse their brood.* For it is more characteristic of witches than of mothers to nurse (*lactare*) their offspring for such misfortune.[99]

Then Job adds the reason for this, which is that, dying in such a way, one loses nothing except the goods that should have been despised. And he makes this clear both in the case of people who enjoy such good things, and in the case of those who do not arrive at their enjoyment, in this place:[100] *Or like one born prematurely.*

93. Jb 3.20.
94. Mt 26.24.
95. Ps 136.9.
96. Wis 7.3.
97. Jer 15.9.
98. Lam 4.3.
99. Albert here plays on two meanings of the verb *lactare,* "to nurse" but also "to dupe," in an effort to convey the sufferings for which Job's mother was preparing him.
100. Jb 3.16.

In the case of those who do enjoy earthly goods, some goods are changeable and some are unchangeable. That is: **[13]** ***For now,*** had I not been born on that day of ominous light, ***I would be sleeping*** with my senses bound fast through death ***and silent,*** that is, I would not be uttering sounds of complaint about the venom of Satan, and I would not be moaning in the midst of so many evils. And interpreting this, he adds: ***and in my sleep,*** namely of death, ***I would be resting,*** having been carried away from the disastrous troubles of Satan. Rv 14:[101] *Blessed are the dead, who die in the Lord. From now on, the Spirit says, they may rest from their labors.* And lest death be considered some great loss, he adds: **[14]** ***with kings.*** The Philosopher calls "kings" those who rule human beings with the perfection of justice.[102] Is 32:[103] *Behold, a king shall reign in justice, and princes shall rule in judgment.* ***and consuls of the earth,*** those are called "consuls" who, by giving their own advice in uncertain affairs, prudently direct the judgments of those who set things into motion. Is 32:[104] *He who is foolish will no longer be prince.* ***who build solitary places for themselves,*** literally "who build in solitude," as the Philosopher says in the book on contemplation.[105] They devote themselves to the pursuit of wisdom and virtue, that they might withdraw themselves from Satan's disturbances, which he stirs up throughout the world. This is what the Brahmin philosophers did, and the first monks in Egypt, who thought little of this present life, lest they be whirled about by the disturbances of Satan. **[15]** ***or with princes,*** namely the chief ones among them, ***who possess gold,*** that is, who had much gold but held it in contempt, lest by the troubles of Satan they destroy the goods of the soul. Job returns to the same idea in what follows: ***and fill their homes with silver.*** Gold signifies contempt for the most precious treasures, and silver signifies contempt for less precious treasures, so that they could secure the goods of the soul, just as Plato is said to have thrown gold down out of his lap, saying:

101. Rv 14.13.
102. Aristotle, *Pol.* 3.14–18.
103. Is 32.1.
104. Is 32.5.
105. See Aristotle, *EN* 9.9.

"It is better to lose gold than one's soul."[106] Bar 3:[107] *They hoard silver and gold, in which humans put their confidence, and there is no end to their acquiring;* and after a few words:[108] *They have been driven away, and they have gone down into hell.* For by the disturbance of Satan they have been taken beyond the boundaries of reason and have been dragged off to hell. Job wishes to declare here: I wish that I had not possessed riches, which every wise person has held in contempt lest they be whirled about by the troubles of Satan, because then Satan's wheel would not have crushed me.

[16] ***Or like one born prematurely and hidden, I would not exist.*** But the sense is: I would not exist, just as one who is born prematurely and hidden does not exist. Supply: who has not tasted either the good or the bad things of this world. One prematurely born is one who was damaged from the beginning, from insemination and conception, before it was formed into a fetus by obtaining a soul and life. ***or those who were conceived,*** formed in the womb, supply: having died too soon, ***but did not see the light,*** namely, the ominous light of this life. Indeed, before they opened their eyes to this light, they died, and thus it was better for them not to exist than to be whirled around by Satan's evils. Hence below, in chapter 31,[109] Job says: *If I have seen the sun when it shone and the moon advancing in brightness, and my heart in secret has rejoiced.* He calls the radiance of greater prosperity "the sun" and the brightness of fortune in lesser goods "the moon."

Then he adds the evils that death prevents us from experiencing: **[17]** ***There the wicked,*** namely those who live in a restless way and who disturb both themselves and others, ***have ceased from tumult,*** by which they have disturbed themselves and others. Indeed, a dead person neither causes nor experiences tumult. Is 25:[110] *You shall reduce the tumult of strangers.*

and there those who are wearied in strength have found rest. The text says "in strength" because while trusting in their own

106. Like Weiss, I was unable to find this quotation.
107. Bar 3.18.
108. Bar 3.19.
109. Jb 31.26–27.
110. Is 25.5.

strength they have oppressed others; from this hardship, the dead, who are wearied, have found rest. Is 25:[111] *As if by the heat under a burning hot cloud, you will make the children of the mighty wither away.*

[18] ***And those who were formerly bound,*** that is, seized, afflicted by strong and tumultuous things, supply: have found rest ***together,*** with them ***without worry;*** that is, they no longer experience worry. Therefore, death is useful because it liberates us from experiencing misfortunes. And, feeling this way, David says:[112] *Woe is me, because my living has been prolonged! I have lived among the inhabitants of Kedar.* And the Lord says in Mk 9:[113] *O unbelieving generation, how long will I endure you? How long will I be with you?*

And Job adds how those who were bound in death are without worry when he supplies: because they ***have not heard the voice of the taskmaster,*** that is, of the oppressing tyrant. Hence in Is 14[114] they say: *Since you have fallen asleep, one will not arise who will cut us down.* And Aristotle says in Book I of the *Ethics* that good and bad things do not enable a dead person to experience good fortune or misfortune.[115]

And, concerning the diversity of those who rest, Job adds: **[19]** ***The small and the great are there,*** supply: they are equals and they are resting equally. Wis 6:[116] *The Lord, who is the ruler of all, does not make an exception for anyone's person, nor fear anyone's greatness, seeing that He Himself made the small and the great and He cares for all equally.* ***and the slave,*** supply: formerly bound, ***is free from his master,*** supply: who does not have a master, but pleases only himself; the former slave and the former master find rest equally. Gn 27:[117] *There will be a time when you will cast off his yoke from your neck.* And so death is desirable because it liberates one from such great evils. Hence the saints, jeering at death, say,

111. Ibid.
112. Ps 119.5.
113. Mk 9.19.
114. Is 14.8.
115. Aristotle, *EN* 1.11.15.
116. Wis 6.8.
117. Gn 27.40.

according to 1 Cor 15:[118] *Where, O death, is your victory? Where, O death, is your sting?*

[20] ***Why has light been given to one who is in misery?***

Here Job shows that the light of life, which has been given into Satan's power, is useless for the one in misery. First he says this, secondly he explains it, and thirdly he amplifies the distress of the one in misery. And that is: ***Why***, that is, for what advantage, ***has light been given to the one who is in misery***, to the one subject to the misfortunes of Satan, for he gains nothing from light except to see his own misery, so that he might feel pain all the more, and therefore light does harm to him. Just as in Gn 3,[119] Adam, since he was miserable, hid himself from the light of God. In such cases, what is said in Jn 3[120] is true: *The light has come into the world, and humans have loved darkness more than the light.* Indeed, nothing is demonstrable in such darkness.

And, explaining this, Job adds: ***and life,*** that is, this exterior life in the light, why has it been given ***to those who are bitter in soul?*** that is, in bitterness that reaches all the way to the soul and even to the soul's destruction. Ru 1:[121] *Call me Mara, that is, bitter, because the Almighty has filled me exceedingly with bitterness.* And a poet says of Hecuba: "Alive but reluctantly, because she lives a life of little worth."[122]

And to explain this further, Job adds: **[21]** ***those who,*** that is, because they ***hope*** with longing ***for death,*** which is the end of misery, ***but it does not come,*** so they are more miserable. Rv 9:[123] *Humans will desire to die, but death flees from them.* Certain people of this kind, because they have become deranged, aim threateningly at their own deaths, as did Ahithophel according to 2 Sm 17,[124] Judas according to Mt 27,[125] and Haman, in sadness, according to Est 7[126]; and Hecuba, calling upon Juno, said: "Make

118. 1 Cor 15.55.
119. Gn 3.8.
120. Jn 3.19.
121. Ru 1.20.
122. *Carmina Burana* 101.22 (c. 1230).
123. Rv 9.6.
124. 2 Sm 17.23.
125. Mt 27.5.
126. Est 7.10.

my body, that of an old woman, wear out by means of a quick end."[127]

Then Job sets forth a parallel to this, adding: ***as if digging for treasure,* [22] *they rejoice greatly when they have found the grave?*** The literal sense is in reverse order, using the figure of speech called "hysteron proteron." In other words, they rejoice as those who are digging for treasure do when they get close to the treasure, and this is because they consider death itself a treasure and a gain, inasmuch as it is the end of their misery. Hence below in chapter 14[128] [Job says]: *Until his desired day comes, as the day of his hired servant.* His day is called "the day of death," and is also called "desired," like the end of work for a hired servant inasmuch as it is the terminus of his miseries. Sir 41:[129] *O death, your verdict is advantageous to the human who is in need and whose strength fails, who is worn out and aged, and who worries about everything.* And so Tobit said to the Lord:[130] *Bring forth your mercy for me, and command that my spirit be received in peace, for it is better for me to die than to live.* In the same way 1 Kgs 19[131] says of Elijah: *He asked for his soul that he might die, and said: "It is enough for me, Lord; take my soul, for I am no better than my fathers."*

And heightening the effect of this, Job adds: **[23] *To a man whose way has been hidden,*** for he does not know whether he will have a good or bad end. Eccl 9:[132] *There are just men and wise men, and their works are in the hand of God; and yet man does not know whether he is worthy of love or hatred. But all things pertaining to the future are kept uncertain.*

Moreover, Job adds the reason for this: ***and,*** that is, because ***God has enveloped him with darkness?*** because he does not know his own end, its nature or its time. Eccl 9:[133] *Man does not know his own end; but just as fish are caught with a hook and birds are captured with a snare, so too men are taken in the evil time when it will*

127. *Carmina Burana* 101.27.
128. Jb 14.6.
129. Sir 41.3–4.
130. Tb 3.6.
131. 1 Kgs 19.4.
132. Eccl 9.1–2.
133. Eccl 9.12.

suddenly come upon them. Prv 14:[134] *There is a way that seems right to a man, but it leads to death at its end.* Ps:[135] *They have not known, nor understood: they walk in darkness.*

[24] ***Before I eat.***

Here Job shows how it happened to himself, and he mentions three points: his mourning concerning his misery, the reason for his mourning, and the innocence of the mourner. And that is: ***Before I eat,*** not for pleasure, but for restoration, ***I sigh,*** under the weight of misery pressing down upon me. In this, many who take their food before they sigh are reproved. Eccl 10:[136] *Woe to the land whose king is a boy and whose princes eat early in the morning* not for restoration, but to satisfy themselves to the full. Lam 1:[137] *My sighs are many and my heart laments.*

and my groaning, in the midst of bewailing and weeping, of course, ***is,*** supply: making a sound ***like overflowing water.*** Is 59:[138] *All of us will bellow like bears and lament like mournful doves.*

And he adds the reason: [25] ***because the fear,*** that is, the reason for the fear, ***which I was fearing*** in each instance ***has happened to me,*** namely with regard to my property, my children, and my person, ***and what I was dreading,*** supply: with respect to my friends and my wife, ***has occurred.*** In chapter 30[139] Job says: *I expected good things, but evil things have come upon me; I waited for light, but darkness has broken out.* And in 31:[140] *I have always feared God as if waves were swelling over me, and I was not able to bear His weight.*

Then, concerning his innocence, Job adds: [26] ***Have I not hidden?*** that is, wishing to conquer with patience the evils that have been inflicted upon me. Rom 12:[141] *Refuse to be conquered by evil, but conquer evil with good.* In such a way Joseph hid the evils inflicted upon him by his own brothers in Gn 45, speaking to his brothers mercifully. ***Have I not kept quiet?*** that is, making

134. Prv 14.12.
135. Ps 81.5.
136. Eccl 10.16.
137. Lam 1.22.
138. Is 59.11.
139. Jb 30.26.
140. Jb 31.23.
141. Rom 12.21.

trouble for no one. For the one who truly rests does so within his very self in the good of virtue. Rom 16:[142] *Watch those who cause dissent and give offense concerning the doctrine that you have learned, and avoid them.* ***Have I not been silent?*** in the midst of tumult and the contradiction of sinners. Ps:[143] *I became silent, and I did not speak about good things, and my sorrow was renewed.* Thus far Job has been keeping quiet about the reason for his misery. ***but indignation,*** that is, a blow from the Lord's indignation, ***has come upon me,*** supply: an innocent man. Lam 2:[144] *He has poured out His own indignation like fire. The Lord has become like an enemy.* Is 59:[145] *He who has withdrawn from evil has opened himself to be prey.*

Job, therefore, said these things in order to set forth the subject matter of the disputation for those who were disputing with him.

142. Rom 16.17.
143. Ps 38.3.
144. Lam 2.4–5.
145. Is 59.15.

CHAPTER 4

THEN RESPONDING. An argument to the contrary is called a response, because Aristotle says that perseverance in a chosen line of skilled argumentation sometimes constitutes the solution.[1] Here the wise man is described by name and by his native land. He is identified by the name ***Eliphaz,*** which means "contempt of the Lord," because he thought that no one was superior to him in wisdom or even close, like the one who said in Is 14,[2] *I will raise my throne above the stars of heaven,* that is, above the teachers of this world. He is also identified by his native land: ***the Temanite,*** which means "the south." For the land of Teman was near Idumea, where there was a zeal for scholarly study and for wisdom. Bar 3:[3] *True wisdom has not been heard in the land of Canaan, nor seen in Teman.* And below this:[4] *The merchants of the land and of Teman, the speakers and those who inquire into wisdom and understanding.* Hence both of these, his name and his native land, function to commend him.

This disputation is principally divided into two parts. In the first part Eliphaz sets forth the topic of the disputation, and in the second he commends and questions Job in order that he might, by means of reason, lead Job to understand rightly, through the end of the fifth chapter, in this place:[5] *See this, as we have investigated.* The first part is further subdivided into two parts. In the first he indicates the necessity that compels him

1. See Aristotle, *APr.* 2.28, and *SE* ch. 18.
2. Is 14.13.
3. Bar 3.22.
4. Bar 3.23.
5. Jb 5.27.

to speak; and in the second he sets the disputation in order, in this place:[6] *Behold, you have taught many.*

And that is: [2] ***If we begin to speak to you,*** that is, by disputing against you, ***perhaps you will take it as annoying.*** For every person is annoyed by an attack on his own position. Indeed Aristotle says in Book VIII of the *Ethics* that the poets actually love their poems as their own children and are bothered by attacks against them.[7]

But who is able to withhold the word that he has conceived? that is, the word in his heart interiorly ordered to the defense of truth. For love of the truth compels one to defend the truth, even if one's friend might be annoyed by this. Sir 4:[8] *Do not honor your neighbor in his fall, nor refrain from speaking at the time of salvation.* In the first book of the *Ethics* Aristotle says: "Comparing friends who are lovers of wisdom to the truth itself, piety requires us to hold the truth in higher esteem."[9]

Although this is the literal interpretation, Gregory proposes an alternative interpretation, concerning people who cannot hold back their speech, but let fly with detractions against their neighbor.[10] Against such people it is said in Sir 19:[11] *Have you heard a word against your neighbor? Let it die inside you, considering that it will not break you apart.* And in the same place:[12] *As an arrow embedded in a dog's leg, so is a word in the mouth of a fool.* For just as a dog that has been hit barks for all to hear, so too the fool fills everyone's ears with a disparaging word that he has heard.

Then follows the beginning of the disputation:

[3] ***Behold, you have taught.***

We should recall to mind what was said above about the positions of these two disputants, namely that Job at first complains that he was not judged according to the order of human justice, and therefore that he was condemned as one who is innocent. Eliphaz, on the contrary, proposes that God punishes only evil

6. Jb 4.3.
7. Aristotle, *EN* 9.7.3; cf. 4.1.20.
8. Sir 4.27–28.
9. Aristotle, *EN* 1.6.1.
10. Gregory, *Mor.* 5.13.30.
11. Sir 19.10.
12. Sir 19.12.

people and rewards good people according to the order of human justice.

This disputation is divided into two parts. In the first part Eliphaz refutes the one who teaches; and in the second he refutes his teaching, in this place:[13] *Call to mind, I beg you.*

The first of these parts has two subdivisions. In the first he recounts what the teacher has done, and in the second how he has fallen short, in this place:[14] *But now.* And that is: ***Behold, you have taught many***. On that passage in Mt 4,[15] *Jesus was going about preaching and teaching,* Chrysostom says that teaching (*doctrina*) pertains to morals.[16] Is 48:[17] *I am the Lord who teaches you useful things and who guides you in the way that you walk.* At the end of Mt:[18] *Teach all nations!* Eliphaz says "many" because many are unlearned, whereas few are learned. Rom 1:[19] *I am one who owes the wise and the foolish.* ***and you have strengthened*** those who are already growing weak, as it were, so that they might not fail with the new strength that they have received, ***weary hands,*** that is, for doing good works. Heb 12:[20] *Lift up the hands that hang slack, strengthen the weak knees, and make straight steps with your feet.*

[4] ***Your words have supported those who were staggering,*** that is, those who were faltering or uncertain. At the end of 2 Mc:[21] *He armed every one of them, not with a shield and spear, but rather with the best words and exhortations.* ***and you have reinforced trembling knees,*** trembling in the way of justice, for weakness is noticeable first in the instability and trembling of the knees. 1 Kgs 18:[22] *How long will you limp on two sides?* as if to say that by strengthening the knees you should not limp. Jos 1:[23] *Take courage and be strong.*

13. Jb 4.7.
14. Jb 4.5.
15. Mt 4.23.
16. See Ps.-Chrysostom, *OIM, hom.* 8.23 (PG 56:677).
17. Is 48.17.
18. Mt 28.19.
19. Rom 1.14.
20. Heb 12.12–13.
21. 2 Mc 15.11.
22. 1 Kgs 18.21.
23. Jos 1.6.

Then Eliphaz adds that Job has fallen short of his own teachings, and this is disgraceful for a teacher: to be chastened for a fault of his own. And that is: [5] ***But now the scourge,*** that is, tribulation, ***has come upon you, and you have fallen,*** murmuring timidly against the one who wounded you. Ps:[24] *At the strength of your hand I have fallen in the midst of your rebukes.* Similarly, Ps:[25] *My life has fallen in suffering, and my years in sighs.* ***it has touched you,*** namely by striking you, ***and you have been thrown into confusion.*** A wise man can be thrown into confusion all the way to the troubling of his heart, but he cannot be confounded all the way to the confusion of reason such that he deduces unseemly things, because the touch of evil does not change him with regard to his reason. Wis 3:[26] *The souls of the just are in the hand of God, and the torment of death will not touch them.* **[6]** ***Where is your fear;*** here Eliphaz brings in his attack against Job, as further below where he says:[27] *As much as you are able, you have cast fear aside.* And because *the fear of the Lord drives out sin,* according to Sir 1,[28] and because, after sin has been driven out, then it produces freedom of conscience and, through freedom, fortitude, he therefore adds: where is ***your fortitude?*** Is 40:[29] *Those who hope in the Lord will renew their fortitude; they will take up wings as eagles, they will run and not be weary, they will fly and not grow weak.* ***and,*** supply: where is ***your patience,*** that is, equanimity in your tolerance for adverse circumstances? Lk 21:[30] *In your patience you will gain your souls.* Sir 51:[31] *I have possessed my heart with them from the beginning; therefore, I will not be forsaken.* ***and the perfection of your ways?*** for the perfection of works is born from patience. Jas 1:[32] *Patience has a perfect work, so that you may be perfect and complete, deficient in nothing.*

24. Ps 38.12.
25. Ps 30.11.
26. Wis 3.1.
27. Jb 15.4.
28. Sir 1.27.
29. Is 40.31.
30. Lk 21.19.
31. Sir 51.28.
32. Jas 1.4.

Disputing by means of persuasive reasoning, Eliphaz adds:

[7] *Call to mind.*

Here he begins to construct his own position, namely that God does not condemn anyone except according to what he deserves. It is divided into two parts: in the first part he constructs his position rationally; and in the second he does so by reason while simultaneously deriding the one who asserts the opposite view, below in this place:[33] *Call then.* The first part is again subdivided into two. At first he sets forth human reasoning, and then divine reasoning, in this place:[34] *Next a secret word was spoken to me.*

In the first of these subdivisions there are two parts: in the first he sets forth human reasoning generally; and in the second he narrows its focus, in this place:[35] *The roaring of the lion.* In the first of these he does two things: indeed he makes clear his view of the order of justice for good people and then for bad people, in this place:[36] *But rather.*

And that is: ***Call to mind, I beg you,*** that is, solemnly swearing to you by oaths of truth, I entreat you, call to mind, if what I am going to say is earnest, and listen carefully to what follows from probable things, which is where you ought to look for support when you oppose your interlocutor. Ps:[37] *I have meditated on all your works, and I meditated on the things that you have made with your hands.* ***who that was innocent has ever perished?*** supply: by the scourges of God. An innocent person, who has done harm to no one, is one against whom neither God nor humans have any complaint. Lk 1:[38] *Both of them were just before God, walking according to all the commandments and just determinations of the Lord without blame.* ***Or when were the upright destroyed?*** The upright are, as Ambrose says, those who have a will that is conformed—in heart, speech, and deed—to the divine will, and who measure all they have according to the rectitude of

33. Jb 5.1.
34. Jb 4.12.
35. Jb 4.10.
36. Jb 4.8.
37. Ps 142.5.
38. Lk 1.6.

virtue.[39] About these a Ps[40] similarly says: *The innocent and the upright have clung to me.* Gn 18:[41] *Far be it from you, who judge the whole earth, to do this, and to slay the just with the wicked, so that what happens to the wicked should happen to the just.* Gn 20:[42] *Will you really destroy a just and innocent people?* Ps:[43] *He will not deprive of good things those who walk in innocence.* And for that reason God said through Daniel in chapter 13:[44] *You shall not kill the innocent and the just.* Eliphaz is asserting that the innocent and the upright are not destroyed finally, although they may be destroyed temporarily, for a time, as Abel was by Cain.[45]

And concerning evil people he adds: **[8]** ***But rather,*** that is, by a higher justice, ***I have seen,*** in my experience, ***those who work iniquity.*** He does not say, "who have worked," because perhaps they have repented, but rather he speaks of those who still work iniquity with a constant will. Mt 7:[46] *Depart from me, you who work iniquity.* For such people are opposed to the upright. ***and sow sorrows,*** that is, by means of wicked plans and machinations, tricks, murmuring, slandering, or even by means of money, such as usurers, who sow money in order that it might multiply further. Mt 13:[47] *The enemy came and sowed weeds.* ***and reap them,*** for they act on account of greed. Is 1:[48] *All of them love bribes, and they seek rewards.* Among those guilty of this sin are judges who, out of zeal for a commission, produce fraudulent legal documents so that a particular case together with its commission might revert to them again.

[9] ***perish by the blowing of God,*** that is, by God judging justly and according to human justice. This is said by way of similitude, for when we blow we draw the external air inside ourselves and drive it out by the force of the lungs and the diaphragm.

39. Like Weiss, I have been unable to find this reference.
40. Ps 24.21.
41. Gn 18.25.
42. Gn 20.4.
43. Ps 83.13.
44. Dn 13.53.
45. Gn 4.8.
46. Mt 7.23.
47. Mt 13.25.
48. Is 1.23.

And so Eliphaz supposes that God examines the deeds of man, weighing them carefully within Himself, and brings forth His judgment as if by blowing. There is a parallel in Is 40:[49] *The grass has withered and the flower has fallen because the breath of the Lord has blown upon it.* Is 30:[50] *The breath of the Lord, like the burning of brimstone, sets it on fire.*

and be consumed by the breath of His wrath. Again this is said by way of human likeness, for Eliphaz was born a man. The repetition of breathing is due to the warming of the blood and evaporation. And breath passes through the face, which is why, for angry people, the face turns red and becomes swollen, the lips broaden, the nostrils open, and then they bring forth vengeance. There is a parallel in Is 2:[51] *Turn away from man, whose breath is in his nostrils.* For even now such a being breathes wrath out of his soul.

Then Eliphaz narrows this general order of justice to his present purpose, adding: **[10]** ***The roaring of the lion,*** he calls Job a lion, as if he ruled in tyranny and by means of oppression. Prv 28:[52] *As a roaring lion and a ravenous bear, a wicked prince rules over his poor people.* ***and the voice of the lioness,*** he calls Job's wife the lioness, as if she were gulping down prey. Nm 23:[53] *Behold, the people will rise up as a lioness, and they will be excited like a lion; the lion will not lie down until it devours its prey and drinks the blood of the slain.*

and the teeth of the lion cubs are broken. Eliphaz is referring to the gluttonous frenzy of Job's children, which he says was crushed when the house fell upon them. Ps:[54] *The lion cubs are roaring and plundering.* And perhaps Eliphaz is using in a negative sense what Job uses in a positive sense below:[55] *I crushed the jaws of the wicked man, and I snatched the prey out of his teeth.*

Then Eliphaz returns to Job, adding: **[11]** ***The tiger has perished.*** The tiger is a cruel animal, swift in pursuing its prey, and

49. Is 40.7.
50. Is 30.33.
51. Is 2.22.
52. Prv 28.15.
53. Nm 23.24.
54. Ps 103.21.
55. Jb 29.17.

fickle. This indicates that Job was cruel inwardly and swift to plunder, although outwardly he pretended to be otherwise. Mt 7:[56] *They come to you in sheep's clothing, but inwardly they are ravenous wolves.* He says that this tiger has perished, has lost its spirit, ***because it does not have prey,*** just as a greedy person becomes great when his purse increases, but perishes when his profits disappear. Ps:[57] *You have broken the teeth of sinners.* ***and the cubs of the lion,*** that is, ministers and officials aiming at plundering, ***are scattered abroad.*** Ezek 19:[58] *She nurtured her cubs in the midst of the young lions.* Na 2:[59] *The lion caught enough for his cubs, and killed for his lionesses; and he filled his caves with prey and his den with what he carried off.* And just after this:[60] *The sword will devour your young lions, and I will banish your prey from the land, and the voice of your messengers will be heard no more.*

[12] ***Next a secret word was spoken to me.***

Because human reasoning about divine things is feeble, here Eliphaz introduces a reason based on a revelation. And it has three parts, namely: the praise of revelation; secondly, the revelation itself, in this place:[61] *Can it be that a human will be made righteous in comparison to God*; and thirdly, confirmation of the revelation using lesser means, in this place:[62] *Behold, those who serve Him.* His praise of revelation is threefold, namely: from the mode of its reception; from the time of the vision, in this place:[63] *In the horror of a nocturnal vision;* and by reverence for the one who was revealing, in this place:[64] *Someone stood there.*

And that is: ***Next,*** thus by continuous probable reasoning I have confirmed what I have said, and if this reasoning about divine matters seems feeble, because it is said in 1 Sm 16,[65] *Humans see those things that are visible, but the Lord looks at the heart,*

56. Mt 7.15.
57. Ps 3.8.
58. Ezek 19.2.
59. Na 2.12.
60. Na 2.13.
61. Jb 4.17.
62. Jb 4.18.
63. Jb 4.13.
64. Jb 4.16.
65. 1 Sm 16.7.

I say "next" for "but," as if to say, "but in order to confirm the truth." ***a secret word was spoken.*** He observes that he received it through an oracle, which is a more certain means of revelation than a dream, as Martial says on the dream of Scipio.[66] ***to me,*** such that it drew near to my heart and my understanding through consent. Rom 10:[67] *The word is near, in your mouth and in your heart.* Indeed, when things that have been revealed are reasonable, then they draw near to the human heart. Jas 1:[68] *With gentleness receive the implanted word.* Ps:[69] *I will hear what the Lord God speaks in me.* But to speak in this way is nothing other than to reveal in the mind by intelligible species the will of God through a sign of His own will. 2 Sm 23:[70] *The Spirit of the Lord has spoken through me, and His word by my tongue.* And Eliphaz says "secret word" because it is concealed from the human community, which attends to sense data and imagination. Rv 2:[71] *To him who conquers I will give the hidden manna; and I will give him a white pebble, and on the pebble a name written, which no one knows except him who receives it.* Gregory: The locution of an interior inspiration cannot be known through its species, which is hidden in the mind, except by someone who is capable of knowing it.[72] Hence it is said in Jn 14[73] concerning the Spirit of God: *Whom the world cannot receive, because it does not see Him, nor does it know Him. But you will come to know Him.*

and as if in secret. He calls the retreat of the pure and simple intellect away from the noise of the senses and the foolishness of mental images a secret action. And this is a good secret action, concerning which that passage in Gn 40,[74] *For in secret I was stolen away out of the land of the Hebrews,* is interpreted spiritually, as is Ru 3:[75] *Ruth came close to a heap of sheaves and hid her-*

66. See Macrobius, *CSS* 1.3.8.
67. Rom 10.8.
68. Jas 1.21.
69. Ps 84.9.
70. 2 Sm 23.2.
71. Rv 2.17.
72. See *Mor.* 5.28.50.
73. Jn 14.17.
74. Gn 40.15.
75. Ru 3.7.

self, and when his cover had been removed, she lay down beside his feet. The heap of sheaves signifies the books of Sacred Scripture, in the piling up of which the one who contemplates hides himself as long as he meditates on Scripture. The feet, however, signify the footprints of God found in creatures, and the cover signifies the veil of the mirror image and of the footprints. The removing of the cover signifies her bare and pure intellect oriented toward Boaz, which means strength; so it signifies coming near the strength of truth by means of hidden contemplation.

my inward ***hearing has received.*** For Basil, on the beginning of Proverbs,[76] says that when the intellect receives by means of a signal, it is called "hearing," just as when the intellect receives by means of an appearance, it is called "vision," and as when the intellect comes into immediate contact with something, it is called "touch." But when the intellect, which is capable of understanding internal realities, receives by means of external stimuli, such as by a certain vapor, it is called "smell"; and when the intellect, capable of understanding internal realities, receives immediately, it is called "taste." Hence in the Ps:[77] *Taste and see how sweet the Lord is.* ***the veins of its whisper.*** He calls the ways and means of revelation, which carry the truth for the purpose of nourishing the intellect, "veins," just as the veins transport blood for the purpose of nourishing the parts of the body. Jb 38:[78] *Show me, if you know, in what way light is scattered.* Bar 3:[79] *They have not known the way of wisdom,* and for this reason they have died. Prv 5:[80] *May your vein be blessed.* Prv 10:[81] *The mouth of the just person is the vein of life.* To be sure, what the ear receives secretly from the mouth is called a "whisper"; and since only one person hears it, those who are with him do not. Hence, according to 1 Sm 3,[82] when the Lord spoke to Samuel in the temple, Eli did not hear it.

Eliphaz commends his revelation for coming at a suitable

76. Basil, *Hom.* 12.14 (*In princ. Prov.*; PG 31:414–15).
77. Ps 33.9.
78. Jb 38.18–19.
79. Bar 3.20.
80. Prv 5.18.
81. Prv 10.11.
82. 1 Sm 3, esp. vv. 4–18.

time, adding: **[13]** ***In the horror of a nocturnal vision.*** By "horror" he signifies its magnitude, for horror comes from something great and astonishing that human nature cannot bear, or can scarcely withstand. By "of a vision" he signifies its certainty, because we have certitude concerning what we see. By "nocturnal" he signifies the concealment of light from the senses, that is to say, when the noise of the senses does not impede the intellect. There is a parallel in Is 21:[83] *From a horrible land a harsh vision was conveyed to me.*

when deep sleep customarily overtakes humans. "Deep sleep" is a profound sleep that binds the imagination and the senses but does not reach the intellect on account of the fact that the power of the intellect is not in the body. Therefore, the intellect is operative to a greater extent in deep sleep because it is not summoned or impeded either by the operation of the senses or by the imagination. Light sleep is also a binding of the senses, but not of mental images or of imagination. Hence Aristotle says in the first book of *On Sleep and Wakefulness* that mental images are excited during wakefulness and to a greater extent in light sleep.[84] What is said in Gn 2[85] is a sign of this: when the Lord wished to reveal to Adam by means of an intellectual revelation how He was going to build the Church from the side of Christ, *He cast a deep sleep over Adam,* so that, with his mind unobstructed, he might clearly perceive the coming revelation. Song 5:[86] *I sleep, but my heart remains awake.* Hence in Nm 24,[87] where a vision is entrusted to Balaam and it says that he beheld visions of Almighty God, this is set forth: *The man whose eye was closed has spoken, he who falls, and so his eyes are opened.* This text intends to show that the more the external eye is closed, the more clearly a person sees within; and the more he falls away from external things and into a deeper sleep, the more his inner eyes are opened for contemplating the truth. Hence Jb 33:[88] *By means of a dream in a night vision, when deep sleep falls*

83. Is 21.1–2.
84. See Aristotle, *Somn.* ch. 1.
85. Gn 2.21.
86. Song 5.2.
87. Nm 24.3–4.
88. Jb 33.15–16.

upon humans and they are sleeping in their beds, then He [*God*] *opens the ears of men, and, teaching them, He instructs them in discipline.* Thus Eliphaz says[89] "overtakes humans" so that humans are understood to possess their rational powers but with their senses overtaken or bound, so that they cannot distract the intellect.

[14] ***fear seized me, and trembling.*** "Fear" is a contraction of the heart, whereas "trembling" is the agitation of the body when the heart has taken flight because of some apparent shock. Indeed, as long as the heart remains contracted, it confines air, heat, and blood within itself, and the external parts of the body tremble because they are devoid of these three things. For the power associated with a feeble part of the body moves it to one position only; but then the lack of heat and air causes it to fall back into the opposite position, and so trembling between two opposite positions results. Hence Damascene says that astonishment is trembling due to an intense mental image or apparition.[90] Ps:[91] *Fear and trembling have come over me, and darkness has covered me.*

and all of my bones were terrified. In the *Topics*[92] Aristotle says that strength and vigor is in the bones and muscles. They are lost when someone is having a vision. Dn 10:[93] *Lord, at the sight of you, my joints were loosened, and no strength remained in me.* Is 21:[94] *I shuddered when I heard it; I was disturbed when I saw it. My heart failed.* And all of this is said by reason of the magnitude of the vision.

[15] ***And when the spirit,*** that is, the higher part of the soul, where the intellect is; ***in my presence,*** that is, before my vision; ***crossed over,*** that is, by suddenly crossing over, it grasped the meaning of the vision, because when even a strong intellect is standing still and at rest in its ordinary mode of existence in this life, we cannot grasp divine realities. This is signified in Gn 28,[95] where Jacob, during sleep while on his journey, saw

89. Here in Jb 4.13.
90. John Damascene, *F.o.* 2.15.
91. Ps 54.6.
92. Aristotle, *Top.* 3.1.
93. Dn 10.16.
94. Is 21.3–4.
95. Gn 28.10–15, esp. vv. 12–13.

angels descending and ascending but not standing still, and he saw the Lord resting on the ladder from above. Although the Lord was standing still, He was not being contemplated by those who stood still. Dn 10:[96] *I, being left alone, saw this great vision; and none of my strength remained, my appearance changed, I fainted, and I did not have any of my bodily strength.*

And this is what follows: ***the hairs of my body bristled up.*** When heat and air have withdrawn to the inner parts of the body, cold creeps up on the exterior or the skin. Due to the skin's contraction, the hairs stand up, and this is called bristling. Dn 10:[97] *How can the servant of my Lord speak with my Lord? For none of my bodily strength remains, and my breath has stopped.*

And all of these words commend the magnitude of the vision, after which he adds a description of the reverence for the one who was revealing Himself. And that is: **[16]** ***Someone stood there.*** Gregory: We are accustomed to saying "someone" of him whom we do not know, for we do not say "someone" except of him whom we either cannot or will not identify.[98] And this is why Eliphaz adds: ***whose countenance I did not know,*** because in this life the countenance of God is not known face-to-face. Hence Jn 1:[99] *But I did not know Him.* Is 53:[100] *His countenance was, as it were, hidden.*

And lest one think that this was a perceptible vision of an actual reality, he adds: ***an image,*** as if to say: "not the reality of a certain one, but rather an image shown in the vision of the imagination," ***before my eyes,*** that is, the eyes of my imagination. Nm 12:[101] *If anyone among you is a prophet of the Lord, I will appear to him in a vision, or I will speak to him in a dream.* Hos 12:[102] *I have used likenesses in the ministry of the prophets.*

and I heard a voice, like a gentle breeze. A gentle breeze (*aura*) moves the ears (*aures*) by a slight whistling and a light hum, that is, without tumult and commotion, where neither the world

96. Dn 10.8.
97. Dn 10.17.
98. See *Mor.* 5.34.61.
99. Jn 1.33.
100. Is 53.3.
101. Nm 12.6.
102. Hos 12.10.

causes confusion nor the flesh makes one unclean nor demons disturb, but rather the gentle breeze of inspiration instructs and teaches concerning spiritual realities. 1 Kgs 19:[103] *Behold, the Lord is going to pass by. And a powerful wind overturning the mountains and crushing the rocks went before the Lord; but the Lord was not in the wind. And after the wind, an earthquake; but the Lord was not in the earthquake. And after the earthquake, a fire; but the Lord was not in the fire. And after the fire, the whistling of a gentle breeze;* the Lord was there. The spirit that crushes the rocks, that is, hard hearts, signifies the breathing of the demons; the earthquake signifies the tumult of the world; the fire signifies the desire of the flesh; and the whistling of whispers signifies the spirit together with the Lord, and the Lord was there. For by means of a gentle breeze, He is breathed into the soul, and therefore He passes over even to his inmost parts. Wis 12:[104] *O how good and sweet is your spirit in all things!* Sir 24:[105] *My spirit is sweeter than honey.*

Then Eliphaz describes the revelation itself that was given to him: **[17]** ***Can it be that a human will be made righteous in comparison to God,*** that is, a human, who is made of mud and whose nature is unclean: "can it be that he will be made righteous?"—that is, will he be able to be just? Below, Jb 14:[106] *Who is able to make him clean who is conceived from unclean seed?* Ps:[107] *Behold, I was conceived in iniquities, and in sins my mother conceived me.* And Eliphaz says "in comparison to God" because he who is unclean considered on his own terms is thoroughly unclean compared to the Lord, because even those things that seem to be clean are unclean compared to God.

And this is what follows: ***or will a man be more pure than his Maker?*** that is: although a man has been made perfect in every virtue, with respect to his own Maker he is unclean. Of this Maker Himself, it is said in Wis 7:[108] *On account of Wisdom's clean-*

103. 1 Kgs 19.11–12.
104. Wis 12.1.
105. Sir 24.27.
106. Jb 14.4.
107. Ps 50.7.
108. Wis 7.24–25.

ness no defiled thing comes into her. Hab 1:[109] *Your eyes are pure, and you are not able to look upon iniquity.* Concerning creation, on the other hand, Is 64:[110] *All of us have become unclean, and all of our righteousness is, as it were, the rag of a menstruating woman.*

And he adds reasoning that confirms what was said [in the revelation], arguing from the smaller or less significant [to the larger or more significant].[111] He first sets forth what seems less significant, and that is: **[18]** ***Behold, those who serve Him,*** that is, for the purpose of serving Him they were made pure and spiritual, such as the angels and saints, ***are not steadfast,*** but can change, supply: toward perversion. For Damascene says that every being that is created is mutable.[112] Below[113] [Job says]: *A human being never remains in the same state.* Ps:[114] *Like clothing you will change them, and they will be changed.*

And he demonstrates this, adding: ***and,*** that is, because ***in His angels He finds perversity,*** namely, the pride by which they fell. Is 14:[115] *How have you fallen from heaven, O Lucifer, who arose early in the morning?* But having first set forth what seems to be the smaller point, Eliphaz goes on to what seems to be the main point.

And that is:

[19] ***How much more.***

And he says two things, namely: he asserts the conclusion that humans will be punished, and the reason that this follows logically. And that is: ***How much more will those who dwell in houses of clay,*** that is, in earthly bodies. Is 64:[116] *Now, O Lord, you*

109. Hab 1.13.

110. Is 64.6.

111. Here Albert understands Eliphaz to be using an argument *a minore ad maius,* from the smaller or less important to the larger or more important point. If God finds perversity in His angels, spiritual creatures whom He made for the very purpose of serving Him ceaselessly, and they fail to remain steadfast (a less significant point for Eliphaz's argument here), how much more will humans, creatures of clay, be consumed (the larger or more significant point).

112. John Damascene, *F.o.* 2.27.

113. Jb 14.2.

114. Ps 101.27.

115. Is 14.12.

116. Is 64.8.

are our Father, and truly we are clay. In Jer 18[117] the Lord says: *As clay in the hand of the potter, so are you in my hand.* And explaining this, Eliphaz adds: ***who have an earthly foundation,*** for human works are based on an earthly body. 1 Cor 15:[118] *The first Adam was from the earth, earthly.* Jn 3:[119] *He who is from the earth speaks about the earth.* ***be consumed as if by a moth?*** A moth is produced from clothing and consumes clothing, and likewise concupiscence is produced from the body and consumes the soul, which inhabits the body. Below[120] [Job says]: *I am going to be consumed as rottenness, and as clothing that is eaten away by a moth.* Is 14:[121] *The moth will be scattered beneath you, and worms will be your covering.*

Then he explains the disorder: **[20]** ***From morning until evening they are consumed,*** that is, continuously, for something is always being lost from this life. Is 38:[122] *From morning until evening you will bring me to an end.* ***and because no one understands*** what he himself is, of course, let alone the Highest Good, to whom there is no comparison. Ps:[123] *I will give you understanding, and I will instruct you.* ***they will perish eternally.*** Hos 4:[124] *The people that does not understand will be beaten.* Ps:[125] *He has refused to understand that he might act rightly. He has devised iniquity in his bed.*

With all of these words Eliphaz intends to declare that human nature is so unclean that no one is able to be without sin; and if someone says he is clean, even though God is punishing him, in fact he is saying that the Lord is unclean by suggesting that He punishes unjustly, and so he prefers himself to and sets himself above his own Maker. But his Maker, as Gregory says, is not an unjust judge of fault.[126]

Then he adds: **[21]** ***And those who will remain,*** namely, those

117. Jer 18.6.
118. 1 Cor. 15.47.
119. Jn 3.31.
120. Jb 13.28.
121. Is 14.11.
122. Is 38.12.
123. Ps 31.8.
124. Hos 4.14.
125. Ps 35.4–5.
126. Like Weiss, I was unable to find this reference.

not consumed by the fault of a filthy nature, ***will be plucked away from them,*** in such a way that they will be neither consumed nor damned with the others. And, as Gregory interprets it, the literal sense is that if some remain who are not consumed immediately by the Lord, and if they differ according to the time of their penance, nevertheless eventually ***they will die*** and be punished, ***and not in wisdom,*** supply: but in foolishness. For the fool will perish eternally. In fact, the root of immortality is in wisdom. Ps:[127] *On that day all their plans will perish.* Wis 15:[128] *To know your justice and your power is the root of immortality.*

127. Ps 145.4.
128. Wis 15.3.

CHAPTER 5

C***ALL THEN, IF THERE is anyone who will respond to you.*** Here Eliphaz begins to object to Job with derision, and his objection has two parts. First he takes up the reasons, in particular, for what has happened to Job; and secondly in general. And in all of this he shows that the Creator of nature is not an unjust judge of fault, in this place:[1] *Nothing on earth happens without a reason.* The first part is subdivided into two. In the first he sets forth his reasoning, and in the second he excludes any tacit objections, in this place:[2] *I have seen a fool.* In the first subdivision he does two things: he derides Job and specifies the cause or reason for this derision, in this place:[3] *Anger kills the foolish man.* And he connects this to a point that he made above,[4] namely that the lion and the tiger and the cubs of the lion are scattered abroad because of the guilt of their plundering, and that in this way Job has been forsaken by God and the good. And if the contrary is supposed to be true, namely that Job was not abandoned by God and the saints, Eliphaz objects to Job:

Call then, that is, invoke God, ***if there is anyone who will respond to you,*** by heeding your prayer. Jb 30:[5] *I will cry out to you, but you will not hear me; I stand up, but you do not look at me. You have turned cruel toward me, and with the severity of your hand you oppose me.* Jn 9:[6] *We know that God does not hear sinners; but if anyone does His will, God heeds him.* And it is as if Eliphaz were saying: "If you

1. Jb 5.6.
2. Jb 5.3.
3. Jb 5.2.
4. Jb 4.10–11.
5. Jb 30.20–21.
6. Jn 9.31.

should cry out when you are afflicted, God would not respond because you have disregarded Him in the time of tranquility." ***and turn to any of the saints,*** that is, to any of the good people, so that they might intercede for you. And it is as if he were saying: "You do not have the saints as your helpers in affliction because you did not have them as your companions in merriment." Is 63:[7] *Abraham has not known us, and Israel has ignored us.* At the end of 1 Jn:[8] *There is a sin that is unto death; I do not say that anyone should pray for him* [*who commits such a mortal sin*].

And, concerning the true reason for his derision toward Job, Eliphaz adds: **[2]** ***Anger kills the foolish man.*** The foolish man is a stupid person who, on account of carelessness and laziness, does not have the ability to discriminate between those things that he should choose and those that he should avoid. In 1 Sm 25[9] it is said of Nabal, whose own name means "foolish": *He is a son of Belial, such that no one is able to speak to him.*

And that is: ***Anger kills the foolish man,*** that is, it makes him worthy of being killed, because in anger he receives everything that he hears and he oppresses both members of his household and his friends. Against this it is said in Sir 4:[10] *Do not be as a lion in your house, destroying the members of your household.* ***and envy slays,*** that is, makes him worthy of being slain, ***the petty one,*** that is, the one who imagines that he is lessened by lacking any possession. In the same way it is said of Haman in Est 5[11] that *he called together his friends and his wife Zeresh, and he related to them the greatness of his wealth and the multitude of his children and with what great glory the king had honored him above all his princes and servants.* And a little later it adds:[12] *And whereas I have all these things, I think that I have nothing as long as I see Mordecai the Jew sitting at the king's gate.* Wis 2:[13] *By the envy of the devil death entered the world, and those who are on his side imitate him.* It is as if Eliphaz were saying: "Irrational rage toward members of your household and envy

7. Is 63.16.
8. 1 Jn 5.16.
9. 1 Sm 25.17.
10. Sir 4.35.
11. Est 5.10–11.
12. Est 5.13.
13. Wis 2.24–25.

toward your fellow citizens have caused you, half-dead, to sit in dung." And because Job could object that many foolish people have prospered, Eliphaz responds that this does not last long, but soon they are completely ruined with regard to their health, their descendants, and their resources. And these three sections that follow correspond to these three ways in which foolish people are destroyed.

And that is: [3] ***I have seen a fool with a strong root,*** that is, firmly rooted. Jer 12:[14] *You have planted them and they have taken root; they prosper and bring forth fruit.* ***and I cursed his beauty immediately.*** The text should be arranged in this way: "immediately I cursed his beauty"; that is, I predicted that he was going to be cursed by God, meaning that his beauty would be brought down into a state of deformity by the curse of God. Dn 4:[15] *Behold, a watcher and a holy one came down from heaven and cried out loudly and said: "Cut down the tree, and lop off its branches, and shake off its leaves, and scatter its fruit."* Ezek 17:[16] *He will pull up its roots, and strip off its fruit, and dry up all the branches that it has sprouted and make them wither.* Wis 4:[17] *Impure plantings will not set deep roots, nor establish a stable foundation. And if they sprout forth branches for a time, because they are not firmly planted they will be shaken by the wind, and they will be uprooted by excessive winds.*

Eliphaz adds how it will be for his descendants: [4] ***His children will be far from safety,*** in the present and in the future, and this is said not only of biological children, but also of imitators of their father's wickedness. Wis 4:[18] *All children who are born of illicit unions are witnesses of wickedness against their parents in their trial.*

And he adds that they are going to be condemned by public justice for their wickedness: ***and they will be crushed at the gate,*** where the public judgment of evildoers takes place. Dt 16:[19] *You shall appoint judges and magistrates at all of your gates.* Hence Dt 21[20] teaches concerning an impudent son that the parents

14. Jer 12.2.
15. Dn 4.10–11.
16. Ezek 17.9.
17. Wis 4.3–4.
18. Wis 4.6.
19. Dt 16.18.
20. Dt 21.18–21.

shall take him to the elders of the community and to the gate of judgment, so that he might be stoned by their verdict.

And because no one is rescued from public judgment, it follows: ***and there will be no one to rescue them.*** Ex 22:[21] *You shall not allow wizards to live.* At the end of Acts[22] it says: *Divine vengeance does not permit him to live.*

Then Eliphaz turns to the plundering of his resources: **[5]** ***Whose,*** namely the fool's, ***harvest,*** that is, good things, gained in whatever way, that he has reaped and collected, ***the hungry man,*** namely the avaricious robber or plunderer whose poverty makes him hungry, ***will eat,*** that is, will devour greedily. Is 16:[23] *The voice of those who trample is rushing in on the produce of your vineyard and on your harvest. And your joy will be carried off.* Jer 48[24] says the same, and Eccl 5:[25] *Riches accumulated to the detriment of their owner. Their loss brings the worst pain: he will father a son who will be in extreme poverty.*

and the armed man, namely the enemy or the devil, who is armed and strengthened against him, ***will drag him off.*** Mt 12[26] and Lk 11:[27] *As long as a strong man who is armed guards his house* ... And this is said of the devil.

and the thirsty, that is, those thirstily desiring his property, ***will drink in,*** that is, gulp down with no difficulty, ***his riches,*** and they will luxuriate, supply: in them. Lk 12:[28] *Whose will be those things that you have prepared?* Hos 7:[29] *Strangers have devoured his strength.*

Eliphaz extends by generalizing what he has described and made clear in particular, saying: **[6]** ***Nothing on earth happens without a reason.*** He says this because he thought Blessed Job was saying that he had been scourged for no reason, and that such scourges come by chance, according to the nature of the elements and of time, and that he had not been stricken for any

21. Ex 22.18.
22. Acts 28.4.
23. Is 16.9–10.
24. Jer 48.33.
25. Eccl 5.12–13.
26. Mt 12.29.
27. Lk 11.21.
28. Lk 12.20.
29. Hos 7.9.

fault. Plato says the same thing as Eliphaz in the *Timaeus*: There is nothing whose origin is not preceded by a legitimate cause.[30] Ezek 18:[31] *The justice of the just man shall be upon him, and the wickedness of the wicked man shall be upon him.*

and, in other words, ***suffering will not spring out of the soil.*** What he calls "soil" is moist earth mixed and tempered to make up human nature. Suffering, that is, the cause of suffering, does not spring forth from it because, as Fulgentius says, God is not the avenger of something of which he is the author.[32] And demonstrating this, Eliphaz adds: **[7]** ***The human,*** the one from the soil (*ex humo*), ***is born to labor,*** without which he does not survive in this mortal life. Gn 3:[33] *By the sweat of your face you shall eat your bread.* ***and the bird is born to fly.*** He wishes to declare that each individual thing is born for the purpose of its own action, and not so that God might afflict it without cause. Wis 1:[34] *God did not make death, nor does He delight in the destruction of the living.* And all of this is said on account of the view, which certain philosophers have asserted, that the human person is directed toward good or toward evil by lucky or unlucky stars in their cycles because, although the Creator does make things, He nevertheless entrusts the government of mutable things to the cycles of the stars and to the random mutability of mortal nature. And Eliphaz was attributing this opinion to Job. Although it is not true, nevertheless, as Rabbi Moses [Maimonides] of Egypt says in the third part of the *Guide of the Perplexed*, ch. 24, this opinion seems to have been held by Aristotle and certain Peripatetics.[35]

[8] ***For this reason.***

Here Eliphaz touches on how through penance Job was able to be restored and reconciled to God, because God is kind in accepting sinners and powerful in restoring them. And Eliphaz

30. Plato, *Ti.* 28A.

31. Ezek 18.20.

32. Fulgentius, *AM* 1.19 (PL 65:167). Cf. Albert, *ST* 2.4.18.2.1 sol., where it is ascribed to Augustine.

33. Gn 3.19.

34. Wis 1.13.

35. See Moses Maimonides, *Dux* 3.23. In referring to Maimonides as "Rabbi Moses of Egypt" here, Albert is indicating the place where the Jewish philosopher lived most of his adult life and died in 1204.

mentions these two things here. And that is: ***For this reason,*** because God punishes for no other reason than sin, ***I will deprecate the Lord.*** "Lord" is a name of power, as Ambrose says.[36] Jdt 8:[37] *Understanding that these punishments are less than our sins, let us believe that these scourges of the Lord, as if they are servants of the Lord with which we are reproved, have happened for our correction, not for our destruction.* Deprecation is prayer for deliverance from evil, as Augustine says.[38] ***and I will set my speech,*** of deprecation and prayer, of course, ***before my God,*** who sees all things. Jas 5:[39] *The constant deprecation of a just person accomplishes much.* And in that same place:[40] *The prayer of faith will save the sick person, and if he has sinned, he will be forgiven.*

Eliphaz shows how powerful God is for salvation, first in general; secondly in particular, in this place:[41] *He bestows rain;* and thirdly he concludes his purpose here, in this place:[42] *Blessed is the man.*

And that is: **[9]** ***He does great things,*** which cannot be done except by great power. Dt 32:[43] *Ascribe greatness to our God; the works of God are perfect.* Hence in great things the magnitude of His power and strength is perceived. Sir 43:[44] *Great is the Lord who made them,* that is, the sky and the sun, ***and inscrutable things,*** inscrutable to wisdom. Rom 11:[45] *O the depth of the riches of the wisdom and the knowledge of God!* Eccl 1:[46] *All things are difficult; the human is not able to explain them with his speech.* ***and marvelous things.*** "Marvelous things" are those of which the human cannot find the cause, although by wondering at them he struggles toward it. Sir 43:[47] *Hearing with our own ears, there we will admire splendid and marvelous works.* ***without number.*** Indeed, just as His

36. Ambrose, *De fide* 1.1.7 (PL 16:530).
37. Jdt 8.27.
38. Augustine, *Ep.* 149.2.13 (CSEL 44.360).
39. Jas 5.16.
40. Jas 5.15.
41. Jb 5.10.
42. Jb 5.17.
43. Dt 32.3–4.
44. Sir 43.5.
45. Rom 11.33.
46. Eccl 1.8.
47. Sir 43.26–27.

power is not limited in its extent, so also it is not limited in number or in variety. For God does not make so many things that He is unable to make more.

Then Eliphaz introduces particular ways [in which God is powerful for salvation]: first in promoting the good; secondly in impeding evil, in this place:[48] *He scatters;* and thirdly in liberating the oppressed, in this place:[49] *On the other hand, He will save.*

And that is: **[10]** ***He bestows rain upon the face of the earth,*** so that it might receive the power of sprouting forth. Is 55:[50] *As the rain and the snow come down from heaven and return there no more, but soak the earth and water it, and make it sprout forth, and give seed to the one who sows and bread to the one who eats.* ***and refreshes all things with water.*** Ps:[51] *You water the mountains from their higher places; the earth will be filled with the fruit of your works.*

And this is the case not only in nature, but also in human affairs. And that is: **[11]** ***He sets the lowly on high.*** Lk 1:[52] *He has exalted the lowly.* Mt 20:[53] *So the last will be first.* ***and he comforts with health those who mourn,*** because of poverty or sickness. Prv 14:[54] *The heart that has known the bitterness of its own soul will have unalloyed joy.* Tb 3:[55] *You do not delight in our destruction; after a storm you produce a calm, and after weeping and wailing you pour out joy.*

Then Eliphaz adds, concerning [how God is powerful in] impeding evil. And that is:

[12] ***He scatters.***

And he asserts two things: that God is an impediment to evil in its execution and in its devious planning. And that is: ***He scatters the plans of the wicked,*** away from the effect and the end at which they aim, so that they end up fighting on behalf of the very one whom they are resisting and opposing with the malice of their wills. And that is: ***so that their hands,*** that is, their actions, ***cannot complete what they had begun,*** that is, what they had be-

48. Jb 5.12.
49. Jb 5.15.
50. Is 55.10.
51. Ps 103.13.
52. Lk 1.52.
53. Mt 20.16.
54. Prv 14.10.
55. Tb 3.22.

gun through their proposed plan. An example of this appears in Gn 37,[56] where his brothers sold Joseph so that they would not be made subject to his authority, but the Lord foiled their plan, bringing it about that as a result of selling him they were made subject to his authority. Similarly in Jn 11,[57] *when the high priests called a meeting of the council,* to kill the Lord, and said, *So that the Romans will not come and destroy our holy place and our nation,* it was on account of the fact that they killed him that the Lord ordained that they would lose [their holy place].[58]

Then Eliphaz explains how God is an impediment to the devious planning of evil: **[13]** ***He catches,*** so that they are not able to proceed, ***the wise,*** that is, the clever and the crafty, ***in their cunning,*** so that their cunning is turned back on their heads, of course. An example of this appears in 2 Sm 17[59] in the counsel of Ahithophel, who *hanged himself* on account of the plan that he devised against David. And another example is in Est 7[60] in the cunning of Haman, who was hanged on the beam *that he had prepared for Mordecai.* And this is what follows: ***and scatters the schemes of the corrupt.*** 2 Sm 15:[61] *Scatter, Lord, the plan of Ahithophel.* Is 8:[62] *Devise a plan, and it will be scattered; speak a word, and it will not be done, because God is with us.*

Eliphaz adds how this happens: **[14]** ***During the day they will meet with darkness.*** They call the bright light of their plan "day,"

56. Gn 37.28.

57. Jn 11.47–48.

58. Albert suggests here the traditional doctrine of Jewish witness, formulated by Augustine, according to which, as punishment for killing the Lord, their own long-awaited Messiah, God stripped the Jews of their holy land and dispersed them throughout the world, where they would continue to serve as unwitting witnesses to the truth of Christianity. On Augustine's doctrine and its reception among medieval theologians and churchmen, see Franklin T. Harkins, "Unwitting Witnesses: Jews and Judaism in the Thought of Augustine," in *Augustine and World Religions,* ed. Brian Brown, John Doody, and Kim Paffenroth (Lanham, MD: Lexington Books, 2008), 37–69; and Jeremy Cohen, *Living Letters of the Law: Ideas of the Jew in Medieval Christianity* (Berkeley: University of California Press, 1999).

59. 2 Sm 17.23.

60. Est 7.10.

61. 2 Sm 15.31, 34.

62. Is 8.10.

through which light they appear to carry out the wickedness of their will. An example of this occurs in Gn 19,[63] where the Sodomites were struck with blindness so that they could not find the door of Lot's house. The same thing occurs in 2 Kgs 6,[64] where the messengers of the king of Syria were struck with blindness so that they would not see Elisha, who stood before their eyes.

And this is what he adds: ***and as if in the night***, supply: having been covered in darkness and concealed, ***they will grope***, that is, they will try to feel their way along, ***at midday***, that is, in the full light of their own deliberations. Wis 17:[65] *The whole world will be illuminated by a clear light, and it was preserved, unhindered in its works. But over them alone had spread a heavy night, an image of the darkness that was going to come over them; but they were more oppressive to themselves than was the darkness.* Is 59:[66] *Like blind people we have groped for the wall, and we have touched it as if without sight. We have stumbled at midday as if in darkness, in dark places as if we were dead.* Jer 15:[67] *Her sun has gone down while it was still day.*

Then Eliphaz adds how powerful God is in liberating the oppressed: **[15]** ***On the other hand, He will save the needy.*** One who wanders from door to door, seeking assistance from others, is called "needy." At the end of Sir:[68] *I was looking for the help of men, but there was none.* Is 63:[69] *From the nations there is not a man with me.* ***from the sword of their mouth,*** namely of the perverse; and this means the sword of the tongue that renounces, slanders, and insults. Prv 30:[70] *There is a generation that has swords for teeth, and grinds with their molars, to devour the needy from the earth and the poor from among men.* ***and,*** in other words, He will liberate ***the poor from the hand of the violent,*** that is, from the power of the one who does violence. Ps:[71] *To you the poor man has been abandoned; you will be a helper to the orphan.*

63. Gn 19.11.
64. 2 Kgs 6.18.
65. Wis 17.19–20.
66. Is 59.10.
67. Jer 15.9.
68. Sir 51.10.
69. Is 63.3.
70. Prv 30.14.
71. Ps 9.35.

[16] ***And,*** supply: in this way ***there will be hope,*** namely God, who is the cause of hope for deliverance ***for the needy.*** Ps:[72] *In you our fathers hoped: they hoped and they were not confounded.* Sir 2:[73] *Consider, my children, the nations of the human race: and know that no one has hoped in the Lord and been confounded, no one has remained in His commandments and been abandoned.* Rom 5:[74] *Hope does not confound.* For hope is a certain expectation that cannot confound. ***but iniquity,*** namely that of the perverse, ***will draw together,*** that is, will close, ***its mouth,*** that is to say, whatever has been confounded and hindered by the effect of the wickedness of its own will.

[17] ***Blessed is the man.***

On the basis of all these things that he has introduced, Eliphaz concludes that Job ought to think that the blow of the Lord was inflicted on him for his sins, and that he should rejoice because he will be healed by means of this blow and he will be restored. And he asserts this first in general; and secondly he makes it clear in particular, in this place:[75] *In the midst of six tribulations.*

And that is: ***Blessed*** by hope ***is the*** rational ***man who is reproved by the Lord*** through tribulations. 1 Cor 11:[76] *As long as we are judged, we are reproved by the Lord, so that we might not be damned with this world.* 2 Mc 6:[77] *It is a sign of great kindness not to allow sinners to continue for a long time according to their purpose, but to punish them immediately.* ***Therefore, do not reject the rebuke of the Lord.*** Rv 3:[78] *Those whom I love, I censure and punish.* Prv 3:[79] *My son, do not reject the discipline of the Lord, and do not falter when you are reproved by Him. For whom the Lord loves, He reproves, just as a father reproves the son in whom he delights.*

Then he adds the reason: **[18]** ***because He wounds, but He cures,*** that is, He cures by wounding. By wounding his patient a surgeon extracts the pus or poison that is the cause of the illness.

72. Ps 21.5–6.
73. Sir 2.11–12.
74. Rom 5.5.
75. Jb 5.19.
76. 1 Cor 11.32.
77. 2 Mc 6.13.
78. Rv 3.19.
79. Prv 3.11–12.

And this is what follows: ***He strikes,*** with punishment, ***but His hands,*** the ones that strike, ***will heal*** from fault. Dt 32:[80] *I will kill and I will make alive, I will strike and I will heal.* Therefore, the Ps[81] says: *Your rod and your staff, they have comforted me.*

Then Eliphaz first touches in particular on those things from which God liberates; and secondly on those things that He restores, in this place:[82] *And you will know that* [*your tent*] *possesses peace.*

And that is: **[19]** ***In the midst of six tribulations,*** which afflict this life, ***He will liberate you.*** Ps:[83] *I am with him in tribulation; I will rescue him.* ***and in the seventh,*** which sometimes is brought on by humans, ***evil will not touch you,*** namely with the touch of deformation.[84] Wis 3:[85] *The souls of the just are in the hand of God, and the torment of death will not touch them.*

Moreover, he specifies the six tribulations: **[20]** ***In famine,*** caused by a shortage of possessions and the destitution of poverty, of course, ***He will redeem you from death,*** so that you do not die destitute. Ps:[86] *I was young, and indeed I have grown old; and I have not seen the just man forsaken, nor his offspring searching for bread.* But if one objects [with the words of] 1 Cor 4,[87] *We hunger and thirst, and we are naked,* it must be said that this is for the purpose of proving virtue, and not for death.

and in war, which is ***from the hand of the sword.*** Gregory says that "war pertains to the enemy," that is, the invasion of the enemy, so that you remain outside of the power of their sword.[88] In Ex 15,[89] where we have, *The Lord is, as it were, a man of war,*

80. Dt 32.39.
81. Ps 22.4.
82. Jb 5.24.
83. Ps 90.15.
84. With the phrase *tactu sc. immutationis* here, Albert has in mind, generally following Augustine, the privation or deformation that is and results from creaturely mutability and decay, which is an impossibility for the souls of the just, as the following scriptural quotation makes clear.
85. Wis 3.1.
86. Ps 36.25.
87. 1 Cor 4.11.
88. Gregory, *Hom. eu.* 2.35.1 (PL 76:1259).
89. Ex 15.3.

another translation has: *The Lord who destroys wars.*[90] Dt 33:[91] *The shield of your help and the sword of your glory is your God. Your enemies will say "no" to you, and you will trample on their necks.*

Then he adds the third tribulation: **[21] *You will be sheltered from the scourge of the tongue.*** The scourge of the tongue is when anyone is beaten by curses or whispers or jeers, and at the end of Sir[92] it is called *the snare of an unjust tongue.* For it says: *You have liberated me from the snare of an unjust tongue and from the words of those who are occupied with lying.* But 1 Pt 2[93] teaches how anyone can be sheltered from this scourge of the tongue: *by doing good you silence human ignorance.*

Eliphaz has articulated these three things because the famine that was brought against Job was from the loss of his possessions, the war from the fact that the Chaldeans formed three squadrons against him, and the scourge of the tongue from the insulting reproach of his wife.

and you will not fear calamity when it comes. The fourth tribulation is punishment. The word "calamity" comes from the [Latin] word *calamus* and the [Greek] word *linos,* that is, "straw" and "string," and it means the stringing up or hindering that someone experiences from the lack of straw and the lack of grains that are produced atop straw, when food and drink become toxic and make bodies ulcerous and diseased, just as Job's body was stricken. Indeed, when sickness is caused by sin, the sickness is healed when the sin is removed by the grace of God. Hence in Mt 9,[94] when the Lord wished to heal the edemic man, he began by saying: *Take heart, son; your sins are forgiven.* Ps:[95] [*The Lord*] *who forgives all your iniquities, who heals all your infirmities.* Gregory says that no adversity will harm you if no iniquity rules over you.[96]

Then Eliphaz adds the fifth tribulation: **[22] *In devastation,*** namely by enemies who destroy the buildings and the works of

90. Origen according to the *GO* on Ex 15.3 (PL 113:227).
91. Dt 33.29.
92. Sir 51.3.
93. 1 Pt 2.15.
94. Mt 9.2.
95. Ps 102.3.
96. See Gregory, *Mor.* 6.30.48.

men, just as the Sabeans and Chaldeans have destroyed yours, ***and famine,*** that is, a lack caused by the devastation, ***you will laugh***. Indeed, when all others are oppressed by devastation and famine, you will delight in abundance and in victory over your enemies, just as Joseph, by providence, enjoyed abundance and, according to Gn 41,[97] provided for his people when famine oppressed Egypt. Prv 3:[98] *So that your barns will be filled with abundance, and your presses will overflow with wine.* Is 30:[99] *The bread of your land will be most plentiful and rich.* Gn 49:[100] *Asher's bread will be rich, and he will provide delicacies to kings.*

Then he adds the sixth tribulation, which is due to the rising of tyrants to power: ***and you will not fear the beasts of the earth.*** They are called "beasts," as if monstrous, on account of the fact that they mangle with their claws and teeth. And he understands that tyrants mangle their citizens and subjects and become more powerful by doing so. This is indicated in 1 Sm 17,[101] where it is said: *I have killed both a bear and a lion.* Sir 47:[102] *He played with lions as with lambs, and he did the same with bears.*

Then he adds the seventh tribulation, in which he cannot be touched by evil. And this is the preservation of good company. For, according to this, even enemies are converted to peace, and at that time nothing is able to harm a man because he is fortified on all sides.

And that is: **[23]** ***But with the stones of the regions,*** that is, with solid men bordering his land, who are called "stones" according to the solidity and strength of their virtue. In the same way it is said in Zec 3[103] that *upon one stone there are seven eyes.* These are the seven spirits looking around, *which,* as it is said in Rv 1,[104] *are in the sight of God.*

There will be ***for you a pact,*** of peace, of course. Prv 12:[105] *Joy*

97. Gn 41.54–57.
98. Prv 3.10.
99. Is 30.23.
100. Gn 49.20.
101. 1 Sm 17.36.
102. Sir 47.3.
103. Zec 3.9.
104. Rv 1.4.
105. Prv 12.20.

follows those who draw up a plan of peace. Heb 12:[106] *Strive for peace and holiness, without which no one will see God.* There was such an agreement between Jacob and Laban, according to Gn 29,[107] that neither of them would cross the boundary stones with evil intent toward the other. And because this pact of peace causes the evil of civil strife to be removed, he adds: ***and the beasts of the earth,*** that is, the quarrelsome people who are living in the land with you, ***will be at peace with you,*** just as, according to Dn 6[108] and 14,[109] the lions became subdued for Daniel. Sir 45:[110] *With his words he has pacified the monsters.* And in the same place:[111] *In the time of wrath there was a reconciliation.*

Then Eliphaz adds three rewards that God will bestow, namely: peaceful property, the multiplication of goods, and a happy consummation in death.

And that is: **[24]** ***And you will know,*** through sensory experience, ***that your tent possesses peace,*** that is, you will possess peacefully all that belongs to you. Ps:[112] *His place has been established in peace.* Is 26:[113] *You will give peace to us, because we have hoped in you, Lord.* And concerning the preservation of peace he adds: ***and visiting your likeness, you will not sin.*** He means "visiting" with comfort and love, as it is said in Gn 21[114] that *the Lord visited Sarah at the time that He had promised.* Lk 1:[115] *Through the depths of the mercy of our God, in which He has visited us.* Our neighbor, in which we see our very selves, as Gregory says,[116] is called a "likeness," and our likeness is visited when our neighbor is loved and benefits thereby. 1 Jn 4:[117] *He who does not love his brother, whom he sees, how can he love God, whom he does not see?* Eliphaz means that

106. Heb 12.14.

107. Although Albert gives Gn 29 as the scriptural reference, the story of the pact between Jacob and Laban is recounted in Gn 31.43–54.

108. Dn 6.22–23.

109. Dn 14.30, 39.

110. Sir 45.2.

111. Sir 44.17.

112. Ps 75.3.

113. Is 26.3.

114. Gn 21.1.

115. Lk 1.78.

116. See Gregory, *Mor.* 6.35.54.

117. 1 Jn 4.20.

he should not at first provoke the citizens and crush his subordinates, but rather recognize himself in them and love and cherish them. Sir 31:[118] *Understand the disposition of your neighbor from your own feelings!* And so he does not do to another what he does not want to be done to himself.

And he adds concerning the multiplication of goods and their development: **[25]** ***And you will know also,*** by experience, of course, ***that your seed,*** as much in your children as in your possessions, ***will be multiplied.*** Jer 31:[119] *I will sow the house of Israel and the house of Judah with the seed of men and with the seed of livestock.* ***and your progeny,*** namely in your grandsons and great-grandsons and other descendants, ***like the grass of the earth,*** which is vigorous, flourishes, and sprouts forth. It is vigorous in virtue, flourishes in integrity, and sprouts forth with fruit. Ex 1:[120] *The children of Israel increased, and they multiplied as if sprouting forth; and having grown exceedingly strong, they filled the land.* At the end of Is:[121] *Your bones will sprout forth like an herb.* 2 Sm 23:[122] *He is my entire salvation, and there is nothing that does not sprout forth from it.*

And he adds concerning a happy consummation: **[26]** ***You will go to your grave in abundance,*** that is to say, leaving all of your people in abundance. It is said in Gn 49[123] that Jacob, full of days, died, leaving his blessing to all of his sons. Sir 44:[124] *Great men of virtue, gifted with prudence,* and after a few words:[125] *Men rich in virtue.* Further along:[126] *A good inheritance continues with their offspring.* And in the same place:[127] *Their bodies are buried in peace, and their names will live for generations.*

as a heap of wheat is brought in. A "heap" is brought together from many, and wheat is more valuable when it buds. And Eliphaz wishes to say that on earth Job will heap up a pile, and he

118. Sir 31.18.
119. Jer 31.27.
120. Ex 1.7.
121. Is 66.14.
122. 2 Sm 23.5.
123. Gn 49.28–29.
124. Sir 44.3.
125. Sir 44.6.
126. Sir 44.11–12.
127. Sir 44.14.

will live in the eternal refreshment of the most valuable goods. Song 7:[128] *Your belly is like a heap of wheat, surrounded by lilies.* For pure and sweet will be the refreshment of the blessed. Ps:[129] *You will fill me with joy with your face: there are delights at your right hand even to the end.*

at its time, that is, when ripe, and Eliphaz wishes to say that he will not die before a ripe old age. Is 65:[130] *An infant of days will be there no more, nor an old man who has not completed his days.* The Psalm[131] speaks in the same way of evil people: *Bloody and deceitful men will not live out half their days.*

And because he argues rhetorically, at the end Eliphaz commends his speech in two ways, namely that it has been proven and that it is true. And thirdly he adds that, on account of this, it should be committed to memory.

And that is: **[27]** ***Behold,*** as if it has been set forth in plain view, ***just as we have investigated it,*** by the clear reasoning of demonstration, of course. Wis 8:[132] *I went about searching, so that I might take wisdom to myself.* ***yes, it is so,*** that is: it is true. 2 Cor 1:[133] *In Him there is not "yes" and "no," but in Him there is only "yes."* ***Consider carefully,*** so that you might see that God does not inflict punishment without reason, ***in your mind,*** that is, by measuring everything with reason, for the word "mind" (*mens*) is derived from the verb "I measure," "you measure" (*metior, metiris*). ***what you have heard,*** namely what you have received by means of your inner hearing. Mt 15:[134] *Hear and understand.* Prv 1:[135] *Consider a parable and its interpretation, the words of the wise and their enigmas.*

128. Song 7.2.
129. Ps 15.11.
130. Is 65.20.
131. Ps 54.24.
132. Wis 8.18.
133. 2 Cor 1.18–19.
134. Mt 15.10.
135. Prv 1.6.

CHAPTER 6

B*UT JOB RESPONDED and said.*

Because of these disputations concerning providence, wherein one person challenges and another responds, the ancients held four opinions about Job. Some said that Job was a Gentile, descended from Esau, who previously was called Jobab, as Gn 36[1] says, and that Eliphaz the Temanite, Bildad the Shuhite, and Zophar the Naamathite were also descended from Esau. These say that all of them were leaders of different parts of Idumea. And they say that Job was the great-grandson of Esau. For the son of Esau was Beor, his grandson was Bela, and his great-grandson was Jobab, who is also called Job. And those who say this are divided into two groups. Some of them assert that Job himself wrote this book; others say that Moses wrote it long after Job's own lifetime.[2] Both of these groups agree that Job was the king or leader of Teman, which is part of the land of Uz, in which wisdom first began to be sought, as Bar 3[3] says. Others said that Job was one of the Babylonian philosophers. They say that he was one of the leaders who came from the East and lived in Babylon after the confusion of languages recounted in Gn 11.[4] Still others said that he was not a real person, but rather that what has been written in this book was devised as a parable to show that divine providence does not govern the world according to the order of human justice, but that the governance of divine providence is utterly dissimilar to the governance and ordering of human justice. For this is made clear in Job, that a simple

1. Gn 36.33.
2. See Gregory, *Praef. in Mor.*
3. Bar 3.23.
4. Gn 11.7–9.

and upright man was stricken and handed over to the power of Satan, which is not consistent with the order of human justice. Therefore, Job responds to Eliphaz, who was holding the view that the world is ruled according to the order of human justice.

And Job's response is divided into two. In the first part he refutes his opponent; and in the second he responds to the objections, further along [in this place]:[5] *Warfare is man's life on earth.* The first part is further divided into four parts according to Job's four refutations of his opponent. The first is that Eliphaz interpreted his words wrongly: for words that were spoken as a manifestation of suffering were understood to have been uttered as blasphemy. The second is that, although they came to comfort him, they fell headlong into reproaches, in this place:[6] *Behold, there is no help for me.* The third is that men who could not craft truthful words in objection to Job were instead composing speeches to rebuke him, in this place:[7] *Teach me and I will be silent.* The fourth is that they were not preserving the character of disputation, but were eager to defeat him in contention, in this place:[8] *Respond, I beg you, without contention.*

The first refutation is divided into two parts: namely, the supposition of Job that his words ought to be attributed to his suffering; and the proof of this supposition, in this place:[9] *Can it be that the wild ass will bellow?*

In the first part there are two things: namely, the magnitude of his pain; and the logical conclusion to be drawn from it, that is, that his words ought to be attributed to his suffering, where he says:[10] *Hence my words.*

And that is: ***But Job responded and said.*** For he responded both to his opponent and to his opponent's objection. Prv 26:[11] *Respond to a fool according to his stupidity, lest he seem wise to himself.*

[2] ***If only my sins,*** that is, mortal sins, ***for which I have deserved wrath,*** eternal punishment, of course. ***and the calamity,*** that is,

5. Jb 7.1.
6. Jb 6.13.
7. Jb 6.24.
8. Jb 6.29.
9. Jb 6.5.
10. Jb 6.3.
11. Prv 26.5.

the tribulation, ***that I suffer,*** namely within and without, ***were weighed.*** Prv 16:[12] *The weight and the balance are the judgments of the Lord.* And in that same place:[13] *The Lord is the weigher of spirits.* ***in a balance,*** that is, on the scales of the order of human justice, so that, just as you say, the punishment would fit the crime. Prv 11:[14] *A just weight is the will of the Lord.* Jb 31:[15] *If I have walked in vanity and my foot has hurried to deceit, may He weigh me in a just balance and may God know my simplicity.*

[3] ***As if the sand of the sea,*** that is, incomparably, just as the sand of the sea, ***this,*** namely my calamity, ***would appear heavier.*** Prv 27:[16] *A stone is heavy and sand is burdensome, but the anger of a fool is heavier than both.* And this is not according to the order of human justice, because, concerning that, Dt 25[17] says: *If the judges see that the one who has sinned deserves to be beaten, they shall lay him down and have him beaten in their presence; and the manner of the beating shall befit the measure of the sin.* Is 27:[18] *In measure against measure, when she will be cast off, you will judge her.*

Because of this he adds: ***Hence my words,*** when I said,[19] *Let the day on which I was born perish,* ***are full of suffering,*** that is, they signify abundant suffering, and they ought to be attributed to suffering and not to the impatience of one who blasphemes. Lam 1:[20] *O all you who pass along the way, pay attention and see if there is any suffering like my suffering.*

Then he adds the reason: [4] ***because the arrows of the Lord are in me,*** that is, His punishments have been driven into me most deeply. Ps:[21] *The sharp arrows of the Mighty One.* ***the anger of which,*** for the arrows are a sign of the divine anger, ***drinks up,*** that is, gulps down without difficulty, ***my spirit,*** which is the bearer of strength and of life, and thus neither strength nor life

12. Prv 16.11.
13. Prv 16.2.
14. Prv 11.1.
15. Jb 31.5–6.
16. Prv 27.3.
17. Dt 25.2.
18. Is 27.8.
19. Jb 3.3.
20. Lam 1.12.
21. Ps 119.4.

is within my power. Lam 2:[22] *He has drawn His bow like a foe, He has strengthened His right hand like an enemy, and He has killed everything that was beautiful to behold in the tabernacles of the daughter of Zion; He has poured out His anger like fire.*

and the terrors of the Lord, concerning worse things still to come, ***wage war,*** supply: continuously, ***against me.*** Ps:[23] *Fear and trembling have come over me, and darkness has covered me.*

Job proves this supposition in what follows.

[5] ***Can it be that the wild ass will bellow?***

And this part has two subdivisions: indeed, first Job proves the supposition; and secondly—in this place,[24] *Who will grant*—he returns to the proof as he had articulated it earlier. There are two things in the proof: first, by means of two metaphors, he demonstrates the absence of anything delightful; then, by means of two other metaphors, he demonstrates the presence of an unremitting and unbearable cause of his sorrow, in this place:[25] *Or can something tasteless be consumed?*

And that is: ***Can it be that the wild ass* (onager) *will bellow,*** that is, a donkey inhabiting the countryside, from [the Greek] *onos,* which is "donkey," and [the Latin] *ager,* [which means "field"]. ***when it has grass?*** that is, a pasture. And he reveals his intention by stating its opposite, as if he were saying, "It will not bellow in the presence of something delightful, but in its absence." Jer 14:[26] *The wild asses stood upon the rocks, and they drew in the wind like dragons; their eyes failed because there was no grass.*

Then Job introduces a second metaphor, revealing his intention in its opposite, as in the earlier metaphor: ***or that the ox will low,*** that is, from the necessity of hunger, ***when it stands before a full trough?*** as if he were saying, "No." Is 1:[27] *The ox knows his owner, and the ass his master's trough.* Jl 1:[28] *Why did the beast groan, why did the herds of cattle low? Because there is no pasture-land for them.* It is as if Job were saying: "If irrational beasts, which

22. Lam 2.4.
23. Ps 54.6.
24. Jb 6.8.
25. Jb 6.6.
26. Jer 14.6.
27. Is 1.3.
28. Jl 1.18.

do not know how to weigh their own punishments, bellow for something delightful that has been lost, what wonder is it if I, a rational being who does weigh my faults and punishments, cry out at the loss of such great goods?"

And he adds a metaphor that shows the presence of some enduring and sorrowful affliction. And that is: **[6]** ***Or can something tasteless,*** that is, unmixed with any flavor of peace, ***be consumed,*** by being incorporated into the body? And explaining this, he adds: ***that is not seasoned with salt,*** namely with some consolation, as if he were saying, "No." Mt 5:[29] *If the salt loses its flavor, with what will it be salted? It is no longer good for anything except to be thrown out and trampled underfoot by humans.*

Then he introduces a second metaphor for the bitterness of his affliction: ***or can anyone taste,*** namely by incorporating into his body, ***what brings death when it is tasted?*** Hence in 2 Kgs 4[30] the sons of the prophets, when they had gathered wild gourds (*coloquintidas*), which are very bitter, cried out: *"Death is in the pot, O man of God!" And they were not able to eat from it.*[31]

But because this was said in general, Job adapts it to his intention, adding: ***For to the soul that is hungry,*** hungry from the absence of anything delectable, of course, ***even things that are bitter,*** provided that they do not cause death, ***seem to be sweet.***[32]

29. Mt 5.13.

30. 2 Kgs 4.39–40.

31. The *Colocynthis* from which the sons of the prophets made a pottage, according to this scriptural text, is *citrullus colocynthis,* commonly known as colocynth or bitter apple, a plant native to the warmer parts of the Mediterranean and Asia, which resembles a watermelon vine but bears a small, hard fruit with a bitter pulp.

32. The words in bold and italics here—*For to the soul that is hungry, even things that are bitter seem to be sweet*—do not appear in most manuscripts of the Vulg. and so neither in most modern editions of the Vulg.. A number of Vulg. manuscripts do have these words, which are from Prv 27.7 according to the LXX and may have been noted in the margin of an early exemplar. See *Biblia Sacra iuxta Latinam Vulgatam Versionem ad codicum fidem, iussu Pii PP. XIII, cura et studio monachorum Abbatiae Pontificiae Sancti Hieronymi in Urbe ordinis sancti Benedicti edita, Libri Hester et Iob ex interpretatione Sancti Hieronymi cum praefationibus et variis capitulorum seriebus* (= Biblia Sacra iuxta Vulg. vers., t. 9) (Rome: Typis Polyglottis Vaticanis, 1951), 109.

Prv 27:[33] *A soul that is full will tread upon the honeycomb, and a soul that is hungry will take something bitter for something sweet.*

Then he appropriates this to himself, saying: [7] ***The things that my soul,*** that is, my animal nature, ***previously was unwilling to touch, now*** in the absence of anything good, ***because of anguish,*** namely the anguish of my present weakness and poverty, ***are my food.*** Jb 30:[34] *Disfigured by disaster and distress, they ate grass and the bark of trees; and the root of junipers was their food.* Likewise, according to Lk 15,[35] the prodigal son, sick with hunger, *desired to fill his stomach with the pods that the pigs were eating.*

Having thus demonstrated his premise, namely that his cry of complaint should be attributed to his suffering, Job returns as it were from the conclusion to the complaint; he is eager for death, which would deprive him of the life that was given over into the power of Satan. And that is:

[8] ***Who will grant.***

He speaks of two things: namely his intended conclusion; and the necessity of this conclusion, in this place:[36] *For what is my strength.*

And that is: ***Who will grant,*** supply: therefore, ***that my petition will come,*** namely the petition that I made, saying:[37] *Let the day on which I was born perish.* According to 1 Kgs 19,[38] Elijah, while he was being persecuted by Jezebel, begged for his soul to die, saying: *It is enough for me, Lord; take my soul, for I am no better than my fathers.*

[9] ***and,*** in other words, ***that God may give me what I hope for?*** that is, death. Tb 3:[39] *Tobit groaned and began to pray with tears, saying.* And after a few verses:[40] *Have mercy on me, and command my spirit to be received in peace; for it is better for me to die than to live.*

and, to put it differently, ***that He who has begun,*** supply: to crush me with infirmities, ***may crush me,*** with death, so that

33. Prv 27.7.
34. Jb 30.3–4.
35. Lk 15.16.
36. Jb 6.11.
37. Jb 3.3.
38. 1 Kgs 19.4.
39. Tb 3.1.
40. Tb 3.6.

I could avoid such great evils. And Moses asked for the same thing, according to Nm 11,[41] because the work of guiding the people was intolerable for him.

Moreover, Job adds how this might happen: ***that He may untie His hand,*** which mercy holds as if bound. Is 9:[42] *Even now His hand is stretched out.* ***and cut me down?*** like a tree. Lk 3:[43] *The ax is laid to the root of the tree.* Dn 4:[44] *Cut down the tree.*

[10] ***And let this be a consolation to me,*** that I might have an end to my desolation, ***that He who afflicts,*** that is, by afflicting, ***me with pain would not spare me,*** supply: but that He bring on death. Jb 3:[45] *As those who dig for a treasure rejoice exceedingly when they have found the grave?* ***and I would not contradict,*** by murmuring or impatiently blaspheming, ***the words,*** of the judgments and sentences, ***of the Holy One,*** that is, of God, in whose presence there can be no injustice. For nothing but destruction is owed to a vessel of clay when it is useless. Rom 9:[46] *Does not the potter have power over the clay, to make from the same lump one vessel for honor and another for dishonor?*

And he confirms this by means of reason, adding: **[11]** ***For what is my strength,*** human strength, of course, ***that I might hold up,*** that is, that I might be able to withstand so many and such great tribulations, as if he were saying, "Nothing." Is 40:[47] *Boys will faint and grow weary, and young men will fall down in weakness.* ***or what is my end,*** which I could reach after such great tribulations, ***that,*** supply: by hoping for that end, ***I should be patient?*** Indeed, Aristotle proves in Book III of the *Ethics* that a strong man does not withstand great evils valiantly and patiently unless by hoping for a great good, which he hopes to gain through great evils.[48] But he who has been delivered into the power of Satan does not hope for a great good. Hence in

41. Nm 11.10–11.
42. Is 9.12.
43. Lk 3.9.
44. Dn 4.11.
45. Jb 3.21–22.
46. Rom 9.21.
47. Is 40.30.
48. See Aristotle, *EN* 3.8.15; cf. Albert, *Eth.* 3.2.2.34 and 3.2.5.43.

2 Cor 4[49] the Apostle, hoping for a great good, said: *What is at present a momentary and slight tribulation for us is working in us an eternal weight of glory beyond measure in its sublimity.* But when he was not hoping for this great good, he said in 2 Cor 1:[50] *We were burdened beyond measure above our strength, such that we were tired even of living.*

Explaining this, Job said: **[12]** ***My strength is not the strength of stones,*** as if I were insensate. 2 Mc 6:[51] *Lord, you who have holy knowledge, you know manifestly that, although I can be freed from death, I withstand terrible bodily pains.* ***nor is my flesh of bronze,*** so that if it is shattered, it could be recast in the same form and appearance and reforged like new. Jb 14:[52] *Do you suppose that a man who has died might live again?* that is, in this mortal life, as if he were saying, "No."

[13] ***Behold, there is no help.***

The second refutation—that, although they came to comfort him, they fell headlong into reproaches—begins here. Job demonstrates this in a threefold way. First, he shows in general that this is evil; secondly, he shows specifically that evil was done in this case, in this place:[53] *My brothers;* thirdly, he shows in particular that evil was done by his friends, in this place:[54] *Now you have come.*

In the first part there are two things, namely the supposition and the exposition of evil.

And that is: ***Behold,*** as if it were evident, ***there is no help for me within myself.*** My property and my children have been lost, and my body has been stricken. Jb 19:[55] *He has stripped me of my glory, and snatched the crown off my head. He has destroyed me on every side, and I am ruined.* ***and those closely associated*** **(necessarii)** ***with me,*** that is, friends who ought to come to help when I am in need (*in necessitate*), ***have withdrawn*** by taking away their love

49. 2 Cor 4.17.
50. 2 Cor 1.8.
51. 2 Mc 6.30.
52. Jb 14.14.
53. Jb 6.15.
54. Jb 6.21.
55. Jb 19.9–10.

from me. Ps:[56] *My friends and neighbors have drawn near and stood against me; and those who were close to me have stood far off.* Jb 19:[57] *My neighbors have forsaken me, and those who knew me have forgotten me.*

And Job shows in general that this is evil. **[14]** ***He who withholds mercy from a friend,*** supply: in a time of need, ***has forsaken the fear of the Lord.*** Indeed, God commands that this should not happen. Sir 6:[58] *A faithful friend is the medicine of life and of immortality; and those who fear the Lord will find him,* that is to say, a friend who is a source of comfort. Likewise, in the same place:[59] *He who fears the Lord likewise will have good friendship, because his friend will be as he is.* But because "to forsake the fear of the Lord" is evil, to withhold mercy from a friend is also evil.

Moreover, Job shows that this happened in his case in three ways, namely by their withdrawal, by covering up their cunning, and by the evidence of their works. In the first of these ways he does two things related to two things that he has proposed. For he shows that it was done and that it was evil.

And that is: **[15]** ***My brothers,*** by profession of good will and of friendship, of course, ***have passed me by,*** such that they flatly refused even to look upon me. Against this it is said in Tb 4:[60] *Do not turn your face away from any poor person.* Ps:[61] *Look upon me and have mercy on me, because I am alone and poor.* Acts 3:[62] *Peter, together with John, looked at the lame man who was also a beggar and said: Look upon us. And that man looked intently at them, hoping that he would receive something from them.*

as the torrent. Water produced from the melting of snow and ice on the mountains by the scorching (*torrore*) of the sun, which water runs headlong down into the lowest regions, is called a "torrent" (*torrens*). ***that rapidly passes through the valleys,*** that is, that quickly goes over into the lowest regions. And Job wishes to say that his friends, elevated with regard to wealth

56. Ps 37.12.
57. Jb 19.14.
58. Sir 6.16.
59. Sir 6.17.
60. Tb 4.7.
61. Ps 24.16.
62. Acts 3.4–5.

and dignity, were at first melted by a sense of loyalty to come to Job, but rapidly and readily passed him by once they saw his actual infirmity, and they withdrew their feelings of loyalty in no time at all. Against this it is said in Sir 4:[63] *Incline your ear without harshness to the poor man, and pay back your debt to him, and answer him peacefully with gentleness.*

And Job shows that this is evil in general first of all: **[16]** ***They who fear the frost,*** that is, the insignificant loss that the needs of a neighbor threaten to impose, ***the snow,*** that is, the great frost of eternal damnation, ***will rush in upon them.*** For Aristotle says in Book II of the *Meteorology* that frost is a little snow, and snow is much frost.[64] The tribulation of the poor man that results from the icy manner of a friend who is not compassionate is called "frost." Ps:[65] *I have become like a wineskin in the frost.* Therefore, he who fears the need of the poor man will be buried by the snow of eternal tribulation and will not find compassion. Ps:[66] *Fire, hail, snow, ice, and wind storms will be the portion of their cup.* Jb 38:[67] *Have you entered the storehouses of the snow, or have you seen the storehouses of the hail, which I have prepared for the time of the enemy, for the day of battle and war?*

And, continuing the metaphor of the torrent, Job adds how this happens. That is: **[17]** ***At the time when they will be scattered,*** just as the ice and snow are scattered from the mountains, they are "scattered" by means of tribulations. ***they will perish,*** by means of eternal destruction, of course. Ps:[68] *Scatter the nations that long for wars.*

And explaining this, he adds: ***and when they have grown hot,*** from tribulations, just as ice and snow on the mountains grow hot by the scorching of the sun, ***they will be melted out of their place,*** supply: and they will flow into the pit of damnation. Jb 21:[69] *They spend their days in prosperity, and in a moment they go*

63. Sir 4.8.

64. See Aristotle, *Mete.* 1.11.

65. Ps 118.83.

66. Ps 148.8 and Ps 10.7, which Albert appears to conflate, understanding them as conveying a single idea and the same divine intention.

67. Jb 38.22–23.

68. Ps 67.31.

69. Jb 21.13.

down to hell. Rv 12:[70] *Their place was not found any more in heaven.* Ps:[71] *I searched, but his place was not found.* Similarly, another Ps:[72] *He will not know his place any more.*

And Job adds, concerning the covering up of their cunning, that his friends did not proceed rightly according to the rule of friendship, but according to the false friendship of cunning. And that is: **[18]** ***The paths of their steps,*** by which they give the impression of approaching a friend, ***are entangled.*** A thing "is entangled" if its ends are hidden, and so one who gives indications of friendship but entangles the end of friendship with the veil of hypocrisy is called an entangled friend. Sir 6:[73] *There is a friend who turns his attention to friendship, and there is a friend who will reveal hatred and strife.* Sir 6:[74] *There is a friend, a companion at the table, but he does not stay during the time of need.* This was the nature of Ahithophel's friendship with David, according to 2 Sm 17.[75] And therefore supply: ***they will walk into the void,*** that is, without profit. Rom 6:[76] *What profit did you then have in those things of which you are now ashamed?* ***and perish,*** deservedly because of such pretense, of course. Ps:[77] *On that day all their plans will perish.*

And Job shows by the evidence of the facts that this happened in his case, adding: **[19]** ***Consider the paths of Teman,*** that is, Eliphaz the Temanite by metonymy, and supply: consider ***the ways of Sheba.*** For Teman is a false friend, and Sheba is a manifest enemy who carried off Job's sheep and oxen and struck his servants down with the sword. Job is implying that the ways of the former and the latter are similar. Prv 27:[78] *The wounds of a friend are better than the deceitful kisses of an enemy.* ***and wait a little while,*** for there is a short time until the judgment. Jas 5:[79] *Behold, the judge stands at the door.*

70. Rv 12.8.
71. Ps 36.36.
72. Ps 102.16.
73. Sir 6.9.
74. Sir 6.10.
75. 2 Sm 17.1–3.
76. Rom 6.21.
77. Ps 145.4.
78. Prv 27.6.
79. Jas 5.9.

[20] ***They have been confounded,*** that is, they will be confused next. Ps:[80] *Let them be covered with their own confusion, as with a cloak.* **because I have hoped,** that is, because I have had hope for the justice of the judge. Jer 17:[81] *Let those who pursue me be confounded, but let me not be confounded.*

And he adds the evidence of the facts: ***likewise they have come all the way to me,*** with something like the loyalty of friendship, ***and they have been covered completely,*** so that they turn friendship into enmity, ***with shame,*** namely the shame of my affliction. But this is not truly characteristic of a friend, for he happily takes the opportunity to come to the help of his friend. Hence it is said in Sir 6[82] concerning a true friend: *A faithful friend is a strong defense, and he who has found him has found a treasure.*

And in order to show that he understands this about his own friends, Job turns toward them and adds: [21] ***Now,*** supply: at the time of my need, ***you have come*** to visit, ***and now,*** supply: although I am really in need, ***seeing my affliction,*** namely with regard to property and personal health, ***you are afraid,*** that is, you fearfully withdraw from sharing your property with me. Against this it is said in 2 Tm 1:[83] *May the Lord grant mercy to the household of Onesiphorus, because he has often refreshed me and he has not been ashamed of my chain.*

He shows how unreasonable this is: [22] ***Can it be that I have said: Bring me,*** supply: something, ***and,*** in other words, ***give me of your substance?*** that is, from your resources, as if he were saying, "No." 2 Cor 11:[84] *In all things I have kept myself from being a burden to you, and so will keep myself.* [23] ***or: Deliver me from the hand of the enemy,*** which, even if it is not an expensive thing to do, is nevertheless burdensome, ***and,*** in other words, ***pluck me out of the hand of the mighty?*** That is: I have sought from you neither gifts nor help, such that you should flee from me. We read, however, in Gn 14[85] that Abraham, with 318 armed men

80. Ps 108.29.
81. Jer 17.18.
82. Sir 6.14.
83. 2 Tm 1.16.
84. 2 Cor 11.9.
85. Gn 14.14.

of his household, attacked the enemy and brought back Lot, his friend, who, though innocent, had been taken captive. And David, according to 1 Sm 30,[86] pursued the Amalekites and brought his men and his wives back from Ziklag as well as the spoils that they had taken. Prv 24:[87] *Pluck up those who are being led to death, and do not hesitate to deliver those who are being dragged off to destruction.*

[24] ***Teach me.***

Here Job sets forth the third refutation of his opponents, namely that they were composing speeches to rebuke him, speeches that had no bearing on the truth. And Job asserts three things, namely: that they did not impede the truth, that they composed rebukes, and that they were impiously rebuking an orphan who had no protector. And that is: ***Teach me.*** To teach is to make clear the cause or reason of something that has been said. Jl 2:[88] *Rejoice in the Lord your God, who has given you a teacher of justice.* ***and I will be silent,*** that is, I will accept your teaching without contradiction. Jb 6:[89] *I would not contradict the words of the Holy One.* ***and if by chance I have been ignorant about anything,*** that is, if I have spoken ignorantly, ***instruct me.*** Indeed, a wise man always wishes to be instructed. Gal 6:[90] *You who are spiritual, instruct him in the spirit of gentleness.*

And seeing that you are not able to do this, supply: **[25]** ***Why have you disparaged the words of truth,*** by which I said that I had been scourged without the cause of deserved evil. 2 Tm 3:[91] *Just as Jannes and Mambres resisted Moses, so too these resist the truth.* Jn 8:[92] *When he tells a lie, he speaks from his own nature, for he is a liar and the father of lies.*

whereas there is none of you who can convict me? namely, of sin, on account of which I have been scourged. Jn 8:[93] *Which of you will convict me of sin? If I speak the truth, why do you not believe me?*

86. 1 Sm 30.18–19.
87. Prv 24.11.
88. Jl 2.23.
89. Jb 6.10.
90. Gal 6.1.
91. 2 Tm 3.8.
92. Jn 8.44.
93. Jn 8.46.

From this Job infers that they are speaking rebukes, and that is: **[26] *You dress up speeches only to rebuke.*** Indeed, it is characteristic of poor disputants and of sophists to accuse their colleague when they do not have something to assert positively in their speech. Against this it is said in 1 Tm 5:[94] *Do not rebuke an older man, but entreat him as a father.* ***and you utter words,*** not for any oratorical purpose but only for *ad hominem* attacks, ***into the wind,*** that is, into empty space. Hos 12:[95] *Ephraim feeds on the wind and pursues the surging heat; all day long he multiplies lies and desolation.* Gregory cites Prv 17:[96] *The source of quarreling is a person who allows water to run away, and before he suffers insult he abandons judgment,* that is, the truth. Gregory explains it in this way: a person who allows water to run away loosens his tongue for a stream of speaking, and thus is the source of disputing. For rebuke is quarreling, because he who does not restrain his tongue completely destroys mutual agreement.[97] And Gregory introduces Prv 25:[98] *As a city that stands open and is not encircled by walls, so is a man who cannot restrain the wind of his own speaking.*[99]

And Job infers that this is wicked: **[27] *You rush in upon the orphan,*** who does not have a protector, but stands alone and fights for the truth. Sir 4:[100] *Fight for justice for your soul, and struggle for justice even unto death.* 1 Kgs 19:[101] *I alone am left, and they seek my life.* ***and you strive to overthrow your friend,*** that is, to turn him from the truth with sophistry. A friend is someone who agrees with us in seeking the truth, even when having a disputation. On the contrary, as Aristotle says in Book VIII of the *Topics,* a perverse companion is one who hinders the common work of searching for truth.[102] Sir 20:[103] *How much better it*

94. 1 Tm 5.1.
95. Hos 12.1.
96. Prv 17.14.
97. See *Mor.* 7.37.57.
98. Prv 25.28.
99. See *Mor.* 7.37.59.
100. Sir 4.33.
101. 1 Kgs 19.10.
102. Aristotle, *Top.* 8.9.
103. Sir 20.1.

is to reprove than to be angry, and not to hinder one who confesses out loud! One who confesses out loud is a professor of the truth.

So that he might not seem to despair of his own position, however, Job adds: **[28]** ***Nevertheless, finish,*** because, although what you are saying is false, nevertheless in disputing there is the opportunity for investigating truth, ***what you have begun,*** namely disputing about providence and God's governing. In Book II of *First Philosophy,* Aristotle says: "It is right to give thanks not only to those who share our opinions, but even to those who have expressed themselves superficially, for these also have accomplished something, for they have helped to develop our habit [of thinking]."[104] His point is that we ought to give thanks not only to those who utter true things in the search for truth, but even to those who articulate false things; for, in articulating false things, they stimulate and develop our habit of seeking the truth. Rom 1:[105] *I am a debtor to the wise and to the foolish.*

But because for the one who denies all things, as the Philosopher says,[106] there can be no syllogism, Job asks that his opponents listen and respond without impudence. And that is: ***give ear,*** supply: for listening. Jb 34:[107] *The ear examines words.* ***and see,*** that is, understand, ***whether I lie.*** Mt 15:[108] *Hear and understand.* Sir 4:[109] *In no way speak against the word of truth, but be dismayed by the lie of your ignorance.*

Here Job sets forth the fourth refutation, namely that they were not preserving the character of disputation, but were eager to defeat him in contention. And that is: **[29]** ***Respond, I beg you*** **(obsecro)**, that is, I entreat you for the sake of the oath (*ob sacramentum*) of truth, ***without contention.*** Ambrose says, and it is also in the *Gloss* on Rom 1: "Contention is fighting against the truth with bold shouting."[110] 2 Tm 2:[111] *But I, testifying before*

104. Aristotle, *Metaph.* 2.1.3.
105. Rom 1.14.
106. See Aristotle, *APr.* 2.22.3.
107. Jb 34.3.
108. Mt 15.10.
109. Sir 4.30.
110. *GO* on Rom. 1.29 (PL 114:474).
111. 2 Tm 2.14.

the Lord, remind them of these things. Do not contend with words: indeed, it is useful for nothing, except for subverting those who listen. ***and speaking,*** that is, answering, ***that which is just, make your judgment.*** For as the Sage[112] says: *He who answers before he listens shows himself to be a fool.*

[30] ***And,*** supply: if you act in this way, ***you will not find iniquity,*** that is, some unjust utterance, ***on my tongue.*** Is 53:[113] *Deceit was not found in his mouth.* Mal 2:[114] *The law of truth was in his mouth, and iniquity was not found on his lips.*

nor in my throat, which, located internally, signifies the heart. For he has not spoken any nonsense from his heart. In fact, everything he says is from his heart. Is 32:[115] *For the fool will speak foolish things, and his heart will work iniquity, so that he might bring about deceit.* Prv 5:[116] *The wicked man shall die, because he has not received instruction, and in the multitude of his follies he will be deceived.* Indeed, Gregory says that a fool is one who does not know what he should do and what he should not do, or what he should say and what he should not say.[117] And therefore Job adds: ***will stupidity resound.***

112. Prv 18.13.
113. Is 53.9.
114. Mal 2.6.
115. Is 32.6.
116. Prv 5.23.
117. Like Weiss, I was unable to find this reference.

CHAPTER 7

W*ARFARE IS man's life on earth.*

Having refuted his perverse companions who, by responding impudently, were hindering their common task, Job returns here to the assertion of his own position. And it is divided into three parts.

In the first part, Job shows that, because of the weariness of life, death should be sought. In the second part, being confident now in his position, he asserts it, confirms it, and concludes it, in this place:[1] *Therefore, I will not restrain.* In the third part, because there is not a remedy, save from God alone, he directs himself toward prayer, in this place:[2] *Spare me, Lord.*

The first part is divided into two: he makes his point first in general; [and] second, specifically in all those things that beset his life, in this place:[3] *Whenever I go to sleep.* In the first [of these two subdivisions], Job does three things. First he sets forth his intended conclusion, secondly he demonstrates it by means of a twofold similitude, and thirdly he applies the demonstration to himself and to human life.

And that is: ***Warfare is man's life on earth.*** The expression must be turned around, namely so that the predicate becomes the subject and vice versa, such that the sense is: "Man's life on earth is warfare." And he says, "Man's life on earth is warfare," because man's life in heaven is not characterized by battle. Hence Rv 12:[4] The dragon who fought with Michael was cast out of heaven, and his angels too, and it adds, *and his place was*

1. Jb 7.11.
2. Jb 7.16.
3. Jb 7.4.
4. Rv 12.7–9.

not found any more in heaven.[5] Concerning the earth, by contrast, it is said in Jb 9:[6] *The earth has been given into the hands of the wicked one.* And therefore Satan, who has taken the resources and the bodies of the good into his power, continuously stirs up war. Indeed, in the same way the *Gloss* on Ex 14 says that Pharaoh brought together his chariots and pursued the children of Israel.[7] That despicable Pharaoh rises up with temptations, but the fighting saints continuously wage war against him. Eph 6:[8] *Our struggle is not against flesh and blood alone, but against principalities and powers, against the rulers of the world of this darkness, against the spiritual powers of wickedness in the heavens.* There is warfare, then, in this life on account of the fact that it has been given over into the power of Satan. Hence another translation reads "temptation."[9] For temptation is, as Hugh of St. Victor says, the incitement to something illicit.[10] Mt 4:[11] *Jesus was led into the desert, to be tempted by the devil,* not only in himself, but also in his bodily members. ***and,*** therefore, ***his days*** are laborious and wearisome, ***are like the days of a hired worker,*** that is, of one drawn to work by the promise of a reward. For his reward is bread, which he eats, and it obliges him to continuous work. Gn 3:[12] *By the sweat of your face you shall eat your bread.* Thus, concerning a life of this sort, nothing should be wished for, except that it might perish.[13]

5. This is a characteristic example of the way in which Albert, perhaps working from memory, provides a general paraphrase of the words found in the Vulg. text that has come down to us. Because his phrase "The dragon ... his angels" summarizes the contents of vv. 7 and 9 of Rv 12, I have not italicized it.

6. Jb 9.24.

7. See *GO* on Ex 14.15–17 (PL 113:226).

8. Eph 6.12.

9. See Origen, *In Ex, hom.* 5.3 (PG 12:329).

10. See Hugh of St. Victor, *De sacr.* 1.7.9 (PL 176:290).

11. Mt 4.1.

12. Gn 3.19.

13. With virtually identical language, Albert here recalls Job's words in 3.3, *Let the day on which I was born perish,* and his own comments on them, namely: "And the entire span of Job's life—in which Satan receives the power to exercise the wickedness of his own will with regard to Job's property, his children, his person, and his friends, whom Satan turns into adversaries—cannot be wished for, except so that it might perish."

And with regard to this [conclusion], Job introduces a twofold similitude: **[2]** ***As a servant,*** namely one bound to the land, ***longs for the shade,*** that is, rest, as if the rest at the end of his work never comes. Ps:[14] *Who will give me wings like a dove, and I will fly and be at rest?* namely so that I might cast off the yoke of servitude. Gn 27:[15] *There will be a time when you will cast his yoke off your neck.* ***and as a hired worker,*** having been drawn by the reward of bread, ***waits,*** supply: with boredom, ***for the end of his work,*** namely to which he has been drawn. And with longing he anticipates its end, so that there might be an end to his weariness and toil. Rv 14:[16] *From now on, says the Spirit, let them rest from their labors.*

Job then applies this to himself, saying: **[3]** ***so too I have spent empty months,*** that is, the daylight of my life has been without reward. Hos 5:[17] *Now the month will devour them together with their portions.* Jerome says: that is, they will be devoured every month.[18] ***and have counted laborious nights,*** that is, the darkness of adversity, ***to myself.*** Jb 30:[19] *At night my bones are pierced with pain,* that is, I was so disgusted that I spent the whole day counting, longing for an end. For the daylight of prosperity is without reward, and now the night brings toil in adversity, too. It is as if Job could conclude his statement and say, as in 3,[20] *Let the day on which I was born perish, and the night in which it was said, "A human being has been conceived!"*

And Job specifically shows this on the basis of those five particularities that beset life, which are the tedium of work, the affliction of pain, the brevity of life, its uselessness, and the impossibility of returning to life. And that is: **[4]** ***Whenever I go to sleep,*** taking rest through sleep, so that tired limbs might be restored. Ps:[21] *I will sleep and I will rest.* ***I say,*** bothered by the weariness of false rest: ***When will I arise?*** For sleep is a nuisance to me

14. Ps 54.7.
15. Gn 27.40.
16. Rv 14.13.
17. Hos 5.7.
18. Jerome, *In Hos.* Bk. I on 5.7 (PL 25:860).
19. Jb 30.17.
20. Jb 3.3.
21. Ps 4.9.

because it is false rest and my sleep is nothing but nightmares; and therefore my sleep does not restore me, but rather afflicts me. Wis 17:[22] *A loud noise coming down disturbed them, and the appearance of gloomy faces frightened them.* Hence Is 21:[23] *Watchman, what of the night? Watchman, what of the night?* ***and again,*** rising in the daylight from weariness, ***I will wait for the evening.*** Hence further along in 17:[24] *My thoughts have been scattered, tormenting my heart. They have turned night into day, and after darkness I hope for light again.*

And this is explained by what follows: ***and,*** because, ***I will be filled with suffering continuously until darkness,*** that is, until nightfall. Ps:[25] *I am poor, and in the midst of labors from my youth.* And Job shows the continuous nature of the pain in his body when he adds: **[5]** ***My flesh is clothed,*** that is, completely covered, ***with rottenness.*** Is 1:[26] *From the sole of his foot all the way to the top of his head, there is no health in him.* ***and with the filth of dust.*** The latter noun should be resolved into an adjective; hence "with the filth of dust" means dusty filth. Blood, when it has hardened, makes a scab, which is reduced to dust when it has become hard and dried up. Jb 25:[27] *Man is rottenness, and the son of man is a worm.* Is 13:[28] *Their appearance shall be as faces burned to ash.* ***My skin has become dry,*** namely not being infused with healthy moisture, ***and has shriveled,*** that is, it has become full of wrinkles as a result of dryness. Lam 4:[29] *Their faces have been made blacker than charcoal, and they are not recognized in the streets; their skin has clung to their bones, and it has become like wood.*

Job also shows this by means of the brevity of life, adding: **[6]** ***My days have passed,*** that is, they have not attained the end of human life due to the evils that Satan imposes, ***more swiftly,*** that is, more quickly, ***than the warp is cut by the weaver.*** For the warp is not cut until the last fiber is introduced into the wo-

22. Wis 17.4.
23. Is 21.11.
24. Jb 17.11–12.
25. Ps 87.16.
26. Is 1.6.
27. Jb 25.6.
28. Is 13.8.
29. Lam 4.8.

ven fabric. Job's life, however, has been cut short, before it has come to its end. Is 38:[30] *My life has been cut short, as by a weaver; while I was still beginning, He cut me off.* Gn 47:[31] *The days of the pilgrimage of my life are one hundred and thirty years, few and evil, and they have not come all the way to the days of my fathers.* **and they are *consumed*,** supply: before their end, by suffering and hardship, ***without any hope*,** supply: of recovery, for there was no hope of recovery by means of inferior causes. Is 38:[32] *From morning all the way until evening you will make an end of me. I will cry out like a young swallow.* Jb 4:[33] *Those who have an earthly foundation will be consumed as if by a moth!*

And concerning the vanity of life, he adds: **[7] *Remember that my life is wind*,** that is, comparable in its temporal brevity to the wind, which can be blown away. Jas 4:[34] *For what is your life? It is a vapor that appears for a little while and then will vanish.* Is 40:[35] *The grass has withered and the flower has fallen because the spirit of the Lord has blown upon it.* **and my eyes will not return to see good things,** namely present realities, for no one returns to enjoy present goods. Wis 2:[36] *No one has been known to have returned from hell.* **[8] *And human vision will not look upon me*,** that is, I will not be able to enjoy seeing and visiting with friends. Is 38:[37] *I will behold man no more, nor the inhabitant of peace.* **but your eyes,** you who are the judge of the living and the dead, ***are upon me*,** supply: they [that is, the living and the dead] are going to be smashed to pieces, ***and I will not subsist*,** supply: any more in this present life. 2 Mc 6:[38] *I will not escape the hand of the Almighty either alive or dead.* Ps:[39] *Where shall I go from your spirit? And where shall I flee from your face?*

30. Is 38.12.
31. Gn 47.9.
32. Is 38.13–14.
33. Jb 4.19.
34. Jas 4.15.
35. Is 40.7.
36. Wis 2.1.
37. Is 38.11.
38. 2 Mc 6.26.
39. Ps 138.7.

And, concerning the impossibility of returning [to this life], Job adds: **[9]** ***As a cloud is consumed,*** namely by being dissolved by the sun, which melts it away, ***and passes away,*** supply: so that it does not exist, that is, it vanishes. Ps:[40] *In His sight the clouds passed away.* ***so too he who will go down to hell,*** that is, to the place of his grave, ***will not come back up,*** such that, to be sure, he should appear in this life again. Is 55:[41] *The rain and the snow come down from heaven, and return there no more.* **[10]** ***And he will return no more to his house.*** 2 Sm 14:[42] *We all die, and like water we fall down into the earth, never to return.* ***and his place,*** namely of this present life, ***will not know him any more.*** Wis 2:[43] *Our body will become extinguished ashes, and our spirit will be poured out as a gentle breeze; and our life will pass away as if it were the trace of a cloud.*

Having shown, on the basis of all these things, that nothing must be said about the day of his birth except that it should perish, Job goes on, adding: **[11]** ***Therefore, I will not restrain my mouth.*** Indeed, having complete faith in the strength of the truth, I will assert my opinion—namely that the day of my birth should perish—with unrestrained speech. 3 Esdras 3:[44] *The truth conquers all.* And in that same book:[45] *The truth endures and increases in power into eternity, and it lives and prevails forever and ever.* ***In the tribulation of my spirit,*** that is, [I am] taking up the argument according to the distress of my spirit, ***I will discuss,*** by disputing, ***in conformity with the bitterness of my soul,*** that is, of my animal life, certainly showing from it [that is, this bitterness of soul] that human life is not ruled or governed according to the order of human justice. Is 38:[46] *I will recount to you all my years in the bitterness of my soul.*

[12] ***Can it be that I am the sea?***

Here Job adds confirmation[47] of the statement that he intro-

40. Ps 17.13.
41. Is 55.10.
42. 2 Sm 14.14.
43. Wis 2.3.
44. 3 Esdras 3.12.
45. 3 Esdras 4.38.
46. Is 38.15.
47. The translation here is of the Latin of MSS F and M, which have *Hic*

duced, namely that the order of divine rule in human life is not according to the order of human justice, which is characterized by repayment for merits, just as Eliphaz said. In the first part [of this second part of the chapter] Job makes this clear with regard to himself; and secondly, once it has been made clear, he concludes the proposition, in this place:[48] *on account of which.*

Moreover, there are two divisions of this first part: in the first Job explains that he is innocent of any fault; and in the second he explains that he has been stricken as a punishment, and this is [where he says]:[49] *Can it be that I am the sea?* Two charges were made against blessed Job: that the restlessness of avarice was constantly driving him to expand his land holdings, just as the sea covers things when it floods and carries them away when it ebbs. Is 57:[50] *The heart of the wicked person is like the raging sea, which is unable to be at rest.* Sir 24:[51] *My stream was made to overflow, and my river came near to the sea.* Is 5:[52] *Woe to you who join house to house and connect field with field, all the way to the end of the territory! Can it be that you alone will live in the middle of the land?*

Therefore, Job denies having this vice, saying: ***Can it be that I am the sea,*** as if to say that it is not as the charge would have it, that he devours and oppresses those subject to him. Jer 51:[53] *He has swallowed me up like a dragon; he has filled his stomach with my tender meat.* Hence Is 27:[54] *The Lord, with His great and hard and strong sword, will visit Leviathan, the twisted serpent, and He will kill the whale that is in the sea.*

Job excuses himself by saying: ***or a whale,*** as if to say: "No, and yet I have been stricken and surrounded by blows." And that is: ***that you have built a prison around me?*** namely so that I

---

ponitur confirmatio rather than simply *Confirmatio est,* as in Weiss's edition. Furthermore, F and M have *humanae* following *secundum ordinem iustitiae* later in this sentence, which I render here for the sake of clarity.

48. Jb 7.15.
49. Jb 7.12.
50. Is 57.20.
51. Sir 24.43.
52. Is 5.8.
53. Jer 51.34.
54. Is 27.1.

might never have the freedom to go out. At the end of 1 Kgs:[55] *Throw this man in prison, and feed him with the bread of tribulation and the water of distress.* Ps:[56] *Lead my soul out of prison.* And Job makes clear in this way that he is in prison, adding: **[13]** ***If I say.*** Arrange the words of the text as follows: ***If, speaking to myself on my couch, I say,*** certainly imagining the hope of some consolation, ***my bed will comfort me,*** by affording me repose so that I can forget my suffering. And that is: ***and I will be refreshed.*** Indeed, he will be relieved of the suffering of his infirmity through sleep. Jn 11:[57] *If he sleeps, he will be well.* Supply: but my hope was a deception, because **[14]** ***You will frighten me with dreams.*** For infirmity that is caused internally does not allow the sick person to dream, except about frightful things. Likewise, it is also said in the practice of medicine that the one on whom a fiery ulcer is produced dreams that he is set on fire by flames; and insofar as dropsy develops, the one who is cold dreams that he is frozen by ice; and the one who is famished dreams that he eats, and the one who is thirsty that he drinks. Is 29:[58] *Just as he who is hungry dreams and eats, but when he has woken up his soul is empty; and just as he who is thirsty dreams and drinks, but when he has woken up he is still weary with thirst,* so we have become. Am 3:[59] *Those who live in Samaria on the scourge of the bed, and on the couch of Damascus. Hear and become sad.* The "scourge of the bed" is a bed with scourges or that scourges.[60] The "couch of Damascus" is a couch contaminated with blood. And such people hear nothing in their dreams, except that whereby they become sad.

And what follows explains this: ***and,*** in other words, ***by means of*** nocturnal ***visions you will shake me with horror.*** Ps:[61] *Every night I will soak my bed; I will water my couch with my tears.*

Having demonstrated this [namely that the order of divine rule in human life is not in accordance with the order of hu-

55. 1 Kgs 22.27.
56. Ps 141.8.
57. Jn 11.12.
58. Is 29.8.
59. Am 3.12–13.
60. See Albert, *In Am* 3.12.
61. Ps 6.7.

man justice], Job reverts to his conclusion, namely that the day should perish on which Satan assumes such great power over innocent people. And that is: **[15]** ***on account of which my soul has chosen suspension***. The soul is suspended from its action and its duty when it does not pour life into the body. Augustine relates, in the book *On the City of God,* that the philosopher Porphyry, when he had heard the opinion of Plato and had learned his proof concerning the necessity of the soul living on after death, cast himself down and said, "If the soul lives on after death, I do not want to live this miserable life."[62] 2 Mc 6:[63] *With a ready mind and bravely, I will endure an honorable death for the sake of the most weighty and most holy laws of God!*

And explaining this, he adds: ***and my bones,*** supply: have chosen, ***death,*** that is, dissolution. Phil 1:[64] *I wish to be dissolved and to be with Christ, a far better thing.* Nm 11:[65] *I pray that you* [*God*] *would kill me, and that I would find grace in your eyes, lest I be afflicted with such great evils.*

Then he adds the reason for this when he supplies: **[16]** ***I have given up hope***. For I do not have the hope of health on the basis of lower causes. ***By no means will I live any longer now.*** Is 38:[66] *Set your house in order, for you will not live.* Sir 41:[67] *O death, your judgment is good to the soul in need and to him whose strength fails, who has grown weak with age, and who worries about everything.*

Now, having demonstrated what he intended [namely that, because of the weariness of life, death should be sought], Job entreats God in prayer for this to happen to him.

And that is: ***Spare me, Lord!***

There are two parts of this prayer: he begs for an end to his most miserable life; and [he begs] that through penance his fault might be cleansed, in this place:[68] *O guardian of men.*

In the first part of his prayer there are three elements: namely the petition, a reason for the petition on the basis of the

62. Cf. Augustine, *Civ.* 22.27.
63. 2 Mc 6.28.
64. Phil 1.23.
65. Nm 11.15.
66. Is 38.1.
67. Sir 41.3–4.
68. Jb 7.20.

worthlessness of nature, and a reason for the same on the basis of the bitterness of the punishment. And that is:

Spare me, Lord! In fact, spare me by putting an end to my life. Tb 3:[69] *Bring forth your mercy for me, and command that my spirit be received in peace!* **For my days are nothing**, that is, they should be compared to nothingness. Ezek 28:[70] *You are nothing, and you will be nothing forever.* Ps:[71] *I was reduced to nothing and I did not know.*

And he adds a reason based on the worthlessness of nature: **[17]** ***What is man?*** This ought to be read with disdain for how worthless he is: in his body, clay; in his condition, a slave; in his course, inconstant; in his action, crooked; in his conception, stained; in his development, weak; in his life, most wretched; and in his death, full of sorrows. ***That you make him so great?*** that is, why should you make him so great, as if to say: "for nought." Ps:[72] *What is man, that you have become known to him? Or the son of man, that you think about him?*

And that is: ***or why do you set***, that is, why should you set, ***your heart upon him***, namely by allowing him, who is of so little value, to live? Ps:[73] *Man has been made to resemble vanity: his days pass away like a shadow.* Is 64:[74] *You are our Father, and we are clay.* Jer 18:[75] *As clay is in the hand of the potter, so are you in my hand, says the Lord.*

[18] ***You visit him at daybreak***, that is, by shining your goodness on him a little, you lift him up with your benefits. Hos 6:[76] *His going out has been prepared as the daybreak.* ***and suddenly***, that is, after a little while, ***you test him***, that is, you make clear what has been established, that he is insignificant and worthy of no esteem. Hos 6:[77] *Your mercy is as a morning cloud, and as the dew that goes away early in the morning.*

69. Tb 3.6.
70. Ezek 28.19.
71. Ps 72.22.
72. Ps 143.3.
73. Ps 143.4.
74. Is 64.8.
75. Jer 18.6.
76. Hos 6.3.
77. Hos 6.4.

Then Job sets forth a reason from the bitterness of misery. [19] ***How long***, that is, for how long, ***will you refuse to spare me?*** Ps:[78] *How long will I receive counsels in my soul, sorrow in my heart throughout the day?* ***and not allow me to swallow,*** that is, to delight in life to such an extent that I can swallow ***my spittle?*** supply: by cutting off life. Salivary fluid, by its nature, conveys flavor to the taste nerves spread around the tongue and also permits swallowing and digestion. So the sense [of the scriptural words] is: "He does not allow me to taste or swallow anything savoring of life." Jb 6:[79] *Can anyone eat something unsavory, which is not seasoned with salt, or taste what brings death when it is tasted?*

And because it can be said that sin hinders God's listening to one's prayers, Job confesses his sin, adding: **[20]** ***I have sinned.*** There is a parallel in 2 Sm 12,[80] where David said, *I have sinned,* and Nathan added, *The Lord has taken your sin from you.* Ps:[81] *I said: against myself I will confess my injustice to the Lord; and you have forgiven the iniquity of my sin.* **What shall I do for you,** that is to say, to obtain forgiveness. Mi 6:[82] *What shall I offer the Lord that is worthy of Him?* ***O guardian of men?*** Ps:[83] *Unless the Lord guards the city, he who guards it keeps watch in vain.* Similarly, Ps:[84] *Behold, He who guards Israel will neither slumber nor sleep.* ***Why have you placed me opposite to you.*** He says, "have you placed," not "have you made," because by smiting Job, God placed him as an opponent, although in his actions he was not an opponent. There is a parallel in 2 Cor 5:[85] *God made Him, who did not know sin, to be sin for us.* Ps:[86] *You have placed us as a reproach to our neighbors.* ***and I have become burdensome to myself?*** that is to say, by means of your beatings. 2 Cor 1:[87] *We have been oppressed beyond measure and beyond our strength, such that we became tired even of living.*

78. Ps 12.2.
79. Jb 6.6.
80. 2 Sm 12.13.
81. Ps 31.5.
82. Mi 6.6.
83. Ps 126.2.
84. Ps 120.4.
85. 2 Cor 5.21.
86. Ps 43.14.
87. 2 Cor 1.8.

And concerning the correction of sin through punishment, Job adds: [21] ***Why***, supply: through punishments at least, ***do you not take away my sin?*** In your leniency, you could at least spare the one who has been stricken. Jer 31:[88] *After you converted me, I did penance.* And just before this:[89] *You chastised me, and I was instructed, as a young untamed bull.* Ps:[90] *The Lord who chastises has chastised me, but He has not delivered me over to death.*

and why do you not remove my iniquity? which, of course, I have committed against my neighbor, considering that about you it is written in Is 27:[91] *Because this is the full fruit of tribulation, that his sin should be taken away.* Is 40:[92] *Her iniquity has been forgiven; she has received from the hand of the Lord double for all her sins.*

Then Job makes clear that he has been smitten, adding: ***Behold, now I lie in the dust,*** that is, with my flesh clothed in rottenness and the filth of dust, I accept the dream of death. Is 47:[93] *Come down, sit in the dust, O virgin daughter of Babylon!* ***and,*** supply: let me die so quickly that ***if you will seek me in the morning,*** namely in this life, ***I will not remain alive.*** Is 24:[94] *It will be removed, as the tent of a single night,* hence it is signified by ivy, about which Jon 4[95] says: *In one night it came into existence, and in one night it perished.*[96]

88. Jer 31.19.
89. Jer 31.18.
90. Ps 117.18.
91. Is 27.9.
92. Is 40.2.
93. Is 47.1.
94. Is 24.20.
95. Jon 4.10.
96. Here Albert connects the "tent of a single night" (*tabernaculum unius noctis*) of Is 24.20 with the shelter or shady retreat (*umbraculum*) that Jonah makes for himself according to Jon 4.5, which Albert seems to identify with the "ivy" (*hedera*) that God prepares for Jonah's protection (4.6). When Jonah grows angry with God after the latter sends a worm to destroy the ivy, God defends Himself by maintaining that it was not Jonah's laboring that made it grow (Jon 4.10). Among the several noteworthy parallels between Jon 4 and Jb 7 is the way the protagonist of each book pleads to God for his own death.

CHAPTER 8

THEN BILDAD ***the Shuhite responded and said.***

Here we return to the position of Bildad.[1] Indeed, he agrees with Eliphaz that the universe is ruled according to the order of human justice,[2] which is repayment according to merits.[3] But Bildad adds two things, namely: that a sinner, through penance, is able to be restored and to escape judgment; and that if God ever punishes in terms of damage to property or health, as long as the one who suffers punishment repents and acts with patience, God will repent in many different ways and will make restitution and restoration for the penitent.

Having noted these things, then, we say that this response of Bildad is divided into two parts. In the first part he sets forth his refutation of his fellow-disputant; and in the second part he sets forth the proof of his own position, which is his solution to the question or the speech, in this place:[4] *Can it be that God.*

And that is: ***Bildad the Shuhite responded.*** He is described by his name and his place. From both he had the reputation for wisdom. For Bildad means "old age alone," and he was so called because it seemed as if he alone had obtained the wisdom of the ancients, for indeed among the ancients were wise men.

1. See Albert's opening comments on ch. 3 above, where he broadly outlines the position of each of the disputants.

2. I follow MSS F and M, which add *humanae* before *iustitiae* here.

3. Cf. Albert's introductory comments on ch. 3 above, where he affirms: "Bildad maintains that divine governance takes place not according to merits, but rather according to the best order in relation to the end of human happiness." See p. 95 above.

4. Jb 8.3.

Thus Graecias[5] criticized Solon, as it is said in Plato's *Timaeus*, by saying, "You Greeks are boys, and there is no gray-haired wisdom among you."[6] Wis 4:[7] *The understanding of a man is his gray hair, and a blameless life is the attainment of old age.* Jb 12:[8] *Among the ancients is wisdom, and in many years prudence.* "Shuhite," however, signifies his "speaking," because Bildad had been zealous for the art of rhetoric and he was eloquent in holding forth. Wis 10:[9] *Wisdom opened the mouths of the mute and made the tongues of infants eloquent.*

and said, that is, by holding forth against Job, he sets out a refutation which any impatient and presumptuous person would deserve. **[2]** ***How long will you say such things***, which suggest your own justification and God's injustice. Ps:[10] *In your sight no living thing will be justified.* Dn 9:[11] *We have sinned against all your justice.* And because Bildad points out such a great spirit in the final words of this verse, he says with his own words: ***and how long will the words of your mouth be a strong spirit?*** namely of anger and indignation and impatience. Is 2:[12] *Turn away from man, whose spirit is in his nostrils.* And in Book III of the *Ethics*, Aristotle cites Homer, who says that powerful men exhaled spirit through their nostrils, and their blood boiled up.[13] Bildad is describing both the spirit of this kind and the speech. Hence Jb 15:[14] *Your iniquity has taught your mouth, and you imitate the speech of blasphemers.* And the text touches on this earlier in the words spoken by Job himself in Jb 6:[15] *If only my sins, for which I have deserved wrath, and the calamity that I suffer were weighed in a balance!* Indeed, these words seem to resound with the notion that some degree of iniquity exists in the one who governs hu-

5. Criteas.
6. Plato, *Ti.* 22B.
7. Wis 4.8–9.
8. Jb 12.12.
9. Wis 10.21.
10. Ps 142.2.
11. Dn 9.15–16.
12. Is 2.22.
13. Aristotle, *EN* 3.11.10.
14. Jb 15.5.
15. Jb 6.2.

man life, as does a spirit of indignation and anger. Hence it also follows:[16] *My words are full of suffering.*

Then Bildad sets forth his response to Job's speech or questioning, and it is divided into two parts: in the first he sets forth his response; and in the second he proves it, in this place:[17] *Inquire.*

In setting forth his response, Bildad makes three points: at first he maintains that there is no iniquity on the part of the Judge; secondly that the one who repents is able to be restored through penance; and thirdly that the restitution of lost property is manifold.

And that is: **[3]** ***Can it be that God trips up,*** that is, casts down, right ***judgment?*** supply: as if to say, "No." For by casting down justice He would cast down His very self, because He is His own justice, from which His proper judgment is formed.[18] Ps:[19] *God is a just judge, strong and patient.* ***and that the Almighty,*** from whom it is neither permitted nor possible to demand anything, ***overthrows what is just?*** as if to say, "No." And Bildad takes the meaning of what is just from the definition of Plato,[20] namely that it is just to repay according to merits. Ezek 18:[21] *Are not My ways right?* And it[22] supplies: *The justice of the just man will be upon him, and the wickedness of the wicked man will be upon him.*

Then, concerning penance, Bildad adds: **[4]** ***Even if,*** that is, although, ***your children have sinned against Him,*** that is, against God. Ps:[23] *Against you alone have I sinned.* ***and,*** supply: therefore, ***He has abandoned them,*** that is, He has cast them down with a sentence of condemnation, ***into the hand,*** that is, into the operation, ***of their own iniquity,*** supply: which they have worked.

16. Jb 6.3.

17. Jb 8.8.

18. Such an affirmation relies on the doctrine of divine simplicity, according to which whatever is predicated of God is not attributed to or predicated of Him accidentally (as in creatures), but rather substantially. So the justice that is proper to God is His very substance or essence, which means that one can make such affirmations as "God is justice" and "God is love."

19. Ps. 7.12.

20. See Plato, *Rep.* Bk. 1. Cf. Albert, *ST* 2.16.104.1.

21. Ezek 18.29.

22. Ezek 18.20.

23. Ps 50.6.

Ezek 18:[24] *In his own injustice, which he has worked, he will die.* Jer 15:[25] *Cast them out from My presence, and let them go forth: those who are destined for death, to death; those who are destined for the sword, to the sword.*

[5] ***Nevertheless, if at dawn,*** that is, quickly. Sir 5:[26] *Do not delay to be converted to the Lord.* **you,** notwithstanding the iniquity of your children. Ezek 18:[27] *The father shall not bear the iniquity of the son.* ***will rise up,*** that is, rise up with all your heart, ***to God,*** namely through penance. Lam 2:[28] *Rise up, and praise the Lord at the beginning of the vigils.* Eph 5:[29] *Rise, you who sleep, and arise from the dead.* ***and make supplication to the Almighty,*** that is to say, in devout prayer. Sir 39:[30] The just man *will give his heart over to keeping watch at dawn for the Lord, who made him, and he will make supplication in the sight of the Most High.*

And because perverse works sometimes contradict one's prayer, Bildad adds: **[6]** ***if you will walk,*** by making progress in this way in your whole way of life, ***pure,*** namely, free from the passions of impatience and anger and concupiscence, ***and upright*** in the work of justice, ***immediately He will wake Himself up for you,*** namely by giving you light and by infusing into you good things, which previously, as if He had been sleeping, He kept hidden. Jer 31:[31] *Just as I have watched over them so that I could uproot and remove and scatter and destroy and crush them, in the same way I will watch over them so that I might build them up and plant them.*

and He will restore peace to the dwelling place of your justice, that is, He builds the merit of justice for you. Ex 1:[32] *Because the midwives feared God, He built homes for them.* Ps:[33] *He will not allow the just to be tossed about forever.*

24. Ezek 18.26.
25. Jer 15.1–2.
26. Sir 5.8.
27. Ezek 18.20.
28. Lam 2.19.
29. Eph 5.14.
30. Sir 39.6.
31. Jer 31.28.
32. Ex 1.21.
33. Ps 54.23.

And what follows explains this: [7] ***to such a degree***, by God's making restitution for your property loss and punishments, ***that if your former things***, that is to say, your property and family, ***were small***, relatively, of course, although they were great in themselves, ***your latter things***, which He will restore after your penance, ***will be multiplied exceedingly***, that is, incomparably. Jl 2:[34] *The threshing floors will be filled again with grain, and presses will overflow with wine and oil. I will restore to you the years that the locust, the grasshopper, the caterpillar, and the blight devoured.* Est 10:[35] *The small spring grew into a river, and turned toward the sun, and overflowed into many waters.*

Bildad proves this demonstration, adding: **[8] *Inquire*.**

And the proof has two parts. In the first part, he proves it; and in the second part, he applies what he has proved to his proposition, in this place:[36] *God will not reject.*

The first part is subdivided into two. For firstly he proves it from authority; and secondly he proves it using the similitude of a metaphor, in this place:[37] *Can it be that the bulrush is able to live?*

In the first subdivision, Bildad does three things: He wakes up his hearer and causes him to pay attention to his demonstration; he shows the force (*necessitatem*) of his demonstration; and he shows its usefulness.

And that is: ***Inquire, indeed, of the former generation***, that is, of the fathers of old. Dt 32:[38] *Inquire of your father, and he will declare to you; of your elders, and they will speak to you.*

and diligently, that is, with zeal, ***investigate the memory of the fathers***, that is, their memorable deeds. Ps:[39] *I reflected upon the days of old, and I had in my mind the everlasting years.* Jer 6:[40] *Stand firm in your ways, and inquire about the ancient paths.* Ps:[41] *I will be mindful of Your wondrous deeds from the beginning.*

34. Jl 2.24–25.
35. Est 10.6.
36. Jb 8.20.
37. Jb 8.11.
38. Dt 32.7.
39. Ps 76.6.
40. Jer 6.16.
41. Ps 76.12.

And he shows the force of this demonstration, saying: **[9]** ***To be sure, we are but of yesterday,*** that is, young, ***and,*** supply: therefore, ***we are ignorant,*** inexperienced, as it were. Aristotle, in Book I of the *Ethics,* says that "it makes no difference whether he is immature in age or in character."[42] Ps:[43] *Do not remember the transgressions of my youth and my ignorance.* ***because like a shadow,*** Ps:[44] *Like a shadow when it declines, I have been carried off,* ***are our days upon the earth,*** according to which a shadow comes into being little by little, stands still scarcely at all, and immediately declines. Wis 5:[45] *All those things have passed away like a shadow, and like a messenger quickly running along.* Ps:[46] *My days have declined like a shadow, and I have dried up like hay.*

And he adds the usefulness of his demonstration: **[10]** ***They,*** namely the fathers by their memorable deeds, ***will teach you,*** those things, of course, that I have said, ***and will bring forth words,*** namely that God does not trip up judgment and the Almighty does not overthrow what is just, ***from their hearts,*** because these words have been contemplated and carefully investigated. Indeed, among all the generations of old one finds that God has done good things for the good and bad things for the wicked. For wise men speak from the heart, whereas the foolish speak only from the mouth. Sir 21:[47] *The mouth of the foolish bubbles up stupidity.* In that same place:[48] *The heart of the foolish is in their mouth, and the mouth of the wise is in their heart.*

Can it be that the bulrush is able to live?

In the second subdivision of the proof, Bildad does three things: he sets forth a similitude; then he modifies it, in this place:[49] *So are the ways;* and, thirdly, he thoroughly develops it so that it might seem to be in accordance with his proposition, in this place:[50] *He seems to be moist.*

42. See Aristotle, *EN* 1.3.
43. Ps 24.7.
44. Ps 108.23.
45. Wis 5.9.
46. Ps 101.12.
47. Sir 21.28.
48. Sir 21.29.
49. Jb 8.13.
50. Jb 8.16.

And that is: **[11]** ***Can it be that the bulrush is able to live without moisture?*** A bulrush is a large rush, and because it exists without any nodes, it has nothing in which its nourishment is stored; and for that reason it is not vigorous unless it draws moisture continuously from an external source.[51] Indeed, in a reed or a plant a node serves the same purpose as the stomach or intestines, which are said to be intricate in humans and animals, namely to store and digest nourishment so that it is not compelled to be concerned constantly about its sustenance. For it would have to be concerned constantly about its sustenance if the nourishment that it received passed through it directly and instantly from an external source. And Bildad intends to say that Job, just like a bulrush, was vigorous on the outside but empty on the inside, and was constantly receiving moisture and nourishment through greediness. Eccl 5:[52] *A greedy man will not be satisfied with money.* Prv 30:[53] *The leech has two daughters who say: Give, give.*

or sedge to come forth without water? "Sedge" is gladiolus,[54] which also has no nodes on its leaves, is vigorous on the outside but is hollow inside; and therefore, like the bulrush, it is not able to live without continuously drawing in water and moisture. But sedge differs in this way: that it spreads out its leaves, which the bulrush does not do. All of its leaves, however, project from its root; none projects from its branch, because it does not have a branch, which is why, according to the science of plants, it is classified as an herb and not as a vegetable. Indeed, as the Philosopher says, what projects many leaves from one root without a branch is an herb.[55]

And by sedge Bildad intends to signify Job's children and household, who were consumed because they were constantly taking in plunder. This is said by means of another metaphor in Prv 30:[56] *The earth is not satisfied by water.*

And he makes this clear, adding: **[12]** ***When it,*** namely the

51. See Albert, *Veg.* 6.2.4; 1.2.1; 2.1.3.
52. Eccl 5.9.
53. Prv 30.15.
54. See Albert, *Veg.* 6.2.8.
55. Aristotle, *Pl.* 1.12.
56. Prv 30.16.

bulrush, ***is still in flower***. And pay close attention to this: that the bulrush does not have a true flower, but rather, in the place of a flower, at its highest point, it sends out certain small and short wands, at the ends of which are formed certain empty seeds, which are in the place of fruit. And Bildad intends by this to say that the integrity with which Job seemed to flourish was not real, but apparent. Jer 48:[57] *Give a flower to Moab, because flourishing it will go out.*

and it, supply: sedge, ***is not plucked up by the hand***. And pay close attention to this: that sedge is twofold: greater and lesser. Greater sedge has leaves whose ends are flat and smooth, whereas the ends of the leaves of lesser sedge are pointed, prickly and very sharp, just as the sickle of a reaper. And this "is not plucked up by the hand" because it would cut the hand of the one plucking it up. And he intends to say that Job so hated rebuke that he was not able to be touched by the hand of the one rebuking him. Hence Jb 4:[58] *But now it has touched you, and you have been thrown into confusion.* For he is thrown into confusion by touch who cannot bear rebuke. Sir 21:[59] *He who hates rebuke, his is the footprint of the sinner.*

it, namely bulrush and sedge, without an influx of moisture, ***withers before all grasses***. Ps:[60] *Let them be as the grass of roofed houses, which dried up before it was plucked up.* Is 18:[61] *Before the harvest everything flourished, and it sprouted forth before it was perfectly mature.*

Moreover, Bildad modifies the metaphor that he has introduced, saying: **[13]** ***So are the ways of all who forget God***. He is said to "forget God" who does not have God before his eyes. Ps:[62] *Let sinners be turned into hell, all the nations that forget God.* And again:[63] *God is not in his sight; his ways are polluted at all times.* Is 57:[64] *Have you lied, and have you not called me to mind or consid-*

57. Jer 48.9.
58. Jb 4.5.
59. Sir 21.7.
60. Ps 128.6.
61. Is 18.5.
62. Ps 9.18.
63. Ps 9.26 (Ps 10.5 according to the Hebrew numbering).
64. Is 57.11.

ered me in your heart? For I am silent and as one who does not see, and you have forgotten me. Jer 2:[65] *My people have forgotten me, in days without number.*

and the hope of the hypocrite will perish. A person who is bewitched, presenting one face to the outside [world] and having another face on the inside, is properly called a "hypocrite." Mt 7:[66] *Beware of false prophets, who come to you in sheep's clothing but inwardly are ravenous wolves.*[67] Wis 5:[68] *The hope of the wicked is as down, which is blown away by the wind.*

And he adds the reason for this: **[14]** ***His madness,*** that is, the hypocrite's, ***will not be pleasing to Him,*** that is, to God. For he who does what is opposed to an upright heart is "mad." Hence Gregory asserts that one who, having a parched garden, pours his water into a river is mad.[69] Prv 12:[70] *He who is vain and mad will lie open to contempt.* Jer 4:[71] *My foolish people have not known me. They are senseless and mad children; they are wise in doing evil, but they do not know how to act rightly.*

and his confidence, that is, his wealth, in which he has confidence, ***will be as the web of a spider,*** that is to say, able to be destroyed easily by scattering. Is 59:[72] *They have woven the webs of a spider.* And after a few words:[73] *Their webs will not be for clothing, nor will they cover themselves with the things they have made. Their works are useless works, and the work of iniquity is in their hands.* Ps:[74] *You make his soul waste away like a spider.*

Bildad adds how this is so: **[15]** ***He will lean,*** that is, he will prop himself up, ***on his own household,*** that is, he will put his confidence in riches and in glory, ***but it will not stand,*** that is, it

65. Jer 2.32.
66. Mt 7.15.
67. Here I follow MSS F and M, which quote this verse completely, unlike Weiss's edition, which has only the first phrase: *Attendite a falsis prophetis.*
68. Wis 5.15.
69. Cf. Ratherius of Verona, *Praeloquia* 1.5.19.
70. Prv 12.8.
71. Jer 4.22.
72. Is 59.5.
73. Is 59.6.
74. Ps 38.12.

will fall. Is 36:[75] *Behold, you put your confidence in this broken staff made of a reed, upon which if a man leans, it will go into his hand and pierce it.*

he will support it, fortifying himself on all sides by the increase of riches, ***but it will not stand up;*** for what has not been established on God is not able to stand up. Mt 7:[76] *The floods came, the winds blew, and they beat upon that house, and it fell, and great was its destruction.* Jb 20:[77] *The offspring of his household will be exposed; they will be pulled down on the day of God's fury.*

[16] ***He seems to be moist.***

Here Bildad thoroughly develops the metaphor, in order to show that it is in accordance with his proposition by referring to three things, namely sprouting, planting, and uprooting.

And that is: ***He seems to be moist.*** For the bulrush lives in marshes, and when it is infused with a great deal of moisture, it grows vigorous, ***before the sun,*** which dries up the marshes with its heat, ***comes up.*** Indeed, the sun signifies God's judgment, which reveals impiety and dries it up. Jas 1:[78] *The sun rose with its heat and made the grass dry, and its flower fell off, and its beautiful shape perished.*

and at his rising, supply: before the sun reaches its peak, ***his bud,*** which is empty, ***will shoot forth.*** Fresh water, by its nature, is potable and easily evaporated by the sun, as Aristotle says.[79] Is 15:[80] *The grass has withered, the bud has failed, all the verdure has passed away. According to the greatness of their work and their visitation also.*

Then, with regard to planting and the place of generation, Bildad adds: **[17]** ***Upon a heap of rocks,*** namely hard and frigid ones, which, as it is said in Book III of *Meteorology,* retain frigid water.[81] ***his roots will be packed together,*** that is, they will be multiplied. He intends to say that the servants and children of Job,

75. Is 36.6.
76. Mt 7.27.
77. Jb 20.28.
78. Jas 1.11.
79. Aristotle, *Mete.* 2.2.
80. Is 15.6–7.
81. Aristotle, *Mete.* 1.14.

in whom he was rooted, were harsh and wicked toward those who were subject to them. Jb 41:[82] *His heart will be hard, as a stone.*

and among the stones he, that is to say, the bulrush, ***will abide.*** And he intends to say that Job refused to interact socially with anyone, except those harsh ones who were insensible to virtue in the manner of stones. 1 Sm 25:[83] *His heart died within him, and he became as a stone.*

Then, concerning loss, Bildad adds: **[18]** ***If one,*** supply: anyone, ***should devour,*** that is, separate, ***him,*** that is to say, the bulrush, ***from his place,*** supply: by uprooting, ***he will say,*** indeed by his works: ***I do not know you.*** For in another place, away from stones and rocks, he does not know how to come forth or to tarry. Jb 19:[84] *As a tree that has been uprooted, He has taken away my hope.* Jer 12:[85] *I will pluck them out of their land.*

And he adds the reason for this: **[19]** ***For this is the joy of his journey,*** that is, of his growth, namely that he exists in such a place. Prv 2:[86] *They rejoice when they have acted wrongly, and they exult in the most wicked things.* ***that in turn,*** through the succession of children, ***others,*** namely other bulrushes, ***might sprout forth,*** that is, be produced, ***out of the earth,*** which is moist and rocky. Wis 4:[87] *Children born of unlawful unions are witnesses of wickedness against their parents.*

Having in this way proven his first point, which is that God does not trip up judgment, Bildad applies it to his main proposition, adding: **[20]** ***God will not reject the simple,*** that is to say, the man of simple virtue. Prv 10:[88] *The strength of the simple is the way of the Lord.* ***nor stretch out His hand,*** that is, the assistance of grace, ***to evildoers.*** Ps:[89] *In His sight the evildoer is brought to nothing.* **[21]** ***until,*** supply: if you will repent, ***your mouth is filled with laughter,*** with abundant laughter, which has no tears. At

82. Jb 41.15.
83. 1 Sm 25.37.
84. Jb 19.10.
85. Jer 12.14.
86. Prv 2.14.
87. Wis 4.6.
88. Prv 10.29.
89. Ps 14.4.

the end of Prv:[90] *She will laugh on the last day.* Lk 6:[91] *Blessed are you who weep now, for you shall laugh.*

and your lips, supply: are filled, ***with rejoicing.*** Gregory says: "When such great joy is conceived in the heart, speech does not convey it, although the mouth utters a sound."[92] Ps:[93] *Blessed is the people who knows rejoicing.* But because Job had the Chaldeans and Sabeans as his enemies,[94] Bildad adds: **[22]** ***Those who hate you will be covered with confusion,*** that is to say, let them be completely buried by confusion. Mi 7:[95] *My enemy will see me, and she will be covered with confusion.* Ps:[96] *Let them be covered with their own confusion, as with a cloak.* ***and the tent of the wicked,*** Gregory says: that is, the edifice of earthly happiness,[97] ***will not stand.*** Is 24:[98] *It will be removed, as the tent of a single night; and its iniquity will weigh it down, and it will fall.*

90. Prv 31.25.
91. Lk 6.21.
92. Gregory, *Mor.* 8.52.88.
93. Ps 88.16.
94. See Jb 1.15–17.
95. Mi 7.10.
96. Ps 108.29.
97. Gregory, *Mor.* 8.54.91.
98. Is 24.20.

CHAPTER 9

A*ND RESPONDING*, *Job said.*

This response of Job to Bildad is divided into two parts. In the first of these, as is certainly the case with a good respondent and a good companion moving their common work forward, Job makes clear that true claims always must be conceded. In the second part, he returns to his own position and demonstrates[1] that human life is not governed according to the order of human justice, and it begins below in this place:[2] *My soul is weary of my life.*

The first of these parts is subdivided into two. In the first subdivision Job proves by many reasons that what must be conceded is true. In the second he says that he did not deny [these claims of his interlocutors], but asserted something else, against which neither Eliphaz nor Bildad has argued, in this place:[3] *One thing there is that I have spoken.*

The first subdivision has two parts. For at first he declares what must be conceded by everyone; and secondly he demonstrates it, in this place:[4] *He is wise in heart.*

In the first part, there are two things: the confession of the truth and the reason for this confession.

And that is: ***And responding, Job said.*** 1 Pt 3:[5] *Being prepared to respond to everyone who asks you with a reason for the hope*

1. Here I read *probat* with MSS TEFM, rather than the *ponit* of Weiss's edition.

2. Jb 10.1.

3. Jb 9.22.

4. Jb 9.4.

5. 1 Pt 3.15.

that is in you. [2] ***Indeed I know,*** that is, by true revelation and true reason. Jn 14:[6] *He [that is, the Holy Spirit] will teach you all things, and supply you with everything.* Sir 17:[7] *He created in them the knowledge of the spirit, He filled their hearts with understanding, and He showed them both evil and good.* ***that this is so,*** as you have said, namely that God does not overthrow judgment and the Almighty does not trip up what is just.[8] ***and,*** likewise supply: "Indeed I know that this is so," as Eliphaz said, ***that man cannot be justified in relation to God.***[9] For every human rectitude is an injustice compared to divine justice. Is 64:[10] *We have sinned, and in our sins we have always existed. All of us have become as someone unclean, and all of our righteousness is, as it were, the rag of a menstruating woman.* Ps[11] and Rom 3:[12] *They have all turned away; they have all become useless together. There is no one who does good, there is not even one.*

Then Job gives the reason for this confession: [3] ***If he wishes to contend with Him,*** supply: in judgment, ***he will not be able to answer one word*** or work that is perfect in justice ***for a thousand,*** that is, for an infinite number of mistaken and imperfect words and works that he puts forward against Him. Hence it is said in the Ps:[13] *Do not enter into judgment with your servant, because in your sight no living thing will be justified.* Jer 2:[14] *I will still contend in judgment with you, says the Lord, and I will dispute with your children.* Mi 6:[15] *Arise, contend in judgment against the mountains, and let the hills hear your voice.* In fact, God convicts everyone. Hence

6. Jn 14.26.
7. Sir 17.6.
8. See Bildad's words in 8.3 above, as well as Albert's comments on 8.10. Notice here that the verbs have been reversed: whereas 8.3 asks whether it can be that God "trips up" (*supplantat*) justice and that the Almighty "overthrows" (*subvertit*) what is just, here Albert's Job recalls Bildad as affirming that God does not "overthrow" (*subvertit*) justice and the Almighty does not "trip up" (*supplantat*) what is just.
9. See Eliphaz's words in 4.17–21.
10. Is 64.5–6.
11. Ps 13.3.
12. Rom 3.12.
13. Ps 142.2.
14. Jer 2.9.
15. Mi 6.1.

Is 64,[16] considering the justice of God, says: *We have all fallen as a leaf, and our iniquities, like the wind, have carried us away.*

Job then adds a demonstration of this, and it has two parts, namely: the demonstration of divine justice; and the adaptation of the demonstration to his proposition, in this place:[17] *What, therefore, am I?*

The demonstration itself has two subdivisions, namely: the demonstration proper; and the conclusion, in this place:[18] *God, whose wrath no one is able to resist.*

In the demonstration proper, he at first proceeds particularly, and then universally in this place:[19] *He who does great things.* He proceeds particularly in two ways, namely: according to God's power (*virtute*), which is the source (*causa*) of His incomparable justice; and according to His work, which is an indication of His justice, in this place:[20] *He who alone stretched out the heavens.*

And that is: **[4]** ***He is wise in heart,*** and therefore perfect for ordering things rightly. Hence in the first book of *First Philosophy,* Aristotle says: "It belongs to the wise man to order, not to be ordered."[21] Ps:[22] *You have made all things in wisdom.*

and mighty in strength, for the purpose, of course, of carrying out whatever works He has ordained. Nm 23[23] and 24:[24] *His strength is like that of the rhinoceros,* which nothing resists, of course. Is 9:[25] *He will be called Wonderful, God, the Mighty.*

Then Job sets forth a proof of this, first in general, and second in particular.

And that is: ***who has resisted Him,*** supply: in judgment, wishing to justify himself. ***and possessed peace?*** That is to say, who has ever relied upon the strength of [his own] justice and remained in peace, without punishment?—as if to say, "No one."

16. Is 64.6.
17. Jb 9.14.
18. Jb 9.13.
19. Jb 9.10.
20. Jb 9.8.
21. Aristotle, *Metaph.* 1.2.1.
22. Ps 103.24.
23. Nm 23.22.
24. Nm 24.8.
25. Is 9.6.

Heb 2:[26] *Every disobedience and transgression has received its just recompense.* 2 Pt 2:[27] *He did not spare the angels who sinned; He did not spare the world at its beginning; and reducing the cities of Sodom and Gomorrah to ashes, He condemned them to destruction.* Jb 7:[28] *You have placed me opposite to you, and I have become burdensome to myself.* Is 57:[29] *There is no peace for the wicked, says the Lord.*

Then he adds this in particular: **[5]** ***He who has removed mountains,*** that is to say, great men from the point of view of the world: Nebuchadnezzar,[30] Holofernes,[31] Sisera,[32] and others. Sir 10:[33] *The kingdom is transferred from one people to another because of injustices and wrongs.* Zec 4:[34] *What are you, O great mountain, you who before Zerubbabel shall become a plain?* Ps:[35] *The mountains will be carried into the heart of the sea.*

and those, namely mountains, ***whom He overthrows in His fury did not know it,*** that is, they were not able to know it beforehand so that they could have avoided it. Ps:[36] *I was reduced to nothing, and I did not know it.* Song 6:[37] *I did not know: my soul has confounded me.* Jb 28:[38] *He has stretched out His hand to the stone, He has overturned mountains from the roots.*

Job then sets forth another proof: **[6]** ***He who shakes the earth,*** that is, those who dwell on the earth, ***out of its place,*** namely by casting them out. Sir 10:[39] *God has destroyed the thrones of proud princes.* And after a few words:[40] *The Lord has overthrown the lands of the giants, and has ruined them all the way to the foundation.*[41]

26. Heb 2.2.
27. 2 Pt 2.4–6.
28. Jb 7.20.
29. Is 57.21.
30. See Dn 4.15–30.
31. See Jdt 13.27–29.
32. See Jgs 4.1–24, esp. v. 21.
33. Sir 10.8.
34. Zec 4.7.
35. Ps 45.3.
36. Ps 72.22.
37. Song 6.11.
38. Jb 28.9.
39. Sir 10.17.
40. Sir 10.19.
41. Although MSS TF and M read, with the Vulg. text, *Terras gentium evertit*

and its pillars, that is, the leaders who hold it up, ***are shattered,*** that is to say, they topple. This is signified in Jgs 16,[42] where Samson, whose name means "powerful sun," shook the pillars that were supporting the house and cast the house down on the Philistines.

And he adds another proof: **[7]** ***He who commands the sun, and it does not rise,*** that is, it does not move through its orbit, just as in Jos 10:[43] *Sun, do not move toward Gibeon, nor you, moon, toward the valley of Aijalon.* Hab 3:[44] *The sun and the moon stood still in their dwelling place.*

and encloses the stars, that is to say, so that they might not shine in consolation, ***as if within a seal*** that obstructs them, keeping life-giving light from shining on sinners. Is 13:[45] *The stars of heaven and their brilliance will not distribute their light; the sun has been made dark in its rising, and the moon will not shine with its light. And I will go to see the evils upon the earth.*

Next Job mentions God's strength in the work of creating and governing: **[8]** ***He who alone,*** that is, without assistance, ***stretched out the heavens.*** Dt 32:[46] *There was no other god with Him.*[47] Moreover, He stretched them out from pole to pole, and from east to west. Ps:[48] *He stretched out heaven like a skin.* But Job says "the heavens" because there are many heavens.

and walks upon the waves of the sea, that is to say, treading upon them and pressing them down, so that they do not exceed

---

Dominus (*The Lord has overthrown the lands of the Gentiles*), with Weiss I read *gigantium* rather than *gentium* in light of Albert's discussion of the "great men," here allegorized as mountains, whom God has overthrown.

42. Jgs 16.29–30.

43. Jos 10.12.

44. Hab 3.11.

45. Is 13.10–11.

46. Dt 32.12.

47. This is an interesting example of Albert's deft appropriation of scriptural intertexts for his exegetical purpose. In the context of Dt 32, Moses is here affirming that the one true God, and no other, guided Jacob or Israel and was "with him" (*cum eo*; v. 12). Here in commenting on Jb 9.8, however, Albert reads Dt 32.12 as an affirmation that God alone was responsible for the work of creation: there was no other god in the beginning "with Him," i.e., with the true God.

48. Ps 103.2.

their boundaries. Jb 38:[49] *He shut up the sea with doors when it burst forth, proceeding as if from the womb.*

[9] ***He who makes Arcturus,***[50] namely the north pole, as the origin of winter cold. Ps:[51] *The north wind and the sea you have created.*

and Orion. Orion is a constellation next to the meridian that shines opposite Sagittarius. When the sun is in Sagittarius, it rises opposite the sun with a cosmic or mundane rising. And it is the source of winter storms when it moves the frigid into the commingling of elements, causing them to thicken and condense, becoming generative.

and Hyades. "Hyades" are so called from the Greek *hydor,* which is water, and they are stars that are declared to be the head of the constellation Taurus.[52] They arise with the cosmic rising in May,[53] and May (*maius*) is also said to be "wetter" (*madius*) because of them. And they move the moisture of generation toward birth and development.

and the inner parts of the South. They are called "the inner parts of the South" because they are opposite the northern axis, near the antarctic pole, and are kept out of sight from us who live in the northern quarter of the earth; hence Lucan says: "This pole is always standing high for us, but that one is touched by the gloomy Styx."[54] And the stars placed there are the origin of heat. Jb 37:[55] *Are your clothes not hot when the south wind blows over the earth?*

And the sense is that heaven is the source of generation. In a certain one of its regions it functions as the origin of cold, in a certain region the origin of heat, in a certain region the origin

49. Jb 38.8.

50. See Albert, *In Am* 5.8.

51. Ps 88.13.

52. For an illuminating study of *hydor* in antiquity, the Christian tradition, and modern science, see Efstratios Th. Theodossiou, Milan S. Dimitrijevic, Vassilios N. Manimanis, and Th. Grammenos, "*Hydor* from Ancient Greek Cosmogonies to Modern Astrophysics," *Transdisciplinarity in Science and Religion* 1 (2007): 137–52.

53. Cf. Albert, *Veg.* 6.1.8.

54. I have been unable to find this dictum in Lucan; rather, see Virgil, *Georg.* 1.242.

55. Jb 37.17.

of the mixing of the elements, and in a certain region the origin of fertile humidity. Bar 3:[56] *He who sends out light and it goes forth; and summons it and it obeys Him with trembling. And the stars have given light during their watches, and they have rejoiced. They were summoned and they said, "Here we are." And with delight they have shown forth for Him who made them.*

Then Job says in general what he has already said in particular: **[10]** ***He who does great things,*** certainly with might and power. Jer 10:[57] *You are great, and your name is great in might.* ***and inscrutable things,*** that is to say, whose cause is not discovered by man. Eccl 1:[58] *All things are difficult; man cannot explain them with words.* ***and marvelous things,*** whose cause is high. Ps:[59] *Marvelous is the Lord on high.* ***which are without number;*** at least relative to the power of the one who does them, they are not limited by any number. Ps:[60] *His wisdom is without number.*

And concerning God's incomprehensibility, Job adds: **[11]** ***If He should come to me,*** appearing in some particular effect of grace or nature, ***I will not,*** supply: perfectly, ***see Him,*** because He infinitely exceeds His visible effects. Jer 32:[61] *The Lord God is incomprehensible in thought.* Ps:[62] *Your footsteps are not knowable.*

if He should depart, namely by withdrawing His effects, ***I will not understand,*** supply: where He is. Jn 3:[63] *You do not know where He comes from or where He goes.* **[12]** ***If He suddenly interrogates,*** namely by setting forth His judgment, ***who will respond to Him?*** that is, who, confident in his own justice, will dare to respond? Rom 9:[64] *O man, who are you, that you should respond to God?* Mt 22:[65] *But he was speechless.* ***or who is able to say: Why do you act***

56. Bar 3.33–35.
57. Jer 10.6.
58. Eccl 1.8.
59. Ps 92.4.
60. Ps 146.5.
61. Jer 32.19.
62. Ps 76.20.
63. Jn 3.8.
64. Rom 9.20.
65. Mt 22.12.

in this way? Rom 9:[66] *Can it be that the thing formed says to Him who formed it: Why have you made me in this way?*

On the basis of all of these proofs, Job concludes universally, adding: [13] ***God, whose wrath no one is able to resist,*** because His wrath is just and reasonable. Jer 49:[67] *Who is able to resist my countenance?* Mal 3:[68] *Who will stand firm to look at Him?*

under whom are bent down those who carry the world? In other words, because princes with their wisdom and power are broken under Him. For those most eminent men will come to nothing. Wis 6:[69] *The mighty will suffer torments mightily.* Sir 24:[70] *By my own power I have trampled upon the necks of the proud and exalted.*

[14] ***What, therefore, am I?***

Job applies to himself what he has demonstrated, arguing, as it were, from the major premise, and it is as if he were saying: "If such great and so many men are not able to respond, I will not be so presumptuous as to respond, confident in my own justice." And that is: ***What, therefore,*** that is, how small, ***am I, that I should respond to Him?*** 1 Sm 9:[71] *Am I not a son of Jemin, from the least of the tribes of Israel? And are my kinsmen not the last among all the families of the tribe of Benjamin?*

and utter my words, namely human words, ***in His presence?*** Gn 18:[72] *I will speak to my Lord, although I am dust and ashes.* Ex 4:[73] *I have never been eloquent, neither yesterday nor the day before, on account of which you have spoken to your servant.*

And Job makes this clear by means of his own perverseness, adding: [15] ***Even if I have something just,*** namely in my actions or in my words, something that seems just according to human reason, ***I will not respond,*** as if relying upon it, in order to dis-

66. Rom 9.20.
67. Jer 49.19.
68. Mal 3.2.
69. Wis 6.7.
70. Sir 24.11.
71. 1 Sm 9.21. The phrase *filius Iemini* in this scriptural text, translated "son of Jemin" here, is the Latin equivalent, in Albert's Vulgate, of "Benjaminite" (*ben* meaning "son of" and *yamîn* meaning "the right hand" in Hebrew).
72. Gn 18.27.
73. Ex 4.10.

pute God's judgments. Ti 3:[74] *Not by the works of justice that we have performed, but according to His own mercy He has saved us.*

but I will pray earnestly to my judge, that is to say, more confident in the clemency and tenderness of the judge than in my own justice. Dn 9:[75] *For we set our prayers before your face not according to our own just actions, but according to your many tender mercies.*

And abasing himself, Job adds: **[16]** ***And if He will hear me when I call,*** that is to say, granting my petition, ***I will not believe that He heard my voice,*** supply: [heard] critically, but rather in His benevolence and mercy. Jl 2:[76] *Turn to the Lord, for He is kind and merciful, and preeminent over wickedness.* Rom 2:[77] *But do you not know that the kindness of God leads you to penance?*

And he adds why he would not believe that he had been heard: **[17]** ***For He crushes me in a whirlwind.*** Through a whirlwind He reveals me, as if a sinner. Is 53:[78] *We considered him abased by God.* Jer 23:[79] *Behold, the whirlwind of the Lord's indignation is coming forth.* Is 25:[80] *The blast of the mighty is like a whirlwind beating against a wall.*

and multiplies my wounds without cause. Jb 16:[81] *He has cut me to pieces with wound after wound.* And Job understands what he says, namely "without cause," to mean without the cause of fault, but not without cause simply. Jb 2:[82] *You have provoked me against him, so that I would afflict him in vain.*[83]

[18] ***He does not allow my spirit to rest,*** supply: but He seizes me with excessive pain. 2 Cor 2:[84] *I had no rest in my spirit.* For the spirit, as has already been said in the foregoing,[85] is the bearer of strength, and, when the spirit has been cut off,

74. Ti 3.5.
75. Dn 9.18.
76. Jl 2.13.
77. Rom 2.4.
78. Is 53.4.
79. Jer 23.19.
80. Is 25.4.
81. Jb 16.15.
82. Jb 2.3.
83. Cf. Albert's quotation of this verse in the commentary on 2.3 above, which omits the phrase "against him."
84. 2 Cor 2.13.
85. See the commentary on 6.4 above.

it is inevitable that strength should fail. Jb 17:[86] *My spirit will be weakened, my days will be shortened.*

and He fills me with bitterness. Lam 1:[87] *My heart is turned in on itself, since I am full of bitterness,* supply: and therefore, in accordance with sin, I seem to have been smitten, and I am not able to respond.

But in order that this might seem more just, Job returns to the strength and justice of God. And that is: **[19]** ***If strength,*** or power, of course, ***is sought, He is the strongest,*** not lacking any power. Ex 15:[88] *Who is like you among the strong, O Lord?* ***if equity of judgment,*** namely by which He judges men, ***no one dares to give testimony for me,*** to the effect that I am innocent, since I have been judged and condemned. Jer 33:[89] *This is what they will call Him: the Lord, our Just one.* Moreover, Job says "no one dares to give testimony" because God Himself is the judge and witness.

[20] ***If I should wish to justify myself,*** supply: against His sentence, ***my own mouth would condemn me,*** that is, it would reveal that I should be condemned. Ps:[90] *Do not incline my heart to words of wickedness, for the purpose of making excuses for sins.*

if, supply: I should wish, ***to show myself innocent,*** that I did not sin at all, ***He will condemn me as perverse,*** because I would be lying about this very thing, and the one who lies is perverse. Wis 1:[91] *The mouth that lies kills the soul.* 1 Jn 1:[92] *If we say that we have no sin, we deceive ourselves and the truth is not in us.*

[21] ***Even if I should be simple,*** by the simplicity of virtue. Jb 1:[93] *A man simple and upright.* ***my soul will be ignorant of this very thing,*** namely whether my simplicity is so great that I can put my hope in it. Eccl 9:[94] *No one knows whether he is deserving of hatred or love.* ***and,*** supply: therefore, ***I will loathe my life,*** which,

86. Jb 17.1.
87. Lam 1.20.
88. Ex 15.11.
89. Jer 33.16.
90. Ps 140.4.
91. Wis 1.11.
92. 1 Jn 1.8.
93. Jb 1.1.
94. Eccl 9.1.

of course, is so irresolute in good things, and by the power of Satan has been so spattered with vain things. Jb 10:[95] *My soul is weary of my life.* Gn 27:[96] *I loathe my life because of the daughters of Heth.*

[22] ***One thing there is that I have spoken.***

Having shown what must be conceded by reason of its truth, Job posits this, which cannot be disputed, as he has asserted. But inquiry must be made into the nature of the providence that governs human life.

And this part of Job's reply is divided into two parts. In the first of these he shows that the innocent man is destroyed, and therefore life is not governed according to the order of human justice. In the second he shows that the smiting of an innocent man and not the failure of reason prevents a response to and a favorable disposition toward this position, in this place:[97] *For I will not respond to a man.*

The first of these parts has two subdivisions: first he shows in general that the life of man is not governed according to the order of human justice; secondly [he shows this] in particular, offering the example of his very self [in this place]:[98] *My days have been swifter.*

In the first subdivision, he does three things: he sets forth the position, and then the singling out of the afflicted person, and from these [two] he infers the general conclusion.

When he says ***One thing there is,*** it is a criticism of his interlocutor, who does not share in his one intention, but who is disputing for some other purpose. About such people it is said in Book VIII of the *Topics,*[99] "he acts with youthful indiscretion, and he employs no syllogisms."

that I have spoken, that is, I have begged, or actually I have spoken. Above, Eliphaz had said that punishments are not inflicted except for sins, and Bildad had tried to defend his opinion. For that reason Job, just as he spoke above against Eliph-

95. Jb 10.1.
96. Gn 27.46.
97. Jb 9.32.
98. Jb 9.25.
99. I was unable to find this quotation in Aristotle's *Top.*, but see Albert, *Top.* 8.1.5.

az and asserted the contrary, so too here he speaks as much against Bildad, showing that punishments are inflicted without sins, because he himself was innocent.

He consumes both the innocent and the wicked.

Indeed, from this it is clearly shown that the life of man is not governed according to the order of human justice, and this is the position of blessed Job. Indeed, no one, having been weighed in the divine balance, is innocent before God, although someone might be found innocent before men. Hence, what Gregory introduces here is affirmed,[100] namely that no one is innocent before God, not even an infant who has lived one day on the earth; for, at the very least, Original Sin must be imputed to him. Eph 2:[101] *We are all born children of wrath.* Ex 34:[102] *No one is innocent in his own right in your presence.*

Then Job adds the singling out of the miserable, which follows from this: **[23]** ***If He scourges,*** that is to say, by daily afflictions, ***let Him kill at once,*** namely by destroying. Jb 3:[103] *They hope for death, but it does not come; as if digging for treasure, they rejoice greatly when they have found the grave.*

and not laugh at the punishments of the innocent, that is, behave in the manner of one laughing; for behaving in this way is cruel, seeing that He rejoices in the punishments of men. Prv 1:[104] *I will laugh at your destruction, and I will mock you when what you feared comes upon you.*

From these things, Job concludes his proposition generally, and therefore supplies: **[24]** ***The,*** supply: entire ***earth,*** insofar as it is for the purpose of human life, ***has been given into the hands of the wicked one,*** that is, of Satan. Hab 1:[105] *The law has been mangled, and judgment does not come all the way to its end; because the wicked one prevails against the just man, perverse judgment therefore goes forth.* Rv 12:[106] *Woe to the earth and to the sea, because the devil*

100. See Gregory, *Mor.* 9.21.32.
101. Eph 2.3.
102. Ex 34.7.
103. Jb 3.21–22.
104. Prv 1.26.
105. Hab 1.4.
106. Rv 12.12.

has come down to you, having great wrath and knowing that he has little time.

And having proved his point, Job rebukes the adversary: ***he,*** namely the wicked one, ***covers the eyes of its,*** that is, the earth's, ***judges.*** The judges of the earth are wise and philosophical men, the same sort as were the friends of Job, whose eyes, he says, are covered because they do not consider the truth that he has so often considered. Dn 13:[107] *You are so foolish, you children of Israel, neither examining nor knowing what is true.* 2 Cor 4:[108] *If our Gospel is hidden,*[109] *it is hidden to those who are ruined; among them the god of this world has blinded the minds of unbelievers.*

but if it is not He, supply: God, the helmsman of life, who in this way has given the earth into the hands of the wicked one, ***then who is it?*** that is to say, who thus condemns the wicked and the innocent? as if to say: "There is no other." Am 3:[110] *Is there evil in a city that the Lord has not made?* Is 45:[111] *I am the Lord, and there is no other God: I form the light and create darkness; I make peace and create evil. I am the Lord who does all these things.*

Then Job proves this in particular, providing the example of his very self. And this is divided into three parts: for first he proves it from a consideration of life, which is vain; secondly from a consideration of works, which are imperfect, in this place:[112] *If I say;* and thirdly from the imperfection of justification, in this place:[113] *If I were washed.*

In the first part he introduces three similes: those of a runner, a ship, and a soaring eagle.

And that is: **[25]** ***My days,*** namely those granted for my life, ***have been swifter than a runner,*** because when a runner passes by, he plants his foot in his stride, interrupting that stride with pauses, because between two movements there is always a rest, as Aristotle says.[114] But my days have not experienced any inter-

107. Dn 13.48.
108. 2 Cor 4.3–4.
109. Here I read *opertum est* rather than Weiss's *apertum est.*
110. Am 3.6.
111. Is 45.6–7.
112. Jb 9.27.
113. Jb 9.30.
114. Aristotle, *Ph.* 8.8.8.

ruption in their passing by. Jer 2:[115] *As a smooth runner traversing his ways.*

they have fled, as a shadow. Jb 8:[116] *My days have passed like a shadow.* ***and they have not seen,*** by the vision of enjoyment, ***good.*** Jb 7:[117] *My eyes will not return to see good things.*

And he adds the simile of a ship: **[26]** ***They have passed by as if ships carrying fruit,*** which ships, of course, leave an aroma behind them as they carry the fruit away. Wis 5:[118] *All those things have passed away like a shadow, and like a messenger quickly running along, and like a ship that passes through the surging sea.*

Then he adds the third simile: ***like an eagle flying toward its prey,*** supply: which, because of its keen desire for its prey, flies quickly. Mt 24:[119] *Wherever the carcass is, there the eagles will be gathered together.* Wis 5:[120] *By moving its wings it has flown across, and afterwards there is no indication of its path.* Jb 39:[121] *The eagle notices its prey and its eyes see it from far away. Its young lap up the blood; and wherever the carcass is, it is there immediately.* And from these similes Job wishes to imply what he said previously in chapter 3:[122] *Let the day on which I was born,* on the earth, namely, for a loathsome life, *perish.*

Then, from a consideration of works, Job adds: **[27]** ***If I say: By no means will I speak in this way,*** that is to say, by considering the vanity of life, because, as Cato says: "Whoever is afraid of death ruins his life and himself."[123] Wis 2:[124] *The time of our life is short and filled with weariness.*

I change my face, that is to say, by considering the works characteristic of the manner of human life. Eccl 2:[125] *I went further to consider wisdom, and errors and folly.* ***and I am tormented by suffer-***

115. Jer 2.23.
116. Jb 8.9.
117. Jb 7.7.
118. Wis 5.9–10.
119. Mt 24.28.
120. Wis 5.11.
121. Jb 39.29–30.
122. Jb 3.3.
123. Cato, *Dist.* 1.22.
124. Wis 2.1.
125. Eccl 2.12.

ing, certainly on account of the fact that I find nothing except sources of my own suffering.

And that is: **[28]** ***I feared all my works,*** namely that they would be bad, because humans ought to fear even good works, for they have been sprinkled with sluggishness, carelessness, and imperfection; and therefore humans should not put their hope in them. Jer 10:[126] *Their works are useless and worthy of ridicule.*

knowing, according to the order of your justice, ***that you did not spare the negligent,*** and much less the perpetrator. Hence Mt 25[127] gives instruction concerning the lazy servant: *Throw him into outer darkness.* Prv 6:[128] *The jealousy and rage of a husband will be merciless on the day of vengeance; and he will neither acquiesce to the prayers of anyone nor accept the greatest number of gifts as a ransom.*

[29] ***But if I am also wicked in this way,*** that is, having been condemned as a wicked person, ***why have I labored in vain?*** Eccl 2:[129] *I detested all my industry, by which I have labored most eagerly under the sun.* And the reason is because I can hope[130] for neither impunity nor reward from such works. Is 49:[131] *I said: I have labored in vain; I have spent my strength without cause and in vain.*

Then, concerning the imperfection of justification, Job adds: **[30]** ***If I were washed,*** namely by the justification of penance, ***as if with water from snow,*** such that I would seem to be restored to the whiteness of snow. Ps:[132] *You shall wash me, and I will be made whiter than snow.* Is 1:[133] *If your sins were as scarlet, they will be made as white as snow.* ***and,*** supply: having been washed in this way, ***my hands were to shine as if most pure,*** that is, the works of my hands. Ps:[134] *I will wash my hands among the innocent.*

[31] ***nevertheless you will immerse me in filth,*** that is, you will show me to be immersed, because I will be found purified from sluggishness and lukewarmness and carelessness and the filthy

126. Jer 10.15.
127. Mt 25.30.
128. Prv 6.34–35.
129. Eccl 2.18.
130. Some MSS read "labor" here instead of "hope."
131. Is 49.4.
132. Ps 50.9.
133. Is 1.18.
134. Ps 25.6.

passions of desire. Is 64:[135] *All of us have become unclean.* ***and my own clothes,*** that is, my manner of life, which is so clothed in filth, ***will abhor me,*** that is, they reveal me as abominable. This is signified in Zec 3:[136] *Joshua was clothed in filthy garments and was standing in the presence of the angel.*

And, as if concluding, Job adds the reason for all these things: **[32]** ***For I will not respond,*** namely contending in judgment, ***to a man,*** one of the male sex, of course, ***who is like me,*** that is to say, who experiences human realities and to whom a similar objection can be raised. Jer 2:[137] *Why do you wish to contend with me in judgment? You have all forsaken me, says the Lord.*

And explaining this, he adds: ***nor to one who can be heard equally with me in judgment,*** that is to say, in the presence of a third judge. For I have no objection against him, as he has against me. Jb 40:[138] *Can it be that you will make my judgment void and that you will condemn me, so that you might be justified?* as if to say: "No."

And heightening this to the greatest extent, Job adds: **[33]** ***There is no one who is powerful enough to convict both of us,*** namely me and that one, because there can be no refutation of Him. Jl 3:[139] *Can it be that you will take your revenge on me?* as if to say: "No."

Explaining this, he adds: ***and to put his hand,*** supply: of reproof, ***between the two of us.*** Seeing the beam in our eyes, we do not find any speck in His.[140] Hab 1:[141] *Your eyes are too pure to look upon evil, and you are not able to gaze at iniquity.*

And he adds that, because he has been struck by such a just judge and helmsman, the beating always seems to be on account of a fault: **[34]** ***Let Him take His rod,*** namely with which He has struck me, ***away from me.*** Lam 3:[142] *I am a man who sees*

135. Is 64.6.
136. Zec 3.3.
137. Jer 2.29.
138. Jb 40.3.
139. Jl 3.4.
140. See Mt 7.3 and Lk 6.41.
141. Hab 1.13.
142. Lam 3.1.

my poverty in the rod of His indignation. Is 27:[143] *Can it be that He has struck him according to the blow of the one who struck Him?* ***and let not fear of Him,*** that is to say, of future beatings, ***terrify me.*** Ps:[144] *Fear and trembling have come upon me, and darkness has covered me.* At the end of Heb:[145] *The sight was so terrible that the eminent Moses said: I have been struck with terror and I am trembling.*

[35] ***I will speak,*** that is to say, I will assert my position, which is that human life is not governed according to the order of human justice, ***and I will not fear him,*** namely an opponent speaking against me. Is 58:[146] *Cry out, don't hold back!* Sir 4:[147] *Strive for justice for your soul and fight for justice continuously until death.*

for I am not able to respond while I am afraid. Indeed, my misfortune (*plaga*) itself is contrary to my words. Jb 16:[148] *My wrinkles give testimony against me, and a liar is stirred up against my face, contradicting me.*

143. Is 27.7.
144. Ps 54.6.
145. Heb 12.21.
146. Is 58.1.
147. Sir 4.33.
148. Jb 16.9.

CHAPTER 10

MY SOUL IS weary of my life.

After blessed Job has made clear that their disputation has not engaged his own proposition, he reveals his proposition here. And this chapter is divided into two parts. In the first of these he shows that human life cannot be governed by the rectitude of unchangeable justice according to the order of human justice. In the second part he shows that no aspect of human affairs, although it may be hidden, escapes the providence of God, in this place:[1] *Although you conceal these things.* The first part is subdivided into two. First, from the dissimilarity between the judgment of God and human judgment, he makes clear that human life does not preserve the rectitude of unchangeable justice. Secondly, from the fragility of nature, he makes clear that human life is not able to preserve it, in this place:[2] *Your hands have made me.*

In the first of these subdivisions there are two things. First he sets forth a certain introduction to this disputation; secondly he proceeds with the disputation, in this place:[3] *I will say to God.* And because these disputations are rhetorical, the introduction fits with the end of what precedes it and with the beginning of what follows.

And that is: ***My soul is weary***, that is, my innermost part is weary on account of all the things that have been said previously, ***of my life***. 2 Cor 1:[4] *Such that we became weary even of living. But*

1. Jb 10.13.
2. Jb 10.8.
3. Jb 10.2.
4. 2 Cor 1.8–9.

we had in ourselves the sentence of death. Mk 14[5] says of the Lord: *He began to be terrified and weary.*

And, supply: therefore, ***I will let my utterance go against me.*** My "utterance" is "against me" because it is about the weariness of human life; [and] "I will let it go" such that I will not adduce any more proofs from it. Ps:[6] *I have established a defense for my mouth when the sinner made a stand against me. I became silent and I did not speak out of good things.*

I will speak, namely searching for arguments elsewhere, ***in the bitterness,*** that is, on account of the bitterness, ***of my soul.*** Is 38:[7] *I will recount to you all my years in the bitterness of my soul.*

And Job begins his disputation, adding: **[2]** ***I will say to God,*** audaciously confident, of course, about his own innocence. Jer 12:[8] *You, indeed, are just, O Lord, if I should debate* (disputem) *with you; nevertheless, I will say just things to you.*

Hence this part is divided into two: first Job expresses his own position, namely that the judgment of God is dissimilar to human judgment; secondly he introduces three reasons for this position, in this place:[9] *Can it be that it seems good?*

And that is: ***Refuse to condemn me,*** that is: Please do not condemn me because you will find in me no reason for condemnation according to the order of human justice. Ps:[10] *Preserve my soul, because I am holy.* Gn 18:[11] *Can it be that you will condemn the just with the wicked?*

show me, by observing the [proper] order of the administration of justice, ***why you judge me,*** namely whether because of a fault or to prove my virtue or as an example for others, ***in this way,*** that is, with so many punishments! For scourges are used in many ways. Is 38:[12] *Lord, I suffer violence; respond for me!*

Then Job introduces reasons that the judgment of God is utterly dissimilar to the judgment of men, both on the part of the

5. Mk 14.33.
6. Ps 38.2–3.
7. Is 38.15.
8. Jer 12.1.
9. Jb 10.3.
10. Ps 85.2.
11. Gn 18.23.
12. Is 38.14.

one who judges and according to the order of the administration of justice.

And that is: [3] ***Can it be that it seems good to you,*** supply: you who are God, from whom nothing is hidden, and you who are the judge and the witness, ***to accuse*** [*me*] ***falsely,*** that is, to search by false pretenses for a reason for a verdict against me, as is the case among men before an unjust judge.

and, supply: in this way, ***to oppress me,*** unjustly, ***the work of your hands,*** that is, even though I am the work of your hands, as if to say: "No." Hos 5:[13] *Ephraim is suffering a false accusation, having been crushed by the verdict.* Is 52:[14] *The Assyrian falsely accused him without any cause.* For it belongs to a prevaricator to destroy without cause a work that someone has made. Gal 2:[15] *If I build up again the things that I have torn down, I set myself up as a prevaricator.*

and, supply: in this calumnious judgment, ***encourage the schemes of the wicked,*** that is to say, of wicked judges? Indeed, it is an abomination to imagine that God would make a false accusation and that wicked judges would be encouraged to make false accusations. Lv 19:[16] *You shall not make a false accusation against your neighbor, nor oppress him with violence.* Indeed, Job's intention is for his argument to deny the consequent. In other words, if God neither makes false accusations nor oppresses anyone with violence, then His judgment is unlike the unjust judgment of a human judge.

But because someone could say that God's judgment is similar to the judgment of a just human judge, Job introduces a second reason that it is not. And that is: [4] ***Can it be that you have eyes of flesh,*** which, to be sure, do not see many things and can be deceived; but God's eyes are by no means like this, so Job expects the answer: "No." Sir 23:[17] *The eyes of the Lord are far brighter than the sun, looking around and seeing all the ways of men.*

And Job explains this further, adding: ***or that as a man sees,***

13. Hos 5.11.
14. Is 52.4.
15. Gal 2.18.
16. Lv 19.13.
17. Sir 23.28.

that is, as a judge who investigates using torture, struggles with hypotheses, and gathers testimony from witnesses; and so supply: ***you also will see?*** as if to say: "No." 1 Sm 16:[18] *Nor do I judge in the way that man sees; for man sees things that are visible, but the Lord looks on the heart.* And Job wants to draw the inference that the judgment of God is also dissimilar to the judgment of a just human judge.

But because someone could say that the order of the divine administration of justice is similar to the order of the human administration of justice, although God as judge is dissimilar to a human judge, therefore in rebuttal Job introduces a third reason, adding: **[5]** ***Can it be that your days are like the days of man.*** "Days" here designates the illumination of those things on which a judgment should be pronounced, and the sense is: "Can it be that by such an illumination as characterizes a human judge you examine the things on which a judgment should be pronounced, such that they become known to you in the same way as to a human judge?" as if he were saying: "No." 1 Cor 4:[19] *Do not pronounce judgment before the time, until the Lord comes, who will shed light on the things hidden in darkness and will reveal the purposes of human hearts.*

And explaining this further, he adds: ***and your years like human time,*** as if he were saying: "No." Ps:[20] *You are always the same, and your years will not come to an end.* Hence it is said in Mi 5:[21] *His going forth is from the beginning, from the days of eternity.* But if the years of God are distinguished, such that they may be called "years" *ad extra* in the plural, they are distinguished only to mark the time whose surpassing measure is eternity; and in this way He who never dies with the passage of time lives for many years.

[6] ***such that,*** supply: according to human order, ***you search for my iniquity,*** which I have committed against my neighbor, ***and probe into,*** according to the order of the human administration of justice, ***my sin,*** which I have committed against my-

18. 1 Sm 16.7.
19. 1 Cor 4.5.
20. Ps 101.28.
21. Mi 5.2.

self or against you? [7] ***And,*** supply: in this way, ***you know that I have done nothing wicked***, such that you might in this way release me from judgment, as if he were saying: "No." For it is said in Dn 7[22] that *the Ancient of Days sat in judgment, and the books were opened.* But the books are the brightness of your foreknowledge, and thus nothing is hidden from you. It is not necessary for you to investigate in a human way, ***although there is no one*** with human purposefulness and strength ***who is able to deliver*** [***me***], either by deceiving or defeating you, ***out of your hand,*** that is, from your power of judgment. Dt 32:[23] *There is no one who is able to deliver out of my hand.* Jn 10:[24] *No one will snatch them out of my hand.* [And:][25] *I and the Father are one.* 2 Mc 6:[26] *I will not escape the hand of the Almighty, either alive or dead.* Heb 4:[27] *All things are naked to His eyes, to whom we must give an account.* In such a way, then, the judgment of God is dissimilar to the judgments of men.

[8] ***Your hands.***

Here Job demonstrates that human weakness does not withstand (*sustinet*) the rectitude of unchangeable justice. And he demonstrates this in a twofold way: namely from the matter (*materia*) that is subject to the Maker; and from the Maker's manner of working, in this place:[28] *Have you not poured me out like milk?*

In the first part Job introduces the work of the Maker as regards the matter. And that is: ***Your hands,*** as opposed to another's. Ps:[29] *Your hands have made me and fashioned me.* And therefore it follows: ***have made me and fashioned* (plasmaverunt) *every part of me all around.*** "To fashion" (*plasmare*) is to form. Is 41:[30] *As a potter* (plastes) *treads clay.* Moreover, that he says "every part of me all around" denotes the aptitude of his limbs, which can

22. Dn 7.9–10.
23. Dt 32.39.
24. Jn 10.28.
25. Jn 10.30.
26. 2 Mc 6.26.
27. Heb 4.13.
28. Jb 10.10.
29. Ps 118.73.
30. Is 41.25.

be made only by the wisdom of God. For the symmetry of his limbs indicates his aptitude for justice, the combination of vital organs indicates his aptitude for temperance, the strength of his body his aptitude for fortitude, and the liveliness and perspicuity of the senses his aptitude for prudence. Sir 17:[31] *God created man from the earth and made him according to His own image, and He clothed him with strength according to Himself.*

and do you suddenly cast me down in this way? that is, while still deliberating, as if to say: "No." For you do not suddenly cast down one whom you have set up with such care; but, in fact, you have a reason in your justice, which is unknown to us. Ps:[32] *He who has formed their hearts one by one, and who understands all their works.* Sir 33:[33] *As the potter's clay is in his hands, to fashion and order it, so all the ways of man are according to God's ordination; man is in the hands of the one who made him, and He will render to him according to His judgment.*

Then Job introduces the worthlessness of the matter: **[9]** ***Remember, I beg you, that you have made me like clay,*** that is, from the earth tempered by moisture. Gn 2:[34] *Then God formed man from the mud of the earth.* ***and you will turn me into dust again,*** namely through death and decaying. Gn 3:[35] *You are dust, and to dust you will return.* Sir 17:[36] *God created man from the earth and He turned him into it again.*

And, concerning the manner of God's making him, Job adds: **[10]** ***Have you not poured me out like milk,*** for seed (*semen*), since it is what remains after the fourth digestion, is at first like milk, and it is poured out through the force of the generative power from all the bodily members.[37]

and curdled me like cheese? For when a drop of the man is

31. Sir 17.1–2.
32. Ps 32.15.
33. Sir 33.13–14.
34. Gn 2.7.
35. Gn 3.19.
36. Sir 17.1–2.
37. See Albert, *QQ. AL* I q. 13, where he explains: "But sperm is warm and moist, and before coitus it descends as if drop by drop through the animal's members and comes to the testicles" (FOTC MC 36, trans. Resnick and Kitchell, p. 36).

joined to a drop of the woman, it enters into it like a vapor, as the spirit enters into the body, and it seizes it with formative power, and it coagulates, just as milk coagulates when a coagulant enters it in the manner of a vapor, as Aristotle says in Book XVI of *On Animals.*[38] Hence Lam 4,[39] where the letter of our text reads: *Her Nazarites were purer than snow, whiter than milk.* The Septuagint reads: *They were curdled like milk.*[40]

[11] ***With skin,*** the third task of the sperm in the drop of the woman is to draw the skin around, so that the spirit might not evaporate; but, moving through every part, the spirit works by going around and pulsating with life. Eccl 1:[41] *Moving through all things, the spirit continues by going around, and it returns according to its cycle.*

and flesh you have clothed me. The fourth task is to diffuse sensation into the flesh that the formative power has drawn together. Wis 7:[42] *In my mother's womb I was fashioned as flesh; in ten months' time I was curdled into blood, from the seed of man.*

[and] with bones and muscles you have bound me together. The fifth task is differentiation, namely of the dissimilar members in which the strength of the body consists. 2 Mc 7:[43] *I myself have not bound together the limbs of each one of you, but rather the Creator of the world, who has fashioned the beginning of each human, has done so.*

And what Job has said about the body, he applies to the soul: **[12]** ***You have granted me life,*** that is, a soul, which is the principle of life. Gn 2:[44] *He breathed into his face the breath of life.* ***and mercy,*** that is, by your mercy you have granted me preservation, so that what you have made would not perish, of course. Lam 3:[45] *The mercies of the Lord, that we have not been destroyed, be-*

38. Aristotle, *GA* 1.20. Cf. Albert, *AL* 16.1.13. Albert seems to have Book 16 of his own work on animals in mind, where he treats this teaching of Aristotle.

39. Lam 4.7.

40. Cf. Origen, *In Lam* 4.7 (PG 16:2294, 2296).

41. Eccl 1.6.

42. Wis 7.1–2.

43. 2 Mc 7.22–23.

44. Gn 2.7.

45. Lam 3.22.

cause His compassion has not failed. ***and your visitation*** **(visitatio)**, that is, your constant vision (*visio*) [of me] through the influx of your kindnesses and graces among the benefits of life. ***has preserved my spirit,*** supply: so that it might not expire. Wis 7:[46] *I was nursed with benefits, and with great care.* Ps:[47] *Visit us with your salvation, that we might see the goodness of your elect.*

Through all these things Job intends to show that man, a fragile vessel, does not withstand (*sustinet*) the rule of unchangeable justice, but rather, as Aristotle says in Book V of the *Ethics* with regard to the governing of human affairs, it is necessary that he use the rule for building employed on Lesbos.[48] For Lesbos is where no stone can be hewn according to a straight edge, so the residents, lest they be without buildings, construct a lead ruler so that, when a stone is not hewn according to the ruler, the ruler is bent to the stone, and, if the curvature is not too great, the stone is kept (*sustineatur*). So it is in human affairs that the laws governing human life must be relaxed according to the weakness of man and must tolerate what has not been distorted too much. Ps:[49] *You shall rule them with an iron rod, and you shall break them into pieces like a potter's vessel.* And that is: If you try to reduce human affairs to iron and to the strict rule of inflexible justice, they will be broken into pieces like a clay vessel.

[13] ***Although you conceal these things.***

Here Job shows that, although it may be hidden, nevertheless no aspect of human affairs escapes God's providence. In the first place he shows this. Secondly, as if returning to his proposition, he shows that life is loathsome and nothing in it ought to be desired, in this place:[50] *Why have you brought me forth from the womb?*

In the first part there are two points, namely: that no aspect of human affairs escapes God's providence; and that the penitent, the wicked, and the just all suffer the evils of Satan in this

46. Wis 7.4.
47. Ps 105.4–5.
48. See Aristotle, *EN* 5.10.7.
49. Ps 2.9.
50. Jb 10.18.

life, and therefore human life is not governed according to the order of human justice, in this place:[51] *If I have sinned.*

And that is: ***Although you conceal these things in your heart,*** for by overlooking them He seems to conceal them, as if He does not care. Indeed, in this it seems that He does not look closely at human deeds. On account of this it is said in the Ps:[52] *They have said: The Lord will not see; nor will the God of Jacob understand.* And again:[53] *Why has the wicked man provoked God? For he has said in his heart: He will not seek to know it.*

nevertheless I know, namely by the illumination of faith, ***that you remember all things,*** that is to say, of human concern. At the end of Jb:[54] *I know that you can do all things, and that no thought is hidden from you.* Jb 23:[55] *He knows my way, and He will test me like gold that passes through the fire.* But Job's statement that the Lord "remembers" is anthropomorphic (*anthropopathos*).[56] For this reason it is said that no past events have escaped His notice. And Job adds that, if life were governed according to human justice, one who is repentant ought to be spared even if he sins.

And that is: **[14]** ***If I have sinned,*** because no one is without sin. 1 Kgs 8:[57] *There is no man who does not sin.* ***and you have spared me,*** namely by overlooking sins, so that you would not scourge me, ***for an hour.*** Wis 11:[58] *Overlooking the sins of men for the sake of repentance.* ***why do you not permit me,*** after being whipped and corrected, ***to be clean,*** that is, to be cleansed, ***from my iniquity?*** so that you can take away these scourges, which, according to the order of human justice, are ill-deserved for anyone who has already been corrected. Dt 25:[59] *The measure of the blows will be according to the measure of the offense.* Ps:[60] *I will*

51. Jb 10.14.
52. Ps 93.7.
53. Ps 10.13.
54. Jb 42.2.
55. Jb 23.10.
56. Cf. the commentary on Jb 2.3 (where God says to Satan, "But you have provoked me"), where Albert also uses this word.
57. 1 Kgs 8.46.
58. Wis 11.24.
59. Dt 25.2.
60. Ps 88.33–34.

visit their iniquities with a rod and their sins with blows. But I will not take my mercy away from him. Since, therefore, you strike someone who has been freed from faults, it is clear that in your governing you do not keep to the order of human justice.

And Job likewise shows this with regard to the wicked man, adding: **[15]** ***And if I am wicked, woe to me,*** not escaping the punishments of Satan. Is 3:[61] *Woe to the wicked man in the midst of evil! The recompense of his hands will be given to him.*

Then he applies this even to the just: ***and if,*** supply: I am, ***just, I will not lift up my head,*** but rather I will hang it according to the evils that I suffer. Is 1:[62] *The whole head is weak, and the whole heart is mournful.* ***being filled with affliction,*** of the body, ***and misery,*** in the loss of property. Lam 3:[63] *He will give his cheek to the one who strikes him; he will be filled with reproaches.*

[16] ***And,*** supply: thus, if I am wicked, ***on account of pride,*** namely by which I condemn you and your commandments, ***you will seize me like a lioness.*** Blessed Gregory here describes the method of capturing lionesses,[64] explaining that a cage, built and fortified with very strong bars, is, to escape notice, placed against a side wall of a deep pit, out of which the lioness is not able to leap. Seeking prey that has been placed above the pit, the lioness falls into it, and, with the hunter harassing her from above with strokes and spears, she is forced to squeeze herself into the cage; and when the lioness has been confined within the bars in this way, the cage is lifted up. And with this analogy Job wishes to assert that he has been harassed and confined by the filth of illness and the strokes of misfortune. Jb 15:[65] *The wicked man is proud all his days, and the number of the years of his tyranny is uncertain. The sound of terror is always in his ears.*

and having returned, supply: if I am repentant, ***you torment me extraordinarily.*** For extraordinary are the scourges that are inflicted on someone who has already been freed from faults. But that he says "having returned" indicates the repetition of

61. Is 3.11.
62. Is 1.5.
63. Lam 3.30.
64. Gregory, *Mor.* 9.57.86.
65. Jb 15.20–21.

scourging that often happens. Lam 3:[66] *He has turned His hand against me alone, again and again, all day long.* Is 14:[67] *I will sweep her away, wearing her out with a broom, says the Lord of hosts.* Supply: and if I am just, **[17]** ***You establish witnesses against me,*** that is, you strengthen them. Indeed, on account of your punishments they are strengthened to say that I was stricken because of sin. There is a parallel in Acts, at the end,[68] where a viper clung to Paul's hand when he had come out of the sea, and the natives said: *This man is certainly a murderer; although he has escaped from the sea, divine vengeance does not allow him to live.*

And this is what follows: ***and you multiply your wrath,*** that is, you show it in many different ways by inflicting punishment. Lam 2:[69] *The Lord has become an enemy.* And Job explains this, adding: ***and punishments war upon me,*** that is, against me. Jb 6:[70] *His punishments war against me, the anger of which drinks up my spirit.*

[18] ***Why have you brought me forth from the womb?***

This is the second part, in which Job returns to the proposition that he first articulated:[71] *Let the day on which I was born perish.* And he makes this clear from the misery of life and from the most miserable fate of the deceased. From the misery of life he shows this in a twofold way, namely from its penal character and from its brevity.

And that is: ***Why have you brought me forth from the womb?*** Jb 3:[72] *Why did I not die in the womb?* ***if only I had been destroyed,*** that is to say, at the beginning of this life, ***so that no eye,*** namely, of my friends, who are disturbed in my presence, ***would have seen me.*** Jer 20:[73] *So that my mother might have become my grave and her womb an everlasting conception!*

[19] ***I should have been as though I had not existed.*** Wis 5:[74] *We,*

66. Lam 3.3.
67. Is 14.23.
68. Acts 28.4.
69. Lam 2.5.
70. Jb 6.4.
71. Jb 3.3.
72. Jb 3.11.
73. Jer 20.17.
74. Wis 5.13.

having been born, immediately ceased to exist. ***carried from the womb to the tomb.*** Jer 20:[75] *Why have I come out of the womb, in order to see hardship and suffering?*[76]

Then, concerning the brevity of life, he adds: **[20]** ***Can it be that the paucity of my days,*** for few are the days during which man lives. Gn 47:[77] *The days of the pilgrimage of my life are few and evil.* ***will not be brought to an end shortly?*** Jb 14:[78] *Man, having been born of woman, living for a short time.* By reason of these things Job concludes that life is miserable and brief.

Allow me to go, then, permitting me to rest a little, ***so that I might lament my suffering a little,*** in order that I might not be carried immediately from one punishment to another. Jer 6:[79] *Make lamentation as for an only child, bitter mourning.* Mt 5:[80] *Blessed are those who mourn, for they will be comforted.*

[21] ***before I go,*** namely by the passing away of death, ***and do not return,*** to this life, for there will be no coming back again after death. Hence in the Ps[81] it is said: *Man, a breeze blowing by and not returning.* Jb 16:[82] *Behold, the years are brief, and I am walking a path by which I will not return.*

to the land that is dark, namely to hell, to which at that time[83] all were descending, which is said to be dark on account of the absence of two kinds of light: both corporeal and spiritual. Jb 17:[84] *Into the deepest hell all that I have will descend.* Ps:[85] *He has established me in darkness, just as the dead of old. My spirit is in agony within me.*

and covered with the gloom of death, that is, with the gloom that death induces. Is 13:[86] *Their countenances will be as faces*

75. Jer 20.18.

76. Cf. the commentary on Jb 3.10 above, where Albert quotes this passage, though differently, reversing the two nouns in the final phrase.

77. Gn 47.9.

78. Jb 14.1.

79. Jer 6.26.

80. Mt 5.5.

81. Ps 77.39.

82. Jb 16.23.

83. Namely, before the advent of Christ.

84. Jb 17.16.

85. Ps 142.3–4.

86. Is 13.8.

burned up. Lam 4:[87] *Their faces have been made blacker than charcoal.*

[22] ***the land of misery,*** in the absence of every good thing, where that rich man begged for a drop of water but did not manage to get it, according to Lk 16,[88] ***and darkness,*** lacking both kinds of light. Jer 13:[89] *Give glory to the Lord before you stumble on the foggy mountains.* ***where the shadow of death.*** He calls images occurring to those who are fearful in darkness "shadows." Wis 17:[90] *Gloomy faces that appeared to them frightened them.* And, concerning the cause, it adds:[91] *For a troubled conscience always foretells grievous things.* ***and no order,*** because not even the elemental qualities maintain their own order there. Hence Gregory: "The flame, which here burns and illuminates, there burns and darkens."[92] Ps:[93] *The voice of the Lord dividing the flame of fire.* Basil says about this verse that although fire's power to burn is sent out to those below, its power to illuminate is sent out to those above.[94]

but everlasting horror dwells. Gregory: Fear is of a future evil. When someone is already suffering that evil, fear of it disappears; but in hell, fear causes agony even during the torments themselves.[95] Is 21:[96] *I shuddered when I heard it; I was disturbed when I saw it. My heart failed. Darkness struck me with amazement.*

87. Lam 4.8.
88. Lk 16.22–26.
89. Jer 13.16.
90. Wis 17.4.
91. Wis 17.10.
92. Gregory, *Mor.* 9.66.100.
93. Ps 28.7.
94. Basil, *Hom.* 6.3 (*In Hexaemeron*; PG 29:121).
95. Gregory, *Mor.* 9.66.100.
96. Is 21.3–4.

CHAPTER 11

BUT ***RESPONDING, Zophar the Naamathite.***

The position of Zophar should be recalled[1] to mind: indeed, it was that providence is the governing of all of human life according to the depths of the wisdom of the divine will, no cause of which ought to be sought because it is, after all, profound wisdom. The law to which man is obliged is complex, and he often sins against it. On this basis Zophar builds his entire argument that Job cannot be innocent.

Now this chapter is divided into two parts. In the first, Zophar extols greatly the wisdom and the manifold laws of God; in the second, he shows that blessed Job has sinned against them, in this place:[2] *A vain man is roused toward pride.*

The first part is subdivided into two. In the first subdivision, he rebukes his fellow disputant; in the second, he sets forth his position and disputes concerning it, in this place:[3] *For you have said.*

And that is: ***But responding, Zophar the Naamathite.*** "Zophar" means the "scattering of speculation" or "scattering the speculator (*speculatorem*)," [and he was so called] on account of the fact that he was so perspicacious that he could put to flight every investigator (*speculatorem*) of learned studies and of science.[4] "Naamathite" means "beautiful," for Zophar was beautiful in

1. Here I read *revocetur* with MSS EFM, rather than *reducetur* with Weiss's edition. See the commentary on 3.1 above, where Albert briefly summarizes Zophar's position.

2. Jb 11.12.

3. Jb 11.4.

4. The Latin word *speculator* means a watchman, spy, scout, explorer, or investigator, and is, of course, related to *specula*, which means both a lookout or watchtower and slight hope or a glimmer of hope. So here, for Albert, the

eloquence. Ti 1:[5] *Embracing the word that is trustworthy in accordance with teaching, so that he may be able to exhort in sound doctrine and to convince those who contradict it.* ***said:*** **[2]** ***Can it be that one who says many things.*** One who "says many things" in disputation is he who says impertinent things and neither confines his propositions to a single syllogistic form nor orders them to one conclusion. Indeed, this is an error (*peccatum*) in disputing questions, as Aristotle says in the second book of *Topics*,[6] and a transgression of the established terminology. Jas 1:[7] *Let every man be quick to listen, but slow to speak.* Prv 14:[8] *Where there are many words, there is often poverty* in works. ***will not,*** that is, will he not, ***also listen?*** as if to say he should. Sir 13:[9] *Do not believe his many words, and do not refrain from speaking with him as an equal.* Indeed, one who disputes must listen to his fellow disputant and [he must] both receive and offer words.

Or will a verbose man be justified? as if to say: "No." Jas 3:[10] *All of us make many mistakes; but anyone who does not make a mistake in speech is a perfect man.*

Then Zophar sets forth another reproach: **[3]** ***Will men refrain from speaking to you alone,*** as if to say: "No." 1 Cor 14:[11] *But if something is revealed to another person sitting [nearby], let the first person be silent. For all of you can prophesy one at a time.*

and when you have mocked others. For rhetorical disputations are characterized by the mocking of one's opponent. Prv 3:[12] *He will mock the mockers.*

will you be refuted by no one? as if to say: "On the contrary, you will be refuted by me, to be sure, I who am able to do this." Is 33:[13] *Woe to you who scorn; will you yourself not also be scorned?*

---

speculator is one who investigates or devotes himself to "speculation" in learned studies or the sciences and thereby hopes to arrive at truth.

5. Ti 1.9.
6. Aristotle, *Top.* 2.1.
7. Jas 1.19.
8. Prv 14.23.
9. Sir 13.14.
10. Jas 3.2.
11. 1 Cor 14.30–31.
12. Prv 3.34.
13. Is 33.1.

And after a few words:[14] *When you have grown weary and stopped despising, you will be despised.*

Then Zophar adds Job's position in order to argue against it. And that is: [4] ***For you have said: My speech is pure,*** that is, without pretense and falsehood. But he said it above in 6[15] in another way: *You will not find iniquity on my tongue, nor in my throat will stupidity resound.*

and, in other words, ***I am clean in your sight,*** supply: O Lord. This is what he understood him to have said when, in 6[16] above, he declared: *If only my sins were weighed, etc.* Is 53:[17] *He has not sinned, neither has deceit been found in his mouth.*

And Zophar makes clear the disposition that he has toward the divine dignity and toward justice. **[5]** ***And, indeed, if only God would speak with you,*** namely by disputing and refuting you, because you could not withstand Him. Ex 20:[18] *You speak to us, but may the Lord not speak to us, lest perhaps we die.* ***and open His lips to you,*** that is to say, so that He might speak directly, not through enigmas or figures. Heb 1:[19] *In many and various ways God formerly spoke to the fathers by the prophets.* **[6]** ***so that He would show you the secrets of wisdom,*** that is, the wisdom by which He knows all hidden things. Ps:[20] *You have made known to me the uncertain and hidden things of your wisdom.* ***and,*** supply: would reveal to you ***that His law,*** namely by which He rules and regulates the actions of men, ***is manifold.*** Hos 8:[21] *I will write to them my manifold laws, which have been regarded as strange,* as if it were saying: "Manifold are the laws, but they [the laws] have been abandoned by them."

and, supply: after He shows to you your transgression of His laws in such a way, ***you would understand that He exacts much less of you,*** supply: with regard to punishments, ***than your iniquity***

14. Is 33.1.
15. Jb 6.30.
16. Jb 6.2.
17. Is 53.9.
18. Ex 20.19.
19. Heb 1.1.
20. Ps 50.8.
21. Hos 8.12.

deserves. What Elihu says is similar. Jb 34:[22] *My father, may Job be tried all the way to the end; may you not desist from the man of iniquity, because he has added blasphemy to his sins*; and Jb 33:[23] *He will look at men, and he will say: I have sinned, and indeed I have failed, and I have not received what I deserved.* On account of this it is said in the Ps:[24] *Lord, do not deal with us according to our sins, or repay us according to our iniquity.*

Then, concerning the incomprehensibility of God and of all divine things, he adds: [7] ***Will you perhaps comprehend the steps of God***, as if to say: "No." For something is comprehended, as Augustine says in the book *On Seeing God*,[25] when the whole of it is hemmed in by the knower and no part of it remains hidden from him. But God is known in this way by no one. Ps:[26] *Your steps shall not be known.*

From here he explains what he has said, adding: ***and***, in other words, ***can you get to know the Almighty perfectly?*** as if to say: "No." For no one can get to know Him in this way because He is infinite, both infinitely powerful and infinitely wise. Jb 9:[27] *If He should come to me, I will not see Him; if He should depart, I will not understand.* [8] ***He is higher than heaven***. 1 Kgs 8:[28] *Heaven and the heavens of heavens do not contain you.* Gregory: "He is higher than heaven because He transcends all things in the encircling of His spirit."[29] ***and what will you do?*** you who are, of course, weak and mortal? Wis 9:[30] *The body, which is corruptible, weighs down the soul, and the earthly dwelling burdens the mind that ponders many things.* ***He is deeper than hell.*** Sir 1:[31] *The depth of the abyss, who will discover it?* Gregory: "Deeper than hell because by transcending the lowest things, He conveys all things upward."[32]

22. Jb 34.36–37.
23. Jb 33.27.
24. Ps 102.10.
25. Augustine, *vid. Deo* 3.
26. Ps 76.20.
27. Jb 9.11.
28. 1 Kgs 8.27.
29. Gregory, *Mor.* 10.9.14.
30. Wis 9.15.
31. Sir 1.2–3.
32. Gregory, *Mor.* 10.9.14.

Heb 1:[33] *Carrying all things by the word of His power.* ***and so how will you know?*** as if he were saying: "You will not be able to." Wis 9:[34] *The thoughts of mortals are timid, and our foresight uncertain.*

[9] ***His measure is longer than the earth.*** Gregory: "Longer than the earth because He exceeds the measure of creation by means of the everlasting nature of eternity."[35] Is 40:[36] *Behold, the nations are like a drop in a bucket, and they are counted like dust on the scales.* Hence a little earlier[37] it says: *Who has weighed out the huge mass of the earth with three fingers?* ***and wider than the sea.*** Gregory: "Because He takes hold of flowing, temporal things and confines them within the presence of His power."[38] Is 40:[39] *Who has measured the waters in His hand?* His height, then, is in His encircling all things, His depth in His conveying all things upward, His length in the immeasurability of eternity, and His width in His embracing transitory things and drawing them together.

And, therefore, because He is so great: **[10]** ***If He should overturn all things,*** that is, reduce them to nothing, ***or compress them into one,*** just as they existed in a single chaos or mixture at the beginning, ***who will speak against Him?*** Wis 12:[40] *Who will accuse you if the nations, which you have made, should perish?* ***Or who will be able to say to Him: Why do you do this?*** Rom 9:[41] *O man, who are you to argue with God?*

Zophar adds that God does not, however, judge unjustly: **[11]** ***For He knows the vanity***[42] ***of men,*** as has been maintained in what has gone before. What is useful for nothing and to no end is vain. Wis 4:[43] *Their fruit is useless, sour to eat, and suitable for*

33. Heb 1.3.
34. Wis 9.14.
35. Gregory, *Mor.* 10.9.14.
36. Is 40.15.
37. Is 40.12.
38. Gregory, *Mor.* 10.9.14.
39. Is 40.12.
40. Wis 12.12.
41. Rom 9.20.
42. Most MSS have "character" here in place of "vanity."
43. Wis 4.5.

nothing. Ps:[44] *The Lord knows the thoughts of men, that they are vain.* ***and when He sees iniquity,*** namely the iniquity of men, which cannot escape His notice, ***does He not consider it?*** supply: with a view to judgment and retribution, as if to say: "Yes." Wis 12:[45] *Since you are just, you order all things justly. You, O Father, consider it alien to your power to condemn him who does not deserve to be punished. For your power is the beginning of justice.*

[12] ***A vain man.***

Here Zophar touches on the fact that Job was not judged unjustly, and it has two parts. In the first, he makes clear Job's sin; in the second, he urges repentance and notes that through it Job can rise again, in this place:[46] *If iniquity.*

In the first part there are two things: namely a general proposition and an adaption. And that is: ***A vain man,*** that is to say, one not devoted to useful pursuits or works, ***is roused toward pride,*** for—having forgotten himself on account of vanity, unaware of his own weakness, and going beyond his own rank—he is praised above others. Wis 13:[47] *All men in whom there is not the knowledge of God are vain.* Ps:[48] *Why do you love vanity and strive for deceit?*

and as if the colt of a wild ass, which is an ass inhabiting the countryside or woodlands, that is to say, one that roams around as it wishes with no master restraining it, ***he thinks that he was born free,*** that is, born for freedom, so that he could not be restrained by any rein of the law or of justice. Jer 2:[49] *A wild ass, accustomed to being alone in the wilderness, in the desire of its soul drew in the wind of the love of itself.*

Then Zophar adapts this to Job, saying: **[13]** ***But you have strengthened,*** that is, you have hardened, ***your heart.*** Jer 7:[50] *They have hardened their necks, and they have done worse than their fathers.*

and, with this supply: because you have hardened your heart

44. Ps 93.11.
45. Wis 12.15–16.
46. Jb 11.14.
47. Wis 13.1.
48. Ps 4.3.
49. Jer 2.24.
50. Jer 7.26.

in this way, ***you have spread out your hands toward God,*** as if you were innocent. Is 1:[51] *When you stretch out your hands, I will turn my eyes away, for your hands are full of blood.*[52]

[14] ***If the iniquity.***

Zophar teaches the true manner of repenting and returning to God, and he specifies two things: namely true repentance; and the fruit of true repentance, in this place:[53] *Then you will be able to lift up.*

And that is: ***If the iniquity, which is in your hand,*** that is, in your works, and the iniquity is said to be the unfairness he showed to his neighbor, ***is removed from yourself,*** namely through repentance. At the end of Hos:[54] *Remove all iniquity, and receive the good.* Jer 15:[55] *If you will separate the precious from the worthless, you will be as my mouth.*

and if injustice, that is, something acquired unjustly that you do not return, ***will not remain in your tent.*** Supply: Tb 2:[56] *Be careful; it might be stolen, so return it to its owner, because it is not lawful for us either to eat or to touch something stolen.* Is 1:[57] *Cease acting perversely, learn to do well.*

Then he describes the fruit of repentance: at first in general, and secondly in particular. And that is: **[15]** ***Then you will be able to lift up your face,*** that is, the intention of your soul, ***without blemish,*** namely the blemish of sin. Eph 5:[58] *Not having a blemish or wrinkle, or anything of this sort.* Song 4:[59] *You are altogether beautiful, my love, and there is not a blemish on you.* And lifting up one's

51. Is 1.15.

52. Here Albert, doubtless working from memory, provides an abbreviated version of this verse, which in the Vulg. reads: *Et cum extenderitis manus vestras, avertam oculos meos a vobis, et cum multiplicaveritis orationem, non exaudiam: manus enim vestrae sanguine plenae sunt.* Such abbreviation may have been intentional on Albert's part, of course: he could have assumed, for example, that the "from you" in the second phrase and the "and when you repeat [your] prayer, I will not hear" that follows would have been redundant or unnecessary here.

53. Jb 11.15.

54. Hos 14.3.

55. Jer 15.19.

56. Tb 2.21.

57. Is 1.16–17.

58. Eph 5.27.

59. Song 4.7.

face is the raising of the mind in prayer. Is 58:[60] *Then you will call, and the Lord will hear; you will cry out, and He will say: Behold, I am here.*

and you will be steadfast, that is, firm in the good, ***and you will not fear*** evil, of course. Ex 14:[61] *Only stand confidently, and the Lord will fight for you against them.* 2 Chr 20:[62] *Do not fear, nor tremble before them. Tomorrow you will go out against them, and the Lord will be with you.* Ps:[63] *The Lord is my helper; I will not fear what man might do to me.*

Then Zophar adds the effects of repentance in particular: three before death and three after death. And that is: **[16]** ***Likewise you will forget misery,*** supply: of the present circumstances, that is to say, your memories will not be bothersome to you. Ps:[64] *According to the multitude of my sorrows in my heart, your consolations have delighted my soul.*

Then he adds the manner of this effect: ***and just like waters,*** supply: of expiation, ***that have passed by,*** that is, after they have passed by, ***you will*** not ***remember it,*** that is, you will have expiation, not affliction, from your present tribulations. Ps:[65] *You have led us out through fire and water, and you have brought us into a place of refreshment.* Gregory brings in this passage from Prv 12:[66] *Whatever befalls the just man will not make him sad*; and this one from Prv 28:[67] *The just man, bold as a lion, will be without fear.*[68]

Then Zophar adds the second fruit, which concerns the obtaining of light: **[17]** ***And brightness like that of midday,*** supply: which shines with its own power and fills everything with light, ***will arise for you,*** that is, for your advantage, ***at evening,*** that is to

60. Is 58.9.

61. Ex 14.25. Only the second half of Albert's quotation here is taken from Ex 14.25; the first (*Tantummodo confidenter state*), however, is from 2 Chr 20.17.

62. 2 Chr 20.17.

63. Ps 117.6.

64. Ps 93.19.

65. Ps 65.12.

66. Prv 12.21.

67. Prv 28.1.

68. Gregory, *Mor.* 10.21.39.

say, for you as you decline in your old age. Is 58:[69] *He will fill your soul with brightness and liberate your bones.*

Then he adds the third effect: ***and when you will have supposed that you have been consumed,*** that is, growing weak in every power, ***you will rise as the morning star,*** which, although it shines on its own, nevertheless is the herald of the perfect light. Prv 4:[70] *The path of the just* [*is*] *as a light shining brightly and growing into perfect day.* Is 58:[71] *Your light will arise, and your darkness will be as midday.*

Then he adds the fourth [effect]: **[18]** ***And you will have confidence,*** that is to say, assurance of heart, ***with hope*** of divine mercy and liberality ***having been set before you.*** Heb 6:[72] *We have the strongest source of consolation, we who have fled for refuge to seize the hope set before us.*

Then, concerning the fruit of repentance after death,[73] he adds: ***and having been exhumed*** **(effossus)**,[74] supply: from the grave, ***you will sleep untroubled,*** namely in the repose of the saints. Acts 7:[75] *He fell asleep in the Lord.* Ps:[76] *In peace I will sleep perfectly, and I will rest.* Jn 11:[77] *If he is asleep, he will be well.*

[19] ***You will rest,*** namely in the good things of God. Rv 14:[78]

69. Is 58.11.
70. Prv 4.18.
71. Is 58.10.
72. Heb 6.18.
73. Above, immediately prior to v. 16, Albert noted that Zophar will proceed to outline six particular effects of repentance, three before death and three after. Although the fourth effect is hope (see on v. 18 above), which may be understood as applying (or at least pointing) to the afterlife, it is not until he comes to this fifth effect that Albert explicitly identifies it as post-mortem in nature.
74. Significantly, whereas the Vulg. here reads *defossus* ("having been buried"), Albert has the sacred text read *effosus* ("having been exhumed" or "having been dug up"), the effect of which is to Christianize the text. That is, for Albert's Zophar, it is only after the body of the deceased has been "exhumed" or "dug up" in the resurrection that he or she "will sleep untroubled" in the everlasting repose of the saints.
75. Acts 7.59.
76. Ps 4.9.
77. Jn 11.12.
78. Rv 14.13.

From now on, says the Spirit, they will rest from their labors. Is 58:[79] *The Lord, your God, will give you rest continually.* ***and there will be no one to make you afraid.*** Rv 21:[80] *Now there will be no more mourning or crying.* ***and many will seek your face,*** that is to say, the face of an intercessor for others. Ps:[81] *All the rich among the people will seek your face.* The brothers of Joseph sought his face in this way in Gn 45.

And Zophar makes this clear with reference to the opposite, adding: **[20]** ***But the eyes of the wicked will fail,*** because they will never be heard. Is 38:[82] *My eyes are weakened, looking upward.* ***and the way of escape,*** that is, by which they might be able to flee, ***will be lost to them.*** 2 Mc 6:[83] *Dead or alive, I will not escape the hand of the Almighty.* ***and their hope,*** that is, those things for which they had hoped, ***the loathing of the soul,*** that is, they make the soul loathsome. Wis 5:[84] *The hope of the wicked is as down, which is blown away by the wind.*

79. Is 58.11.
80. Rv 21.4.
81. Ps 44.13.
82. Is 38.14.
83. 2 Mc 6.26.
84. Wis 5.15.

CHAPTER 12

B*UT RESPONDING, Job said.*

This response of blessed Job is divided into two parts.[1] In the first of these he rebukes the one who is disputing badly; in the second he returns to the demonstration of his proposed intention, around the middle of chapter 13 at this place:[2] *Hear my word and understand the enigmas.*

The first part is subdivided into two. In the first subdivision he argues that they dispute in an undisciplined way; in the second he admonishes them so that they might receive correction, after the beginning of chapter 13, in this place:[3] *Therefore, hear my corrections.*

The first subdivision is divided again into two sections. In the first of these he shows that his fellow disputants are undisciplined and the things they say are trivial; in the second he shows that their words are also perverse, in chapter 13 at this place:[4] *Behold all things.*

In the first of these sections there are three points. For he shows that they are arrogant and insulting. Second, by using a counterexample, he shows that they were mistaken, in this place:[5] *For the simplicity of the just man is mocked.* Third, he shows that in their speech they were trivial and were setting forth commonplaces, in this place:[6] *Without a doubt.*

And that is: ***But responding, Job said.*** Is 38:[7] *Lord, I suffer vi-*

1. Job's entire response constitutes chapters 12–14.
2. Jb 13.17.
3. Jb 13.6.
4. Jb 13.1.
5. Jb 12.4.
6. Jb 12.7.
7. Is 38.14.

olence; respond for me. [2] ***Therefore, you alone are men,*** that is, in your opinion, the only ones having understanding of the truth. Aristotle, *Ethics,* Book X, [says that] man alone has understanding.[8] Sir 17:[9] *He gave men a heart for thinking things through, and He filled them with the knowledge of understanding.* ***and,*** if this is true, ***would wisdom stay*** **(moretur)**, that is, remain, ***with you?*** He is asking a question: "Are you alone men such that wisdom remains with you?" Eccl 2:[10] *Wisdom also remained with me.* Or "will die" (*morietur*), as Gregory reads the text. For he speaks in this way: "Indeed, what other than this very thing—that wisdom will die with him—does the one who judges that he alone has understanding suppose?"[11] 1 Cor 1:[12] *I will destroy the wisdom of the wise, and I will reject the prudence of the prudent.*

Then he demonstrates that they understand nothing pertaining to the world, adding: [3] ***For who is ignorant of these things that you know?*** as if he were saying: "The things that you say are clear to the bleary-eyed and to barbers."[13] Jb 15:[14] *What do you know that we are ignorant of? Or what do you understand that we do not know?*

Hence he said beforehand: ***I too have a heart just as you do.***[15] The "heart" is understood here as teachable and capable of wisdom. 1 Kgs 3:[16] *Give to your servant a teachable heart, so that it can judge your people and discern between good and evil.* ***and I am not inferior to you,*** namely in wisdom. Eccl 1:[17] *I have become great, and in wisdom I have surpassed all who were before me.*

Then he adds that they are insulting: [4] ***He who is mocked by his friends,*** that is, he who is exposed to derision, ***as I am,***

8. *EN* 10.7 passim.
9. Sir 17.5.
10. Eccl 2.9.
11. Gregory, *Mor.* 10.25.44.
12. 1 Cor 1.19.
13. Cf. Horace, *Sat.* 1.7.3.
14. Jb 15.9.
15. These words constitute the first half of 12.3, whereas the question that Albert has just explicated—*For who is ignorant of these things that you know?*—comes from the second half of this verse.
16. 1 Kgs 3.9.
17. Eccl 1.16.

supply: by you. Lam 3:[18] *You have heard their reproach, Lord, all their deliberations against me.* Ps:[19] *You have made me a reproach to the fool.* ***will call upon God,*** in prayer, of course, ***and He will hear him.*** Ps:[20] *When I called upon Him, the God of my justice heard me.*

And he provides an example against their speech, first concerning good people and second concerning evil people: ***For the simplicity of the just man is mocked,*** that is, because he is simple in virtue but entangled in great misfortune. Prv 9:[21] *He who teaches a mocker does injury to himself.* Prv 14:[22] *A mocker seeks wisdom, but he does not find it.*

[5] ***A lamp despised,*** that is, the simplicity of the just man is a lamp despised. I say "lamp" on account of its transparent sexual purity, its piety—infused with oil, as it were—its fiery charity, and the luminous integrity of its manner of life. Song 8:[23] *Its lamps are lamps of fire and flames.* "Despised," I say, ***in the thoughts of the rich,*** who love darkness. Jn 3:[24] *Men loved darkness rather than the light.* ***is ready,*** that is, prepared, ***for the appointed time,*** namely appointed by God, when it is going to be revealed. Is 62:[25] *Until her just one comes forth as splendor, and her savior is lit like a lamp.*

Then he adds an example concerning evil people: **[6]** ***The tents of robbers,*** who both do violence and pillage the property of others, ***overflow.*** Jer 12:[26] *It goes well for all who transgress and act unjustly.* ***and audaciously,*** that is, impudently, ***they provoke God,*** supply: armed with the gifts of God against Him. Acts 7:[27] *With a stiff neck and untamable heart, you always resist the Holy Spirit.* Ps:[28] *Their iniquity has sprung forth, as if from corpulence.* ***whereas He Himself has given all things into their hands,*** supply: and so

18. Lam 3.61.
19. Ps 38.9.
20. Ps 4.2.
21. Prv 9.7.
22. Prv 14.6.
23. Song 8.6.
24. Jn 3.19.
25. Is 62.1.
26. Jer 12.1.
27. Acts 7.51.
28. Ps 72.7.

they were ungrateful for such great benefits. Sir 29:[29] *He who is of an ungrateful mind will forsake the one who liberated him.*

Then he continues by showing that their words were trivial and quite commonplace, and he says two things: namely, that their words were trivial; and that greater attention should be paid to his own words, in this place:[30] *Does not the ear discern words?*

In the first part, he says[31] three things: namely, that their words can be taught by any creature whatsoever, because none is ignorant of them; and he points out what they are. And that is: [7] ***Without a doubt,*** that is, certainly, ***ask the beasts of burden,*** that is, those who carry our burdens, ***and they will teach you,*** the same things you brag about, as if you were so wise. In the letter of Jude:[32] *The animal, accustomed to the yoke, rebuked the foolishness of the prophet.*

and supply: ask ***the birds of the air, and they will show you,*** namely the species, measure, and order according to which God has created them. Ps:[33] *The birds of the air and the fishes of the sea, which traverse the routes of the sea.*

[8] ***Speak to the earth,*** namely the place of generation and habitation, ***and it will answer you,*** concerning the power and wisdom of God, of course. Ps:[34] *You have made all things in wisdom; the earth is filled with your riches.* ***and the fishes of the sea will tell.*** *He is referring to everything ever born,* hence it is said of creatures in the Ps:[35] *Their sound has gone forth into all the earth, and their words to the ends of the world.*

Then he shows that they [that is, the words of his fellow disputants] are generally known, adding: [9] ***Who does not know,*** or: who can be ignorant, provided that he pays attention. Is 46:[36]

29. Sir 29.22.

30. Jb 12.11.

31. Here I read *dicit* with MSS ETFM, rather than *facit* with Weiss's edition.

32. Albert may have in mind Jude 10–11 here, but his words more directly follow 2 Pt 2.16. The story of Balaam and his ass—the prophet and the animal referred to in 2 Pt 2.16—is narrated in Nm 22.20–34.

33. Ps 8.9.

34. Ps 103.24.

35. Ps 18.5.

36. Is 46.8.

Recall, recall it to mind, you transgressors. ***that the hand of the Lord,*** that is, His operative power, ***has made all these things,*** namely present created things, hence all things proclaim what is said in the Ps:[37] *He made us, and not we ourselves.* Is 40:[38] *He has measured the seas by the handful, and He has weighed the heavens in His palm.*

[10] ***in whose hand,*** that is, in whose power, ***is the soul of every living,*** that is, ensouled, ***thing.*** Ps:[39] *You will send forth your spirit and they will be created, and you will renew the face of the earth.* And below:[40] *You will take away their spirit and they will pass away.* ***and the spirit of all human flesh,*** that is, the rational soul, which is in man? Prv 16:[41] *The Lord is the weigher of spirits.* Dn 5:[42] *You have not glorified God, who holds your breath in His hand, and all your ways.*

Then he adds that his own words should be listened to better than they have been listened to. **[11]** ***Does not the ear discern words,*** that is, it ought to discern. On account of this Basil says that it is hollowed out, so that it might take in words more deeply; imbued with common wax, so as to hold them; perfected by a dry drum, so that it might perceive them easily; and full of calm air, so that no commotion disturbs it.[43] Mt 15:[44] *Hear and understand.* ***and the palate,*** that is, as the palate, ***of the one eating,*** supply: discerns ***the taste?*** For the palate frequently discerns the taste of food that has been chewed and probed on every side. Is 55:[45] *Listen, you who hear me: eat what is good, and your soul will*

37. Ps 99.3.
38. Is 40.12.
39. Ps 103.30.
40. Ps 103.29. Albert's *infra* ("below") here suggests that he is recalling this scriptural passage from memory, as the words he quotes here are, in the Vulg. text of Ps 103 that has come down to us, immediately *above* those he has just invoked. It is perfectly understandable that Albert would recall the scriptural words according to the natural order of creatures (i.e., their coming into being prior to their demise).
41. Prv 16.2.
42. Dn 5.23.
43. Like Weiss, I have been unable to find this reference in the works of Basil.
44. Mt 15.10.
45. Is 55.2.

take pleasure in fatness. Jer 15:[46] *I found your words, and I ate them.* For in meditation, the word ought to be chewed and dissolved, and then it can be discerned.

He continues by setting forth in advance a general proposition by which it is shown that God is supremely wise and supremely strong.

[12] ***Among the ancients is wisdom.***

"Wisdom" is used in two ways, as Aristotle says in Book VI of the *Ethics.*[47] For wisdom denotes knowledge (*scientia*), which contains its own end and reason for knowing, and it is difficult for man to have it, and so it is called wisdom strictly speaking. Generally, however, wisdom means the excellence (*virtus*) of a science or an art: that is to say, when someone who practices a particular art or science reaches the point where he grasps the order concerning the things that pertain to that science or art. And whichever way "wisdom" is said, one does not possess it without a great deal of experience.

And therefore he says: ***Among the ancients is wisdom.*** Wis 4:[48] *The understanding of a man is his gray hair, and a blameless life is the attainment of old age.* Prv 20:[49] *The dignity of old men is their gray hair.* And this is understood as the gray hair of the mind. ***and in many years prudence.*** "Prudence" concerns bringing ideas together, which one must learn through many attempts. Sir 25:[50] *How beautiful is the wisdom of the old man, and how renowned his understanding and counsel! Much knowledge gained by experience is the crown of old men.* He is silent about knowledge, because knowledge (*scientia*) concerns demonstrable and necessary things, for which one is a middle term, and young men see this more readily than old men. In Book I of the *Metaphysics* Aristotle says: "Experience produces an art; inexperience, a fall."[51]

[13] ***With Him.***

By means of effect, he shows that prudence, wisdom, and

46. Jer 15.16.
47. *EN* 6.7.1–5.
48. Wis 4.8–9.
49. Prv 20.29.
50. Sir 25.7–8.
51. Aristotle, *Metaph.* 1.1.

strength are with God; and he does this in two ways: among natural realities; and among men, in this place:[52] *With Him is strength.*

And that is: ***With Him is wisdom.*** It is said to be "with Him" on account of the fact that it is always at hand; "wisdom," moreover, is that by which He disposes and ordains all things. Sir 1:[53] *All wisdom is from the Lord God, and has always been with Him, and is before all time.* ***and strength,*** namely for carrying out whatever has been ordained. Wis 8:[54] *She reaches from end to end with strength, and orders all things sweetly.* Nm 24:[55] *God, whose strength is like that of a rhinoceros, has led him out of Egypt.*

He has counsel. Gregory: The counsel of God is an immutable definition of what must be done.[56] Is 9:[57] *He shall be called Wonderful, Counselor.* ***and understanding* (intelligentia)**. "Understanding" is the habit (*habitus*) and conception of principles, by which both things going to be known and things going to be done are governed. Prv 8:[58] *I, wisdom, dwell* (habito) *in counsel, and I am present in learned thoughts.* And after a few words:[59] *Counsel and equity are mine; prudence and strength are mine.*

Then he proposes the effect of God's nature. **[14]** ***If He destroys*** any natural or human things whatsoever, ***there is no one to rebuild,*** that is, able to rebuild, except Him, of course. For just as He made all things from nothing, so He is able to rebuild things that have been destroyed. There is an example in the Sodomites, whom He destroyed without the hope of rebuilding; but finally He restored them.[60] Jb 34:[61] *He will crush many*

52. Jb 12.6.
53. Sir 1.1.
54. Wis 8.1.
55. Nm 24.8.
56. Gregory, *Mor.* 11.8.11; cf. Albert, *ST* 1.15.62 ad 1.
57. Is 9.6.
58. Prv 8.12.
59. Prv 8.14.
60. The destruction of Sodom is recounted in Gn 19. Concerning its restoration, Albert may have in mind the words of the Lord related in the vision of Isaiah concerning Judah and Jerusalem (see Is 1, particularly vv. 7–26).
61. Jb 34.24.

and innumerable men, and He will make others stand in their place. There is an example in the Flood.[62]

If He closes a man up, namely in the prison of infirmity or tribulation, ***there is no one who can open,*** supply: besides Him. Rv 3:[63] *He has the key of David, He who closes and no one opens; He opens and no one closes.* Is 22:[64] *He will close, and there will be no one who can open; He will open, and there will be no one who can close.*

[15] ***If He holds back the waters,*** namely of rain or of doctrine, ***all things will dry up,*** both hearts and the ground. Jer 14:[65] *They [the farmers of Judah and Jerusalem] were confounded and afflicted, and they covered their heads: on account of the devastation of the land, because rain did not come upon the earth.* Is 5:[66] *I will command my clouds not to rain on it.* There is an example in 1 Kgs 17,[67] where immediately after the words of Elijah it did not rain on the land for three years and six months. Jas 5:[68] *Elijah was a man, capable of emotions just as we are; and he prayed fervently that it might not rain on the land, and it did not rain for three years and six months.*

and if He sends them out, that is to say, the waters of rain or of doctrine, ***they will overwhelm the land*** either of the heart or of the ground. Gn 7:[69] *All the fountains of the great deep burst forth, and the flood gates of heaven were opened; and rain fell on the earth.*

[16] ***With Him is strength.***

Here he touches on the effect among humans, first particularly; and second universally, in this place:[70] *He multiplies nations.* Particularly he touches on five things, namely the reversal of the deceiver and the deceived, the reversal of the worthy and the unworthy, the reversal of the one with truthful lips and the one with lying lips, the reversal of the honorable and the contemptible, and the reversal of what is deep in darkness and what is made visible in the light.

62. See Gn 6–9.
63. Rv 3.7.
64. Is 22.22.
65. Jer 14.3–4.
66. Is 5.6.
67. 1 Kgs 17.1.
68. Jas 5.17.
69. Gn 7.11–12.
70. Jb 12.23.

But first he sets forth a general proposition, which he demonstrates through what follows.

And that is: ***With Him is strength***, namely of doing what He wills. Ex 15:[71] *Who is like you among the strong, O Lord?* ***and wisdom***, namely of ordaining and disposing. Jb 9:[72] *He is wise in heart, and mighty in strength.*

Then he sets forth the first effect: ***He knows both the deceiver***, that is, the ways in which he deceives, ***and him who is deceived***, that is, whether he is deceived through simplicity or folly or willfulness. Jer 20:[73] *You have deceived me, Lord, and I have been deceived; you have been stronger than I, and you have prevailed.* Supply: and because He has known this: **[17]** ***He brings counselors***, namely those drawing up and devising the most wicked counsels, ***to a foolish end***, so that they cannot arrive at their intended end. Jb 5:[74] *He catches the wise in their cunning, and scatters the schemes of the corrupt.* **and**, supply: he brings ***judges to bewilderment***, that is, so that they do not know what is just and unjust, and subvert the legal process. Dn 13:[75] *Unfairness came forth from the older judges, who seemed to rule the people.* Is 1:[76] *They do not judge in favor of the orphan, and the cause of the widow will not come to them.*

Then he adds the second reversal: **[18]** ***He loosens the belt of kings.*** The "belt" is the royal or military or sacerdotal belt by which the dignity of a person is made clear. Hence 1 Sm 18:[77] *Jonathan stripped himself of the tunic with which he was clothed, and he gave it to David together with the rest of his garments, all the way to his sword and bow and even to his belt.* ***and ties a rope around their waist.*** I mean ropes by means of which they are bound like the vile and debased. Prv 5:[78] *His own iniquities seize the wicked man, and he is bound with the ropes of his own sins.* **[19]** ***He leads away priests***, that is, those who had been priests, ***without glory***. This

71. Ex 15.11.
72. Jb 9.4.
73. Jer 20.7.
74. Jb 5.13.
75. Dn 13.5.
76. Is 1.23.
77. 1 Sm 18.4.
78. Prv 5.22.

is a description of history, for example, of Shebna.[79] Is 22:[80] *Behold, the Lord will cause you to be carried away, just as a gallinaceous cock is carried away, and He will remove you like a cloak.* ***and overthrows great men.*** What he said concerning kings[81] provides the explanation of this phrase. Am 6:[82] *The great men, the heads of the people, entering the house of Israel with pomp.* And after a few lines:[83] *Now they will depart at the head of those going into exile, and the faction of the lascivious will be taken away.*

And he adds the third effect: **[20]** ***He changes the words of those who speak the truth,*** that is, such that those who have been accustomed to speaking verities speak falsehoods. There is an example in 1 Kgs 13,[84] where the prophet who was living in Bethel, changing the words of truth into a lie, said to the prophet of the Lord: *An angel spoke a word to me, saying: Bring him back into your house!* And he explains this, adding: ***and,*** that is, ***He takes away the learning of old men.*** "Old men" are so called on account of the old age of their minds, which are at times turned to folly on account of the fact that they squander wisdom. Hence, among the things that God hates, Prv 6[85] specifies *a foolish old man.*[86] Heb 5:[87] *Although by this time you ought to be masters, you need to be taught again the first elements of the word of justice.* Rom 2:[88] *You who teach another, do you not teach yourself?*

Then he adds the fourth effect: **[21]** ***He pours,*** abundantly, of course, ***contempt on princes,*** supply: so that those who were respected might become contemptible. There is an example in Nebuchadnezzar, Dn 4:[89] *They will cast you out from among men, and your dwelling will be with wild beasts.* Is 52:[90] *As many have been*

79. See 2 Kgs 18–19 and Is 36–37.
80. Is 22.17.
81. Namely, above in v. 18.
82. Am 6.1.
83. Am 6.7.
84. 1 Kgs 13.11–18.
85. Prv 6.16.
86. Cf. Sir 25.3–4.
87. Heb 5.12.
88. Rom 2.21.
89. Dn 4.22.
90. Is 52.14.

astonished at him, so will his appearance be without glory among men. ***and lifts up those who have been oppressed.*** 1 Sm 2:[91] *He rouses the destitute man from the dust, and raises the poor man from the dung heap, so that he might sit with princes and possess the throne of glory.*

And he adds the fifth effect: **[22]** ***He reveals deep things out of the darkness,*** that is, hidden places. Dn 2:[92] *There is a God in heaven who reveals mysteries.* ***and brings the shadow of death,*** that is, what was shut up, like the shadow of death, ***out into the light,*** that is, into plain view. Jb 34:[93] *There is no darkness, and there is no shadow of death where those who work iniquity can hide.*

Then he adds the effect among humans universally, and he speaks of two universal effects, namely the subversion of the nations and the subversion of the senses.

And that is: **[23]** ***He multiplies nations.*** That is to say, *from one man He made all the races of men,* as Acts 17[94] says. Is 51:[95] *I called him alone, and I blessed him, and I multiplied him.* ***and destroys them,*** namely by famine and by pestilence and by the sword. Ps:[96] *Your hand has destroyed the nations, and you have planted them; you have afflicted the peoples and driven them out.* ***and, after they have been overthrown, completely restores them again.*** Gn 40:[97] *Pharaoh will remember your service, and he will restore you to your former position.* Jb 34:[98] *He will crush many and innumerable men, and He will make others stand in their place.*

[24] ***He changes the heart of the princes of the people of the earth,*** namely so that, as if foolish, they do not know what they are doing. Rom 1:[99] *Declaring themselves to be wise, they were made fools; and their foolish heart was darkened.*

And he explains this, adding: ***and,*** that is, ***deceives them,*** that is, permits them to be deceived, ***so that they walk in vain through an impassable place,*** that is to say, not arriving at their intended

91. 1 Sm 2.8.
92. Dn 2.28.
93. Jb 34.22.
94. Acts 17.26.
95. Is 51.2.
96. Ps 43.3.
97. Gn 40.13.
98. Jb 34.24.
99. Rom 1.22, 21.

end. There is an example in Ahab, at the end of 1 Kgs,[100] who, while he was thinking about capturing Ramoth in Gilead, was deceived by a false spirit in the mouth of the prophets and was killed.

Then he explains this, adding: **[25]** ***They will grope as if in darkness,*** that is to say, feeling with their hands, as they go astray; ***and not in the light,*** that is, possessing none of the light of reason. Is 59:[101] *We, like blind people, have groped for the wall, and we have touched it as if we had no eyes.* **and He will make them stagger,** namely by taking away the light of understanding, ***as if they were drunk.*** Is 28:[102] *In drunkenness they have not known Him who sees, and they have been ignorant of judgment.* Ps:[103] *He made them wander through an impassable place and not on a road.*

100. 1 Kgs 22.1–40.
101. Is 59.10.
102. Is 28.7.
103. Ps 106.40.

CHAPTER 13

B*EHOLD ALL these things.*

Here begins the part in which Job shows that they [that is, his fellow disputants] are perverse in their teachings, and it has three sections. In the first of these he shows that he is not inferior to them in knowledge; second, that this is not the reason for the disputation; and third, that their teaching is perverse.

And that is: ***Behold all these things,*** supply: which have been said. ***my eyes have seen,*** namely in the presence of divine light. Sir 48:[1] *With a great spirit he saw the highest things.* ***and my ears,*** interior ears, of course, ***have heard.*** 1 Sm 3:[2] *Speak, Lord, for your servant is listening.* **and I have understood each one** by comparing one to another. Dn 10:[3] *One needs understanding in the case of a vision.* Gregory: "For if understanding is not granted when something is shown or heard, then there is no prophecy at all."[4] And Job intends to say that God performs all the things that happened not according to the order of human justice, but by a governance that is dissimilar to human governance.

And this is: **[2]** ***In accordance with your knowledge,*** which comes, of course, from seeing works and hearing words, ***I too know.*** Wis 7:[5] *He has given me true knowledge of the things that are, so that I might know the orderly arrangement of the whole world.* ***and I am not inferior to you,*** namely in the virtue pertaining to life. And by moderating his words, he says less and signifies more.

1. Sir 48.27.
2. 1 Sm 3.9.
3. Dn 10.1.
4. Gregory, *Mor.* 11.20.31.
5. Wis 7.17.

For he was superior to them, as it is said in Jb 1:[6] *There is no one like him on the earth.* Sir 44:[7] *There was not found one like him.*

Then he adds that this was not the reason for the disputation, but a certain demonstration of wisdom. And that is: **[3]** ***But nevertheless I will speak to the Almighty,*** in whose presence, of course, there is no injustice. Ex 15:[8] *Almighty is His name.* Est 13:[9] *All things have been established in your power, and there is no one who can resist your will.* ***and,*** that is, ***I want to debate*** **(disputare)** ***with God,*** concerning the mode of providence and the reason behind His governance of human life. Jer 12:[10] *You, indeed, are just, O Lord, if I should debate* (disputem) *with you; nevertheless, I will say just things to you.*

Then, concerning the refutation of his fellow disputants for their perverse teaching, he adds: **[4]** ***Earlier,*** supply: which purpose of mine I will confine within the disputation, ***I showed you,*** supply: to be ***fashioners of lies.*** Gregory: "Truth arises not from fabrication, but from nature; but a lie is fabricated, for just as a building is fabricated from stones, so too a lie is fabricated from words."[11] Jer 9:[12] *They have taught their tongues to speak lies, as they have labored to act wickedly.* Ps:[13] *Your tongue crafted deceits.* ***and cultivators of perverse teachings,*** for he who defends his own teaching as if it honors the divine should not, on those grounds, be followed. Moreover, it is a perverse teaching to say that divine governance is regulated by any alien rule, such as the order of human justice. Jer 9:[14] *Through deceit they have refused to know me, says the Lord.*

And because perverse teaching does harm, he adds: **[5]** ***But if only you would remain silent,*** not revealing your own stupidity, of course, ***so that you might be thought to be wise,*** namely in my

6. Jb 1.8.
7. Sir 44.20.
8. Ex 15.3.
9. Est 13.9.
10. Jer 12.1.
11. Gregory, *Mor.* 11.23.34.
12. Jer 9.5.
13. Ps 49.19.
14. Jer 9.6.

heart. Jer 10:[15] *They will be shown to be senseless and foolish by the teaching of their vanity.*

[6] *Hear, therefore.*

Here begins the part of Job's response wherein he corrects his fellow disputants, and it has two subdivisions. For first he shows that perverse teaching is displeasing to God; second, that it does not engage his proposition, in this place:[16] *Why do I tear my flesh?*

There are three points in the first subdivision, namely: switching over to truthful correction; showing that the deceitful and misleading proposition is displeasing to the Lord; and showing that the divine refutation and retribution are coming for such things.

And that is: ***Hear therefore my reproof,*** the reason why you are culpable. Prv 1:[17] *Be converted at my reproof. Behold, I will bring forth my spirit for you, and I will show you my words.* And this is what follows: ***and pay attention to the judgment of my lips,*** that is, of the words articulated by my lips. Jb 6:[18] *Speaking that which is just, judge me. And you will not find iniquity on my tongue, nor in my throat will stupidity resound.*

And he adds that lying is not pleasing to God. And that is: **[7] *Can it be that God needs your lying?*** Gregory: "Truth does not need to be supported by falsehood."[19] Jn 8:[20] *He did not stand in the truth, for he is a liar and the father of lies.* Rom 3:[21] *God is truthful, but every man is a liar.* ***such that you should speak deceit on His behalf?*** He who flatters anyone while speaking contrary to the truth "speaks deceit." Jer 9:[22] *Your dwelling is in the midst of deceit.* Mal 2:[23] *The law of truth was in his mouth, and iniquity was not found on his lips.* **[8] *Can it be that you have become so partial to him,*** for when they said—contrary to the truth—that man's

15. Jer 10.8.
16. Jb 13.14.
17. Prv 1.23.
18. Jb 6.29–30.
19. Gregory, *Mor.* 11.26.37.
20. Jn 8.44.
21. Rom 3.4.
22. Jer 9.6.
23. Mal 2.6.

life is governed according to the order of human justice, they showed their partiality for God. That is, they were flattering Him, so that God would not seem to be punishing the innocent unjustly.

Then, explaining this, he adds: ***and,*** that is, ***do you endeavor to judge for God,*** supply: contrary to the truth? This is wholly perverse because what is contrary to the truth cannot be for God. 2 Cor 13:[24] *For we cannot do anything against the truth, but all things for the truth.*

[9] ***Or will it please Him,*** namely God, ***from whom nothing,*** supply: mendacious, ***can be concealed?*** as if he were saying: "No." Wis 1:[25] *The mouth that lies kills the soul.* Heb 4:[26] *All things are naked and manifest to His eyes.* ***or will He be deceived as a man,*** who is able to be deceived, of course, ***by your knavish ways,*** that is, faulty flatteries? as if he were saying: "No." Prv 8:[27] *I detest arrogance and pride, and a perverse way, and a double-tongued mouth.*

Then he shows that the divine refutation and retribution proceed against such things, adding: **[10]** ***He will accuse you,*** that is, show that you have been accused. Ps:[28] *I will convict you, and I will set your evil deeds before your face.* ***since in secret,*** that is, in the secret place of the heart, ***you have been partial to Him,*** namely by flattering Him, so that He might seem just before men, and by speaking contrary to the truth. Jas 2:[29] *Have faith in the glory of our Lord Jesus Christ, but without partiality.* Acts 10:[30] *Truly I have realized that God shows no partiality.*

And he adds concerning retribution: **[11]** ***Immediately when He incites Himself,*** namely having been provoked by the accusation of lying, ***He will throw you into confusion,*** by means of punishment, of course. Wis 5:[31] *Seeing it, they will be thrown into confusion by horrible fear.* ***and His terror*** with a great punishment

24. 2 Cor 13.8.
25. Wis 1.11.
26. Heb 4.13.
27. Prv 8.13.
28. Ps 49.21.
29. Jas 2.1.
30. Acts 10.34.
31. Wis 5.2.

will rush in powerfully ***upon you,*** who certainly are going to be overwhelmed. Is 30:[32] *His wrath burns and is heavy to bear.*

[12] ***and,*** supply: then ***your memory,*** which presently you are trying to construe as false wisdom, ***will be compared to ashes,*** which are carried away by the wind. Ps:[33] *Their memory has perished with a loud sound.* Similarly, Ps:[34] *Let them become as dust in the presence of the wind.* **and your necks,** which now are stiffened by an impudence against the truth, ***will be reduced to clay,*** that is to say, made worthless and soft. Is 48:[35] *For I knew that you are stubborn, and your neck is as an iron sinew, and your forehead as bronze.* Ps:[36] *I will wipe them out, like the dirt in the streets.*

From these things Job infers that what his fellow disputants say is not relevant to his proposition.[37] And in doing this he has three points: he asks them to listen, he shows them the reasons for his words, and he proves his ways in comparison to divine scrutiny.

And that is: **[13]** ***Be silent for a short time,*** that is, momentarily, until I finish, ***so that I might speak,*** not foolishly, of course, but ***whatever my mind may suggest to me,*** that is, reason measuring all things according to the standard of the truth. 1 Cor 14:[38] *I will pray with the spirit, I will pray with the mind also.*

And, concerning the reason for his words, he adds: **[14]** ***Why do I tear my flesh,*** that is, expose the wounds, ***with my teeth,*** that is, with biting words. Mi 3:[39] *They have eaten the flesh of my people, and they have flayed their skin off them.* **and carry my soul,** that is, animal life, ***in my hands?*** as if to offer it to Him who immediately pierces it. Ps:[40] *My soul is always in my hands.* Jb 7:[41] *My soul*

32. Is 30.27.
33. Ps 9.7.
34. Ps 34.5.
35. Is 48.4.
36. Ps 17.43.
37. Here begins what Albert understands as the second subdivision of the part of Job's response (constituting chs. 12–14) wherein he corrects the perverse teaching of his fellow disputants. See Albert's twofold division of this part in his comments on v. 6 above.
38. 1 Cor 14.15.
39. Mi 3.3.
40. Ps 118.109.
41. Jb 7.15.

has chosen hanging. It is as if he were saying: "I do not bring forward words of desperation in order for you to interpret them." And this is what follows. Supply: because **[15]** ***Even if He should kill me, I will hope in Him***. Rom 5:[42] *Hope does not confound*. Heb 6:[43] *We have fled for refuge to seize the hope set before us, which we have as an anchor for the soul, safe and secure*. Hence these words are not said for this reason,[44] but on account of their truth. And supply: Even if I am just and am found to be just, if I should be judged, ***nevertheless I will criticize my ways***, supply: set forth [to view] and in comparison to divine scrutiny, ***in His presence***, that is, I will show that they are open to critique, because in comparison to divine rectitude nothing is sufficiently just. Is 64:[45] *All of us have become unclean*. Ps:[46] *Their judges were joined to the rock and have been swallowed up*; that is, the holy ones,[47] who are judges according to righteousness (*per iustitiam*), when joined through comparison to Christ, the rock, have been swallowed up by the firmness of divine justice, that is, have been considered unjust.

[16] ***And***, supply: so, on account of the humility of confession and on account of the hope that I have in Him, ***He will be my Savior***. Dn 13:[48] *All the people cried out with a loud voice and blessed God, who saves those who hope in Him*. ***for no hypocrite***, supply: as you are, you who, of course, appear to speak for God when you speak contrary to the truth, ***will come into His presence***, that is, into the light of His grace. Jb 8:[49] *The hope of the hypocrite will perish. His madness will not be pleasing to Him*.

[17] ***Hear my speech***.

Here Job returns to his own proposition and confirms it, and this has two subdivisions.[50] First he shows that he has not been punished on account of sin; second, that human frailty cannot

42. Rom 5.5.
43. Heb 6.18–19.
44. Namely so that God might kill him.
45. Is 64.6.
46. Ps 140.6.
47. Albert later identifies these as angels.
48. Dn 13.60.
49. Jb 8.13–14.
50. Here, with v. 17, Job begins the second major part of his response in chapters 12–14, according to Albert. See Albert's comments on 12.1 above.

withstand the strictness of divine justice, in this place:[51] *Against a leaf that is carried off by the wind.* In the first subdivision, there are three points, namely: an exhibition of his own justice, a petition aimed at removing his blows, and an inquiry into the iniquity that is, in fact, punished.

And that is: ***Hear,*** interiorly, of course, ***my speech.*** Mt 13:[52] *He who has ears to hear, let him hear.* ***and receive enigmas,*** that is, the similitudes by means of which I argue, ***with your ears.*** Prv 1:[53] *Turn your mind to a parable and its interpretation, the words of the wise and their enigmas.*

[18] ***If I will be judged,*** namely according to the order of human justice, ***I know that I will be found just.*** Ps:[54] *You have examined my heart and visited it by night; you have tried me by fire, and iniquity has not been found in me.* **[19]** ***Who is there who will be judged with me,*** that is, contend with me in judgment***? Let him come!*** supply: and convict me. Is 50:[55] *He who justifies me is near; who will speak against me? Let us stand together; who is my adversary? Let him come to me.* Jn 8:[56] *Which of you will convict me of sin?*

Supply: and since no one appears, ***Why am I consumed while remaining silent?*** supply: because I am not speaking on behalf of the truth. And he says "am I consumed" because interiorly, within himself, he was indignant about their lies. Sir 4:[57] *Fight for justice for your soul, and struggle for justice even unto death.* Jer 20:[58] *The word of the Lord came to me as if a burning fire shut up in my bones, and I was wearied, not able to bear it.*

Then, begging that the arguments of one who speaks falsely be removed from him, Job sets forth the punishments with which he has been beaten. For Dt 28[59] specifies the punishments with which the transgressor of the law is beaten; and

51. Jb 13.25.
52. Mt 13.9.
53. Prv 1.6.
54. Ps 16.3.
55. Is 50.8.
56. Jn 8.46.
57. Sir 4.33.
58. Jer 20.9.
59. Dt 28.15–68.

therefore there seems to be a transgression of the law where these punishments are found.

And that is: **[20]** ***Only do not do two things to me,*** that is, reveal me as guilty by beating me, and threaten me with future beatings. And that is: ***and then I will not hide from your face,*** that is, from the presence of your truth. For the truth does not seek out corners, but falsehood and sin do. Gn 3:[60] *I heard your voice and I hid myself because I was naked.*

And he specifies those two things: **[21]** ***Withdraw your hand,*** supply: which beats me, ***far from me,*** namely so that your hand beating me might not cause me to appear to be a sinner. Ps:[61] *I have become silent and I have not opened my mouth because you have done this; remove your blows from me.* ***and let not your dread,***[62] namely by which I fear that you are going to beat me again, ***terrify me,*** because the beating would give support to those who falsely maintain that I have been beaten on account of my iniquity. Jb 3:[63] *The fear that I was fearing has happened to me, and what I was dreading has occurred.* Jb 23:[64] *I do not want Him to contend against me with much strength, nor overwhelm me with the weight of His greatness. Let Him display fairness toward me.* Supply: and then **[22]** ***Call me,*** O Eliphaz and your friends, ***and I will answer you,*** giving a reason for the truth, ***or at least I will speak,*** supply: by opposing falsehood. ***and you answer me,*** giving a reason for your assertion. 1 Pt 3:[65] *Being prepared to respond to everyone who asks you with a reason for the hope that is in you.*

And for that reason he then inquires concerning his own iniquity of the judge who sees all things. And that is: **[23]** ***How great are my iniquities.*** Iniquity is called "great" when it is intensified by quantity and aggravated by circumstances; and, to be sure, an "iniquity" is a sin committed with injury to one's neighbor. Is 59:[66] *Your iniquities have separated you and your God.* ***and***

60. Gn 3.10.

61. Ps 38.10–11.

62. Here I read *formido* with MSS ETFM, rather than *fortitudo* with Weiss's edition.

63. Jb 3.25.

64. Jb 23.6–7.

65. 1 Pt 3.15.

66. Is 59.2.

sins. A "sin" is a disgraceful and corrupt deed resulting from a lack of the good of grace. Ps:[67] *My sin is always against me.*

My crimes. A "crime" is, as Augustine says, what is deserving of accusation in a judgment.[68] Hos 6:[69] *They have committed crimes.* ***and transgressions*** **(delicta)**, which refer to derelictions, that is, to sins of omission, ***show to me:*** for which of these are you punishing me in this way? Jb 10:[70] *Show me why you judge me in this way.*

Supply: and if I have no sins for you to punish, **[24]** ***Why do you hide your face,*** that is, why do you not permit the light of your grace to shine upon me? Is 54:[71] *In a moment of indignation I have hidden my face from you for a little while.* ***and consider me your enemy?*** supply: although I am not, yet as a result of your judgment, by your beating me, you place me as an enemy. Jb 7:[72] *You have placed me against you, and I have become burdensome to myself.* Lam 2:[73] *The Lord has become like an enemy; He has cast down Israel headlong, all of its walls.*

[25] ***Against a leaf.***

Here begins the part in which, on account of the miseries and vanity of human life, Job shows that man is not able to withstand the rule of unchangeable justice,[74] and it is divided into two. For in the first subdivision he presents his plea; in the second, he asks that God spare and protect him, in this place:[75] *Who will grant me.*

The first subdivision is further divided into two sections: in the first section, he shows from these things pertaining to life that life is empty and short; in the second section, he shows

67. Ps 50.5.
68. See Augustine, *mend.* 1.21.
69. Hos 6.9.
70. Jb 10.2.
71. Is 54.8.
72. Jb 7.20.
73. Lam 2.5.
74. Albert understands this as the second division of the second major part of Job's response in chapters 12–14, as is clear from his division of the text at 13.17 above.
75. Jb 14.13.

the same thing from the impossibility of returning to life after death, in this place:[76] *A tree has hope.*

In the first of these sections there are three subsections: in the first subsection, indeed, he shows the weakness and emptiness [of life] from man's weakness; in the second subsection, from man's birth, in this place:[77] *Man, born;* and in the third subsection, from life's brevity, in this place:[78] *The days of man are short.*

In the first of these subsections there are two points, namely: showing man's weakness; and showing that it is impossible for it to withstand the rule of strict rectitude.

And that is: ***Against a leaf,*** that is, a light and most lowly thing, ***that is carried off by the wind,*** that is, by a gentle blowing. Is 64:[79] *We have all fallen as a leaf; and our iniquities, like the wind, have carried us away.* **you show your power,** namely of your rectitude, which is infinite and overwhelming and not able to be borne by human weakness. Wis 16:[80] *It is you who have the power of life and death.* **and you persecute a dry straw,** that is to say, one dried up by the squalor of misery. For "persecution" is when what is not capable of rectitude is driven back to rectitude. Ps:[81] *Make them like a wheel, and as straw in the presence of the wind.* Is 1:[82] *Your strength will be as the ashes of flax.*

Job shows, moreover, that he is being persecuted, adding: **[26]** ***For you write,*** that is, you retain in memory as if in writing, ***bitter things against me,*** that is, the causes of bitterness, namely sins. Mal 3:[83] *A book of remembrance was written in His presence.* ***and,*** supply: so ***you wish to consume,*** that is, to condemn, ***me,*** driving me back to strict rectitude, ***for the sins,*** that is, according to the sins, ***of my youth.*** He says "youth" because that stage

76. Jb 14.7.
77. Jb 14.1.
78. Jb 14.5.
79. Is 64.6.
80. Wis 16.13.
81. Ps 82.14.
82. Is 1.31.
83. Mal 3.16.

of life is fleeting and unstable and devoted to wantonness. Ps:[84] *Do not remember the transgressions of my youth and my ignorance.*

Job also adds the way that God writes: **[27]** ***You have put my feet in shackles,*** that is, you have bound me such that I am not able to flee from your surveying gaze or, if I am bound, to go farther away. Sir 23:[85] *The eyes of the Lord are looking around and seeing all the ways of men, and the depths of the abyss, and the hearts of men, looking into the hidden places.*

and, in other words, ***you have kept a close watch over all my paths.*** "Paths" are thoughts and plans that are narrower than ways, and of them God is not ignorant. Lam 3:[86] *He has closed off my ways with square stones,* so that I cannot go out. ***and you have inspected,*** namely in order that you might set apart and examine according to strict justice and rectitude ***the steps,*** that is, the works, ***of my feet,*** that is, of my affections. Mt 12:[87] *For every idle word that men have spoken, they will render an account on the day of judgment.* Eccl 12:[88] *God will bring everything that has been done into judgment according to every error, whether it is good or evil.*

But I am not able to withstand such rectitude, **[28]** ***who am going to be consumed as rottenness,*** that is to say, by being united with the moist earth, ***and as a garment,*** that is, clothing for the bodily members, ***that is eaten away,*** that is, consumed, ***by a moth,*** that is, by natural heat, as if by a moth. Is 14:[89] *The moth will be scattered beneath you, and worms will be your covering.*

And he shows this very thing by looking at man's generation in three ways: in its beginning, its progress, and its conclusion. And that is: **[14.1]** ***Man, born of a woman,***[90] and therefore soft and tender. For a woman (*mulier*) is so called from *mollire,* "to be soft," on account of which it is said concerning the sons of

84. Ps 24.7.
85. Sir 23.28.
86. Lam 3.9.
87. Mt 12.36.
88. Eccl 12.14.
89. Is 14.11.
90. Note that the commentary on chapter 14 begins here, apparently seamlessly since chs. 12–14 constitute a single response from Job. As indicated in the translation below, the rubric "CAPITULUM XIV." appears just prior to v. 5 in Weiss's edition and in the several manuscripts that I have consulted.

God in Jn 1:[91] *Who are born not of blood, nor of the will of the flesh, nor of the will of man.* This text of John uses "flesh" for woman.[92] Jb 15:[93] *What is man that he should be spotless, and having been born of a woman that he should appear just?* ***living for a short time.*** Jas 4:[94] *For what is your life? It is a vapor that appears for a little while.* Gregory: "The more his life is constricted, the more his misery is expanded."[95] And this is what follows: ***is filled with many miseries,*** for all present realities are some sort of misery. Rv 3:[96] *You do not realize that you are wretched, and miserable, and poor, and naked, and blind.*

And he adds concerning the progress [of man's life]: **[14.2]** ***He comes forth like a flower,*** for the stage of infancy and youth is a time of blooming. Is 40:[97] *Truly the people is grass, and all its glory as a flower of the field.* ***and is destroyed,*** namely by the continuous process of consumption. For heat consumes moisture continuously. Ps:[98] *Exhaust their strength.* Is 40:[99] *The grass has withered and the flower has fallen.*

Then he adds concerning the conclusion [of man's life]: ***and he flees as a shadow,*** supply: declining. Ps:[100] *Like a shadow when it declines, I have been carried off.* ***and never remains in the same state.*** Indeed, because the wet and dry elements and the hot and cold ones are battling one another, man's mixed state cannot be one. Jas 1:[101] *As the flower of the grass he will pass away. The sun rose with its heat and made the grass dry, and its flower fell off, and its beautiful shape perished.* On account of this it is said in Gn 3:[102] *You are dust, and to dust you will return;* and it says "you will return" beautifully because man never stands fixed, but moves

91. Jn 1.13.
92. Cf. Albert, *Super Ioh.* 1.13.
93. Jb 15.14.
94. Jas 4.15.
95. Gregory, *Mor.* 11.49.66.
96. Rv 3.17.
97. Is 40.7, 6.
98. See, e.g., Ps 9.36 and 58.14–17; see also Office of Matins, Response 3 for the first Sunday in October.
99. Is 40.8.
100. Ps 108.23.
101. Jas 1.10–11.
102. Gn 3.19.

constantly. And comparing [man's] weakness to [God's] strict rectitude, Job adds: **[14.3]** ***And you think that it is appropriate to open your eyes,*** namely so that you might inspect and enumerate all his deeds, ***upon one of this sort,*** so miserable and so unstable. Ps:[103] *What is man, that you have become known to him? Or the son of man, that you think about him?* ***and,*** in other words, ***to bring him into judgment with you?*** that is, after being examined by your strict rectitude. Ps:[104] *Do not enter into judgment with your servant, because in your sight no living thing will be justified.* Mal 3:[105] *Who will be able to imagine the day of His coming? Who will stand firm to look at Him?*

And he adds concerning the corrupt origin [of man]: **[14.4]** ***Who is able to make clean,*** that is, to purify from every blemish of uncleanness, ***one who was conceived from unclean seed?*** Seed is called "unclean," as Augustine says, on account of the conjoined desire, which is the tinder and fuel for a flagrant will toward what is forbidden.[106] Sir 34:[107] *What can be made clean from what is unclean? And what truth can be spoken by a liar?*

And so he adds: ***Is it not you who are alone?*** For He is "alone" who is clean of every defect. Indeed, everything that has been made possesses some mixture of potency and non-existence, and therefore it is not clean, which is why He is called "Holy of Holies" antonomastically in Dn 9.[108] For Dionysius, in the book *On the Divine Names,* chapter XII, says that holiness is perfect cleanness that is free from every impurity.[109]

103. Ps 143.3.
104. Ps 142.2.
105. Mal 3.2.
106. See Augustine, *c. Iul.* 5.13.
107. Sir 34.4.
108. Dn 9.24.
109. Dionysius, *DN* 12.3.

CHAPTER 14

T***HE DAYS OF man are short.***

Here Job shows the emptiness of life from its brevity, and he asserts two things, namely: its emptiness, and that the wretched man should therefore be spared.

And that is: ***The days of man are short,*** at least in relation to eternity. Gn 47:[1] *The days of the pilgrimage of my life are few and evil.* Is 38:[2] *From morning until evening you will bring me to an end.* ***the number of his months,*** that is, of renewals and vicissitudes, ***is with you.*** Am 5:[3] *Now the month will devour them together with their children.*

And he explains this, adding: ***you have established his boundaries,*** namely of life, ***which cannot be surpassed,*** which you alone know. Acts 1:[4] *It is not for you to know the times and moments, which the Father has established according to His own power.* Acts 17:[5] *From one man He made all nations of men to dwell upon the entire face of the earth, and He determined the established times and the boundaries of their habitation.*

Then he begs God to spare such a wretched man, adding: **[6]** ***Therefore, withdraw a little from him,*** that is, remove the scourging hand, ***so that he can rest,*** from the pain of the blows, of course. At the end of 2 Sm:[6] *The Lord had mercy on their suffering, and said to the angel who was smiting the people: That is enough; now stop your hand!* ***until, wished for, there comes his day;*** arrange the words of the text in this way: "until his wished-for

1. Gn 47.9.
2. Is 38.12.
3. These words are not from Am 5, but rather from Hos 5.7.
4. Acts 1.7.
5. Acts 17.26.
6. 2 Sm 24.16.

day comes." ***even as that of a hired worker.*** For the day of death is wished for and waited for by the one subsisting by honest work, just as the payday of a hired worker is the ultimate end of his work and the beginning of his reward. Jb 3:[7] *They rejoice greatly when they have found the grave.* Jer 31:[8] *Let your voice rest from wailing and your eyes from tears, because there is a reward for your work.*

By means of all these words Job intends [to show] that no man is capable of the strict rectitude [of God], and therefore the rule by which he is governed in such a life is dissimilar to every rule of human justice. Indeed, this was the position of blessed Job, which his friends were attacking.

[7] ***A tree has hope.***

Here, by describing the impossibility of returning to this life after death, Job magnifies man's misery. And he asserts two things, namely: that man is more miserable than plants, which possess the lowest form of life; and that by himself he is withering and he is not able to rise again except by divine power, in this place:[9] *Just as if the waters should recede.* And that is: ***A tree has hope,*** that is, a natural expectation, namely that it might come to life again, hence Aristotle, in the book *On Plants,* says that the youth of a plant returns from within.[10]

Then he explains this hope, adding: ***if it is cut off,*** as a little branch, ***it turns green again,*** when grafted, of course. There is a parallel in Rom 11:[11] *Or, contrary to nature, you were grafted onto a good olive tree; and you were made a partaker of the roots and of the abundance of the olive tree.* Jer 17:[12] *He will be like a green tree, which sends out its roots toward moisture.* ***and its branches spring forth,*** namely from the engrafted switch. Ps:[13] *It stretched forth its branches to the sea, and its shoots to the river.* And this is one way that a plant returns to its youth.

And he adds a second way: **[8]** ***If its roots grow old in the ground,*** that is, if, having matured to old age, they become dry

7. Jb 3.22.
8. Jer 31.16.
9. Jb 14.11.
10. Aristotle, *Pl.* 1.7.
11. Rom 11.24, 17.
12. Jer 17.8.
13. Ps 72.12.

because of an obstruction of the pores. And explaining this, he adds: ***and***, in other words, ***its trunk dies***, such that it is not able, of course, to put forth leaves, blossom, and bear fruit, ***in the dust***, that is, the cold and dry ground. In the letter of Jude:[14] *Trees of autumn, unfruitful, twice dead, uprooted.* **[9]** ***At the scent of water***, that is, at the source of water vapor, ***it will sprout forth***, that is, it will begin to sprout forth. Jer 17:[15] *It sends out its roots toward moisture, and it will not fear when the heat comes. And its leaf will be green.* Jb 29:[16] *My roots have spread out beside the water, and the dew will remain for my harvest.* ***and it will produce foliage***, namely of leaves, flowers, and fruits, ***as when it was first planted***. At the end of Hos:[17] *Its roots will burst forth as those of Lebanon. Its branches will spread, and its glory will be as the olive tree.* And Job is touching on an aspect of country life, which Aristotle, in the book *On Plants*,[18] and Palladius, in the book *On Agriculture*,[19] also mention: namely that an older tree, when the skin of its roots has become hard and its pores restricted, is not able to send moisture to its innermost parts, and so the tree withers up and produces no fruit. But if the larger roots are stripped and split with an ax, and stones are placed within the fissures so that they cannot close again, and manure is put down and completely covers the ground, the tree begins to draw moisture into the fissures; and it returns to its youth and is covered with leaves, and it is adorned with flowers, and it bears fruit. Lk 13:[20] *Look, for three years I have come seeking fruit on this fig tree, and I have found none. Cut it down, then. Why does it still occupy the ground? But responding, the man said to him: Lord, leave it alone for one more year, until I dig around it and put some manure down.*

Then by means of the opposite he shows the misery of the human condition, adding: **[10]** ***But man, when he has died*** by the loss of his soul ***and been stripped*** of his strength by exhaling his

14. Jude 12.
15. Jer 17.8.
16. Jb 29.19.
17. Hos 14.6–7.
18. Aristotle, *Pl.* 1.17.
19. See Palladius, *OA* 2.15.9.
20. Lk 13.7–8.

spirit ***and consumed*** by the rotting of his body. Jb 1:[21] *Naked I came from my mother's womb, and naked will I return there.* ***where, I ask, is he?*** Neither by engrafting nor by cultivation does he return to his youth. 1 Mc 2:[22] *He is extolled today, but tomorrow will not be found, because he has returned into his earth.*

Then he offers two similes for this, adding: **[11]** ***Just as if the waters should recede from the sea,*** which, as the philosophers say, ebbs and flows according to the moon's orbit,[23] ***and a river,*** supply: enlarged by drops of rainwater, ***having been emptied,*** namely of water, ***should dry up,*** just as if there were a deluge of fire, as in the myth of Phaethon that Plato recounts.[24] Ps:[25] *Why is it, O sea, that you fled, and that you, O Jordan, turned back?* **[12]** ***so man, when he has fallen asleep,*** namely into the sleep of death. Ps:[26] *On account of your rebuke, O God of Jacob, those who mounted horses have fallen asleep.* ***will not rise again,*** supply: by natural power, of course. Ps:[27] *Can it be that you will perform miracles for the dead? Or will physicians raise them up and give praise to you?* And he adds that he will rise again by a higher power: ***until heaven is worn away.*** Heaven is able to be "worn away" in two ways: according to substance, and in this way heaven will not be worn away; and according to function, according to which it stimulates generation and corruption, and in this way it will be worn away, when it will come to a halt at the end of the world. Mt 24:[28] *Heaven and earth will pass away.* ***he will not wake up.*** Wakefulness is the diffusion of breath, warmth, and strength to the sense organs. ***nor will he rise up,*** namely in body and soul, ***from his sleep,*** that is, from death. Dn 12:[29] *Many of those who sleep in the dust of the earth will awake, some to eternal life, others to reproach, so that they will see it always.*

[13] ***Who will grant me.***

Here begins something like a conclusion. Because life's van-

21. Jb 1.21.
22. 1 Mc 2.63.
23. See Aristotle, *Mund.* ch. 4.
24. Plato, *Ti.* 22C. Cf. Aristotle, *Mund.* ch. 6.
25. Ps 113.5.
26. Ps 75.7.
27. Ps 87.11.
28. Mt 24.35.
29. Dn 12.2.

ity is such that it cannot be made to fit under a rule, and because it affords no rest on account of Satan's provocations, Job begs that he might be granted rest, at least after death.

And this conclusion has three parts: in the first he sets forth his petition; in the second, the reason for his petition, in this place:[30] *Do you believe;* and in the third, an amplification of the inconstancy of life, in this place:[31] *A falling mountain disappears.*

And that is: ***Who will grant me.*** He suggests that he does not have it on his own. 1 Cor 4:[32] *What do you have that you have not received?* ***that in hell* (in inferno)**, that is to say, in the places of refuge for souls,[33] ***you will protect me,*** namely from the provocations of Satan. Ps:[34] *You have delivered my soul, so that it will not perish.* Hos 13:[35] *From death I will redeem them; from the hand of death I will deliver them.* ***and shelter me,*** namely so that the malice of Satan does not touch me. Ps:[36] *You will protect them in your tabernacle from the contradiction of tongues.* ***until your wrath,*** which you reveal in your strict judgment, of course, ***passes by.*** Ps:[37] *Can it be that He will be angry with us forever?* Indeed, the wrath of the Lord passes away, but His mercy does not pass away. Jer 29:[38] *I have plans of peace and not of suffering.* ***and you establish a time for me in which you will remember me?*** namely by putting an end to my tribulation and by comforting me through your mercy. At the end of Dn:[39] *You have remembered me, O God, and you have not abandoned those who love you.*

Then Job adds the reason for his petition, and he says two

30. Jb 14.14.
31. Jb 14.18.
32. 1 Cor 4.7.
33. See the comments on Jb 17.16 below, where Albert makes clear that *infernum*, even *profundissimum infernum*, does not always mean the lowest part of hell in which the damned are punished eternally, but rather the limbo that is the place of refuge of holy souls that will, *post Christum*, be liberated and attain to the beatific vision. Note that Albert draws on Jb 14.13 explicitly in elucidating 17.16.
34. Cf. Ps 85.13.
35. Hos 13.14.
36. Ps 30.21.
37. Ps 84.6.
38. Jer 29.11.
39. Dn 14.37.

things. For he sets forth the reason for the petition; and then he removes what is contrary to the petition, in this place:[40] *You certainly have numbered my steps.*

And that is: [14] ***Do you believe that man, once he has died, will live again?*** that is to say, can live this mortal life, as if he were saying "No"; because although he will live again, he will live an immortal life by the power of God. Phil 3:[41] *He will transform our body, making it like the body of His glory.* And supply: therefore, while I live ***all the days in which I now wage war,*** supply: against the provocations of Satan. Jb 7:[42] *Warfare is man's life on earth.* ***I am waiting,*** that is to say, with hope and desire, ***until my change comes,*** namely the transformation of mortality into immortality. 1 Cor 15:[43] *The dead will rise incorruptible, and we will be changed.* Indeed, then we will not experience the provocations of Satan. Rv 21:[44] *Now there will be no more mourning or crying, nor any pain.* 1 Cor 15:[45] *When the mortal* [*body*] *has put on immortality, then the word that is written will be fulfilled: Death has been swallowed up in victory.* [15] ***You will call me,*** namely to change, ***and I will answer you*** through obedience. Gregory: "We will truly answer God who calls us when, at the command of the Supreme Incorruption, we rise incorruptible."[46] Gn 22:[47] having been called by the Lord, *he answered: Here I am.* Mt 20:[48] *Call the laborers and give them their reward.* Then he explains how his answer is possible. Supply: because ***to the work of your hands you will stretch out your right hand,*** that is, efficacious help, by means of which I am able to arrive at immortality. Ps:[49] *The right hand of the Lord has wrought power; the right hand of the Lord has exalted me.* Prv 3:[50] *Length of days is in her right hand.*

40. Jb 14.16.
41. Phil 3.21.
42. Jb 7.1.
43. 1 Cor 15.52.
44. Rv 21.4.
45. 1 Cor 15.54.
46. Gregory, *Mor.* 12.14.18.
47. Gn 22.1.
48. Mt 20.8.
49. Ps 117.16.
50. Prv 3.16.

Then Job removes what is contrary to his petition, adding: **[16]** ***You certainly have numbered my steps,*** that is, my works and thoughts to be repaid, of course, with good and with evil. Is 27:[51] *In measure against measure, when she will be cast off, you will judge her.* ***but,*** because from the point of view of the strictness of your justice nothing is sufficiently upright, ***spare my sins.*** Jl 2:[52] *Spare, O Lord, spare your people, and do not make your inheritance a reproach.*

Moreover, Job adds how God has counted his sins out one by one: **[17]** ***You have sealed my offenses as if in a little bag.*** Gregory: "He seals our offenses in a little bag in that He pays close attention to them in the secrecy of His own judgment, in order to punish us."[53] At the end of Eccl:[54] *He will bring everything that has been done into judgment.* ***but have healed my iniquity,*** namely by means of scourges. Is 27:[55] *This is the full fruit, that his iniquity should be taken away.* At the end of Mi:[56] *Who, O God, is like you, who takes away iniquity and passes over the sins of the remnant of your inheritance?*

Job continues by amplifying the inconstancy of this present life, and he says three things, namely: that he is continuously consumed; that his life is ending without any hope of return; and that he is robbed of the good things of this present age.

And that is: **[18]** ***A falling mountain disappears,*** supply: gradually, although it is great; and the greatness of the present age falls in this way. Is 40:[57] *Every mountain and hill will be made low.* ***and a rock,*** although it is hard, ***is removed from its place.*** And he means that, although the life of any particular man may be vigorous and strong, nevertheless eventually he will be carried off from this present age by death. Is 2:[58] *The day of the Lord will be upon the tall and lofty cedars of Lebanon, and upon all the oaks of*

51. Is 27.8.
52. Jl 2.17.
53. Gregory, *Mor.* 12.17.21.
54. Eccl 12.14.
55. Is 27.9.
56. Mi 7.18.
57. Is 40.4.
58. Is 2.12–13.

Bashan. And after a few lines:[59] *And the loftiness of men will be bent down, and the haughtiness of men will be humbled.*

Then he adds a third metaphor: **[19]** ***Water wears away stones,*** hence the proverb: Drops wear away a stone, not by force but by falling frequently.[60] And he means that by constant consumption life continuously wastes away. Jb 4:[61] *From morning until evening they are cut down.*[62]

And he sets forth a fourth metaphor: ***and by flooding, the earth is consumed little by little,*** meaning that life is continuously destroyed by the drawing away of vital moisture. 2 Sm 14:[63] *We all die, and like water we fall down into the earth.* And this is what follows: ***similarly, then, you will destroy men,*** namely by gradual consumption. 1 Cor 15:[64] *I die daily on account of your glory, brothers.*

He adds, however, that too little remains: **[20]** ***You have strengthened him a little bit*** by leading him to an increase of substance and a perfection of power. Is 40:[65] *He gives power to the weary, and increases strength and vigor for those who are not,* but this is only a little bit. Ps:[66] *You have made his soul waste away like a spider.* ***so that,*** expressing result here, not purpose, ***he passes away forever,*** that is to say, never to return to this mortal life. Is 38:[67] *My eyes will not return to see good things.* Jb 16:[68] *Brief years pass away, and I am walking a path by which I will not return.*[69]

Moreover, he adds how this happens: ***you will change his appearance,*** that is to say, barring him from the light of this present life so that he might not see it again. Ps:[70] *As a cloak you will*

59. Is 2.17.

60. See Ovid, *Ep. ex Ponto* 4.10.5.

61. Jb 4.20.

62. The verb that appears in Albert's quotation of this verse here is *succiduntur,* whereas *consumuntur* appears in the verse when he is commenting on it above in chapter 4.

63. 2 Sm 14.14.

64. 1 Cor 15.31.

65. Is 40.29.

66. Ps 38.12.

67. This is not from Is 38, but rather is Jb 7.7.

68. Jb 16.23.

69. Cf. Albert's quotation of this verse in his comments on Jb 10.21 above, where the wording of the verse appears somewhat differently.

70. Ps 101.27. The words quoted here are exactly those of Heb 1.12. Ps 101.27

change them, and they will be changed. ***and cast him out,*** namely beyond the light of the present life into the darkness of death. Lam 3:[71] *He has driven me, and He has led me into darkness.* Ps:[72] *He has established me in darkness, just as the dead of old.*

[21] ***Whether his children will be prominent,*** that is, distinguished, ***or obscure,*** that is, abject and unfortunate, ***he will not know,*** after death, of course. Gregory: "Just as the living are ignorant of where the souls of the dead are kept, so too the dead, who lived in the flesh, do not know how the lives of those who are established in the flesh after them are ordered."[73] Is 38:[74] *I will behold man no more, nor the inhabitant of peace.* On account of this Aristotle, in the first Book of the *Ethics,* says that if any good or bad fortune of the living overflows all the way to the dead, it would seem to be something weak and insufficient, either in itself or for them, and not enough to make them happy.[75] And he means that after death there will be no consolation for man either in the good things of the present age or in friends, as if the hope of that consolation would make it easier for him to bear the weariness of this life.[76]

And this is what follows: **[22]** ***Nevertheless his flesh,*** that is, his body, ***while he lives*** this present life ***will suffer pain;*** that is, it will endure the pains of the body. Is 50:[77] *This has happened to you by my hand; you will sleep in pain.* Jb 30:[78] *At night my bones are pierced with pain, and those who eat away at me do not sleep.* ***and his soul will grieve over him,*** that is, over the straits of his own life. Wis 7:[79] *The first sound that I uttered was crying, like everyone else.* Lam 1:[80] *Weeping, she wept in the night,* that is, in the straits of life.

---

expresses the same idea with only slightly different words (viz., it begins with *sicut opertorium* rather than *velut amictum*).

71. Lam 3.2.

72. Ps 142.3.

73. Gregory, *Mor.* 12.21.26.

74. Is 38.11.

75. Aristotle, *EN* 1.11.5.

76. Here I read *taedium istius vitae* with MSS FM, rather than *taedia vitae* with Weiss's edition.

77. Is 50.11.

78. Jb 30.17.

79. Wis 7.3.

80. Lam 1.2.

CHAPTER 15

A*ND RESPONDING, Eliphaz the Temanite said.*

The second cycle of the disputation begins here, and it continues all the way to chapter 22. And we should recall to mind the position of Eliphaz,[1] who said that God governs human affairs by rendering good things to good people and bad things to bad people, and in this *the ways of the Lord are just,* as it is said in Ezek 18.[2] And Job was justifying himself earlier, saying:[3] *Before I eat, I sigh,* suggesting that the fear of God had preserved him from sin, and therefore he had not been stricken on account of sin. For that reason Eliphaz disputes against this, wishing to show that that fear came forth from an evil conscience, according to what is said in Wis 17:[4] *Whenever wickedness is fearful, it is attributed to the condemnation of the ungodly.*[5]

And so this chapter is divided into two parts. In the first he reproves Job for his manner of speaking and for the falsity of his words. In the second he points out his wickedness and that he is fearful on account of his wickedness, in this place:[6] *For he has stretched out against God.*[7]

The first part is divided into two. Indeed, in the first subdi-

1. See the commentary on 4.7–9 above.

2. Ezek 18.29.

3. Jb 3.24.

4. Wis 17.10.

5. See Albert's citations of Wis 17.10b in his comments on Jb 15.21a and 15.21b below.

6. Jb 15.25.

7. Interestingly, in quoting the beginning of this verse, Albert here has the verb *extendit,* rather than *tetendit,* which he uses when he comes to 15.25 below. The meanings of these two verbs are essentially identical, so his use of *extendit* here rather than *tetendit* suggests Albert's greater concern to convey

vision he reproves his words. In the second he shows that Job is obstinate in evil, in this place:[8] *I will show you; listen to me.*

The first of these subdivisions is further divided into two sections. For in the first section he reproves his mode of speaking; in the second section he reveals the falsity in his words, in this place:[9] *Can it be that you were the first man?*

In the first section there are two points, namely: the inappropriate mode of his speech; and its source, in this place:[10] *For your iniquity has taught.*

He points out two inappropriate aspects of his mode, namely in the speech and in the one who speaks, and that is: ***And responding, Eliphaz the Temanite said.*** It has been said[11] that Eliphaz means "contempt of the Lord," because he did not think that there was anyone superior to him in wisdom; he is called "the Temanite" because in Teman there was a zeal for scholarly study, as it is said in Bar 3.[12] Hence Jb 12:[13] *You alone are men, and wisdom would stay with you.*

And he reproves the mode of his speech, adding: **[2]** ***Can it be that a wise man,*** namely who gives forethought to what and what kinds of things he might say, ***will respond as if speaking into the wind?*** that is, with useless things that feed only the wind, as if to say, "No." Hos 12:[14] *Ephraim feeds on the wind and pursues the surging heat; all day long he multiplies lies and desolation.*

Then he adds a reproof of the one speaking; supply: and ***Can it be that the wise man will fill his stomach with burning heat?*** namely of anger and indignation against his fellow disputant. This is a metaphor, for foul-smelling fumes are belched forth when the stomach is full of burning heat. And these compan-

---

the fundamental meaning of the sacred text than to employ perfect verbal consistency in its conveyance.

8. Jb 15.17.

9. Jb 15.7.

10. Jb 15.5.

11. See the commentary on 2.11 and 4.1 above.

12. Bar 3.22.

13. Jb 12.2.

14. Hos 12.1.

ions were interpreting what Job said above:[15] *Why have you disparaged the words of truth,* as the result of indignation.

And he makes this clear, adding: **[3]** ***With words you accuse Him who is not equal to you,*** that is, God, and in this way you speak from the burning heat of the stomach. 1 Tm 5:[16] *Do not rebuke an older man, but entreat him as a father.* But Eliphaz says this on account of the fact that Job had said in 6:[17] *If only my sins, for which I deserved wrath, and the calamity that I suffer were weighed in a balance!* Jb 19:[18] *At least now understand that God has not afflicted me with a just judgment.* And because Job brings forth unsuitable words, Eliphaz adds: ***and you say what is not appropriate for you.*** Jb 6:[19] *You utter words into the wind.* And concluding from this, he adds: **[4]** ***Inasmuch as it is in you, you have nullified fear,*** namely of God. But God deprives nothing of its being inasmuch as it is in itself. Rather, it is man who rejects God. Ps:[20] *The fear of God is not before their eyes.* ***and you have carried away,*** that is, you have removed, ***prayers from the presence of God,*** that is, your prayers do not have a place in the presence of God. Jn 9:[21] *God does not hear sinners.* Is 1:[22] *When you offer many prayers, I will not listen.*

Then he adds the reason for these things: **[5]** ***For your iniquity,*** which overflows in your heart, of course, ***has taught your mouth.*** Mt 12:[23] *Out of the abundance of the heart the mouth speaks.* And in the same place:[24] *An evil man brings evil things out of an evil treasure chest.* Gregory: "From a perverse life you have learned to speak perverse words."[25] ***and,*** supply: therefore, ***you imitate the speech of blasphemers,*** namely by imposing on God a false accusation, that He has inflicted punishment on you without cause, as though He took delight in the punishments and

15. Jb 6.25.
16. 1 Tm 5.1.
17. Jb 6.2.
18. Jb 19.6.
19. Jb 6.26.
20. Ps 13.3.
21. Jn 9.31.
22. Is 1.15.
23. Mt 12.34.
24. Mt 12.35.
25. Gregory, *Mor.* 12.25.30.

destruction of men. Wis 1:[26] *God did not make death, nor does He delight in the destruction of the living.* Supply: hence or therefore **[6]** ***Your own mouth will condemn you,*** that is, your words make clear that you are worthy of condemnation, ***and not I;*** he says this so that he might seem to have compassion. Mt 12:[27] *By your words you will be justified, and by your words you will be condemned.* ***and your own lips,*** that is, the words of your lips which were produced separately, ***will respond to you;*** that is, they supply the material for the one who responds. Mt 24:[28] *From your own mouth I judge you, wicked servant!* Lam 3:[29] *The lips of those who rise up, O Lord, and their plans against me all day long,* supply: you have seen.

And he continues by reproving first the ignorance and afterwards the falsity of Job's words, and that is: **[7]** ***Can it be that you were the first man born?*** The letter of the text should be arranged in this way: "You, O man born from the earth, of course, can it be that you were the first?" as if to say, "No." And he means that, since he is the last, he is not able to know things higher than himself, and that, since he is from the earth, he is not able to reach divine realities. Sir 3:[30] *Do not seek things that are higher than you, and do not search out things that are mightier than you.* ***and were you formed before the hills?*** as if you were able to investigate the wisdom of God, and he is alluding to what is said in Prv 8:[31] *Before the hills I was brought forth.*

And therefore it follows: **[8]** ***Can it be that you have heard God's plan?*** existing before all things, of course. Gregory: "So that you are able to speak about the eternal and dispute concerning His purpose."[32] Is 40:[33] *Who has helped the spirit of the Lord? Or who has been His counselor?* Rom 11:[34] *Who has known the*

26. Wis 1.13.
27. Mt 12.37.
28. Two MSS, F and M, cite this as Mt 12. Cf. Mt 12.37 and 25.26; and Lk 19.22.
29. Lam 3.62.
30. Sir 3.22.
31. Prv 8.25.
32. Gregory, *Mor.* 12.27.32.
33. Is 40.13.
34. Rom 11.34.

thoughts of the Lord? Or who has been His counselor? ***and that His wisdom is inferior to you?*** that is, will follow after you; as if to say, "No." Sir 1:[35] *Who will investigate the wisdom of God that goes before all things?* Wis 9:[36] *Who will investigate the things that are in heaven? And who will know your thoughts?* And Eliphaz means that divine realities, because they are in God, cannot be investigated, and so it is foolish to say that human affairs are governed not according to the merits of men but only from the depths of God's own plan.

Therefore, concerning men he adds: **[9]** ***What,*** namely among human matters, ***have you come to know that we are ignorant of? What,*** namely among divine matters that have been learned from human matters, ***do you understand that we do not know?*** Jb 13:[37] *In accordance with your knowledge I too have known; and I am not inferior to you.* **[10]** ***There are among us both old men,*** namely minds of old age, ***and ancient men,*** who gained experience, from whom we receive teaching suitable to their authority and proven by their experience. Wis 4:[38] *The understanding of a man is his gray hair, and a blameless life is the attainment of old age.* ***much older than your fathers,*** that is, those who formed you in wisdom. Jb 12:[39] *Among the ancients is wisdom, and in many years prudence.* He is alluding to what is said in 1 Kgs 12,[40] where Rehoboam submitted to the advice of the younger men and departed from the advice of the older men, and therefore his kingdom was divided. In Book III of the *Topics* Aristotle says: "No one chooses young leaders because it is not certain that they are wise."[41]

He adds, moreover, what injury has occurred on account of this: **[11]** ***Is it a grand thing that God,*** who comforts every penitent and good man, ***should comfort you?*** At the end of Is:[42] *As one whom a mother caresses, so I will comfort you.* ***But your perverse***

35. Sir 1.3.
36. Wis 9.16–17.
37. Jb 13.2.
38. Wis 4.8–9.
39. Jb 12.12.
40. 1 Kgs 12.8.
41. Aristotle, *Top.* 3.2.7.
42. Is 66.13.

words, that is to say, the decisions of your unrepentant heart, ***hinder this***. For sin hinders the reception of divine consolation. Jer 3:[43] *You have polluted the land with your fornications and your wickedness. For that reason the drops of rain have been withheld, and there has been no rainy season.*

And on account of this injury he takes the opportunity to reprove Job, adding, supply: therefore **[12]** ***Why does your heart***, whose lifting up is harmful to you, ***lift you up?*** Is 10:[44] *I will punish the fruit of the proud heart of the king of Assyria.* Ps:[45] *Do not lift up your heart on high; do not speak iniquity against God.* ***and why do you have thunderstruck eyes, as if you were thinking great***, or lofty, ***things?*** Gregory: "Often the hearts of the just are lifted up to contemplate higher things such that outwardly their faces appear to be stupefied,"[46] and in this way they are thought to be thunderstruck. Hence even the Lord was thought by His disciples to have become mad. Mk 3:[47] *Indeed His disciples went out to restrain Him, for they were saying: He has gone mad.*

And after this he introduces something more by way of reproof: **[13]** ***Why does your spirit swell against God?*** Gregory: "The swelling of the mind is an obstacle to truth."[48] Rom 11:[49] *Do not be proud, but fear!* ***such that you bring forth***, namely out in public, ***from your***, that is, your very own, ***mouth***, which the Holy Spirit does not move. Ps:[50] *Your mouth abounded in malice, and your tongue prepared deceits.* ***words of this sort?*** namely by means of which you accuse God so that you might justify yourself. Jb 40:[51] *Can it be that you will make my judgment void and that you will condemn me, so that you will be justified?*

And he goes on by proving the impossibility of Job's words, using an argument *a fortiori*, supposing what seems to be less and inferring what seems to be more. Nevertheless, before both

43. Jer 3.2–3.
44. Is 10.12.
45. Ps 74.6.
46. Gregory, *Mor.* 12.30.35.
47. Mk 3.21.
48. Gregory, *Mor.* 23.17.31.
49. Rom 11.20.
50. Ps 49.19.
51. Jb 40.3.

of these, he sets forth his intended conclusion in the mode of a question. And that is: **[14]** ***What is man,*** that is, how worthless is man, ***that he should be spotless,*** that is, that he should be able to be spotless, to whom so many stains cling because of his earthly manner of life? Is 6:[52] *I am a man of unclean lips, and I live among a people possessing unclean lips.* Is 64:[53] *All of us have become unclean,* and corrupt by nature. Hence he adds: ***and,*** supply: who is man, ***having been born of a woman,*** namely who was the first drinker of corruption, ***that he should appear just?*** Ps:[54] *For behold I was conceived in iniquities, and my mother conceived me in sins.*

And he sets forth first what seems to be less: **[15]** ***Behold among the holy ones,*** that is to say, the angels, ***none is immutable,*** by nature, that is, ***and,*** in other words, ***the heavens,*** that is, celestial beings, ***are not pure,*** supply: through themselves (*per se ipsos*), ***in His sight,*** that is, by comparison with Him, but this seems to be the lesser point. Ps:[55] *Their judges were joined to the rock and have been swallowed up.* For our judges are the holy angels, and when they are joined by comparison with the rock, that is, the solidity of Christ and of God, they are swallowed up, that is, thought to be nothing.[56]

Then he introduces what seems to be more, adding: **[16]** ***How much more abominable,*** namely in a corrupted nature, ***and useless,*** namely in works, ***is man.*** Ps:[57] *They have become abominable and useless.* ***who drinks in,*** that is, without difficulty, and customarily gulps down, ***iniquity as if it were water?*** Water does not hinder swallowing by having either a sharp taste or a thick substance. Jb 34:[58] *What man is there like Job, who drinks in scorn as if it were water? Who goes with those who work iniquity and walks with wicked men?* Ps:[59] *He put on a curse like a garment, and it entered his entrails as if it were water.*

[17] ***I will show you.***

52. Is 6.5.
53. Is 64.6.
54. Ps 50.7.
55. Ps 140.6.
56. Cf. Albert's comments on 13.15 above.
57. Ps 13.1.
58. Jb 34.7–8.
59. Ps 108.18.

Here he shows that one who is obstinate in evil is always fearful, not with the fear that excludes sin, but with the fear that seizes the wicked man, who can hope for nothing except punishment because he is conscious of sin, as it is said of Cain in Gn 4:[60] *Behold, today you cast me out from the face of the earth, and I will be hidden from your presence. Anyone, therefore, who finds me will kill me.* And this part is divided into two parts.

Indeed in the first of these subdivisions he teaches that such fear belongs to the obstinate person; in the second he shows the cause of his fear, in this place:[61] *For he has stretched out against God.*

There are two points in the first subdivision: namely the commending of this teaching; and what he teaches, in this place:[62] *All his days.* The commending of the teaching consists in two things: in arousing one to listen and in the authority of the teaching.

And that is: ***I will show you,*** namely by the method of teaching; ***listen to me,*** that is to say, with an interior hearing. Is 50:[63] *The Lord has opened my ear, and I have not opposed Him; I have not turned back.* And in the same place:[64] *He awakens my ear so that I may hear Him as a master.* ***I will tell you what I have seen,*** namely in similitudes and in personal experience. But he says this because there are two senses related to teaching—hearing and sight—and sight is more certain than hearing. Horace: "Things that fall on the ears excite the soul more slowly than those that are exposed to reliable eyes."[65] Jn 3:[66] *He testifies to what he has seen and heard.*

And concerning the authority of the teaching he adds: **[18]** ***Wise men confess,*** that is, acknowledge simultaneously. For Aristotle says in Book I of the *Topics* that among probable things the more probable is what seems to be true to the wise or to

60. Gn 4.14.
61. Jb 15.25.
62. Jb 15.20.
63. Is 50.5.
64. Is 50.4.
65. Horace, *AP* ll.180–81.
66. Jn 3.11.

all or to many.[67] At the end of Eccl:[68] *The words of the wise are as goads, and as nails deeply embedded.*

Lest, however, it be thought that wise men contrived these wise words, he adds: ***and they do not hide their fathers***, namely those from whom they received wisdom. And it says "they do not hide" because they were demonstrable in wisdom. And teachers are called "fathers" because just as a father forms his child with regard to human nature, so too a teacher forms his student with regard to wisdom. Sir 4:[69] *Wisdom breathes life into her children; she supports those who seek her and will go before them in the way of justice.*

And praising these men, he adds: **[19]** ***to whom alone the earth was given***, that is, the judgment and knowledge of terrestrial realities. Hence 1 Cor 2:[70] *Which none of the princes of this world knew.* The Gloss says that the princes of the world are philosophers and wise men who make judgments about secular matters.[71]

And this is what follows: ***and no stranger***, namely to wisdom, ***will pass through them***, that is, the wise men. For he does not have fellowship with them. Eccl 2:[72] *I have seen that wisdom surpasses foolishness, as much as light differs from darkness. The eyes of a wise man are in his head; the fool walks in darkness.* Eccl 1:[73] *I proposed in my mind to seek and investigate wisely all things that occur under the sun.*

He adds, moreover, what he teaches: **[20]** ***All his days the wicked man is proud***, that is, he possesses the will to be haughty and

67. I was unable to find this in Aristotle's *Top.*, but see Albert, *Top.* 1.3.1.

68. Eccl 12.11.

69. Sir 4.12.

70. 1 Cor 2.8.

71. See *GO* vol. 4, where the words *principum huius saeculi* are glossed interlinearly thus: *demonum vel philosophorum uel doctorum in lege*. Given the fluidity of the glosses that were constitutive of the *GO* on any scriptural book across time and space in the High Middle Ages, Albert may have had access to one or more manuscripts whose gloss on these words were closer to, or even identical with, what he relates here. For an excellent general study of the *GO*, see Lesley Smith, *The* Glossa Ordinaria*: The Making of a Medieval Bible Commentary* (Leiden: Brill, 2009), esp. pp. 73–79 on its fluid textual tradition.

72. Eccl 2.13–14.

73. Eccl 1.13.

to exalt himself above others. Ps:[74] *The pride of those who hate you rises up continually*. ***and,*** supply: this is remarkable because ***the number of the years of his tyranny is uncertain***. A tyrant, as Boethius says, is one who wickedly subverts the rule of the state in a manner that is harmful to the people but to his own advantage.[75] On account of this Aristotle says in the first Book of the *Ethics* that tyranny is a corruption of the power to rule.[76] Hence it is said in 2 Mc 4[77] of Jason that he came into Jerusalem *possessing nothing indeed worthy of the priesthood, but having the mind of a cruel tyrant and the fury of a wild beast.* And Eliphaz means that blessed Job was ruling among the people tyrannically.

And because *wickedness is fearful,* as it is said in Wis 17,[78] therefore it follows: **[21]** ***The sound of terror,*** that is, the hearing of terror, ***is always in his ears***. The reverse is said about the untroubled mind in a Psalm:[79] *He will not fear evil news*. Wis 17:[80] *When the conscience rebukes, the worst thoughts tend to preoccupy the mind.*

Further amplifying this fear, he adds: ***and when there is peace,*** that is, when no one plots any evil thing, ***he,*** namely the wicked man, ***always suspects treachery***. Dt 32:[81] *The sword will devastate them without, and terror within.* Gregory: "Just as a good mind is always calm, a perverse mind is always in distress, because either it is planning evil deeds to be carried out or it fears that they might be carried out by others against it."[82] Prv 15:[83] *An untroubled mind is like a perennial feast.* Wis 17:[84] *A troubled conscience always anticipates cruel things.*

He adds how the troubled conscience is amplified by despair: **[22]** ***He does not believe that he can return,*** supply: by means of penance, ***from darkness,*** namely the darkness of his distress,

74. Ps 73.23.
75. Boethius, *CP* 2.6 and 3.5 (PL 63:703 and 740).
76. Aristotle, *EN* 8.10.2.
77. 2 Mc 4.25.
78. Wis 17.10.
79. Ps 111.7.
80. Wis 17.10. Cf. Albert's somewhat different citation of the same verse in the following paragraph.
81. Dt 32.25.
82. Gregory, *Mor.* 12.39.44.
83. Prv 15.15.
84. Wis 17.10.

to the light of consolation, ***looking around*** with despair ***every-where,*** that is, at every motive, ***for the sword,*** which is the avenger of iniquity. Jb 19:[85] *The sword is the avenger of iniquities.* Hence in Gn 4[86] Cain said: *Anyone who finds me will kill me.* In fact, since he did not find a killer, he killed himself,[87] just as Judas in Mt 27[88] and Ahithophel in 2 Sm 17[89] and Haman in Est 7.[90]

And he shows that this condition endures even when tending to life's necessities, adding: **[23]** ***When he moves himself to seek bread,*** that is, the necessities of life, ***he knows,*** that is, he supposes without doubt, ***that the day of darkness,*** that is, of death, ***has been provided*** supply: to him ***in his hand,*** that is, in his works. At the end of Lam:[91] *Our lives were in peril from the edge of the sword as we fetched our bread.*

And he adds: **[24]** ***Tribulation,*** anticipated externally, of course, ***will terrify him.*** Ps:[92] *I have discovered tribulation and sorrow.* ***and distress*** of the heart within ***will surround him.*** Is 21:[93] *My heart has failed; darkness has stupefied me.* ***as a king who is preparing for battle,*** who always fears that, having been left behind by his own soldiers and betrayed, he will be killed by the enemy. Dt 28:[94] *The Lord*[95] *will give you a fearful heart and failing eyes and a soul consumed with grief; and your life will be as if hanging*[96] *before you. You will be afraid at night and during the day, and you will not trust your life.*

[25] ***He has stretched out.***

85. Jb 19.29.

86. Gn 4.14.

87. I have been unable to find a source, either scriptural or traditional, for Albert's statement that Cain committed suicide. This may be Albert's own supposition concerning the demise of Cain, whom he takes as illustrative of the truth that the troubled conscience of a wicked man is amplified by despair.

88. Mt 27.5.

89. 2 Sm 17.23.

90. Est 7.10.

91. Lam 5.9.

92. Ps 114.3.

93. Is 21.4.

94. Dt 28.65–66.

95. Here I read with MSS FM, which omit the *In fine* with which this scriptural quotation begins in Weiss's edition.

96. Here I read *pendens* with MSS ETFM, rather than *precedens* of Weiss's edition.

Here he specifies that the cause of his fear is cowardly wickedness; and secondly he introduces the punishment, in this place:[97] *He will dwell.* Thirdly he returns to the cause, so that the punishment might seem more justified, in this place:[98] *For the congregation of the hypocrite.*

And that is: ***For he has stretched out his hand against God***. Gregory: "To stretch out one's hand against God is to persist in perverse activity while disdaining His judgments."[99] Hos 7:[100] *He stretched out his hand with scorners.* ***and has strengthened himself against the Almighty***. Gregory: "He is strengthened against God because he is permitted to be successful in his own evil deeds."[101] Ex 15:[102] *Trembling seized the strong men of Moab.*

[26] ***He has run against God with an erect neck.*** Gregory: "Someone has run in evil when he has not had any obstacle or adversity in his evildoing."[103] Prv 1:[104] *Their feet run toward evil.* And he adds what an "erect neck" is: ***and,*** in other words, ***with a fat neck,*** that is, fattened[105] by pride, ***he is armed,*** that is, he has presented his bodily members as weapons of iniquity, contrary to what is said in Rom 6:[106] *Do not present your members as weapons of iniquity for sin.* Ps:[107] *Their iniquity has sprung forth, as if from corpulence.* Thus 1 Sm 15:[108] *Agag, very fat and trembling, was presented to Samuel.* For Agag means "solemn with feasting," because he always wished to be in the midst of the delights of a solemn feast; and Eliphaz adds that this induced in him a mental blindness: **[27]** ***Thickness has covered his face,*** that is, the vision of his mind. Gregory: "The desired abundance of earthly

97. Jb 15.28.
98. Jb 15.34.
99. Gregory, *Mor.* 12.43.48.
100. Hos 7.5.
101. Gregory, *Mor.* 12.43.48.
102. Ex 15.15.
103. Gregory, *Mor.* 12.43.49.
104. Prv 1.16.
105. Here I read *saginata* with MSS TEFM, rather than *opulenta* with Weiss's edition.
106. Rom 6.13.
107. Ps 72.7.
108. 1 Sm 15.32.

delights pressed upon the eyes of his mind."[109] Ps:[110] *God is not in his sight; his ways are polluted at all times.* Is:[111] *Because of this the sovereign Lord, the Lord of Hosts, will send leanness among His fat ones.* ***and the fat hangs down from his sides,*** that is, from his associates and friends who are at his side. Gregory: "Whoever associates with one who is unjustly powerful, he himself also becomes puffed up with that one's power as if from fatness."[112] Sir 13:[113] *Whoever touches pitch will become dirty from it; and whoever associates with a proud person will put on pride.*

Because of all these wicked deeds he introduces the expected punishment, and he says two things, namely: what the expected punishment is; and he demonstrates it by means of a metaphor, in this place:[114] *His grapes will be struck as a vine.* He describes the punishment in a twofold way: by type (*speciem*); and by swiftness, in this place:[115] *Before his days.* By type in a twofold way, namely: its quality; and that he cannot be saved from it, in this place:[116] *May he not believe in vain.* He describes its quality by referring to the society of the wicked, the ruining of a house, the destruction of the body, and the elimination of posterity.

And that is: **[28]** ***He has dwelt in desolate cities;*** that is, with love he has dwelt in the society of sinners, which has been forsaken by every good man. Ps:[117] *I have seen iniquity and contradiction in the city.* Is 25:[118] *You have made the city a heap, the strong city a ruin, a house of strangers, so that it is not a city.* ***and in abandoned houses that have been reduced to heaps,*** and this is his ruining of a house. For a house has been ruined when it has collapsed and been reduced to a heap. Is 6:[119] *The cities have been left with-*

109. Gregory, *Mor.* 12.44.50.

110. Ps 9.26. Weiss's edition has an incorrect citation here, namely 10.5, as is also the case when Albert quotes this verse in commenting on Jb 1.1 and Jb 8.13 above.

111. Is 10.16.

112. Gregory, *Mor.* 12.45.51.

113. Sir 13.1.

114. Jb 15.33.

115. Jb 15.32.

116. Jb 15.31.

117. Ps 54.10.

118. Is 25.2.

119. Is 6.11.

out inhabitants, and the houses without human beings. Moreover, he shows every particular way that a household may be ruined. For Aristotle says that a household is built by four virtues, namely: magisterial virtue, which is knowing how to use one's servants or attendants or stewards; chrematistic or economic virtue, which is the knowledge of enriching the household, so that its profits do not run out through repeated use; marital virtue, which is the knowledge of producing heirs of the household, lest outsiders be brought in as heirs; and the knowledge of managing one's children, so that rooted in its families, the city will grow.[120] And Eliphaz shows that these virtues have been ruined, each in turn.

As to the first, he says: **[29]** ***He will not be enriched,*** not after the death of his stewards, to whom one's possessions must be entrusted at interest. Mt 25:[121] *He called his servants and gave them his possessions.* And he said:[122] *Trade until I come.*

As to the second, he says: ***neither will his substance persist,*** that is, his investments will not be returned. Lk 15:[123] *He squandered his substance by living luxuriously with prostitutes.* Ps:[124] *May the money-lender carefully examine his entire substance, and may strangers plunder his efforts.*

As to the third, he says: ***nor will he send his root into the earth,*** namely because his wife is either barren or adulterous, bringing in another's child as an heir. Sir 23:[125] *For a man who is a fornicator all bread is sweet;* and further along:[126] *Every woman who leaves her husband and brings in an heir by another marriage sins.* Wis 4:[127] *Adulterated plantings will not set deep roots.* **[30]** ***He will not escape from darkness,*** that is, from distress. Lam 3:[128] *He has driven me and He has led me into darkness.*

120. Aristotle, *Pol.* 1.3. Cf. the commentary on Jb 1.3 above, where Albert explains that Job managed his household with these four virtues.

121. Mt 25.14.

122. Lk 19.13.

123. Lk 15.13.

124. Ps 108.11.

125. Sir 23.24.

126. Sir 23.32.

127. Wis 4.3.

128. Lam 3.2.

As to the fourth, he says: ***the flame,*** that is, consuming judgment, ***will dry up his branches,*** namely the succession of his children and descendants. Ps:[129] *May his children perish; in one generation may his name be blotted out.* Is 14:[130] *I will destroy the name of Babylon, and the remnant, and the progeny, and the shoot.*

Then, concerning the destruction of Job's person, he adds: ***and he will be swept away,*** from the land of the living, of course, ***by the breath of his own mouth,*** supply: [the breath] having been swept away. Ps:[131] *His breath will pass away, and he will return into his earth.* 1 Mc 2:[132] *The glory of the sinful man is dung and worms: he is extolled today, but tomorrow will not be found, because he has returned into his earth.*

Also, concerning the impossibility of redemption, he adds: **[31]** ***May he not believe in vain;*** for if he were to believe, he would be disappointed, ***having been misled by error,*** because, although it is written in Prv 13,[133] *The ransom of a man's soul is his own riches,* nevertheless they do not save him from the judgment of God. And that is: ***that he is going to be redeemed with any price.*** Prv 6:[134] *He will not even accept the greatest number of gifts as a ransom.*

Then he adds that he will be condemned quickly. And that is: **[32]** ***Before his days,*** namely of a natural lifespan, ***are completed, he will perish.*** Ps 5:[135] *The Lord will abhor a bloodthirsty and deceitful man.* ***and his hands will wither up,*** that is, his power of operation and his works. Eccl 9:[136] *There will be neither work, nor reason, nor knowledge, nor wisdom in hell, to which place you are going quickly.*

And he sets forth a metaphor for this: **[33]** ***His grapes,*** that is, his fruit, ***will be struck as a vine in first flower,*** namely when it is dried up by a light frost and burned by a little heat. Jb 8:[137] *When it is still in flower and it is not plucked up by the hand, it withers before*

129. Ps 108.13.
130. Is 14.22.
131. Ps 145.4.
132. 1 Mc 2.62–63.
133. Prv 13.8.
134. Prv 6.35.
135. Ps 5.7.
136. Eccl 9.10.
137. Jb 8.12.

all grasses. ***and*** supply: will be struck ***as an olive tree casting down its flower,*** that is, a tree that sheds its flower and degenerates into a wild olive tree, which is barren and does not bear fruit. Jl 1:[138] *He has laid waste to my vine, and he has stripped the bark off my fig tree.* Dt 28:[139] *You will have olive trees in all your borders, but you will not be anointed with oil because the olives will fall off and die.*

And so that the punishment might seem more just, he returns to the offense (*culpam*) and responds to a tacit objection. For someone could say that blessed Job was outwardly well-composed, but Eliphaz attributes it to hypocrisy.

And that is: **[34]** ***For the congregation of the hypocrite is barren,*** that is, things having been collected by the hypocrite, supply: and so they are not useful. Jb 8:[140] *The hope of the hypocrite will perish.* And because on the inside a hypocrite is like an avaricious wolf, he adds: ***and fire,*** of the eternal conflagration, of course, ***will devour*** or consume ***the tents,*** that is, the resources, families, and bodies, ***of those who accept bribes with pleasure,*** that is, with the pleasure of greed. Is 1:[141] *All of them love bribes, and they seek rewards.* And it follows:[142] *Your strength will be as the ashes of flax, and your work as a spark; and both will burn together, and there will be no one to quench it.*

And Eliphaz adds that in this way he perseveres in evil: **[35]** ***He has conceived sorrow,*** namely by thinking and being jealous, ***and has given birth to iniquity,*** namely by what he has done and by what he has failed to do. Ps:[143] *He has conceived sorrow and has given birth to iniquity.* ***and his womb,*** that is, his will, fertile with regard to evils, ***prepares deceits.*** Is 59:[144] *We have conceived and have spoken from our heart words of falsehood.* Jer 9:[145] *Your dwelling is in the midst of deceit. Through deceit they have refused to know me, says the Lord.*

138. Jl 1.7.
139. Dt 28.40.
140. Jb 8.13.
141. Is 1.23.
142. Is 1.31.
143. Ps 7.15.
144. Is 59.13.
145. Jer 9.6.

CHAPTER 16

THEN RESPONDING, *Job said.*

This response of Job builds on his argument that human life in the present is not governed according to good or bad merits, although in the future good people will be repaid with good things and evil people with bad things. But for certain other purposes, such as to test virtue or to provide a model of perseverance or to manifest God's glory, many bad things are inflicted upon good people and many good things happen to evil people. And therefore Job insists on showing that he has suffered many things without iniquity.

His response is divided into two parts on account of the fact that the disputation, which makes use of exclamations, refutations, and invectives, is rhetorical. Hence at first he sets forth a refutation; and then a proof of his proposition, in this place:[1] *I who was once wealthy*.

In the first part he sets forth a refutation of his fellow disputants; in the second part he says that he has been distressed about interrupting them on behalf of the truth and remaining silent on account of their words of opposition, which charge in against him, in this place:[2] *But what shall I do?*

In the first part he refutes his friends concerning four things, namely: their frequent and futile repetition of the same things; their burdensome comforting; their arrogant and windy proposition, and that his friends are not set straight by words; and fourthly he wishes that they might receive instruction even by feeling punishments.

1. Jb 16.13.
2. Jb 16.7.

And that is: ***Then responding,*** supply: against Eliphaz, ***Job said:*** For the wise man refutes falsehood. 2 Cor 13:[3] *For we cannot do anything against the truth, but all things for the truth.* **[2]** ***I have often heard things of this sort,*** supply: without advantage and repeated worthlessly. Mt 6:[4] *They think that in their loquaciousness they will be heard.* For it is characteristic of the foolish, when they grow weak in their thinking, to rely on a multitude of words, not paying attention to what is said in Prv 14:[5] *Where there are many words, there is often poverty in works.*

And concerning their burdensome comforting, he adds: ***all of you,*** who appear to be my friends, ***are burdensome comforters,*** that is, piling on a heavy burden instead of consolation. Gregory: "Be careful that a rebuke not be given in a time of sorrow. If certain people should rightly be rebuked, nevertheless do not do it in the midst of suffering, lest he who ought to alleviate their suffering only increase it."[6] Jer 23:[7] *You are a burden, and I will certainly cast you away, says the Lord.* Ps:[8] *They have added to the pain of my wounds.*

And, concerning their windy proposition, he adds: **[3]** ***Can it be that windy words,*** that is, immoderate words spoken swiftly and arrogantly, ***will have no end?*** Jb 6:[9] *You dress up speeches only to rebuke, and you utter words into the wind.* ***Or is it not somewhat distressing,*** that is, shameful, ***for you,*** O Eliphaz, ***to speak?*** For the impudent person is not ashamed of lying. Jer 3:[10] *Your face has become like that of a prostitute, and have you refused to blush?* Against this Eccl 5[11] says: *Do not say anything rashly, nor let your heart be hasty to bring forth a word in the presence of God.*

Then, to set them straight by his own example, he adds: **[4]** ***I too could,*** that is to say, if discipline did not restrain me, ***say***

3. 2 Cor 13.8.
4. Mt 6.7.
5. Prv 14.23.
6. Gregory, *Mor.* 13.3.3.
7. Jer 23.33.
8. Ps 68.27.
9. Jb 6.26.
10. Jer 3.3.
11. Eccl 5.1.

things like you. Ps:[12] *I was disturbed, and I did not speak.* 1 Cor 4[13] is similar: *We are reviled, and we bless; we are blasphemed, and we endure it.* 1 Pt 2:[14] *When He was reviled, He did not revile in return.* Sir 31:[15] *He who could have transgressed has not transgressed.*

But because they are not set straight by words, he wishes that they might at least be set straight by the rod. And that is: ***and if only your soul*** **(anima)**, that is, your animal and sensible life, ***were in the place of my soul!*** that is, in the midst of affliction just as I am afflicted. Is 26:[16] *They have sought you in distress; in the tribulation of murmuring your teaching was with them.* **[5]** ***And I would comfort you,*** namely with true consolation, ***with words,*** with gentle ones, of course, not as you are comforting me. Is 40:[17] *Comfort, O comfort, my people.* At the end of 1 Thes:[18] *Comfort the discouraged, support the weak.* ***and I would move my head over you.*** For the movement of the head signifies the bending of the mind towards compassion, and sometimes it signifies the cruelty of derision. Lam 2:[19] *They have hissed at and moved their heads over daughter Jerusalem.* **[6]** ***And I would encourage you with my mouth,*** that is, with gentle words I would strengthen you toward forbearance. Near the end of 2 Mc:[20] *He armed every one of them, not with the protection of shield and spear, but rather with the best words and exhortations.* ***and I would move my lips,*** namely with a gentle coaxing motion, ***as if sparing you,*** namely correcting with restrained invective the things that should be reproved among you. Song 4:[21] *Honey and milk are under your tongue.* Ps:[22] *Grace is poured out over your lips.*

Then he describes the perplexity and anguish of his decision: **[7]** ***But what shall I do?*** It is as if he were saying: "I do not

12. Ps 76.5.
13. 1 Cor 4.12.
14. 1 Pt 2.23.
15. Sir 31.10.
16. Is 26.16.
17. Is 40.1.
18. 1 Thes 5.14.
19. Lam 2.15.
20. 2 Mc 15.11.
21. Song 4.11.
22. Ps 44.3.

know whether I should speak on behalf of the truth, since even that would cause me to suffer, or whether I should be silent and yield to falsehood so that the rebuke of my friends would cease." Near the end of 2 Sm:[23] *I am hemmed in exceedingly on all sides.* Dn 13:[24] *There are straits for me on all sides.*

And he considers each of the two possibilities: ***If I speak,*** supply: on behalf of the truth, ***my pain will not cease,*** thereby giving strength to my opponents' arguments. Hence Is 53[25] cries out: *Who would believe our report?* For my pain is so great that I seem to have been punished for sin. Is 53:[26] *We considered him as a leper, one stricken and humbled by God.* ***and if I remain silent,*** namely conceding to falsehood, ***it,*** namely pain, ***will not depart from me,*** because I see truth being overcome. This is similar to what was suffered by Jeremiah according to Jer 20:[27] *The word of the Lord has become for me a source of reproach and derision all day long. And I said: I will not remember Him, nor speak anymore in His name. Then the word of the Lord came to me like a burning fire in my heart and shut up in my bones, and I was wearied, not able to bear it.*

He adds, moreover, that his pain provides evidence against him: **[8]** ***Now, however,*** that is, indeed, ***my pain has overwhelmed me.*** Is 38:[28] *Like a lion He has broken all my bones.*

And, amplifying the force of his pain, he adds: ***and all my limbs,*** that is, my bodily members, ***have been reduced to nothing,*** supply: even now distending to corruption. 2 Tm 4:[29] *I am already being poured out, and the time of my dissolution approaches.* Ps:[30] *I was reduced to nothing and I did not know it.*

And he adds that the intensity of the beating that he received served to strengthen the arguments of his opponents for four reasons, namely: the instigation of lying, the fury of the one speaking against him, the opening of the mouth for the

23. 2 Sm 24.14.
24. Dn 13.22.
25. Is 53.1.
26. Is 53.4.
27. Jer 20.8–9.
28. Is 38.13.
29. 2 Tm 4.6.
30. Ps 72.22.

purpose of reproving, and the closing of the mouth of the one defending the truth.

And that is: **[9]** ***My wrinkles,*** namely by means of which my tight skin has become full of creases because of the intensity of my infirmity, ***bear witness against me,*** namely that I have been stricken on account of sin. Jb 7:[31] *My flesh is clothed with rottenness and with the filth of dust; my skin has become dry and has tightened.* ***and,*** supply: therefore, ***a liar is roused,*** as if waking up, ***against my face,*** that is, face to face, ***contradicting me.*** Hab 1:[32] *Because the wicked one prevails against the just man, perverse judgment goes forth.*

And to show his zeal for speaking the truth, he adds: **[10]** ***He has amassed his fury against me.*** Ps:[33] *Their fury is like that of a serpent.* ***and threatening me,*** that is, speaking in a menacing way, ***he has gnashed his teeth at me.*** Ps:[34] *The sinner will see and will be angry, and he will gnash his teeth and waste away.* Acts 7:[35] *But hearing these things, they were cut to their hearts, and they gnashed their teeth at him.* ***My enemy,*** namely he who ought to have been my ally in the disputation, ***has stared at me with terrible eyes,*** in order, of course, to make me afraid to speak the truth. This is similar to what happened [to Esther] in Est 15:[36] *When he* [*King Ahasuerus*] *had lifted up his face and with fiery eyes had shown the fury of a sinner, the queen collapsed, and her color turned pale, and she rested her fallen head on her handmaid.*

And because the audacity of an opponent opens his mouth, Job adds: **[11]** ***They have opened their mouths against me,*** that is, they have contradicted me openly. Ps:[37] *They have opened their mouths against me, like a lion rapacious and roaring.* Jer 12:[38] *It* [*a lion in the woods*] *has lifted up its voice against me.* ***and, reproaching me, they have struck my jaw.*** The literal reading is not that they have slapped blessed Job. Rather, the purpose of the jaw is to hold in place those things that are chewed by the teeth, and in

31. Jb 7.5.
32. Hab 1.4.
33. Ps 57.5.
34. Ps 111.10.
35. Acts 7.54.
36. Est 15.10.
37. Ps 21.14.
38. Jer 12.8.

a certain spiritual way things are chewed when repeated mental processing breaks them apart into the true and the false. When the memory holds these things in place so that they may be broken apart by the mind, it is called the jaw. And this jaw is said to have been struck when what the mind has reflected on well is met by a contradiction, and this can be the reason why he said "reproaching me, they have struck," not "they have struck me with their hands." Mi 5:[39] *With a rod he has struck the jaw of the judge of Israel.* ***and they are filled,*** that is, fed and restored inwardly, ***with my punishment,*** which is cruel. Lam 3:[40] *He will give his jaw to the one who strikes him; he will be filled with reproaches.*

And so supply: **[12]** ***The Lord has shut me up with the unjust man,*** so that He might hold me captive and I may not be able to speak against Him. Lam 3:[41] *He has closed off my ways with square stones; he has overturned my paths.* ***and,*** in other words, ***has delivered me into the hands of the wicked,*** that is, to the power of those attacking the truth. Jb 9:[42] *The earth has been given into the hands of the wicked one; he covers the eyes of its judges.*

[13] ***I who was once.***

Here begins the second part, in which Job shows by his own example that God does not reward justice with temporal goods in this life, and neither does He punish sin with temporal evils. And it has two sections. In the first he proves what has been said; in the second, he begs God that he might be freed from the evils of life, which Satan is heaping upon him, below in this place:[43] *My spirit will be weakened.*

The first section is divided into three subdivisions: in the first subdivision he enumerates the evils that he has suffered; in the second he makes clear that he has suffered without sinning, in this place:[44] *These things I have suffered;* in the third, he invokes God as his witness concerning these things, in this place:[45] *O earth, do not cover.*

39. Mi 5.1.
40. Lam 3.30.
41. Lam 3.9.
42. Jb 9.24.
43. Jb 17.1.
44. Jb 16.18.
45. Jb 16.19.

In the first subdivision he says three things, namely that he has been crushed by sorrows, how cruelly he has been crushed, and how humbly he has endured it.

And that is: ***I who was once wealthy***. He says this for a greater sense of misery, for misery afflicts to a greater extent one who has become accustomed to living in luxury; hence Boethius: "The most extreme form of misfortune is to have been fortunate at one time."[46] 1 Mc 6:[47] *Into how much tribulation I have come, and into what great floods of sorrow, in which I now am; but I was pleasant and beloved in my power.* Jb 29[48] and 30:[49] *And when I sat as a king, with an army gathered around me, yet I was a comforter of those who mourned. But now the younger in time mock me.* In the first book of the *Ethics,* Aristotle calls such people spun by Priam's luck, because they are brought down from the summit of terrestrial fortune to the lowest level of misfortune.[50]

suddenly, that is, contrary to expectation, ***I have been crushed.*** Jb 30:[51] *I expected good things, but evil things have come upon me; I waited for light, but darkness has burst forth.* And he enumerates the afflictions that he has endured. ***He has grabbed my neck,*** that is, He has choked me. From the back part of the head[52] motor nerves in the neck descend into the whole body. The evidence for this is that if someone is choked at the back of the neck his entire body is rendered immobile. He wishes to say, then, that God choked him with punishments in such a way that he was not able to move. At the end of Lam:[53] *We were driven by our necks;*[54] *we were weary and no rest was given to us.* ***He has broken me into pieces,*** into limbs and bones, in which strength resides.

46. Boethius, *CP* 2.4 (PL 63:677).
47. 1 Mc 6.11.
48. Jb 29.25.
49. Jb 30.1.
50. Aristotle, *EN* 1.10.14.
51. Jb 30.26.
52. Modern scientists know this part as the brain stem or base of the brain, through which the nerve connections of the motor and sensory systems from the main part of the brain (i.e., what Albert here calls the "head") pass to the rest of the body. The brain stem also plays a crucial role in the regulation of cardiac and respiratory functioning, as Albert rightly suggests.
53. Lam 5.5.
54. That is, as if yoked animals.

Is 38:[55] *Like a lion He has broken all my bones.* ***and He has set me up as if His target,*** namely toward which He would direct the arrows of His punishments. Jb 6:[56] *The arrows of the Lord are in me, the anger of which drinks up my spirit.* Lam 2:[57] *He has drawn His bow like a foe; He has strengthened His right hand like an enemy, and He has killed everything that was beautiful to behold in the tabernacles of the daughter of Zion.*

[14] ***He has encircled me with His lances.*** Wis 5:[58] *He will sharpen His awful wrath into a lance.* Thus the sense is: He has so multiplied the punishments with which His wrath has struck me that there was no way of escaping without falling upon a spear. Lam 3:[59] *Against me alone He has turned and returned His hand all day long.* ***He has severely wounded my loins.*** The loins are the seat of pleasure, and the sense is that He has dragged every pleasure down into bitterness. Lam 3:[60] *He has drawn His bow, and set me as a mark for His arrows. He has shot into my kidneys the daughters of His quiver.*

Moreover, he adds how cruelly this has happened: ***He has not acted sparingly,*** so as to introduce some peace or consolation. For Satan, into whose power Job was given, does not intend to act sparingly. Hab 1:[61] *He will never spare the nations from destruction.* ***and has poured out my bowels onto the earth,*** that is, my vital parts, namely my children and my own body. Lam 2:[62] *He poured out my liver onto the earth.*

[15] ***He has cut me to pieces with wound after wound.*** Is 1:[63] *From the sole of his foot all the way to the top of his head, there is no health in him.* Ps:[64] *They have added to the pain of my wounds.* ***He has rushed headlong against me like a giant,*** that is, a mighty one

55. Is 38.13.
56. Jb 6.4.
57. Lam 2.4.
58. Wis 5.21.
59. Lam 3.3.
60. Lam 3.12–13.
61. Hab 1.17.
62. Lam 2.11.
63. Is 1.6.
64. Ps 68.27.

and a tyrant. Gn 6:[65] *Giants were on the earth in those days; powerful, renowned men of old.* Is 14:[66] *It [hell] will stir up the giants for you.*

And he adds how humbly he has accepted this [suffering]: **[16] *I have sewed sackcloth over my skin,*** so that I could bring harshness together with harshness. Jon 3:[67] *The king of Nineveh,* which means "beautiful,"[68] *dressed himself in sackcloth.* ***and I have covered my body in ashes,*** in memory of mortality, of course. Sir 7:[69] *Remember your last [day], and you will never sin.* Gregory: Ashes and a hairshirt are the weapons of penitents.[70]

And because weeping pertains to the penitent, he adds: **[17] *My face has become swollen from weeping.*** Jer 9:[71] *Who will offer water for my head, and a fountain of tears for my eyes? And I will weep day and night?* ***and my eyelids have grown dark.*** Basil says that the darkness of the eyelids is placed all around the eyes so that the visual ray might be directed to a certain object.[72] Hence the sense is that Job's vision has grown dark; so what contains is written for what is contained.[73] Lam 2:[74] *My eyes have grown weak from weeping; my stomach is upset.*

And he adds that he suffered this innocently: **[18] *These things I have suffered with no iniquity of my hand,*** that is, of my work. Is 53[75] and in 1 Pt 2:[76] *He did not commit a sin, nor was deceit found in his mouth.* ***since I have offered to God pure prayers,*** which

65. Gn 6.4.
66. Is 14.9.
67. Jon 3.6.
68. See Jerome, *Prol. in Nahum.*
69. Sir 7.40.
70. See Gregory, *Mor.* 35.6.7 and 9.65.97.
71. Jer 9.1.
72. See Basil, *HS* 2.15 (PG 30:59). Following Galen, the standard ancient and medieval view of visual perception was what is described today as emission or extramission theory, which proposed that sight was accomplished by rays of light emitted from the eyes and directed to the external object. This view has been replaced in the modern period by intromission theory, which maintains that sight occurs when rays of light reflected from the external object enter the eyes.
73. That is, "eyelids" is written for vision or sight.
74. Lam 2.11.
75. Is 53.12.
76. 1 Pt 2.22.

no wicked life has contradicted, of course. Jn 9:[77] *We know that God does not hear sinners; but if anyone is a servant of God and does His will, God hears him.*

And Job says all these things in order to show that God does not reward the just temporally and does not punish the wicked temporally. Wis 12:[78] *Since you are just, you order all things justly. You, O Father, condemn him who does not deserve to be punished, and you consider him alien to your power.*

Moreover, he proves this with God as his witness, adding: **[19]** ***O earth,*** that is, the earthly fantasy (*phantasia*) that imagines that human affairs are governed by God according to the order of human justice, ***do not cover my blood,*** that is to say, such that my blood, having been poured out by so many punishments, might not testify to this truth, namely that God does not reward good people temporally but He governs with something else in view, permitting good people to be punished, either to test them or to manifest the glory of God or for this reason, so that their crown and their reward in the future might be increased, or certainly, as Gregory says, so that the wicked, seeing that even the holy are punished, might contemplate the punishments they will deserve if they do not return to their senses.[79] Lk 23:[80] *If they do these things among the green wood, what will happen when it is dry?*

Hence, explaining what he has said, he adds: ***neither let my cry find a hiding place in you,*** O earthly fantasy, so that it will always testify to the truth.[81] For my blood cries out on behalf of the truth. Heb 12:[82] *You have come* [...] *to the sprinkling of blood that speaks better than that of Abel.*

And concerning this he invokes God as a witness: **[20]** ***For behold, my witness is in heaven,*** where there is nothing that is not just (*rectum*). For from heaven God, punishing good peo-

77. Jn 9.31.

78. Wis 12.15.

79. See Gregory, *Mor.* 14.6.7.

80. Lk 23.31.

81. This is the earthly fiction just mentioned, namely that God governs human affairs according to the order of human justice.

82. Heb 12.22–24.

ple and permitting them to prosper, testifies to this. Ps:[83] *You have caused judgment to be heard from heaven.* ***and my confidant is on high,*** that is, in Him who is exalted, having been lifted up beyond the erroneous fantasy,[84] and therefore He has no fellowship with falsehood. Prv 8:[85] *All my words are just, and there is nothing wicked or perverse in them.*

But because those who have been deceived by error do not accept the truth, he adds: **[21]** ***My friends are verbose,*** that is, speaking boldly in their words against me as they were engaging in the disputation, and therefore not receiving the truth. Jb 11:[86] *Can it be that one who says many things will not also listen? Or will a verbose man be justified?* And therefore supply: because I do not find the truth among humans, ***my eye pours out tears to God,*** who is the judge and witness of the truth. But an eye pouring out tears signifies suppliant and upright prayer. Sir 35:[87] *The prayer of him who humbles himself will pierce the clouds, and he will not be comforted until he draws near.*

And having compassion on them, he adds: **[22]** ***And if only a man were to be judged by God,*** that is, in the presence of God, ***in the same way that the son of man is judged by his fellow man,*** namely according to merits, so that good things might come forth for good people and bad things for wicked people, supply: because then evil would not have befallen me. Jb 6[88] is similar: *If only my sins, for which I have deserved wrath, and the calamity that I suffer were weighed in a balance.* But that it is not so is said in Tb 3:[89] *Your plan is not in the power of man.*

He adds, moreover, that the temporal reward is brief: **[23]** ***For behold, brief years pass away;*** the justice of the saints will not be able to be rewarded fittingly (*condigne*) in a brief and transitory period of time. 2 Cor 4:[90] *What is at present a momentary and slight*

83. Ps 75.9.
84. Namely that God governs human affairs according to the order of human justice.
85. Prv 8.8.
86. Jb 11.2.
87. Sir 35.21.
88. Jb 6.2.
89. Tb 3.20.
90. 2 Cor 4.17.

tribulation for us is working in us an eternal weight of glory beyond measure in its sublimity. ***and I am walking,*** that is, I am advancing without delay toward death, ***a path,*** that is, a brief shortcut through life, ***by which I will not return*** to these temporal benefits or misfortunes (*bona vel mala*), supply: and so such things should not be hoped for.[91] Is 38:[92] *I will behold man no more, nor the inhabitant of peace.*

91. Here I read *speranda* with MSS EFM, rather than *toleranda* with Weiss's edition.

92. Is 38.11.

CHAPTER 17

MY SPIRIT WILL BE *weakened.*

In this section,[1] since the evidence [for his proposition] is not accepted [by his fellow disputants], Job begs for the help of liberation from the evils of life, which have been given into Satan's power, even among good people, whom Satan frequently punishes, and which evils are for the purpose of proving his proposition. And it is divided into two subsections.

In the first subsection he begs to be freed from his adversaries [in the disputation] on account of the fact that his having suffered evils innocently did not convince them of the falsehood of their error. In the second subsection, in order to convince them, he adduces the inconsolable nature of his suffering, in this place:[2] *My days have passed away.*

In the first subsection he does five things: first, in fact, he affirms that he has suffered pain innocently. Secondly, he shows the obstinacy of his adversaries, in this place:[3] *Their hearts.* Thirdly, he sets forth his own indignation against those who are opposed to the truth, in this place:[4] *My eye has grown dark.* Fourthly, he shows the progress of good people as a result of the declaration of the truth, in this place:[5] *The just will be astonished.* Fifthly, out of compassion he calls his adversaries back

1. Here begins the second section of the second part of Job's response (see Albert's *divisio textus* on 16.13 above), wherein he begs God that he might be freed from the evils of this life, which Satan is heaping upon him.

2. Jb 17.11.

3. Jb 17.4.

4. Jb 17.7.

5. Jb 17.8.

and teaches them the way to return to the truth, in this place:[6] *Therefore, all of you.*

The first [of these five things] is further divided into two: for he sets forth evidence of the truth, and, because it is not accepted [by his adversaries], he begs for the help of divine liberation, in this place:[7] *Deliver me, O Lord.*

And that is: ***My spirit will be weakened,*** namely such that it can no longer be the bearer of power and of life through the body. Eccl 12:[8] *The dust will return into its earth, from which it came, and the spirit returns to the Lord, who gave it.* Ps:[9] *His spirit will pass away, and he,* supply: [his] body, *will return into his earth.* Similarly, Ps:[10] *You will take away their spirit, and they will pass away.* And, supply: because "my spirit will be weakened," ***my days will be shortened,*** that is, the days of my life. Is 38:[11] *My life has been cut short, as by a weaver.* Jb 14:[12] *The days of man are short.* ***and only the grave remains for me,*** that is, my wound is so great that nothing is left except death and the grave. Jer 30:[13] *Your fracture is the worst; your wound is incurable.*[14] Who will heal you?

[2] ***I have not sinned,*** that is to say, by a sin for which I have deserved this wound. Is 53:[15] *He did not commit a sin, nor was deceit found in his mouth.* ***and,*** supply: nevertheless, ***my eye abides in bitterness.*** For it is not only touched by affliction, but by remaining in affliction it abides [there] weeping. Lam 1:[16] *See, O Lord, that I am in distress. My stomach is upset; my heart is turned in on itself, since I am full of bitterness.* And he means that such a great wound being inflicted without sin is an argument for the truth

6. Jb 17.10.
7. Jb 17.3.
8. Eccl 12.7.
9. Ps 145.4.
10. Ps 103.29.
11. Is 38.12.
12. Jb 14.5.
13. Jer 30.12.
14. Here Albert quotes Jer 30.12 in a way different from that in which he does above in commenting on 2.7. There he has this scriptural text including the question that follows the quotation here: *quis medebitur tibi?*
15. Is 53.12.
16. Lam 1.20.

that in this life God does not reward good people and punish evil people.

But because his adversaries do not accept this truth, he begs for the help of liberation, and that is: [3] ***Deliver me,*** namely from the vehemence of those attacking the truth, ***and set me near you,*** that is, as a witness to your manifest truth. Hence earlier he said:[17] *My friends are verbose; my eye pours out tears to God.* Ps:[18] *Deliver me from blood, O God, my God, and my tongue will extol your justice.* Near the end of 2 Tm:[19] *At my first defense no one was present with me, but everyone abandoned me.* And after a few lines:[20] *But the Lord has delivered me from every evil work.*

and let the hand, that is, the power, ***of anyone fight against me.*** Rom 8:[21] *If God is for us, who is against us?* Is 50:[22] *God who justifies me* [*is near*]; *who will speak against me? The Lord God is my helper; who, therefore, is there who will condemn me?*

He adds, moreover, why he begs to be liberated, namely because his adversaries do not receive understanding of the truth, and that is: [4] ***Their hearts you have caused to be,*** that is, you have permitted to become, ***far from understanding,*** of the truth, of course. Understanding is far away, however, when their hearts have been filled with ideas contrary to the principles of the truth; then, indeed, the truth is repugnant to the heart. Jer 13:[23] *If an Ethiopian is able to change his skin or a leopard its spots, you too are able to act well even when you have learned evil.* ***therefore they will not be exalted,*** namely through understanding of divine truth, which is not understood except by a heart exalted beyond earthly realities and the fantasies (*phantasiis*) of earthly people. Ps:[24] *The human may come to a lofty heart, but God will be exalted.*

And concerning their shamelessness before the truth[25] he

17. Jb 16.21.
18. Ps 50.16.
19. 2 Tm 4.16.
20. 2 Tm 4.18.
21. Rom 8.31.
22. Is 50.8–9.
23. Jer 13.23.
24. Ps 63.7–8.
25. Although Weiss notes no variants here, I read *veritatem* with MS F, which I consulted directly, rather than Weiss's *varietatem.*

adds: [5] ***He***, the one having been roused against my face, ***promises the prey to his companions,*** namely to those lying. [Recall] Jb 16.[26] "He promises to his companions," to his own who are attacking the truth, "the prey," that is to say, that they might violently subjugate me. Is 33:[27] *Woe to you who prey on others! Will you yourself not also be preyed upon?*

But what follows is the consolation [for Job]: ***and the eyes of his children will fail***. Those who imitate his [Job's adversary's] errors are called "his children"; and [it says "the eyes" here] because wherever love is treated, there the word "eye" is used. It is said that "the eyes fail" when the things hoped for and loved do not happen.

And because he disputed by mocking the truth, Job therefore adds: **[6]** ***He has made me as it were a byword of the common people,*** namely so that the common people might use me as a byword of derision and of curse. Ps:[28] *All who have seen me have mocked me; they have spoken with their lips, and they have wagged their heads.* And this is what follows: ***and I am an example,*** that is, publicly, ***before them,*** namely the common people. Lam 2:[29] *All your enemies have opened their mouths against you; they hiss and gnash their teeth.* And in the same book:[30] *I am their song.*

And he goes on about his indignation against falsehood out of zeal for the truth, and that is: [7] ***My eye has grown dark on account of indignation***. Jb 16:[31] *My face has become swollen from weeping, and my eyelids have grown dark.* Is 38:[32] *My eyes are weakened, looking upward.* Lam 2:[33] *My eyes have grown weak from weeping; my stomach is upset.* ***and my limbs,*** by a failure of strength, of course, ***have been reduced as if to nothing,*** that is to say, such that even now my life is, so to speak, cut off. Jb 33:[34] *His soul will*

26. Jb 16.9, where Job affirms that *a liar is roused against my face, contradicting me.*

27. Is 33.1.

28. Ps 21.8.

29. Lam 2.16.

30. Lam 3.36.

31. Jb 16.17.

32. Is 38.14.

33. Lam 2.11.

34. Jb 33.22.

draw near to corruption, and his life to those who bring death. Ps:[35] *My feet were almost moved, my steps nearly slipped, because I was zealous concerning the unjust.*

That the good make progress on account of this, however, he adds: **[8]** ***The just will be astonished by this,*** namely that falsehood opposes itself to the truth. Jer 2:[36] *Be astounded, O heavens, by this.* ***and the innocent,*** namely the defender of the truth, ***will be aroused against the hypocrite.*** "Hypocrite" designates someone who attacks the truth under the cloak of feigned justice, just as the sophists and heretics do, about whom it is said in Mt 7:[37] *They come to you in sheep's clothing, but inwardly they are ravenous wolves.* 2 Cor 13:[38] *For we cannot do anything against the truth, but all things for the truth.* Hence the innocent one is roused by zeal for the truth. 1 Cor 15:[39] *Be vigilant, O just ones, and refuse to sin; for some people have no knowledge of God.*

[9] ***And,*** supply: after defending the truth, ***the just man will hold fast to his own way,*** and he will not turn toward errors. Jb 27:[40] *My justification, which I have begun to hold fast, I will not forsake.* ***and he who has clean hands,*** that is, good works, ***will increase his strength,*** that is to say, so that he might make progress in them and persevere. Is 40:[41] *Those who hope in the Lord will renew*[42] *their strength; they will take up wings as eagles; they will run and not be weary; they will fly and not grow weak.*

And because he desires their conversion, he adds: **[10]** ***Therefore all of you,*** supply: who oppose the truth, ***be converted,*** to the truth, of course, ***and come*** by means of the imitation of the truth. Is 21:[43] *If you seek, seek; be converted and come!*

Then he teaches the method whereby they are able to accept [his] instruction: ***and I will not find among you any wise man,***

35. Ps 72.2–3.
36. Jer 2.12.
37. Mt 7.15.
38. 2 Cor 13.8.
39. 1 Cor 15.34.
40. Jb 27.6.
41. Is 40.31.
42. Although Weiss notes no variants here, I read *mutabunt* with MS F, which I consulted directly, rather than Weiss's *unitabunt.*
43. Is 21.12.

that is, one relying upon his own wisdom in a fantastical mode (*phantastice*).[44] Ob:[45] *I will destroy the wise from Edom, and prudence from the mountain of Esau.* 1 Cor 1:[46] *I will destroy the wisdom of the wise, and I will reject the prudence of the prudent.*

[11] *My days have passed away.*

Here he proves his proposition from the inconsolable nature of the suffering of good people, who nevertheless are not punished for sinning.

And he asserts three things: the inconsolable nature [of the suffering of the good]; the reason for its inconsolable nature, in this place:[47] *If I endure;* and his intended conclusion from these points, in this place:[48] *Where, therefore, is.*

And that is: ***My days have passed away,*** that is, the days given to causing my life have already passed away, and the days given to experiencing its effects still pass by. Wis 5:[49] *All those things have passed away like a shadow, and like a messenger quickly running ahead.* And in the midst of the days passing away, ***my plans* (cogitationes) *have been scattered,*** that is, into many little parts. Lk 10:[50] *Martha, Martha, you are worried and troubled about many things.* ***tormenting my heart,*** with worry, of course. Ps:[51] *My heart is troubled within me, my strength has left me, and the very light of my eyes is not with me.* Is 24:[52] *By breaking, the earth will be broken into pieces; by grinding, the earth will be worn away.*

He adds, moreover, how much weariness this heaps up: **[12] *They have turned night into day,*** that is, the calm of night into the struggle of daytime and of wakefulness. Jb 7:[53] *Whenever I*

44. By *phantastice* here Albert means in a mode or way related to the ideas or images characteristic of their human minds alone. See the comments on 16.19 and 17.4, where Albert uses *phantasia* of the earthly idea or fantasy that imagines God as governing human affairs according to the order of human justice.

45. Ob 8.

46. 1 Cor 1.19.

47. Jb 17.13.

48. Jb 17.15.

49. Wis 5.9.

50. Lk 10.41.

51. Ps 37.11.

52. Is 24.19.

53. Jb 7.4.

go to sleep, I say: When will I rise? And again I will wait for evening, and I will be filled with suffering continuously until darkness. And this is what follows: ***and again after darkness,*** namely during the night when I should be at peace, ***I hope for light;*** that is, I long for it. And this is the sense: "I hope for the light, which is after the darkness." Jb 30:[54] *At night my bones are pierced with pain, and those who eat away at me do not sleep.* Mi 7:[55] *If I sit in darkness, the Lord is my light.*[56]

Then he adds the reason for the inconsolable nature [of the suffering of the good] because of the end of life both in the soul and in the body, and that is: **[13]** ***If I endure,*** supply: patiently, supply: the end is not a source of comfort because ***hell is my house,*** that is, the repository for my soul. For when the price [of human redemption] had not been paid and the door [to heaven] had not been opened, the fathers went down to limbo, and Job calls this "hell" here. But such an end holds no consolation. Gn 37:[57] *He refused to receive consolation, but said: I will go down into hell to my son, mourning.* And Job explains this, adding: ***and,*** in other words, ***in darkness,*** namely the darkness of hell, ***I have made my bed,*** that is, in the peaceful sleep of limbo I will wait for the light of divine vision. Lam 3:[58] *He has driven me, and He has led me into darkness.*

And, concerning the inconsolable end of the body, he adds: **[14]** ***I have said,*** having understood by examination, of course, ***to rottenness: You are my father,*** for I have been born from a seed that is rotting and of one who is rotting. Jb 25:[59] *Man, who is rottenness, and the son of man, who is a worm.* ***and,*** supply: I have said, ***my mother,*** because my material beginning possessed rot-

54. Jb 30.17.
55. Mi 7.8.
56. Cf. the comments on Jb 1.6 and on 3.4 above, where Albert also invokes Mi 7.8. Interestingly, though, he has the final part of the verse beginning with a different word in each of these citations: *cum sedero ...* (*when I sit ...*) in the first instance (on 1.6); *dum sedero ...* (*as long as I sit ...*) in the second (on 3.4); and *Si sedero ...* (*If I sit ...*) here. This suggests that Albert was recalling Mi 7.8 from memory and in so doing was more concerned with the gist of the scriptural text than its exact wording as attested in any particular manuscript.
57. Gn 37.35.
58. Lam 3.2.
59. Jb 25.6.

tenness. Wis 7:[60] *I was pressed together into blood, from the seed of man and the delight of conjugal sleep.* ***and,*** supply: I have said, ***my sister to worms,*** as though to those already born or going to be born with me from the same rottenness. Sir 10:[61] *When a man dies, he will inherit serpents, and beasts, and worms.*

From these two points he concludes that the suffering [of the good] is inconsolable, adding: **[15]** ***Where, therefore, is,*** that is, in what consolation, ***now,*** that is, which I may reach in the present, ***my expectation?*** that is, the good that I might expect when after death I have rest neither in the soul nor in the body, as if he were saying, "in nothing." Jb 6:[62] *What is my strength, that I might hold up? Or what is my end, that I should be patient?* ***and who is carefully considering,*** supply: for the purpose of repaying, that is to say, seeing that neither has the blood of redemption been shed nor the door of salvation been opened, according to what is said afterwards, ***my patience?*** supply: which meanwhile I have in the midst of my sufferings. Heb 10:[63] *Patience is necessary for you, so that, doing the will of God, you might receive the promises.* Jas 5:[64] *Behold, we call blessed those who have endured.*

And he adds the reason and it is supplied: **[16]** ***Into the deepest hell.*** Gregory: With respect to heaven, the earth is deep, the place of graves deeper, and limbo and the repository for souls the deepest.[65] The superlative "deepest," then, denotes not an extreme in comparison to the places of hell, as if he is saying that he will go down to the place of the damned, but rather in the comparison that has been mentioned.[66] Or "the deepest" can be interpreted as "very deep." For Priscian says that when no comparison is specified, a superlative adjective has a positive sense like the adverb "very."[67]

all that I have will descend. That is to say, according to Gregory, all things pertaining to the soul (*animalia*), because the

60. Wis 7.2.
61. Sir 10.13.
62. Jb 6.11.
63. Heb 10.36.
64. Jas 5.11.
65. See Gregory, *Mor.* 13.48.53.
66. That of Gregory immediately above.
67. Priscian, *IG* 3.18.

whole is wherever he can sense what he takes in; or all, that is, all his works and everything that he has done.[68] Rv 14:[69] *For their works follow them.*

And because no one is free from anxiety concerning their reward, he therefore adds: ***Do you think at least,*** from the fact, of course, that I have no peace in this life, ***that there,*** that is, in hell, ***I will have rest?*** namely the rest of beatitude. Jb 14:[70] *Who will grant me that in hell you will protect me and shelter me until your wrath passes by, and will establish a time for me in which you might remember me?* Gregory: "It should be considered whether any of us will be free from anxiety concerning rest if even the very one whom the Judge praises is afraid of these things."[71]

68. Gregory, *Mor.* 13.48.54.
69. Rv 14.13.
70. Jb 14.13.
71. Gregory, *Mor.* 13.49.55.

CHAPTER 18

T*HEN RESPONDING***,** ***Bildad the Shuhite said.***

We should recall to mind the position of Bildad, who agrees with Eliphaz in this: that in this life God repays according to what is deserved, good things to good people and bad things to bad people. And if it should happen differently, such that good things should come forth for bad people, and bad things for good people, in the end, since fate moves in the opposite direction—insofar as good people return to good things and bad people fall back on bad things—they are compensated with compound interest. And this is Bildad's own addition to the position of Eliphaz.[1]

The Gloss says that this chapter is divided into two parts:[2]

For in the first part he accuses Job of boastful speech; in the second, of a wicked way of life, in this place:[3] *Will not the light of the wicked person.*

In the first place, then, he continues and shows how this chapter is introduced, and that is: ***Then responding, Bildad.*** In our consideration above, we said that Bildad means "old age"; thus he appeared[4] to possess an aged wisdom; and ***the Shuhite*** means "speaking"; thus the ignorance in his speaking stood out.[5] Sir 32:[6] *Speak, you who are older, for it is fitting for you.* ***said,*** responding, of course, both to the human being [namely Job]

1. For other summary statements of Bildad's position, see the commentary on 3.1 and 8.1 above; for Eliphaz's position, see on 3.1, 4.7–9, and 15.1.

2. See *GO* on Jb 18 (PL 113:805–7).

3. Jb 18.5.

4. Here I read *videbatur* with MSS FM, rather than *dicebatur* with Weiss's edition.

5. See the commentary on 3.1 and 8.1 above.

6. Sir 32.4.

and to his prayer. For he responds to the human being by reproaching his boasting; and he responds to the prayer by showing that the wicked person does not prosper. 1 Pt 3:[7] *Being always prepared to respond to everyone who asks you with a reason for the hope that is in you.* Jn 9:[8] *He is of age; let him speak for himself.*

[2] ***To what end.***

He finds fault with four things about Job's manner of speaking, things that seem to express boasting, namely: that, as a hasty talker, he responds before he understands; that he despises and reproaches those with whom he speaks; that, having been stirred up, he speaks out of rage; and that his own words fall short of persuading.

And that is: ***To what end will you fling out words?*** This can be understood of the end of a duration, and so the sense is that he pours forth speech without end, just as it is said in Sir 15[9] that a fool *cannot restrain his own breath in speaking.* Or it can be understood of the end of an intention, and so the sense is that he speaks uselessly on account of the fact that nothing follows because of his words. And Bildad has said the very same thing in Jb 8:[10] *How long will you say such things, while the breath of your mouth is jumbled up?*[11] For he is a braggart who usurps for himself wisdom that he does not have. Is 16:[12] *He is exceedingly proud. His pride and his arrogance are greater than his strength.*

And he sets forth the first proof, saying: ***Understand first, and so let us speak.*** Prv 18:[13] *He who answers before he listens shows himself to be a fool and very deserving of reproof.* But when Bildad says, "and so let us speak," he wants to be understood first, so that his speech will fit in, because above it was said in Jb 12:[14] *The ear discerns words; and the palate of the one eating, the taste.*

7. 1 Pt 3.15.

8. Jn 9.21.

9. The words that follow are taken not from Sir 15, but rather from Prv 25.28.

10. Jb 8.2.

11. Here Albert cites the second half of this verse in a way different from that in which he does in chapter 8 above.

12. Is 16.6.

13. Prv 18.13.

14. Jb 12.11.

And he introduces the second proof: [3] ***Why have we been thought of as beasts,*** namely animals without understanding, who would not comprehend the truth in what you said above in 12:[15] *Without a doubt ask the beasts, and they will teach you.* ***and been vile,*** that is, thought of as vile in this life, ***in your sight?*** we who are, of course, beautiful and distinguished before others. And Bildad says this especially because of what was said by Job above in 6:[16] *Why have you disparaged the words of truth, whereas there is none of you who can convict me?* And in the same place:[17] *You rush in upon the orphan, and you strive to overthrow your friend.* For one who disputes in this way is vulgar and disreputable.

And he sets forth the third proof: [4] ***You who destroy your soul in your fury.*** The soul is destroyed in fury in a twofold way. [First,] with regard to seeing the truth. Cato: "Anger obstructs the mind, so that it is not able to discern the truth."[18] Ps:[19] *Fire has fallen, and they have not seen the sun.* For when the fire of anger falls into the mind, it is not permitted to discern the sun of clear truth. And [second] it destroys the soul by the guilt of sin. Jas 1:[20] *The anger of man does not produce the justice of God.*

Then he sets forth his fourth criticism: ***can it be that the earth will be forsaken,*** supply: by God, ***because of you.*** Now the earth is called "forsaken" if its governance according to the rule of human justice is abandoned. Explaining this, he adds: ***and that rocks,*** that is, solid truths, ***will be moved from their place?*** that is, from the place of immovable truth. And he calls the principles of the governance of justice "rocks" according to the same metaphor by which it is said in Mt 16[21] concerning the confession of Peter: *You are Peter, and upon this rock I will build my Church.* For Peter, in the language of Syria, means "rock," and he received the name Peter because of the solidity of the truth that he confessed. Prv 30:[22] *The little rabbit, the weak people, makes its*

15. Jb 12.7.
16. Jb 6.25.
17. Jb 6.27.
18. Cato, *Dist.* 2.4.
19. Ps 57.9.
20. Jas 1.20.
21. Mt 16.18.
22. Prv 30.26.

bed in the rock, that is, in the solidity of the truth. Bildad said something similar above in 8:[23] *Can it be that God trips up justice, and that the Almighty overthrows what is right?*

[5] ***Will not the light of the wicked person.***

This [second part of the chapter] touches on the punishment for an evil way of life. This was treated at first in chapter 13, and afterwards a general conclusion is provided in this place:[24] *These, therefore, are.* Foremost is the punishment of the swift annihilation of prosperity, and that is:

Will not the light, that is, the prosperity, ***of the wicked person be extinguished,*** that is, pass away. 1 Mc 2:[25] *He is extolled today, but tomorrow will not be found.* Prv 13:[26] *The light of the just brings joy, but the lamp of the wicked will be extinguished.* And explaining this, he adds something first with a view to the wicked person and second with a view to his home.

And that is: ***and the flame of his fire not shine?*** "A flame," as Aristotle says, "is vapor having been set on fire."[27] And it signifies prosperity, which is constituted from avarice and desire. Jas 4:[28] *It is a vapor that appears for a little while and then will be snuffed out.*

And concerning the home of the wicked person he adds: **[6]** ***The light,*** that is to say, prosperity, ***will grow dark in his tabernacle.*** Sir 20:[29] *The way of the wicked is dark; they do not know where they might fall.* And concerning the condemned Babylon, Rv 18[30] says: *The light of the lamp will shine no more in it.*

And he adds the annihilation of prosperity with respect to the city and the nation: ***and the lamp that is over him,*** that is, his reputation, ***will be extinguished,*** certainly on account of the fact that it is not maintained and supplied with the oil of piety. Mt 25:[31] *Give us some of your oil, because our lamps are extinguished.*

23. Jb 8.3.
24. Jb 18.21.
25. 1 Mc 2.63.
26. Prv 13.9.
27. Aristotle, *GC* 2.4.6.
28. Jas 4.15.
29. The following scriptural text is not from Sir 20, but rather is Prv 4.19.
30. Rv 18.23.
31. Mt 25.8.

Prv, at the end,[32] says the opposite about good people: *Her lamp will not be extinguished in the night.*

The loss of prosperity is followed by the loss of liberty; and concerning this Bildad adds secondly: [7] ***The steps of his strength,*** that is, the freedom that he possesses because of his wealth and fame to go where he wishes in his work, ***will be limited.*** Hos 2:[33] *I will close off your way with thorns, and she will not find her paths.*

And so that the punishment might seem more just, Bildad repeats the offense: ***and his own scheme will throw him down.*** A deliberate decision to do evil is called a "scheme." Prv 1:[34] *They will eat, therefore, the fruit of their own way, and they will be filled with their own schemes.* Gn 49:[35] *May my soul not enter into their scheme.*

[8] ***For he has thrust his feet,*** that is, the desire with which he advances toward evil, ***into a net,*** that is, capture by the devil. Hab 1:[36] *He drew all of them with his drag-net, and he gathered them into his net.* The opposite is said concerning good people in Prv 1:[37] *A net is cast in vain before the eyes of those who have wings.* ***and in its mesh,*** that is, the net's, ***he walks,*** that is, he advances in evil. 2 Tm 3:[38] *Evil people proceed to more wicked things, going astray and leading others astray.*

[9] ***His heel will be caught in a snare,*** namely by which he is dragged into punishment in the end. This end is signified by the heel, which is the end of the human. Is 24:[39] *The one who will set himself free from the pit will be caught in a snare.*

and his thirst will be inflamed against him, because even when he is no longer able to perpetrate evil, he does not lose his thirst, that is, his desire for evil. At the end of 1 Tm:[40] *Those who wish to become rich fall into temptation and into the snare of the devil,*

32. Prv 31.18.
33. Hos 2.6.
34. Prv 1.31.
35. Gn 49.6.
36. Hab 1.15.
37. Prv 1.17.
38. 2 Tm 3.13.
39. Is 24.18.
40. 1 Tm 6.9.

and into many harmful desires that plunge man into destruction and perdition.

Moreover, in the third place Bildad adds how the wicked person is deceived: **[10]** ***His shackle has been hidden in the earth,*** that is, by means of an earthly affection. A hidden snare binding the foot is called a "shackle." Eccl 9:[41] *Just as birds are captured with a snare and fish with a hook, so too men are taken in an evil time when it suddenly comes upon them.*[42] ***and the trap of that one,*** supply: of the devil, ***on the path,*** that is, over the works of the wicked person. Wis 14:[43] *Creatures have become objects of hatred and mousetraps for the feet of the foolish.*

[11] ***Terrors will frighten him on every side.*** Gregory: "Because what he does to others he fears from others."[44] Is 24:[45] *Fear and the pit and the snare are upon you, O you inhabitant of the earth!* ***and entangle his feet,*** namely because he will not have the freedom to do what he wishes. Is 22:[46] *Your leaders have fled simultaneously and they have been bound tightly.*

Fifth, Bildad desires that, just as he had become fat from riches, he would now become thin from the hunger of poverty, and that is: **[12]** ***May his strength be weakened by hunger,*** namely so that he might be led toward debility. Ps:[47] *They will suffer hunger like dogs, and they will wander through the city.* At the end of Is:[48] *My servants will eat, but you will be hungry; my servants will drink, but you will be thirsty.* ***and may starvation,*** that is to say, devouring hunger, ***invade his ribs,*** that is, lead him to such emaciation that his ribs are visible, and *the fat* that *hangs down from his sides,* as was said above,[49] is turned into extreme hunger.

Sixth, concerning the failure of beauty and strength, Bildad adds: **[13]** ***May it devour the beauty of his skin.*** At the end

41. Eccl 9.12.

42. Compare the commentary on 3.23 above, where Albert quotes this verse somewhat differently.

43. Wis 14.11.

44. Gregory, *Mor.* 14.13.15.

45. Is 24.17.

46. Is 22.3.

47. Ps 58.7.

48. Is 65.13.

49. Jb 15.27.

of Lam:[50] *Our skin has burned up like an oven, from the scorching heat of famine.* ***may the first-born death consume his arms,*** that is, the help of his strength. The "first-born" is what has been born from sin; and the sense is: may he be annihilated by a most bitter death according to the multitude of his sins. Wis 1:[51] *Injustice is the acquisition of death. The wicked, moreover, have summoned death by their works and words; and considering it a friend, they have fallen. And they have made solemn promises to it, because they are worthy of death who have a share in it,* that is, in death.

Seventh, concerning the complete annihilation of the wicked person, Bildad adds—at first, indeed, how he is annihilated in his tent—**[14]** ***May his confidence,*** that is, the confidence that he has had in the resources and the family of his tent, ***be ripped out of his tent.*** Bildad said the same thing in Jb 8:[52] *He will lean on his own household, but it will not stand.* Jer 4:[53] *Suddenly my tents were destroyed, my curtains in a moment.* Is 24:[54] *It will be removed, as the tent of a single night; and its iniquity will weigh it down.* ***and,*** in other words, ***may destruction trample on him as a king would do,*** that is, as if powerful and exercising dominion. But this king is Satan, into whose power he is handed over. Rv 6:[55] *Behold, a pale horse! And the name of the one who sat upon it was Death, and hell followed him. And power over the four parts of the earth was given to him, to kill with the sword, with famine, with death, and with the beasts of the earth.*

Eighth, Bildad adds a statement of abandonment, and that is: **[15]** ***May the companions of him who no longer exists,*** that is, the companions of solitude and of demons, who have been led to nothingness, ***dwell in his tent,*** which is his at present. Is 34:[56] *It will be a den for snakes and a pasture for ostriches. Demons will meet, and hairy donkey-centaurs will call out to one another.*

Ninth, concerning the continuous cause of barrenness, he adds: ***may sulfur,*** that is to say, the tinder of continuous confla-

50. Lam 5.10.
51. Wis 1.15–16.
52. Jb 8.15.
53. Jer 4.20.
54. Is 24.20.
55. Rv 6.8.
56. Is 34.13–14.

gration, of stench, and of barrenness, ***be sprinkled in his tent,*** that is, on the property that he occupies. Is 34:[57] *His streams will be turned into pitch, and his soil into sulfur; and his land will become burning pitch. Night and day it will not be extinguished, into eternity.*

Tenth, concerning the destruction of his posterity, Bildad adds: **[16]** ***May his roots be dried up below,*** namely the children, grandchildren, and great-grandchildren descending from him. Ps:[58] *He will tear you out of your tent, and your root from the land of the living.* ***and may his harvest,*** that is, inheritance, from which he receives a harvest, ***be destroyed above,*** namely among his ancestors. Am 2:[59] *In their presence I destroyed the Amorite, whose height was like the height of cedars and who was strong as an oak. And I destroyed his fruit above and his root beneath.*

Eleventh, he continues concerning his destruction from memory, and that is: **[17]** ***May his memory perish from the earth.*** Ps:[60] *May the memory of them perish from the earth, because he* [*the wicked man*] *did not remember to show mercy.* Prv 10:[61] *The memory of the just is praised, but the name of the wicked will rot.* And explaining this, he adds: ***and,*** in other words, ***may his name not be honored in the streets.*** A "street" (*platea*) is so called from the Greek *platos,* which means "wide." And Bildad wishes to say that a memorial to his name should not be honored among the breadth of the people. Hence it is written in the deeds of the Romans that when Domitian was killed by the Senate, it was decreed that his inauspicious name should be stricken from wooden writing-tablets and stone monuments.[62] Ps:[63] *I will wipe them out, like the dirt in the streets,* that is, as if worthless and fit to be trampled.

Twelfth, concerning final condemnation, Bildad describes the privation of light and the place of punishment. And that is: **[18]** ***He will drive him out from the light,*** supply: the light of this

57. Is 34.9–10.
58. Ps 51.7.
59. Am 2.9.
60. Ps 108.15–16.
61. Prv 10.7.
62. See Macrobius, *Satu.* 1.12.37; and Suetonius, *VC* 8.23.
63. Ps 17.43.

life, ***into the darkness,*** namely outer darkness, where no light will ever shine. Mt 25:[64] *Throw him into outer darkness, where there will be weeping and gnashing of teeth.* And he describes the place of damnation: ***and from the,*** supply: higher ***world, He will carry him*** into the gloomy world of hell, of course. Is 14:[65] *You will be dragged down into hell, to the bottom of the pit.* On account of this Isaac [Israeli], speaking according to the Stoics in *The Book of Definitions,* asserts that the wicked man will be forced down into the gloomy underworld and will burn there in a great fire.[66]

And amplifying this, he adds: **[19]** ***His seed will not subsist.*** Ps:[67] *The seed of the wicked will perish.* Is 14:[68] *The seed of the most wicked will not arise for all eternity.* ***nor his descendants among his people,*** namely those derived from his seed, ***nor any remnant,*** however insignificant, ***in his country,*** in which he has gloried. Is 14:[69] *I will destroy the name of Babylon, and the remnant, and the progeny, and the shoot.* As proof of this, according to 2 Kgs 9[70] and 10,[71] God, by means of Jehu, expunged from the house of Ahab the one who urinates against the wall.[72]

Thirteenth, he adds how the one having been condemned is driven to amazement by seeing all of this, and that is: **[20]** ***On his day,*** that is, the day of condemnation, ***the youngest*** among the people, of course, ***will be amazed, and horror,*** because of the intensity of the condemnation and punishment, ***will fall upon the first ones,*** namely magnates and leaders. Is 21:[73] *I shuddered when I heard it; I was disturbed when I saw it. My heart failed. Darkness struck me with amazement.*

Then, by way of conclusion, Bildad adds why he has said all

64. Mt 25.30.
65. Is 14.15, 19.
66. See Isaac Israeli, *Def.* 2; and Albert, *NOA* 2.11.
67. Ps 36.28.
68. Is 14.20.
69. Is 14.22.
70. 2 Kgs 9.8.
71. 2 Kgs 10.11.
72. As his own scriptural references indicate, Albert appears to conflate these two verses from 2 Kgs 9 and 10, according to which God, through Jehu, destroys the entire house of Ahab, including the imprisoned, the very young, and social misfits.
73. Is 21.3–4.

these things: [21] ***These are the tents of the wicked man***, supply: that have been reduced to nothingness in this way on account of iniquity. Ps:[74] *May sinners pass away from the earth, and the wicked, so that they might be no more.* **and this**, namely hell, ***is the place of him who does not know God***, that is, who does not have God before his eyes. 1 Cor 14:[75] *He who does not know will not be known.* Mt 7:[76] *I will declare to them that I never knew you.* Mt 25:[77] *I do not know you. Go, accursed ones, into the eternal fire.* Rv 12:[78] *Their place was not found any more in heaven.*

74. Ps 103.35.
75. 1 Cor 14.38.
76. Mt 7.23.
77. Mt 25.41.
78. Rv 12.8.

CHAPTER 19

T*HEN RESPONDING, Job said.*

This response of Job is divided into two parts. In the first, he responds to his fellow human beings; in the second, to their speech, in this place:[1] *Behold, I will cry out.*

The first part has three sections: in the first, he shows that his human interlocutors' words are not helpful; in the second, he shows that they are unfitting, in this place:[2] *To be sure, if I have been ignorant;* in the third, that even in their manner of hearing, his interlocutors are impudent, in this place:[3] *At least now.*

And that is: ***Then responding, Job said.*** Prv 26:[4] *Respond to a fool according to his stupidity, lest he seem wise to himself.* **[2]** ***How long will you afflict my soul,*** which has been afflicted by many tribulations, to be sure. Ps:[5] *He persecuted the poor and beggarly man, and the contrite of heart [in order] to destroy him.* ***and grind me down with words?*** supply: as if with teeth. Ps:[6] *They have sharpened their tongues like a serpent's.* Jer 9:[7] *Their tongue, a piercing arrow, has spoken deceit.*

[3] ***Behold, you have confounded me ten times,*** that is to say, five times by refuting my speech and five times by flinging out false accusations at me, and Gregory proves this as follows: Job has responded five times from the beginning up to this point: the first time in Jb 6, the second time in Jb 9, the third time in

1. Jb 19.7.
2. Jb 19.4.
3. Jb 19.6.
4. Prv 26.5.
5. Ps 108.17.
6. Ps 139.4.
7. Jer 9.8.

Jb 12, the fourth time in Jb 16, and the fifth time in Jb 19. And with each exchange, they flung out false accusations instead of proper responses.[8] Ps:[9] *You have made me a reproach to the fool.* Jer 15:[10] *Refuse to support me in your patience; know that on account of you I have suffered reproach.* ***and you have not been ashamed to oppress me,*** which is nevertheless shameful. For it is not helpful to accuse the one who has been afflicted, even if he really should be refuted. Jer 3:[11] *You had a harlot's forehead, but you refused to blush.* Jb 16:[12] *Can it be that windy words will have no end? Or is it not somewhat distressing for you to speak?*

And Job shows that their response is unfitting, adding: **[4]** ***To be sure, if I have been ignorant,*** supply: as you are alleging against me, especially as Eliphaz alleged above in 15:[13] *Can it be that you have heard God's plan, and that His wisdom is inferior to you?* Indeed, they said this because he did not know God's plan: ***my ignorance will remain with me.*** For I humbly confess that I do not know the profundities of God, and so my ignorance will remain with me. Ps:[14] *I studied so that I might know this; it is a task set before me, until I enter into the sanctuary of God and understand according to their last ends.*

[5] ***But you have set yourselves up against me;*** that is, out of pride you have accused me. Nm 16:[15] *You are too exalted, sons of Levi.* Lam 1:[16] *The enemy is lifted up.*[17] ***and you blame me for my reproaches,*** that is, for the reproaches brought forth against me. Jb 16:[18] *Reproaching me, they have struck my jaw.* Lam 3:[19] *He will give his cheek to the one who strikes him; he will be filled with reproaches.*

And he shows that they are impudent with regard to hear-

8. See Gregory, *Mor.* 14.26.30.
9. Ps 38.9.
10. Jer 15.15.
11. Jer 3.3.
12. Jb 16.3.
13. Jb 15.8.
14. Ps 72.16–17.
15. Nm 16.7.
16. Lam 1.9.
17. Here I read *erectus est* with MS F rather than Weiss's *rectus est.*
18. Jb 16.11.
19. Lam 3.30.

ing: **[6]** ***At least now understand*** the statements that in your earlier impudence you refused to understand. Jas 1:[20] *Let every man be quick to listen, but slow to speak.* ***that God has not afflicted me with an equitable judgment,*** namely the judgment of that justice that is repayment for my merits. Hence in Jb 2[21] the Lord says: *You have provoked me against him,*[22] *so that I would afflict him for no reason.* ***and,*** in other words, ***He has surrounded me with His scourges.*** Job says "His," not "my," because he did not merit them. And he says that he was "surrounded" because he was scourged on every side and bound tightly by scourges. Jb 2:[23] *He struck Job with the worst type of ulcer from the sole of his foot all the way to the top of his head.*

And enumerating the scourges, Job adds: first, what he has suffered from God; second, what he has suffered from his fellow human beings, in this place:[24] *At once His troops have come*; and third he turns to pray for mercy, describing the misery that he has endured, in this place:[25] *To my skin.*

[7] ***Behold, I, suffering violence,*** namely the violence of anguish, ***will cry out.*** Is 38:[26] *Lord, I suffer violence; respond for me.* ***but no one will hear me,*** namely for the purpose of deliverance. Jb 30:[27] *I will cry out to you, but you will not hear me. I stand up, but you do not look at me. You have changed into one who is cruel toward me, and with the hardness of your hand you have opposed me.* ***I will shout,*** uttering querulous words in prayer, ***but there is no one who will judge,*** supply: my cause. Hab 1:[28] *How long, O Lord, will I cry out, and will you not hear me? Will I, suffering violence, shout out to you, and will you not save?*

[8] ***He has enclosed,*** namely by means of straits and tribulations, ***my path,*** that is, the way of profit, which, of course, I

20. Jas 1.19.

21. Jb 2.3.

22. Cf. above at Jb 2.3, where, in setting forth this verse, Albert omits the *adversus eum* found here.

23. Jb 2.7.

24. Jb 19.12.

25. Jb 19.20.

26. Is 38.14.

27. Jb 30.20–21.

28. Hab 1.2.

have become accustomed to traveling with regard to the management of my property. ***and***, supply: therefore, ***I am not able to pass***, namely to freedom. Hos 2:[29] *Behold, I will close off your way with thorns, and I will close it off with a wall, and she will not find her paths.* Lam 3:[30] *He has closed off my ways with square stones, so that I might not go out,* that is, He has closed them off with the strongest severity.

and over my path, supply: which I have become accustomed to walking on in overseeing my property, ***He has set darkness***, so that I might not see the way of escape by means of reason. Jb 3:[31] *To a man whose way has been hidden, and God has enveloped him in darkness.* Lam 3:[32] *He has put me in dark places, just as those who are dead forever.* **[9]** ***He has stripped me of my glory***, that is, of my dignity, in which there is glory. Hence Jb 2:[33] *He scraped the discharged pus with a potsherd while sitting on a dung heap.*

And he expands upon this, adding: ***and He has snatched the crown***, namely the royal crown, ***from my head***. Lam 5:[34] *The crown has fallen from our head; our singing has turned into mourning.* Indeed, God is said to have done this when He gave power to Satan. Ezek 21:[35] *Remove the diadem, take off the crown.*

Then he adds generally: **[10]** ***He has destroyed me on every side***, that is, with regard to all good things, ***and I am ruined***, namely from a consideration of inferior causes. There is a parallel in Is 38:[36] *Set your house in order, for you will die and not live.* Lam 3:[37] *My soul is driven away; I have forgotten good things. And I said: My purpose has perished, and my hope away from the Lord.*

And adding this example, he makes clear: ***and as though a tree torn out [of the ground]***, supply: by the roots, ***He has uprooted my hope***, namely of rising again. Ps:[38] *God will destroy you forever.*

29. Hos 2.6.
30. Lam 3.9, 7.
31. Jb 3.23.
32. Lam 3.6.
33. Jb 2.8.
34. Lam 5.16, 15.
35. Ezek 21.26.
36. Is 38.1.
37. Lam 3.17–18.
38. Ps 51.7.

He will tear you out and remove you from your tent, and your root from the land of the living. For I have no place from which to drink in the spirit of consolation; and on account of this, supply: it is certain that **[11]** ***His wrath has been kindled against me.*** Is 30:[39] *His wrath burns and is heavy to bear.* ***and so He has considered me His enemy,*** namely by punishing me in many different ways. Lam 2:[40] *He has drawn His bow like a foe, He has strengthened His right hand like an enemy, and He has killed everything that was beautiful.*

[12] ***At once His troops have come.***

Here Job touches on what he has suffered from his fellow human beings, according to every different kind of human.

And that is: ***At once His troops have come,*** that is, quickly one after another. Jb 1:[41] *While he was still speaking, another also came in and said.* And they are called "the troops of God" because He gave them power. ***and have made for themselves a way through me,*** that is to say, running over me and my possessions as they wished. Jb 30:[42] *As when a wall has been broken and a door opened, they have rushed in upon me, and they have fallen headlong upon my miseries.* ***and they,*** namely the Chaldeans and Sabeans and fire and wind, ***have besieged my tent all around,*** so that there is no escape, of course. Lam 3:[43] *He has built all around me; He has surrounded me with bitterness and hardship.*

He has suffered this from his enemies. He also adds what he has suffered from his brothers: **[13]** ***He has put my brothers far from me,*** namely by turning friendships into enmity. Jer 9:[44] *A man does not have faith in any brother of his, because every brother will utterly supplant.* ***and those familiar to me,*** namely members of my household, ***have departed from me like strangers.*** Jer 9:[45] *Every friend will walk deceitfully. And a man will mock his brother.*

And amplifying this further, he adds: **[14]** ***My relatives have forsaken me.*** Ps:[46] *My friends and neighbors have drawn near and*

39. Is 30.27.
40. Lam 2.4.
41. Jb 1.18.
42. Jb 30.14.
43. Lam 3.5.
44. Jer 9.4.
45. Jer 9.4–5.
46. Ps 37.12.

stood against me. ***and those who knew me,*** namely those to whom the benefits of my generosity came, ***have forgotten me,*** that is to say, repaying none of these benefits, although it is nevertheless written in Sir 29:[47] *Do not forget the kindness of your guarantor.*

Then he amplifies still more: **[15]** ***The inhabitants of my house,*** that is, those who were nourished and who dwelt in my household, of whom I took care, ***and my maidservants,*** who were appointed for service, ***have considered me a stranger,*** for whom, of course, they have done nothing, which is among the greatest evils. Prv 30:[48] *By three things the earth is disturbed, and a fourth, which it cannot bear: by a servant when he reigns.* And after a few words:[49] *By a maidservant when she is co-heir with her mistress.* ***and I have become like an alien in their eyes,*** I who was entertaining no disrespectful thoughts about them, of course. Jer 14:[50] *Why will you be like an alien in the land, and like a traveler turning aside to spend the night?* as if to say: "It is unfitting."

[16] ***I called to my slave,*** born and bought for obedience, ***but he did not answer,*** namely by obeying me. 2 Sm 19:[51] *O Lord, my King, my slave has disregarded me.* ***I entreated him with my own mouth.*** Jn 1:[52] *He came to his own, and his own did not accept Him.*

And he expands more, adding: **[17]** ***My wife shuddered at my breath,*** supply: as if it had a foul odor. Tb 2:[53] *His wife, being enraged, responded: Your hope is clearly in vain, and your almsgiving has become visible now. With these and other words of this kind she reproached him.*

And he adds what he has suffered from his children, that is, from those whom he loved as his children, and that is: ***and I entreated the children of my loins,*** since it has been written in Prv 30:[54] *The eye that mocks his father and despises his own mother's giving birth* [*to him*], *may the ravens of the rushing streams pluck it out and may the young eagles devour it!*

47. Sir 29.19.
48. Prv 30.21–22.
49. Prv 30.23.
50. Jer 14.8.
51. 2 Sm 19.26.
52. Jn 1.11.
53. Tb 2.22–23.
54. Prv 30.17.

And, concerning fools among the people, he adds: **[18]** ***Even fools,*** and those despised by others, ***despised me.*** Jb 30:[55] *Now younger men deride me, those whose fathers I did not deem worthy to put together with my sheepdogs.* ***and when I had retreated*** far away ***from them, they spoke against me.*** Ps:[56] *Instead of loving me, they detracted from me.*

Then, concerning wise men, he adds: **[19]** ***Those who were formerly my counselors,*** namely those who were aware of my private thoughts, ***have hated me.*** And Job understands betrayal in the same way that Ahithophel betrayed David according to 2 Sm 15,[57] namely a counselor reveals private thoughts because he is evil. Is 19:[58] *The wise counselors of Pharaoh have given foolish advice.* Mi 4:[59] *Can it be that you have no king, or that your counselor has perished, because pain has seized you like a woman in labor?* ***and he whom I loved most,*** among my counselors, namely Eliphaz, ***has turned against me.*** Sir 6:[60] *Let many be amicable to you, but let your counselor be one in a thousand.* Ps:[61] *Truly you are a single-minded man, my guide, and well-known to me. You also ate delightful fare with me.*

[20] ***To my skin.***

Here Job begins to adduce his misery and to beg for mercy, and it has two parts. In the first part, he begs for mercy and confesses the righteousness of faith. In the second, he concludes by chastising those who were attacking him, a just man, in this place:[62] *Why, then, do you say now?*

In the first part there are two sections: the plea for mercy; and the confession of justice, in this place:[63] *Who will grant me this?*

In the first sections, first he adduces his misery; second, he begs for mercy; and third, he rebukes the harshness of his at-

55. Jb 30.1.
56. Ps 108.4.
57. 2 Sm 15.31.
58. Is 19.11.
59. Mi 4.9.
60. Sir 6.6.
61. Ps 54.14–15.
62. Jb 19.28.
63. Jb 19.23.

tackers. And that is: ***To my skin,*** that is to say, to the dry and parched hide, ***my bones have clung,*** so that my bones are covered by skin alone, ***after my flesh was consumed,*** because of excessive leanness and the experience of famine. Jb 7:[64] *My flesh is clothed with rottenness and the filth of dust; my skin has become dry and has tightened.* ***and only lips,*** possessing no fullness, to be sure, ***are left around my teeth.*** Lam 4:[65] *Their skin has clung to their bones, and it has become like wood.* At the end of Lam:[66] *Our skin has burned up like an oven, from the scorching heat of famine.*

On account of this misery he begs for mercy: **[21]** ***Have mercy on me, have mercy on me!*** He repeats this utterance so as to bring about mercy. Mt 18:[67] *Should you not also have mercy on your fellow servant, just as I have had mercy on you?* ***at least you, my friends,*** even if others, of course, may not have shown mercy. For it is a characteristic of friends that the disposition of one depends on the disposition of the other. Sir 6:[68] *He is a friend who turns his attention to friendship.* And after a few lines:[69] *A faithful friend is a strong defense.* And in the same place:[70] *A faithful friend is the medicine of life.*

because the hand of the Lord, supply: of the one beating me, ***has touched me.*** For Satan would not have been able to touch me if God had not permitted it. Jb 4:[71] *Now the scourge has come upon you, and you have fallen; it has touched you, and you have been thrown into confusion.* Jb 2:[72] *Satan said: Stretch out your hand and touch his flesh and his bone.*

Because of these miseries, Job blames his attackers for their harshness: **[22]** ***Why do you, like God, persecute me?*** Indeed, God persecutes an innocent man in order that He might prove him or to manifest His own glory. You fellows, however, have no rea-

64. Jb 7.5.
65. Lam 4.8.
66. Lam 5.10.
67. Mt 18.33.
68. Sir 6.9.
69. Sir 6.14.
70. Sir 6.16.
71. Jb 4.5.
72. Jb 2.5.

son to persecute an innocent man. Ps:[73] *The human persecuted the poor and beggarly man, and the contrite of heart* [*in order*] *to destroy him.*[74]

Moreover, he adds why they might do this: ***and,*** that is, because ***you sate yourselves with my flesh?*** that is, you feed lavishly on my weaknesses, which are in my flesh. For he who increases the punishment of someone who has been afflicted is sated by punishments and refreshed. Jb 10:[75] *Being filled with affliction and misery.*

[23] ***Who will grant me.***

Here Job comes to a confession of faith and of justice, so that he might seem more innocent, and he declares three things: namely that his confession should endure as an everlasting memory of the event; second, he sets forth a true confession; and third, he declares that his hope is in the equitable administration of justice.

And that is: ***Who will grant me this,*** namely satisfying my desire, ***that,*** for posterity's sake, ***my words be written down?*** Hab 2:[76] *Write down what you have seen, and make it plain on tablets, so that whoever reads it might run through it quickly.* And he wishes that they be written indelibly, and that is: ***Who will allow me to mark them down in a book?*** that is, on durable material, as if in a book, ***with an iron stylus,*** which is able to write on durable material. Something durable, although it receives written words with difficulty, nevertheless retains them quite firmly. ***or with a sheet of lead,*** that is, on a sheet of lead. Although lead is soft,

73. Ps 108.17.

74. Cf. the commentary on 19.2 above, where Albert quotes this same verse. There the first half of the verse reads *Persecutus est hominem inopem et mendicum,* "He persecuted the poor and beggarly man," with "man" or "human" (*hominem*) functioning as a direct object in the accusative case. Here, however, the first half of the verse reads *Persecutus est homo inopem et mendicum,* "The human persecuted the poor and beggarly man," with *homo* in the nominative case serving as the subject. Although *homo* (rather than *hominem*) here could reflect an oral or aural mistake made during Albert's lecture and/or a scribal error, it seems more likely that Albert is "remembering" the phrase differently here in order to make his point that "the human," unlike God, persecutes the innocent for no good reason or with no good end in view.

75. Jb 10.15.

76. Hab 2.2.

it lasts for a long time, because it forms a patina when left in a moist place. ***or with a chisel.*** The noun "chisel" (*celte*) is indeclinable, and it is a tool used by a stonemason for carving very hard stones. And that is: ***to carve them in stone?*** And Job understands by "book" the human heart in general, by "iron stylus" deep inscription, by "sheet of lead" the hearts of the most serious people, and by "stone" the hearts of the cruelest people. Is 8:[77] *Take for yourself a large book, and write in it with a human stylus.* A parallel case is set in opposition to this one in Jer 17:[78] *The sin of Judah has been written with an iron stylus with a point as hard as a diamond; it has been engraved on the tablet of their heart.*

Moreover, he adds what should be written down: **[25]** ***For I know,*** namely by revelation and faith, ***that my Redeemer lives.*** 1 Tm 6:[79] *He alone has immortality.* ***and on the last day,*** supply: of this world, namely when the heavens will be worn away, ***I will rise out of the earth.*** 1 Cor 15:[80] *For the trumpet will sound, and the dead will rise incorruptible.* ***and I will be clothed again with my skin,*** that is to say, with my flesh and bones. Ezek 37:[81] *And behold, the tendons and flesh came upon the bones, and the skin was stretched out over them.*

And this is what follows: ***and in my flesh I will see my God,*** supply: as my judge, not my condemner but my savior. Dn 12:[82] *At that time all of your people who will have been found written in the book of life will be saved.*

[27] ***Whom I myself,*** that is to say, by myself, ***will see, and my eyes,*** not only of the heart, but also of the body, ***will gaze upon.*** Rv 1:[83] *Behold, He comes with the clouds; and every eye will see Him.* ***and not another.*** For no one is able to send a deputy instead of himself. 2 Cor 5:[84] *Every one of us must appear before the judgment seat of Christ, so that each one might receive the proper things of the body, according to what he has done.*

77. Is 8.1.
78. Jer 17.1.
79. 1 Tm 6.16.
80. 1 Cor 15.52.
81. Ezek 37.8.
82. Dn 12.1.
83. Rv 1.7.
84. 2 Cor 5.10.

And because I am just, I do not fear judgment, but I hope in Him. And that is: ***This hope of mine is stored up in my breast,*** that is, in the secret place of my heart. And it is clear from this that I am innocent; for if I were guilty, I would fear judgment. Heb 6:[85] *We have the strongest source of consolation, we who have fled for refuge to seize the hope set before us, which we have as an anchor for the soul, safe and secure.*

On the basis of all these things, Job rebukes his attackers, and that is: **[28]** ***Why, then, do you say now,*** namely with equal consent: ***Let us persecute him,*** by contradicting him with words, of which Jer 18[86] speaks: *Come, and let us strike him with the tongue, and let us pay no attention to all his words.* Jer 20:[87] *I heard the insults of many and terrors all around: "Persecute him" and "let us persecute him," from all the men who had been amicable to me.* ***and let us find the root of a word against him?*** that is, a word in which we can establish the roots of contradiction. Heb 12:[88] *He [Christ] endured such contradiction from sinners.*

[29] ***Flee, therefore,*** certainly so that you might not fall under judgment, ***from the face,*** that is, from the presence ***of the sword,*** namely of the one who vindicates in judgment. Is 21:[89] *For they have fled from the face of the sword, from the face of the bent bow, from the presence of the battleground.* ***seeing that the sword is the avenger of iniquities,*** that is, the final sentence of the judge. Rv 1:[90] *A sharp, two-edged sword came out of His mouth.* Rom 13:[91] *If you do evil, be afraid; for He does not bear the sword in vain. Indeed, He is the minister of God, an avenger to execute wrath upon him who does evil.* ***and understand that there is judgment.*** At the end of Eccl:[92] *God will bring everything that has been done into judgment, and every error, whether it is good or evil.*

85. Heb 6.18–19.
86. Jer 18.18.
87. Jer 20.10.
88. Heb 12.3.
89. Is 21.15.
90. Rv 1.16.
91. Rom 13.4.
92. Eccl 12.14.

CHAPTER 20

BUT ZOPHAR *the Naamathite responded and said.*

We should recall to mind the position of Zophar, which was partly the same as Eliphaz's position in that he said that in this life good things happen to good people and bad things happen to the wicked. But he adds this: that if life sometimes happens otherwise, this occurs according to God's profound plan, which we are not able to understand. Nevertheless, Zophar maintains that in the end, on the burial mound of retributions, it will be revealed that this plan [of God] is wise and just, as it is said in Rv 22,[1] *He who is filthy, let him be filthy still,* and in 2 Mc 6,[2] *So that, because they had fallen back into their sins in the end, He might finally take vengeance on them.* And 1 Thes 2:[3] *So that they might always bring their sins to completion; for God's wrath comes upon them continuously to the end.* And, indeed, Bildad also said this, but Zophar added that this happens according to God's profound and just plan. And in accordance with this, the response of this chapter is divided into two parts. For in the first part, Zophar responds to the man [Job]; and in the second, to his speech, in this place:[4] *This I know from the beginning.*

There are three points in the first part. First, he says that he treats various things by bringing them together in the reasoning process; second, he specifies his thought process; third, he notes the discovery of the truth.

And that is: ***But Zophar,*** which means "scatterer of speculation," [and he was so called] because with his acumen he scattered every speculation of their arguments, ***the Naamathite,*** that

1. Rv 22.11.
2. 2 Mc 6.15.
3. 1 Thes 2.16.
4. Jb 20.4.

is “beautiful,” and he is so called because he set forth all the things that he understood with the beauty of delightful speech, ***responded.*** Wis 7:[5] *Wisdom, the maker of all things, has taught me.* And Wis 8:[6] *I will be admired in the sight of the mighty, and the faces of princes will marvel at me. They will wait for me when I am silent, and they will watch me when I speak.* ***and said,*** that is, he proposed to make a sound more boldly from his own mouth. Jerome: “I do not know what hidden energy a living voice possesses; flowing from the mouth of the teacher, it resounds loudly in the student’s ear.”[7]

[2] ***Therefore, my thoughts,*** which are called thoughts, as it were, because in combining diverse realities in the reasoning process he thinks about the things that he examines; and this is a sign of foolishness and of imperfect knowledge. And that is: ***variously follow one another.***[8] Indeed, in those cases where knowledge has been made known, to investigate “various” things and things that are not suitable is foolishness. Sir 27:[9] *A holy person remains in wisdom, as the sun; but a fool is changed, as the moon.*

and my mind **(mens)**, which is so called from “measuring” (*metiendo*) on account of the fact that it measures (*mensurat*) all things according to what is right, ***is carried off to different things,*** which can only happen by mental images wandering from the truth. For true understanding is in one reality, which is the principle of truth. Prv 15:[10] *The lips of the wise will disseminate knowledge; the heart of the foolish will be different.*

And he adds the reason: **[3]** ***I will listen to,*** so that I might smash to pieces, of course, ***the doctrine of which you accuse me,***

5. Wis 7.21.

6. Wis 8.11–12.

7. Jerome, *Ep. 53 (alia 103) ad Paulinum* (PL 22:541).

8. The Vulg. text of the first half of v. 2, which Albert reproduces here, reads, *Idcirco cogitationes meae variae succedunt sibi,* and is more literally translated, “Therefore, my various thoughts follow one another.” Because Albert separates this half verse here in his commentary, I have rendered *variae* more loosely as “variously.”

9. Sir 27.12.

10. Prv 15.7.

certainly by disapproving of my position. Jas 1:[11] *Let every man be quick to listen.* Is 51:[12] *Listen to me, you who follow what is just and you who seek the Lord.*

And concerning the revelation of the truth, he adds: ***and the spirit of my understanding,*** that is, inspiring in me understanding of the truth. Jb 32:[13] *The inspiration of the Most High grants understanding.* ***will respond for me,*** concerning the particulars of what is true and what is false. Jn 14:[14] *He will teach you all things, and supply you with everything.*

[4] ***This I know.***

Here he responds to the speech [of Job], and it is subdivided into two parts. In the first, he shows that manifold iniquity will be changed by God's great plan into manifold punishment. In the second, he shows at what time this plan will be revealed, in this place:[15] *The heavens will reveal.*

The first of these subdivisions is further divided into two. First, he shows that all the prosperity (*fortunam*) of the wicked person is transitory; second, he shows that his iniquity passes over into punishment, in this place:[16] *His bones.* In the first [of these sections], he proves [first] from authority that the glory of the wicked person is short-lived; second, he proves this from the vanity of the glory in which he prides himself; third, that it passes away irretrievably; and fourth, that it passes away miserably.

And that is: ***This I know,*** supply: with the Spirit responding, ***from the beginning,*** of the world, of course, ***when man was placed on the earth,*** after he had been cast out of Paradise. Gn 3:[17] *The Lord drove him out of the Paradise of pleasure, to till the earth from which he was taken.* Supply: According to the opinion of all wise people, [5] ***that the praise of the wicked,*** that is, the prosperity (*fortuna*) for which the wicked seek to be praised, ***is short-lived.***

11. Jas 1.19.
12. Is 51.1.
13. Jb 32.8.
14. Jn 14.26.
15. Jb 20.27.
16. Jb 20.11.
17. Gn 3.23.

1 Mc 2:[18] *He is extolled today, but tomorrow will not be found.* Jas 4:[19] *It [your life] is a vapor that appears for a little while and then will be snuffed out.*

and the joy of the hypocrite, that is, the prosperity (*fortuna*) in which he rejoices, ***but for a moment,*** which is no length of time at all compared to eternity. Anselm, in the *Monologion:* "Just as one 'now' of time includes every place and all things that are in each place, however distant the places may be from one another, so too the one 'now' of eternity includes every time and all things that are in each time, however much the periods of time may be separated from one another."[20] Jb 21:[21] *In a moment they go down to hell.*

And he shows this from the vanity of the prosperity [of the wicked person]. And that is: **[6]** ***If his pride,*** that is, his ambition, ***mounts all the way up to heaven,*** that is, to a divine and celestial height. Is 14:[22] *I will ascend into heaven; I will exalt my throne above the stars of heaven.* ***and his head,*** that is, his ambitious mind, ***touches the clouds,*** that is, the greatest human heights, as we read in 2 Mc 9[23] of Antiochus that *he seemed to himself to rule over the waves of the sea, full of pride beyond the human limit, and to weigh the heights of the mountains in a balance.*

[7] ***in the end he will be destroyed like a,*** supply: worthless, ***dung heap.*** Ob:[24] *Although you have been exalted like an eagle and have built your nest among the stars, I will drag you down from there, says the Lord.* Is 14:[25] *Your pride has been dragged down to hell; your dead body has collapsed.* 1 Mc 2:[26] *Their glory is dung and worms.* ***And those who had seen him,*** supply: previously in the midst of glory, ***will say,*** when he suddenly vanishes, of course: ***Where is he?***

18. 1 Mc 2.63.
19. Jas 4.15.
20. Anselm, *Mon.* 22; cf. *Conc.* 1.5.
21. Jb 21.13.
22. Is 14.13.
23. 2 Mc 9.8.
24. Ob 4.
25. Is 14.11.
26. 1 Mc 2.62.

Ps:[27] *I passed by and, behold, he was not.* Wis 2:[28] *We were born from nothing, and after this we will be as if we had not existed.*

And he sets forth this comparison: **[8]** ***As a,*** supply: an imaginary, ***dream*** that vanishes into oblivion, ***he will not be found,*** supply: among others. Rv 12:[29] *Their place was not found any more in heaven.* Ps:[30] *I searched, but his place was not found.*

Moreover, he adds the reason: ***he will pass*** **(transiet),** that is, according to classical grammar, "he shall pass" (*transibit*), ***like a vision in the night,*** supply: in a dream state. Ps:[31] *Man passes away like an image; and, indeed, he is thrown into confusion for no reason.* Wis 5:[32] *These things have passed away like a shadow.*

Then he adds that the glory of the wicked person passes away irretrievably: **[9]** ***The eyes,*** certainly of those rejoicing with him, ***that had seen him,*** with a delightful look, ***will not see him,*** supply: any more; ***neither will his place,*** that is, the goods pertaining to his place, ***look upon him favorably any longer.*** Is 38:[33] *I will behold man no more, nor the inhabitant of peace.*

And he explains this, adding: **[10]** ***His children will be worn down by poverty.*** Jb 30:[34] *Barren with poverty and hunger.* Ps:[35] *May his children wander about and beg, and may they be cast out of their dwelling places.*

Then he adds how the wicked person's glory passes away miserably: ***and his hands,*** that is, his works, ***will return pain to him.*** Is 50:[36] *This has happened to you by my hand; you will sleep in pain.* Is 3:[37] *Woe to the wicked man in the midst of evil! The recompense of his hands will be given to him.*

[11] ***His bones.***

Here he shows how iniquity passes over into punishment, and it has two parts. In the first part, he explains justice, which

27. Ps 36.36.
28. Wis 2.2.
29. Rv 12.8.
30. Ps 36.36.
31. Ps 38.7.
32. Wis 5.9.
33. Is 38.11.
34. Jb 30.3.
35. Ps 108.10.
36. Is 50.11.
37. Is 3.11.

draws iniquity toward punishment. In the second part, he shows the implication for justice of [the wicked man's] wishing for joy, in this place:[38] *If only his stomach were filled.* There are two subdivisions in the first part, namely: a description of the punishments into which the delight of fault is changed; and secondly, a repetition of the fault, so that damnation might seem more just, in this place:[39] *Because he destroyed the house of the poor man.* In the first subdivision, there are two further sections. In the first, he describes the punishment in particular; in the second, in general, in this place:[40] *He will be punished for everything that he has done.* In the first of these sections, there are five points, namely: that he will be punished profoundly, that he will be punished bitterly, that he will be punished by the loss of all delightful things, that he will be punished in a death-dealing way, and that he will be punished without consolation.

And that is: ***His bones,*** the deepest receptacles of his innermost secrets, of course, ***will be filled with the vices of his youth,*** that is to say, with the fatness of the pleasure of vices. Ezek 32:[41] *Their iniquities were in their bones.* ***and they will sleep with him,*** namely the wicked man who does not abandon his vices, ***in the dust,*** into which he himself will be turned after death. Prv 22:[42] *This is a proverb: A young man who remains close to his way will not depart from it even when he grows old.* At the end of Is:[43] *A sinner who is a hundred years old will be accursed.*

He explains the reason for this, adding: **[12]** ***For although evil,*** namely the evil of fault, ***is sweet in his mouth,*** the mouth of his heart, of course. Ps:[44] *Their iniquity has sprung forth, as if from corpulence: they have passed into the affection of the heart.* ***he hides it under his tongue,*** with flattering speech and excuses. Ps:[45] *Do not incline my heart to words of wickedness for the purpose of making excuses for sins.*

38. Jb 20.23.
39. Jb 20.19.
40. Jb 20.18.
41. Ezek 32.27.
42. Prv 22.6.
43. Is 65.20.
44. Ps 72.7.
45. Ps 140.4.

[13] ***He will keep it,*** namely the delightful fault. Gregory: "He keeps the evil deed that he loves. He neither attacks it by means of repentance, nor will he abandon it."[46] And that is: ***and he will not abandon it,*** through repentance, of course. This is characteristic of weak people, who, always keeping it to themselves, do not want to suffer any sadness in repenting, contrary to what is said in Jb 10:[47] *I will let my utterance go against me; I will speak in the bitterness of my soul.* ***and he will hide it in his throat,*** namely the evil deed, contrary to what is said in Jb 31:[48] *I have not given my throat to sin.* And after a few lines:[49] *If, as a man, I have hidden my sin, and I have concealed my iniquity in my bosom.* For what is concealed in the throat is concealed for this purpose, so that it might be savored for a long time and the throat might delight in it for a long time.

Then he adds that the wicked person will be punished bitterly. **[14]** ***His bread,*** that is, the refreshment of iniquity. Prv 4:[50] *They eat the bread of impiety and drink the wine of iniquity.* That this bread, however, will be changed into bitterness follows: ***in his belly,*** that is, in his innermost parts, ***will be turned,*** supply: through punishment, ***into the venom of asps inside him.*** Prv 20:[51] *The bread of lying is sweet to a man, but afterwards his mouth will be filled with pebbles.* Sir 31:[52] *The city will murmur against the most worthless bread.* And he says "the venom of asps" to signify something death-dealing. Dt 32:[53] *The venom of asps is incurable.*

He also adds that the wicked person will be punished by the loss of all delightful things: **[15]** ***The riches that he has devoured,*** supply here: by living luxuriously. Lk 15:[54] *He has devoured his own resources by living luxuriously with prostitutes.* Moreover, "to devour" means to gulp down with gluttony. Jer 51:[55] *He has swal-*

46. Gregory, *Mor.* 15.12.14.
47. Jb 10.1.
48. Jb 31.30.
49. Jb 31.33.
50. Prv 4.17.
51. Prv 20.17.
52. Sir 31.29.
53. Dt 32.33.
54. Lk 15.30.
55. Jer 51.34.

lowed me up like a dragon; he has filled his stomach with my tender meat. ***he will vomit up***. What is delightful when it is devoured is vile when it is vomited; and this means that an offense, although delightful when it is committed, is vile when it is punished. Is 28:[56] *All the tables were full of vomit and filth, so that there was not a place remaining.* ***and God will draw them out of his stomach***. This is signified in Tb 6,[57] where the angel instructed Tobit, saying: *Gut this fish.* For the fish signifies something pleasant, which is gutted when what it has devoured with pleasure is forced to be vomited up with poisonous bile.

And he adds that the wicked person will be punished in a death-dealing way: **[16]** ***He will suck the head of asps***. An asp is a snake that does not hear the musician [who seeks to charm it] but has a death-dealing venom; and it signifies demons, who have power over the obstinate but do not hear the teachers (*doctores*). He "sucks its head" who chooses with pleasure to accept the beginnings of its suggestion. This is described by means of another metaphor in Is 59:[58] *They have broken the eggs of asps and have woven the webs of spiders.* Ps:[59] *Like the deaf asp that stops up its ears, which will not hear the voice of the charmers.*

Then, amplifying this, he adds: ***and the viper's tongue will kill him***. The "viper" (*vipera*) is so called on account of the fact that it brings forth by force (*vi pariat*), which signifies the violent temptation of a demon. Whereas the demon seems pleasant to one whom he tempts, the person is killed when he consents. Indeed, the "tongue" signifies the persuasion of the serpent. Of this kind of persuasion it is said in Lk 3:[60] *You brood of vipers, who has warned you to flee from the wrath to come?* At the end of Acts:[61] *A viper, when it had come out of the fire, attacked his hand.*

And he adds that the wicked person will be punished without consolation: **[17]** ***May he not see***, in his own experience, of course, ***the streams of the river***, that is, the streams overflowing with divine goodness, ***torrents***, that is, set free by the warmth of

56. Is 28.8.
57. Tb 6.5.
58. Is 59.5.
59. Ps 57.5–6.
60. Lk 3.7.
61. Acts 28.3.

divine charity burning hot, ***of honey,*** that is, of divine sweetness, ***and butter,*** which signifies the thick richness (*crassitudinem*) of the delight of divine consolation. Concerning this it is said of the saints in Ps:[62] *They will be inebriated by the abundance of your house, and you will make them drink of the torrent of your pleasure.* At the end of Is:[63] *Behold, I will bring among you as it were a river of peace, and as an overflowing torrent the glory of the Gentiles, which you will imbibe.* Is 55:[64] *Listen carefully to me, and eat what is good, and your soul will be delighted in thick richness* (crassitudine). All of these things, in fact, will be taken away from the damned, on account of which they are able to say this in Hos 13:[65] *Consolation has been hidden from my eyes.*

Then he adds a description of the punishment in general: **[18]** ***He will be punished for everything that he has done.*** Eccl 12:[66] *Concerning every error God will bring you into judgment.* ***yet he will not be consumed.*** Bernard: He always dies in such a way that he is never completely extinguished.[67] Jb 21:[68] *He will remain watchful on the heap of the dead.* For a dead person remains watchful whose life is always cut off but is never completely extinguished. Rv 9:[69] *They will desire to die, but death will flee from them.* ***according to the multitude of their devices,*** that is, of their recent sins, ***so also he will suffer,*** in the midst of punishments, of course. Rv 18:[70] *As much as she has glorified herself and lived among pleasures, give to her so much torment and sorrow.*

And, so that damnation might seem more just, he repeats the fault of impiety, which is cupidity, as Gregory says.[71] 1 Tm 6:[72] *Cupidity is the root of all evils.* And that is: **[19]** ***Because destroying it,*** supply: violently, ***he stripped,*** that is, he plundered, ***the house***

62. Ps 35.9.
63. Is 66.12.
64. Is 55.2.
65. Hos 13.14.
66. Eccl 12.14.
67. See Bernard of Clairvaux, *Cons.* 5.12.26; and Gregory, *Mor.* 15.17.21.
68. Jb 21.32.
69. Rv 9.6.
70. Rv 18.7.
71. Gregory, *Mor.* 15.18.22.
72. 1 Tm 6.10.

of the poor man. Is 3:[73] *The plunder of the poor is in your house. Why do you consume my people and grind down the faces of the poor?* And amplifying this, he adds: ***He has carried off the house,*** that is, the resources of the house, and thus he was unjust by carrying off another's possessions. Hab 2:[74] *Woe to him who heaps up what is not his own! And how long will he load himself down with thick clay?* ***that he did not build,*** in other words, by threatening some benefit to a certain poor man, an image of which is described in Lk 16:[75] *Lazarus was longing to be filled with the crumbs that fell from the rich man's table, but no one gave him anything.* Hab 2:[76] *Woe to him who brings together a wicked avarice in his own house, so that his nest may be on high.*

[20] ***And still his stomach,*** that is, his avarice, ***has not been satisfied.*** Prv 13:[77] *The stomach of the wicked is incapable of being satisfied.* Eccl 5:[78] *A greedy man will not be satisfied with money.* ***and when he has the things that he coveted,*** supply: through avarice, ***he will not be able to possess them,*** being thwarted by death, of course. Lk 12:[79] *This night they demand your soul back from you, and whose will those things that you have provided be?* Eccl 5:[80] *Riches kept safe to the harm of their owner; indeed, they are lost in the midst of the worst affliction.*

And Zophar adds the reason: **[21]** ***None of his food,*** which he would have offered to the poor, of course, ***remained.*** Ezek 16:[81] *This was the iniquity of Sodom, your sister: pride, being full of bread, and abundance, and her own idleness and that of her daughters; and they did not extend a hand to the needy and to the poor.*

and nothing of his goods will endure, in fact, he is robbed of every good thing. Hab 2:[82] *Because you have robbed many nations, all*

73. Is 3.14–15.
74. Hab 2.6.
75. Lk 16.21.
76. Hab 2.9.
77. Prv 13.25.
78. Eccl 5.9.
79. Lk 12.20.
80. Eccl 5.12–13.
81. Ezek 16.49.
82. Hab 2.8.

who will be left of the peoples will rob you. Ps:[83] *They have slept their sleep, and all the men of wealth have found nothing in their hands.* [22] ***When he will be satisfied,*** in other words, when by the abundance of riches he will give satisfaction to his own desire, ***he will be closed in,*** namely by loneliness. Near the end of 2 Sm:[84] *I am hemmed in exceedingly on all sides.* ***he will burn,*** namely with the anxiety of losing what he has. Dn 13:[85] *There are straits for me on all sides.* ***and every pain,*** that is, perfect pain, ***will rush in upon him.*** He says "will rush in" because pain will hold him with violent force. 1 Thes 5:[86] *When they will say "Peace and security," then sudden destruction will come upon them, as labor pains upon one who is with child, and they will not escape.* Near the end of 1 Tm:[87] *Those who desire to be rich fall into temptation and into the snare of the devil, and into many harmful desires, which plunge the human into destruction and perdition.*

[23] ***If only.***

Zophar touches on the implication for justice of [the wicked man's] wishing for joy, and he makes five points: that the fury of the Judge burns hot, that the condemned person has no way of escape, that the one to be tortured is handed over to the cruel, that he is attacked by every element; and fifthly he adds that the offspring of his iniquity is revealed in this.

And that is: ***If only his stomach were filled,*** that is, the depth of his entire capacity, so that it might be completely full with punishments, of course, ***so that God may send forth upon him,*** him whom, to be sure, He has preserved according to His mercy up until now, ***the wrath of His fury,*** that is, the wrath of God's seething with zeal for punishment. Dt 32:[88] *A fire has been kindled in my wrath, and it will burn.* Zep 3:[89] *I will pour out upon them my indignation, all the wrath of my fury.* ***and rain down,*** namely by way of well-ordered drops of punishments, ***His war,*** that is, punishments by means of which he is attacked unremittingly, ***upon***

83. Ps 75.6.
84. 2 Sm 24.14.
85. Dn 13.22.
86. 1 Thes 5.3.
87. 1 Tm 6.9.
88. Dt 32.22.
89. Zep 3.8.

him, namely the wicked man. Jb 38:[90] *Can it be that you have entered into the storehouses of the snow, or have you beheld the storehouses of the hail, which I have prepared for the time of the enemy, for the day of battle and of war?* Ps:[91] *He has rained snares upon sinners: fire and brimstone and stormy winds.*

And he adds that [the condemned person] will suffer without an escape route, and that is: **[24]** ***He will flee from weapons of iron.*** Here iron, which vanquishes other metals, as it is said in Dn 2,[92] indicates the present punishment by which God is armed for the purpose of vanquishing the wicked. Wis 5:[93] *His zeal will take up armor.*

But the wicked, who resist repentance, flee from this punishment. Ps:[94] *They do not experience the hardship of men, and they will not be scourged like other men. For that reason pride has possessed them.* ***and he will run headlong into a bow of brass.*** Zophar calls this alloy of copper or tin or lead "brass," which, because it is not liable to corruption, signifies eternal punishment. He says "bow," however, because it strikes from far off and deeply. Wis 5:[95] *Bolts of lightning will go straight out of the clouds, and they will be shot out as if from a well*—that is, strongly—*bent bow.* **[25]** ***It,*** supply: namely the bow, ***is drawn out*** by the powerful right hand of the archer ***and comes forth from its scabbard.*** They call a stretched [animal] skin in which archers carry their bow a "scabbard," and the scabbard signifies the hidden judgment of God, which will be made manifest at that time. But the bow signifies Scripture, by whose truth [the wicked] will be condemned. Jb 29:[96] *The bow in my hand will be renewed.* ***and it flashes brightly***, that is, sending forth the arrows of judgment (*spicula sententiae*) with clear justice, ***in his bitterness,*** that is, the bitterness of the wicked man. And this is what is said in Mt 25:[97] *Go, accursed ones,*

90. Jb 38.22–23.
91. Ps 10.7.
92. Dn 2.40.
93. Wis 5.18.
94. Ps 72.5–6.
95. Wis 5.22.
96. Jb 29.20.
97. Mt 25.41.

into the eternal fire. Ps:[98] *The sharp arrows of the Mighty One.* 2 Kgs 9:[99] *Jehu drew his bow with his hand, and he struck Joram between the shoulders; and the arrow came out through his heart.* Joram means "river," and he signifies the one flowing down into concupiscence. Jehu, however, means "evildoer," and he signifies the devil, who strikes the wicked by the authority of God. Ps:[100] *He sent forth His arrows, and He scattered them. He multiplied lightning bolts, and He confounded them.*

Then he adds how the one to be tortured will be handed over to the cruel. And that is: ***the horrible ones,*** namely demons, ***will advance*** at first by persuading him to commit a fault ***and will come*** by inflicting punishment ***upon him,*** namely the wicked man. Hab 1:[101] *He is horrible and terrible, and from his very self judgment and his burden will come forth.* And in the same place:[102] *He is cruel and will have no mercy.* Is 19:[103] *I will deliver Egypt into the hand of cruel masters.*

[26] ***All darkness,*** that is, perfect darkness, ***is hidden in his secret places,*** that is, in the consciences of sinners, and this darkness is interior. Ps:[104] *They have not known nor understood: they walk in darkness.* And with these the wicked man will be thrown into outer darkness. Mt 24:[105] *Throw him into outer darkness, where there will be weeping and gnashing of teeth.*

And Zophar adds how the wicked man is attacked by the elements of the earth, and first by fire: ***a fire*** that afflicts and burns, of course, ***that is not kindled,*** supply: by a human, but rather by the wrath of God, ***will devour him.*** Is 30:[106] *His burning place* (Tophet) *has been prepared since yesterday, prepared by the king, deep and wide. Its nourishment is fire and much wood, and the breath of the Lord, like the burning of brimstone, sets it on fire.*

he will be afflicted when left in his tent. Indeed, after the res-

98. Ps 119.4.
99. 2 Kgs 9.24.
100. Ps 17.15.
101. Hab 1.7.
102. The following words are not from Hab 1, but rather are from Jer 6.23.
103. Is 19.4.
104. Ps 81.5.
105. The following words are not from Mt 24, but rather are from Mt 8.12.
106. Is 30.33.

urrection he will be punished in his body and his soul, for the body is called a "tent" in Jb 15:[107] *Fire will devour the tents of those who accept bribes with pleasure.*

And he adds that heaven will reveal what is hidden, and that is: **[27]** ***The heavens,*** that is, the holy angels of heaven, ***will reveal his iniquity.*** Dt 31:[108] *I will call heaven and earth as witnesses against them.* And this is what follows: ***and the earth,*** that is, those of the earth, ***will rise up against him.*** Wis 5:[109] *The entire earth will fight with him against those who are senseless.*

Then Zophar adds how what he planted in the home of conscience will be revealed, and that is: supply: And then ***the offspring of his house will be exposed.*** Gregory:[110] "Every evil that was born in one's conscience is revealed at the coming of the Judge." Sir 7:[111] *My son, do not sow evils in furrows of injustice, and you will not reap them sevenfold.* ***he will be dragged down,*** namely by the weight of his own iniquity, ***on the day of God's wrath,*** that is, on the day of judgment, when God will make His fury known. 2 Pt 2:[112] *He handed them over—those who had been dragged down by the ropes of hell into the infernal region—to be tormented.*

After all these things, Zophar says by way of conclusion: **[29]** ***This is the portion of the wicked man from God,*** that is, the portion that will be allotted [to him] by God. Ps:[113] *Fire, hail, snow, ice, and wind storms will be the portion of their cup.* Indeed, everything is very bad, of which this is a portion, and Zophar explains this by adding: ***and,*** that is, ***the inheritance of his words,*** namely the words of God, because He foretold these things in the Scriptures, ***from the Lord,*** namely a just judgment from the one who judges. Sir 10:[114] *When a man dies, he will inherit serpents, and beasts, and worms.*

107. Jb 15.34.
108. Dt 31.28.
109. Wis 5.21.
110. Gregory, *Mor.* 15.32.38.
111. Sir 7.3.
112. 2 Pt 2.4.
113. Albert here conflates Ps 148.8 and Ps 10.7, as he does above in commenting on Jb 6.16.
114. Sir 10.13.

CHAPTER 21

THEN JOB RESPONDED and said.

Just as the other three interlocutors were fashioning their entire objection from circumstances that are peripheral to a wicked man's debt of justice, so too Job develops every part of his response on the basis of particular cases that run contrary to their universal claims. For they believed that just as a circumstance peripheral to the subject of discussion can be inferred once the subject has been proposed (for example: This man is a thief; it follows, therefore, that he is wandering around at night), so, on the contrary, the subject can be inferred from the peripheral circumstance (for example: This man is wandering around at night; therefore, he is a thief). But one cannot invert these consequences without falling into the fallacy of the consequent, as Aristotle says near the beginning of *On Sophistical Refutations.*[1] Because Job's interlocutors understood that a wicked person must be punished by the exacting of justice and that there is no injustice on the part of the Judge, they were arguing that the one who should have been punished had been punished. And they accepted as true the inverse of these consequences, namely that if he had been punished, then he is wicked. Hence all the objections of the three interlocutors err according to the fallacy of the consequent. By contrast, however, Job develops all of his arguments from particular cases that run contrary to the general position that in this life God repays according to merits, giving good things to good people and bad things to bad people, which position Eliphaz plainly has asserted; and that, if God ignores the prosperity of bad people and the adversity of good people, He compensates for

1. See Aristotle, *SE* ch. 5.

these realities in the end by piling up repayment, which Bildad plainly has asserted; or that God permits these things according to His lofty purpose, so that the wicked person might fall more profoundly and the good person might be restored to a greater blessedness, which Zophar manifestly has asserted. Here Job responds against this general position by bringing in clearer counterexamples than he has produced thus far, and therefore he earnestly begs to be heard.

This chapter is divided into two parts: first, indeed, he responds to the man [Zophar], and secondly he responds to his speech, in this place:[2] *Why, therefore, do the wicked live?* The first of these parts has three points: that attention should be paid to Job's speech; that its profundity should be feared; and that it should be marveled at.

And that is: ***Then Job responded,*** both to the man and to his speech, ***and said.*** For it is just that a wise man should respond to charges [leveled against him], should inform those who are ignorant, and should restrain their arrogance. Hos 5:[3] *The arrogance of Israel will respond to His [God's] face.* Sir 5:[4] *If you have understanding, respond to your neighbor.*

[2] ***Listen, I beg you, to my words.*** Is 55:[5] *Listen, you who hear me.* Prv 1:[6] *A wise man who listens will be wiser.* ***and do penance,*** namely by retracting your error. Near the end of Jb:[7] *I blame myself and I do penance.* And because listening pertains to one who is willing, and because certain people listen reluctantly, Job therefore urges them to listen patiently at least. And that is: **[3]** ***Bear with me, so that I might speak.*** Near the end of Heb:[8] *May you bear this word of consolation.* Wis 8:[9] *They will bear with me when I am silent, and they will look to me when I speak.* ***and afterwards, if it seems right,*** supply: good to you, ***laugh at my words,*** supply: if they are

2. Jb 21.7.
3. Hos 5.5.
4. Sir 5.14.
5. Is 55.2.
6. Prv 1.5.
7. Jb 42.6.
8. Heb 13.22.
9. Wis 8.12.

deserving of laughter. Is 59:[10] *Their works are useless and deserving of laughter.*

Then Job adds that his speech should be feared: **[4] *Can it be that my debate* (disputatio) *is against man*,** that is, about human deeds, as if he were saying, "No indeed, it is about divine deeds." Jb 13:[11] *I want to debate* (disputare) *with God.* Jer 12:[12] *You, indeed, are just, O Lord, if I should debate* (disputem) *with you; nevertheless, I will say just things to you.* ***that I should not rightly be saddened?*** that is, be shaken up by fear. Jb 9:[13] *If I wish to contend with Him, I will not respond to Him one word for a thousand.* And in the same place:[14] *For I will not respond to a man, who is like me, nor to one who can be heard equally with me in judgment.*

And he adds that his speech should be marveled at: **[5] *Pay attention to me*,** supply: as I speak, ***and be astounded*,** in wonder at the judgments of God. Jer 2:[15] *Be astounded, O heavens, by this.* ***and put your finger over your mouth*,** that is, press your lips together, lest you contradict [me]. Wis 8:[16] *If I discuss many things, they will put their hands over their mouths.*

Then he adds the reason for the bewilderment: **[6] *And when I remember*,** supply: the judgments of the Lord, ***I become very afraid*,** before such great profundity, of course. Gn 18:[17] *I will speak to my Lord, although I am dust and ashes.* ***and trembling seizes my flesh*,** that is, my weakness. Jb 9:[18] *What am I, that I should respond to Him and utter my words in His presence?* Hab 3:[19] *O Lord, I heard of your renown, and I was afraid.*

[7] *Why, therefore.*

Here Job responds to the speech [of Zophar], and it is divided into two parts. In the first he describes the present reality; but because someone might suppose that he wishes to correct

10. Is 59.6, conflated with Jer 51.18.
11. Jb 13.3.
12. Jer 12.1.
13. Jb 9.3.
14. Jb 9.32.
15. Jer 2.12.
16. Wis 8.12.
17. Gn 18.27.
18. Jb 9.14.
19. Hab 3.2.

the judgments of God, in the second part he explains this, in this place:[20] *Can it be that anyone will teach God?*

The first of these parts is divided into two sections. In the first of these Job points out the prosperity of the wicked; but because it could be said that they are not completely wicked and obstinate, in the second part he makes clear that they are, in this place:[21] *Who have said to God: Depart from us.*

In the first part Job shows how the wicked prosper personally, in their heirs, and in the good things and the delights of this world. And that is: ***Why, therefore,*** supply: if, in truth, you all say that in this life God renders good things to good people and bad things to bad people,[22] this conjunctive phrase should be read as contradicting this view. ***do the wicked live,*** supply: when they are deserving of death. Rom 1:[23] *Those who do such things are deserving of death; not only those who do them, but also those who are of the same mind as those who do them.* ***why are they placed in elevated positions,*** supply: as dignitaries. Eccl 3:[24] *I saw under heaven impiety in the place of judgment, and iniquity in the place of justice.* Eccl 10:[25] *The fool is placed in a position of high dignity, and the rich man sits beneath him.*

But because their dignity is reinforced by riches, Job adds: ***and why are they strengthened with riches?*** Jb 41:[26] *There is no power on earth that can be compared to Him.* Jas 2:[27] *Do not the rich oppress you with their power?* And he explains this point by point, adding: **[8]** ***Their offspring,*** that is to say, the children of the unjust, ***continue,*** namely in prosperity, ***in their presence,*** so that they might delight in their children, of course, although, on

20. Jb 21.22.
21. Jb 21.14.
22. Albert takes this to be the basic position on divine providence of all three of his friends, though, within this understanding, the three also differ in important ways. For summaries of the positions of Eliphaz, Bildad, and Zophar, see Albert's comments on 3.1, 15.1, 18.1, and 20.1 above.
23. Rom 1.32.
24. Eccl 3.16.
25. Eccl 10.6.
26. Jb 41.24.
27. Jas 2.6.

the basis of what they deserve, they ought to be driven away. Wis 4:[28] *All children who are born of the unjust are witnesses of wickedness against their parents.* Wis 3:[29] *Children of adulterers will not come to perfection, and offspring from an illicit bed will be driven away.* ***a multitude of relatives,*** namely of descendants from their offspring, ***and of grandchildren in their sight,*** supply: they continue in prosperity, even though concerning the order of justice it is written in Wis 4:[30] *The varied multitude of the wicked will not thrive, and adulterated plantings will not set deep roots.*

And he adds that they prosper with regard to their resources: **[9]** ***Their homes,*** that is,[31] the resources that pertain to the home, ***are secure,*** that is to say, no one is assailing them. Jgs 18:[32] *We will come to a people that is secure, into a spacious country.* Ps:[33] *I was zealous concerning the unjust, seeing the peace of sinners.* ***and peaceful.*** Mt 12:[34] *As long as a strong man, fully armed, guards his house, all that he possesses remains in a state of peace.* ***and the rod,*** that is, the discipline, ***of God is not upon them.*** Ps 72:[35] *They do not experience the hardship of men, and they will not be scourged like other men.*

Their cows have conceived, that is, a multitude of cattle; and conception indicates that the misfortune of sterility has been removed from them. But because cows that have conceived sometimes birth aborted calves, Job adds this: ***and have not miscarried.*** Similarly, because the fetus sometimes fails to develop on account of a nutritional defect, he adds: ***their cow has given birth and it is not deprived of its young,*** supply: due to a nutritional defect. Hos 9:[36] *Their glory* [*is*] *from birth and from the womb and from conception.*

28. Wis 4.6.
29. Wis 3.16.
30. Wis 4.3.
31. Here I read *hoc est* with MS EFM, rather than *hae sunt* with Weiss's edition.
32. Jgs 18.10.
33. Ps 72.3.
34. Although the MSS, and thus Weiss's edition, indicate Mt 12 here, the following words are, in fact, from Lk 11.21.
35. Ps 72.5.
36. Hos 9.11.

Then Job adds how the wicked prosper in the delights of this world: **[11] *Their little ones go out like a flock,*** supply: having been multiplied. Ex 1:[37] *They multiplied as if sprouting forth; and having grown exceedingly strong, they filled the land.* ***and their infants.*** He calls the sons of the family who did not yet have an independent voice with which to speak, "infants." ***jump around and play games,*** leaping and dancing, of course. Jer 31:[38] *Again you will be adorned with your tambourines, and you will go forth in the dance of the merrymakers.*

And he adds how they play: **[12] *They hold the tambourine,*** which makes a sound when it is struck, ***and the zither,*** which makes a sound when the strings or cords are moved, ***and they rejoice at the sound of the organ,*** certainly among pipes and voices, on account of which every kind of music is distinguished. Ex 15:[39] *All the women came out after Miriam with tambourines and dancing.* 1 Sm 18:[40] *Women came out of all the cities of Israel, singing and dancing, to meet King Saul, with tambourines of joy and metallic rattles. And the women sang as they played.*

[13] *They spend their days in the midst of good things;* that is, they spend on delights the resources granted to them for this life. Wis 2:[41] *Let us enjoy the good things that exist, and let us make use of creation as we did hastily in youth. Let us take our fill of costly wine and perfumes.*

And because someone could say that they will hold death in check, Job adds: ***and in a moment,*** that is, in the end, as if in an indivisible point of time, ***they go down to hell*** by means of death, as if he were saying: "This small amount of time, which pays back nature's debt, does not diminish the prosperity of the whole of life." Lk 16:[42] *Son, you have received good things during your life.*

Job shows that there are wicked people, however, who prosper in this way; and he makes two points, namely: that they are

37. Ex 1.7.
38. Jer 31.4.
39. Ex 15.20.
40. 1 Sm 18.6–7.
41. Wis 2.6–7.
42. Lk 16.25.

wicked, and that they are obstinate, in this place:[43] *How often will the lamp.* In the first part as well he makes two points: one is that they are wicked *per se,* and the other that they are wicked *per accidens,* in this place:[44] *Nevertheless.* He demonstrates, moreover, that they are wicked [*per se*] in two ways, namely: that they do not know God, and that they hold God in contempt.

And that is: **[14]** ***Who,*** that is, they, ***have said to God,*** and if not with words, nevertheless with their behavior: ***Depart from us.*** Is 30:[45] *Let the Holy One of Israel cease to be in our presence.* The Gloss[46] introduces this place in the Ps:[47] *The fool has said in his heart: There is no God.* Job also adds how they have said these things: ***we refuse to have knowledge of your ways,*** that is, of your laws. Is 59:[48] *We have turned away so that we would not follow after our God.* Wis 5:[49] *We have wandered from the way of truth, and the light of justice has not shone on us.*

Then, concerning their contempt [for God], he adds: **[15]** ***Who is the Almighty;*** this should be read with disdain, as if he were saying: "We hold Him in contempt." ***that we should serve Him?*** Pharaoh said something similar according to Ex 5:[50] *I do not know the Lord, and I will not let Israel go.* ***and what does it profit us,*** that is, we have expected no reward, ***if we pray to Him?*** namely with our hearts, mouths, and works. Mal 3:[51] *You have said: He who serves God labors in vain. And what advantage is it that we have kept His commandments, and we who are sorrowful have walked in the presence of the Lord of Hosts?* Wis 2:[52] *They did not know the mysteries of God* (sacramenta Dei), *nor did they hope for the reward of justice, nor did they esteem the honor of holy souls.*

Moreover, Job says that they are wicked *per accidens,* adding that he does not agree with their way of thinking that the wick-

43. Jb 21.17.
44. Jb 21.16.
45. Is 30.11.
46. *GO* on Jb 21.15.
47. Ps 13.1.
48. Is 59.13.
49. Wis 5.6.
50. Ex 5.2.
51. Mal 3.14.
52. Wis 2.22.

ed man himself will not be judged. **[16]** ***And,*** that is, ***neverthe-less,*** although the wicked speak such words, ***because their good things,*** namely in which they prosper, ***are not in their hands,*** that is, in their power, but rather are in the power of God. Lk 12:[53] *You fool, this night they demand your soul back from you, and whose will those things that you have prepared be?* Eccl 6:[54] *The man to whom God has given riches, possessions, and honors such that his soul lacks none of all the things that he desires; God does not enable him to enjoy these things, but a stranger will devour them.* ***may the scheme of the wicked,*** namely by which they, holding eternal realities in contempt, have chosen to cling to present realities, ***be far from me.*** Gn 49:[55] *May my soul not enter into their scheme.* Ps:[56] *The scheme of the wicked will perish.*

Then he adds that the wicked are obstinate. They are set straight neither by punishments, nor by love for their posterity, nor by the desire for a longer life. And that is: **[17]** ***How often will the lamp of the wicked be extinguished.*** All that illuminates the eyes by delighting the vision is called a "lamp." Hence, according to 2 Sm 14,[57] the woman said concerning her son, whom she loved: *They seek to extinguish my only remaining spark.* And Job, speaking of the time when he lived in prosperity, said in Jb 29:[58] [*Who will grant that I might be as*] *when His lamp shone over my head and I walked according to His light in the midst of darkness?* This lamp is extinguished when prosperity is taken away from the wicked man, and the fear of that prosperity's being extinguished does not draw him back from wickedness. And this is signified in 1 Sm 3,[59] where Eli did not see *the lamp of God before it was extinguished.*

and, supply: how often, ***will a flood,*** namely of affliction on account of iniquity, ***come upon them,*** namely the wicked; supply: and this consideration also does not draw the wicked man back

53. Lk 12.20.
54. Eccl 6.2.
55. Gn 49.6.
56. Ps 111.10. Cf. Ps 1.6 and Ps 36.28.
57. 2 Sm 14.7.
58. Jb 29.3.
59. 1 Sm 3.2–3.

[from his wickedness]. Lam 3:[60] *Waters have flowed over my head. I said: I have been destroyed.*

and, supply: how often, ***will God distribute the pains* (dolores)**, that is, will He wield various pains, ***of His wrath?*** that is, of God's wrath; supply: this also does not draw him back [from wickedness], but rather he clings obstinately to iniquity. Jer 5:[61] *You have struck them, but they have not suffered pain* (doluerunt); *you have worn them down, but they have refused to receive correction.*

Then Job amplifies this, saying: **[18] *They will be like chaff,*** namely beaten and broken, ***in the presence of the wind,*** that is, of the blowing of divine judgment.[62] Ps:[63] *Make them like a wheel, and as straw in the presence of the wind.* ***and as ashes,*** already burned up, of course, by the fire of concupiscence, ***that the whirlwind,*** namely of the Lord's indignation, ***scatters.*** Is 1:[64] *Your strength will be as the ashes of flax, and your work as a spark; both will burn together, and there will be no one who will extinguish them.* Job means that the wicked man, although he considers all these things, is so obstinate that he does not withdraw from his wickedness.

Moreover, concerning the cause of this obstinacy from the side of divine permission, he adds: **[19] *God has stored up the pain* (dolorem) *of the father,*** namely in fault and in punishment, ***for his children,*** not only according to natural lineage but also in imitation of his wickedness. Ex 20:[65] *I am a jealous God, visiting the sins of the fathers upon their children to the third and fourth generation.* ***and when He,*** supply: God, ***repays it,*** supply: the pain, ***then he will know.*** The Gloss:[66] "A fault closes the eyes, but punishment opens them." There is an example in 2 Mc 9:[67] Antiochus, on account of the pain he suffered, came to his senses and said, *It is right to be subject to God, and that mortals should not think that they are equal to God.* Supply: and then **[20] *His eyes,***

60. Lam 3.54.
61. Jer 5.3.
62. Cf. Jb 4.9 and Albert's comments on it above.
63. Ps 82.14.
64. Is 1.31.
65. Ex 20.5.
66. See Gregory, *Mor.* 15.41.58.
67. 2 Mc 9.12.

namely the eyes of the heart of the wicked man rather than the eyes of the body, ***will see his own destruction***, that is, the cause of his destruction. Wis 5:[68] *They will speak to one another, groaning in anguish of spirit.* And after a few lines:[69] *Therefore, we have wandered from the way of truth.* ***and***, supply: then, ***he***, namely the wicked man, ***will drink of the wrath of the Almighty***. Jer 25:[70] *Drink, become drunk, and vomit; fall down and refuse to get up.* Ps 74:[71] *The dregs of it* [*the cup of God's judgment*] *have not been emptied; all the sinners of the earth will drink.*

Then Job adds that the wicked man is not drawn back [from his wickedness] by love for his posterity, although he knows that his posterity will be destroyed on account of his own sin. And that is: **[21]** ***For why does what happens***, namely concerning taking delight in sin, ***to his house***, supply: which is going to be completely destroyed on account of his iniquity, ***after him concern him?*** for as long as he is able to act unjustly, he does not worry about the destruction of his house. Is 14:[72] *The seed of the most wicked will not arise for all eternity. Prepare his children for slaughter.*

And he adds that the desire for a longer life also does not draw the wicked man back from iniquity. And that is: ***and if the number of his months should be cut in half?*** For he knows what is written in the Ps:[73] *Bloody and deceitful men will not live out half their days.* Indeed, the lust for sin is so great that he does not abandon sinning on account of any loss or danger incurred. Ps:[74] *The unjust man said to himself that he would sin. There is no fear of God before his eyes.*

[22] ***Can it be that anyone will teach God?***

Having set forth these points, here Job concludes his argument. And this conclusion[75] has three parts, namely: the con-

68. Wis 5.3.
69. Wis 5.6.
70. Jer 25.27.
71. Ps 74.9.
72. Is 14.20–21.
73. Ps 54.24.
74. Ps 35.2.
75. This conclusion constitutes the second part of the second major division of chapter 21 (viz., Job's response to Zophar's speech), according to Albert. Recall the *divisio textus* that Albert sets forth in introducing v. 7 above.

clusion of the argument; a verbal assault against his adversary, in this place:[76] *Certainly I know;* and a refutation of his falsehood, in this place:[77] *How, then, do you comfort me.*

In the first part there are three points, namely: that there is no acknowledgment of injustice on the part of God; Job provides an explanation of the present reality of the wicked man; and he affirms that those who were dissimilar in life come to a similar death.

And that is: ***Can it be that anyone will teach,*** that is, will be able to teach, ***God,*** who knows all things and governs all things, of course, ***knowledge*** of their orderly arrangement or of inferior realities? Is 40:[78] *Who has helped the spirit of the Lord? Or who has been His counselor and has taught Him? With whom has He entered into deliberation, and who has instructed Him, and taught Him the path of justice, and taught Him knowledge, and shown Him the way of wisdom?*

And he adds the reason why God is not able to be taught: ***who,*** that is, because He ***judges those that are on high?*** that is, angels and celestial natures, by means of which inferior things are governed and disposed. On account of this, the stars are actually called, in Wis 13,[79] *rulers of the world.* Sir 17:[80] *Over every nation He has set rulers.* And this is to be understood as indicating the angels. If, therefore, God rules those who rule, He has complete control over inferior things. Ps:[81] *The scepter of your kingdom is a scepter of ruling rightly.* Indeed, all four disputants acknowledged that there was no injustice on the part of the God who rules, as has been indicated in the arguments considered previously.

Then Job explains the present reality, as it appears more evidently. **[23]** ***One man,*** namely the wicked man who is obstinate, ***dies strong,*** namely vigorous and with a [secure] household, ***and healthy,*** in body, having been stricken with no sickness during his entire life, ***rich*** in resources ***and happy*** on account of politi-

76. Jb 21.27.
77. Jb 21.34.
78. Is 40.13–14.
79. Wis 13.2.
80. Sir 17.14.
81. Ps 44.7.

cal power and fame. And he explains this [further] by means of particulars: **[24]** ***His bowels,*** that is, his intimate relatives, such as his children and his descendants, ***are full of fat,*** that is, of good fortune.[82] Jb 15:[83] *Thickness has covered his face, and the fat hangs down from his sides.* and **his bones,** that is, his friends who comfort him, ***are refreshed*** for the sake of continuous nourishment ***with*** sweet, rich, and pleasant ***marrow.*** Jer 48:[84] *Moab has been fruitful from his youth, he has rested on his dregs; he has not been poured out from vessel to vessel, nor has he gone into exile; therefore, his flavor has remained in him, and his aroma has not changed,* as if to say: "He never suffered any misfortune during his entire life." The rich man who feasted, according to Lk 16,[85] serves as an example. **[25]** ***But another man,*** dissimilar in fortune, ***dies in the bitterness of his soul,*** which experienced no prosperity whatsoever during his entire life, ***without any resources,*** which might have brought either power or wealth, as this place in Lam 3[86] confirms concerning him: *God has filled me with bitterness; He has inebriated me with wormwood.* Lazarus, the good pauper, serves as an example.[87] Ps:[88] *I am poor, and in the midst of labors from my youth.* Hence Abraham said concerning both of them:[89] *Son, you have received good things during your life, and Lazarus evil things, of course.* But neither [the rich man nor Lazarus] received according to his merits in this life, which indeed is confounding to many people. Solomon discusses this in Eccl 5,[90] and he teaches: *Do not say in the presence of the angel: There is no providence.* And after a few lines:[91] *If you see the oppression of the poor, and violent judgments, and justice subverted in the province, do not be confounded by this state of affairs.*

82. Here I read *bona fortuna* with MSS EFM, rather than *pingui fortuna* with Weiss's edition.

83. Jb 15.27.

84. Jer 48.11.

85. Lk 16.19.

86. Lam 3.15.

87. See Lk 16.20–21.

88. Ps 87.16.

89. Lk 16.25.

90. Eccl 5.5.

91. Eccl 5.7.

[26] ***nevertheless,*** supply: although they were dissimilar in life, ***in the dust,*** into which they will be changed, of course, ***they will sleep together,*** that is, they will receive a similar end. Thus the evil person is not repaid in this life with what is evil, nor is the good person repaid with what is good. Solomon also overthrew this view in Eccl 2:[92] *I said in my heart: If the death of the fool and my own will be one, what benefit is it to me that I have devoted myself more to the study of wisdom?* ***and worms will cover them,*** as they decay, of course. Is 14:[93] *The moth will be scattered beneath you, and worms will be your covering.*

After these words, moreover, Job mounts a verbal assault against the adversaries of truth, and that is: **[27]** ***Certainly I know your thoughts,*** that is, the thinking or reasoning you have introduced. Ps:[94] *The Lord knows the thoughts of men, that they are vain.* ***and your judgments,*** that is, conclusions, supply: introduced ***against me,*** supply: are ***unjust,*** [that is,] false. Jb 16:[95] *A liar is roused against my face, contradicting me.*

Job adds, however, how their judgments are false: **[28]** ***For you say,*** objecting to me: ***Where is the house of the prince?*** namely of the tyrant and the oppressor, as if to say: "God does not permit them to rule, but rather He destroys their houses." Indeed, Eliphaz said this above in chapter 4:[96] *Call to mind, I beg you, who that was innocent has ever perished? Or when were the upright destroyed? But rather, I have seen those who sow sorrows and reap them perish by the blowing of God and be consumed by the breath of His wrath.*

and, supply: you say: ***where,*** are, of course, ***the tents of the wicked?*** which were destroyed, you all affirm, by the judgment of God. Eliphaz said this above:[97] *Fire will devour the tents of those who accept bribes with pleasure.* Your opinion, therefore, is proven to be both unjust and false.

92. Eccl 2.15.
93. Is 14.11.
94. Ps 93.11.
95. Jb 16.9.
96. Jb 4.7–9.
97. Jb 15.34.

And Job confirms this, adding: **[29]** ***Ask any wayfarer whatever,*** who crosses many lands and sees many things in various places. Heb 11:[98] *Confessing that they are pilgrims and strangers on the earth.* ***and you will realize that he understands these same things,*** supply: that I am saying concerning the wicked man and the good man. For it is apparent to sense perception that God does not repay in this life according to merits. Jer 31:[99] *All people will know me, from the greatest of them all the way down to the least of them.*

Then he adds the reason why the wicked man prospers: **[30]** ***Because the wicked*** and obstinate ***man is preserved,*** supply: in prosperity, ***for the day of perdition,*** namely the last day, when he will be destroyed in soul and in body, ***and,*** supply: in this way having been deceived by the prosperity of good fortune, ***he will be led to the day of wrath,*** when he will endure the burning anger of God. 2 Mc 6:[100] *Concerning the other nations, the Lord waits patiently so that, when the day of judgment arrives, He may punish them according to the fullness of their sins.* Ps:[101] *When I appoint the time, I will judge just conduct.* Dt 32:[102] *If I sharpen my sword like lightning and my hand takes hold of judgment, I will repay my enemies with vengeance.*

Job adds, moreover, that this does not constitute any injustice on God's part: **[31]** ***Who will find fault,*** that is, is able to find fault, ***with His ways in His presence?*** that is, with the ways of God, which are always in His presence, that is, in the light of His presence. Jb 40:[103] *Can it be that you will make my judgment void and that you will condemn me, so that you will be justified?* ***and who will repay Him,*** supply: God, ***for what He has done?*** by preserving the wicked man in prosperity and by afflicting the just man with adversity. Jb 9:[104] *Who is able to say: Why do you act in*

98. Heb 11.13.
99. Jer 31.34.
100. 2 Mc 6.14.
101. Ps 74.3.
102. Dt 32.41.
103. Jb 40.3.
104. Jb 9.12.

this way? Wis 12:[105] *For who will say to you: What have you done? Or who will stand firm against your judgment?*

And God repays the wicked man: **[32]** ***He,*** namely the wicked man having been seduced by his prosperity, ***will be led to the graves,*** with his soul buried in hell—as the rich man was buried due to his feasting, according to Lk 16[106]—and with his body buried in the earth. Ps:[107] *Their graves will be their homes eternally.* ***and,*** having been condemned to pay the penalty, ***he will remain watchful on the heap of the dead,*** that is, where the evil deceased are piled up in hell. Someone who has the faculties of sense perception in actuality (*actu*) with a view toward imitation is said "to remain watchful"; thus, since they feel punishment in actuality (*actu*), the damned are said to remain watchful. Ezek 32:[108] *Their graves have been established in the lowest parts of the pit, and his multitude lay encircling his grave.*

Job also adds how the wicked man was led to such a grave: **[33]** ***He was delightful to the gravel of Cocytus.*** "Cocytus," as the philosophers say, is an infernal river.[109] The Latin equivalent of the word is *luctus,*[110] and it signifies concupiscence, which drags one down into lamentation. And "gravel" consists of small stones that the rushing current of a river drags down, and it signifies those who are dragged down to destruction by concupiscence. Dn 7:[111] *A rapid river of fire flowed forth from His presence,* the presence of the Judge, of course.

Furthermore, Job adds how efficient this river is: ***and it,*** supply: Cocytus, ***will drag down every human,*** namely wise one (*sapientem*), ***after it*** into the ground. For he cannot withstand the waves of concupiscence. Jgs 5:[112] *The torrent of the Kishon dragged their corpses down.* "Kishon" means "vomiting forth suffering for men"; and it signifies the infernal river, which drags down the

105. Wis 12.12.
106. Lk 16.22.
107. Ps 48.12.
108. Ezek 32.23.
109. See Virgil, *Aen.* 6.297; Cicero, *ND* 3.17, and *TD* 1.5.10; and Thomas Aquinas, *Exp. Iob* 21.33.
110. *Luctus* = "lamentation."
111. Dn 7.10.
112. Jgs 5.21.

corpses of those who live in concupiscence. ***and,*** supply: the same river violently drives down ***innumerable humans before it.*** Indeed, there are many who, even while resisting, are thrown down by the violence of concupiscence. In Book VII of the *Ethics,* Aristotle calls these people incontinent: indeed, they have a sound faculty of reason, but they are conquered by the force of their passions.[113] After it says, *The torrent of the Kishon dragged their corpses down,* Jgs 5[114] adds: *the torrent of the Kedumim.* But "Kedumim" means "the sea of the ancients"; that is, the sea of concupiscence buries all people, and it violently drives down even those who possess ancient and hoary reason.

After saying all these things, therefore, Job confirms his proposition: **[34]** ***How, then,*** this conjunction denotes a verbal assault, ***do you comfort me in vain,*** namely by saying that I should act with patience because punishment is a purgation from sin. Jb 16:[115] *All of you are burdensome comforters.* ***since your responses,*** by means of which you attack me, of course, ***have been shown to be repugnant to the truth?*** 2 Tm 2:[116] *A servant of the Lord ought not dispute, but rather be gentle toward all people, teachable, patient, and reproving with moderation those who oppose the truth.* In a preface in which he defends himself, Jerome says:[117] "Indeed, a sacred simplicity of life is advantageous only for him who practices it. And as much as he builds up the Church of God by the merit of his life, he harms it as much if he does not oppose those who seek to destroy it."

113. Aristotle, *EN* 7.7.1.
114. Jgs 5.21.
115. Jb 16.2.
116. 2 Tm 2.24–25.
117. Jerome, *Ep. ad Paulinum* 53.3 (PL 22:542).

INDICES

GENERAL INDEX

INDEX OF HOLY SCRIPTURE

Old Testament

New Testament

RECENT VOLUMES IN THE FATHERS OF THE CHURCH, MEDIAEVAL CONTINUATION

ST. HILDEGARD OF BINGEN, *The Book of Divine Works,* translated by Nathaniel M. Campbell, Volume 18 (2018)

ALBERT THE GREAT, *On the Body of the Lord,* translated by Sr. Albert Marie Surmanski, OP, Volume 17 (2017)

PETER THE VENERABLE, *Writings Against the Saracens,* translated by Irven M. Resnick, Volume 16 (2016)

JOHN DUNS SCOTUS, *Questions on Aristotle's* Categories, translated by Lloyd A. Newton, Volume 15 (2014)

PETER THE VENERABLE, *Against the Inveterate Obduracy of the Jews,* translated by Irven M. Resnick, Volume 14 (2013)

ROBERT GROSSETESTE, *On the Cessation of the Laws,* translated by Stephen M. Hildebrand, Volume 13 (2012)

PETER ABELARD, *Commentary on the Epistle to the Romans,* translated by Steven R. Cartwright, Volume 12 (2011)

THOMAS AQUINAS, *The Academic Sermons,* translated by Mark-Robin Hoogland, CP, Volume 11 (2010)

LANFRANC OF CANTERBURY, *On the Body and Blood of the Lord,* and GUITMUND OF AVERSA, *On the Truth of the Body and Blood of Christ in the Eucharist,* translated by Mark G. Vaillancourt, Volume 10 (2009)

WORKS OF ST. ALBERT THE GREAT IN THIS SERIES

Questions Concerning Aristotle's On Animals, translated by Irven M. Resnick and Kenneth F. Kitchell, Jr., Fathers of the Church, Mediaeval Continuation 9 (2008)

On the Body of the Lord, translated by Sr. Albert Marie Surmanski, OP, Fathers of the Church, Mediaeval Continuation 17 (2017)

On Job, Volume 1, translated by Franklin T. Harkins, Fathers of the Church, Mediaeval Continuation 19 (2019)